Sophie Tucker

SOPHIE TUCKER

First Lady of Show Business

by ARMOND FIELDS

McFarland & Company, Inc., Publishers
Jefferson, North Carolina, and London

ALSO BY ARMOND FIELDS
AND FROM MCFARLAND

Fred Stone: Circus Performer and Musical Comedy Star (2002)

*James J. Corbett: A Biography of the Heavyweight Boxing
Champion and Popular Theater Headliner* (2001)

Eddie Foy: A Biography of the Early Popular Stage Comedian (1999)

Lillian Russell: A Biography of "America's Beauty" (1999)

FRONTISPIECE: When she appeared on stage in her finest regalia, Sophie's gowns received almost as much attention as her performances. She was known to be one of the most beautifully attired performers on Broadway. (Museum of the City of New York)

LIBRARY OF CONGRESS CATALOGUING-IN-PUBLICATION DATA

Fields, Armond, 1930–
Sophie Tucker : first lady of show business / by Armond Fields.
p.   cm.
Includes bibliographical references and index.

ISBN 0-7864-1577-0 (softcover : 50# alkaline paper)

1. Tucker, Sophie, 1884–1966.
2. Singers—United States—Biography.   I. Title.
ML420.T89F5   2003   782.42164'092—dc21   2003006011
British Library cataloguing data are available

©2003 Armond Fields. All rights reserved

*No part of this book may be reproduced or transmitted in any form
or by any means, electronic or mechanical, including photocopying
or recording, or by any information storage and retrieval system,
without permission in writing from the publisher.*

Cover photograph: Sophie Tucker, 1918 (Museum of the City of New York)
Background image ©2003 EyeWire

Manufactured in the United States of America

*McFarland & Company, Inc., Publishers
Box 611, Jefferson, North Carolina 28640
www.mcfarlandpub.com*

Acknowledgments

Biographies depend upon the collection of historical papers, archives' preserving them, and archivists' making them available to researchers. I am grateful to the following sources, all of whom carefully preserved Sophie's personal and professional history and allowed me to study the material freely.

New York Public Library, Performing Arts Division
Marty Jacobs, Museum of the City of New York
Mary Ann Chach, Shubert Archive
John Ahouse, University of Southern California, Special Collections Library
Ned Comstock, University of Southern California, Cinema Library
University of Texas, Harry Ransom Humanities Research Center
American Jewish Archives, The Jacob Rader Marcus Center
Marsha Lotstein, Jewish Historical Society, Hartford, CT
Academy of Motion Picture Arts and Sciences
The Museum of Television and Radio
The Theatre Museum, London, England
The New York Historical Society

My special thanks go to a group of intrepid researchers: Shirley and Stu Tolley; Emily Kelley; Mary Jane McIntire; Giao Luong; Heity Hyun; and Seth Fields.

To John Farrell, my longtime editor, my gratitude for another fine job.

Finally, loving appreciation to my wife, Sara Fields, who has supported me through every phase of my exploration of the artists who made popular theater a dynamic and living history.

Contents

Acknowledgments	v
Introduction	1
1. Welcome to America	7
2. Breaking In	18
3. The Mary Garden of Ragtime (1)	32
4. The Mary Garden of Ragtime (2)	44
5. Vaudeville Stardom	55
6. Celebrating Cabarets	71
7. Risky Business	85
8. At the Top of Her Game	102
9. Burning Up the Boards	123
10. Honky Tonk	136
11. Escape to London	148
12. Looking Back Over Her Shoulder	164
13. The Labor Union Blues	184
14. Fast Becoming a Legend	194
15. The Glory Years	210
16. A Fabulous Character	227
Epilogue	246
Notes	251
Selected Bibliography and Source Material	255
Index	259

Introduction

Broadway, 1906. The Miracle Mile. The Street of Fun and Fantasy. The Great White Way.

Flourishing brightly and with evident arrogance night and day, Broadway seemed a city unto itself, stretching for almost two miles of Manhattan, from Madison Square to Longacre Square. As Lloyd Morris once described it, Broadway had become a "national highway of pleasure, saturated in legend; and the exploits of its transient sovereigns often seemed as fabulous as those of ancient gods."

Perhaps not as romantically poetic as Morris's description, Broadway, nevertheless, pulsated with both anticipated and unexpected delights. It was not just the effervescent mix of citizens that strolled the street—from the Four Hundred of high society, playboys, celebrities, and greatest stars of the theater, to streetwalkers, pickpockets, and panhandlers—it was the exuberant, self-promoting image the street had created, a thoroughfare where sensual joy, amusement, romance, and excitement could be easily experienced twenty-four hours a day.

Broadway in 1906 was lined with electric street lights, a glittering effect heightened to dazzling splendor by the blazing marquees of department stores, restaurants and theaters. Automobiles, cable cars, and hansoms (two-wheeled cabs) crowded the street. So noisy and dense was the traffic that any attempt by pedestrians to cross Broadway was deemed extremely hazardous, if not death-defying.

In Manhattan, there were more than fifty-eight theaters, legitimate and popular, almost half of them situated on or adjacent to Broadway. Many were located in that area between Thirty-seventh and Forty-second streets, fondly called the Rialto by its denizens. Gathered there was anything labeled theatrical, from performers and promoters, to tour groups bent on getting a glimpse of their favorite stars "up close." Gibson-girl styles were all the vogue, thanks to the elegant drawings in *Life* magazine by Charles Dana Gibson, the city's acclaimed purveyor of new fashions.

Shoulder to shoulder with the theaters stood Macy's and Wanamaker's department stores, exhibiting the finest in women's wear, elegant rococo-styled hotels like the Astor, Knickerbocker, St. Nicholas, and the area's newest jeweled addition, the Waldorf Astoria. At the lower end of the street near Madison Square was Delmonico's Restaurant, the most famous resort for sumptuous dining among theater's first-nighters. Up the street were Shanley's Lobster Palace, known for its "sporting crowd," and Rector's, near Forty-fourth street, with its ceiling-high mirrors and its Louis XIV decor rich in green and gold—the "supreme shrine of the cult of pleasure," where, if one could obtain a table for an after-theater dinner, one had surely "arrived."

On the esplanade between Forty-second and Forty-seventh streets known as Longacre Square, Adolph S. Ochs, publisher of the *New York Times,* had built a monument to himself and his newspaper that soon became known to all the world as Times Square. His newspaper was one of the first to report the appearance of "rainy-daisy" skirts on Broadway. The hems of such garments rose a scandalous six inches off the ground, and young women used the quickly swelling fad to openly declare their independence by breaking with traditional fashions.

It seemed to Broadway adherents that new theaters and new productions opened every week. The Hippodrome, a monstrous building occupying the entire Sixth Avenue frontage between Forty-third and Forty-fourth streets, claimed to seat 5,200 people and cost more than $1.5 million to build. Lew Fields had recently opened the third theater bearing his name. The more intimate Liberty Theater opened next door. So close were the two venues that their crowds mingled freely before each performance and patrons sometimes found themselves in the wrong theater.

During the early part of the twentieth century, many of the stage's most familiar performers were at the height of their popularity: Maude Adams, in "The Little Minister"; Mrs. Fiske in "Leah Kleschna"; David Warfield in "The Music Master." Not to be overshadowed by the fascination legitimate theater received along Broadway, popular headliners played to packed houses. Vaudeville and burlesque (satire, travesty, and farce comedy, not girlie shows) were in their heyday, starring such noteworthy performers as The Three Keatons, with little Buster now receiving separate billing; Houdini and his death-defying escapes; W.C. Fields, comic juggler; and the Dockstater Minstrels. Musical comedy featured such lavish presentations as "The Yankee Consul," "The College Widow," and the "The Prince of Pilsen," and were influenced by the innovative productions of George M. Cohan's "Forty-Five Minutes from Broadway" and Lew Fields' "It Happened in Nordland." Tin Pan Alley songwriters churned out popular tunes by the hundreds, igniting a sheet music industry whose customers seemed unable to satiate their appetite for these tuneful songs to play and sing at home. And the phonograph record was not far behind.

Full-page newspaper advertisements appeared every week, promoting the latest songs and the performers interpreting them. It was a commercial alliance that offered financial advantages to both parties. Songs like "In My Merry Oldsmobile," "Wait Till the Sun Shines, Nellie," "Coming Through the Rye," and "My Gal Sal" had become instant hits due to the cooperation of music publisher and popular singer, reaching audiences in vaudeville houses across the country.

The moving picture business had only recently graduated from nickelodeons into vaudeville houses. At first used as "chasers" to empty the theater at the end of a program, "movies" soon became acts in their own right, presenting sporting events, natural disasters (film of the San Francisco earthquake arrived in New York theaters only two weeks after the catastrophe), and stories of scientific discoveries. Edison Films led the group of moving picture entrepreneurs by preparing short subjects and human-interest stories. Not to be outdone, Biograph, Pathé, Vitograph, Lubin, and Selig were astute and aggressive competitors already experimenting with longer features, although detractors of the new medium counseled that no audience would sit for more than fifteen minutes to watch a film.

To add to the sensory clutter along Broadway, products like Mennen's Talcum Powder, Horlick's Malted Milk, Pond's Cold Cream, O'Sullivan's Heels, and Cracker Jack were featured on large billboards and building broadsides. Quaker Puffed Rice erected a sign that simulated cereal popping out of a bowl, an astonishing display that stopped onlookers in their tracks.

But not all of Broadway's theaters featured electric lights, plush box seats, and attractive, veteran headliners. For every theater that advertised top vaudeville actors, there was another that promoted little-known performers whose acts were not yet deemed sufficiently unique to command a spot on a high-class bill. These performers played what was called "the secondary circuit." Whether in New York or in small New England towns, theaters on this circuit could afford only low-priced vaudeville companies. This circuit also served as the venue for newcomers to show biz, to help them develop their routines, build their stage personae, and learn the intricacies and idiosyncrasies that they hoped would enhance their budding stage careers. Most of these eager dreamers never made it to the big-time. Some were just good enough to extend their stage lives on the secondary circuit. Only a select few made the successful jump to high-class theaters.

Another opportunity for little-known or less talented performers were various venues not usually associated with theaters but nevertheless offering popular entertainment. Among these were beer gardens, night clubs, and bordellos. Beer gardens were the most prevalent and the most willing to give would-be performers a trial. They featured an amateur night each week, played to an audience that often included agents seeking new talent. For their efforts, performers selected to participate received a free meal and a beer. Beginners were acutely aware that a good number of the most popular Broadway stars had begun their careers performing at beer gardens. It was a tough and sometimes dangerous atmosphere in which to play, yet it provided an excellent learning experience if one were willing and intelligent enough to persevere through a rigorous training period.

In the summer of 1906, armed with nothing but the names of a few Tin Pan Alley songwriters and encouragement from a number of small-time entertainers who happened to be good customers of the Abuza Kosher Restaurant in Hartford, Connecticut, twenty-year-old Sophie Tuck arrived at New York's Grand Central Station to seek a career on the popular stage. It did not take her long to comprehend the formidable obstacles she faced.

The impact on women of early twentieth-century popular theater had been enormous. During the first few years of the 1900s, women were gaining more freedom from the home and independence from Victorian values regarding their role in society. As a result, a new culture was established, one in which traditional boundaries between the sexes were rapidly being erased.

Women now had more leisure time, resulting from a combination of mechanical conveniences in the home and the onslaught of advertising in women's magazines that offered them greater personal identity and life-style emancipation. One of the most significant forms of personal enfranchisement came with the development and maturation of American popular theater. It was not surprising that the more women attended the theater, the more theater prospered.

By 1910, it was estimated that more than forty percent of popular theater audiences were made up of women. The percentage was even higher at legitimate theater venues. With the appearance of such larger-than-life, self-promoting actresses as Lillian Russell, Elsie Janis, Nora Bayes, and Eva Tanguay, astute critics and theater managers talked enthusiastically about the "feminization of the stage" and its attendant financial benefits. At the same time, since more women attended the theater, more of them became interested in the acting profession; and, by doing so, they discovered encouraging opportunities. Theater managers quickly perceived the financial rewards brought by increasingly female audiences and charismatic female entertainers who themselves became role models for their enthusiastic audiences.

The media phenomenon of "the stage-struck girl" had been translated into many more women than men seeking theatrical employment, a ratio of twenty-five girls to one man, according to agents. In supposed horror, the moralistic (and male-dominated) *Dramatic Mirror,* a weekly theatrical newspaper, derided young women for viewing the stage "though rose-colored spectacles," without having the slightest idea of the "studying, training, drudging, and hard work" that awaited them if they chose to enter the profession. At the same time, the *Mirror's* classified pages were filled with ads recruiting women performers.

Though only a very few aspirants ever enjoyed sufficient success to earn even a journeyman's salary, the bleak prospects did nothing to discourage women from trying. They may or may not have been aware that their lives would be viewed as atypical, if not immoral; yet the goals of visibility, independence, and success more than motivated them to the challenge. No question, it was worth the effort, the risk, the personal gamble, to better their otherwise dull and repressive lives.

To recognize the increasing interest women expressed, newspapers published columns like "The Matinee Girl" and "About Women," dedicated to their interests in the stage and its female performers. The introduction of the matinee itself, a Saturday afternoon event, attracted a majority of women and created a venue, unseen before at theaters, for the open sharing of fashions, gossip, and adoration of performers. Of even greater significance, in order to openly express their newly found independence, women came to these matinees without male escorts.

Reciprocally, predominantly female audiences gave actresses the opportunity to express their values and personae more freely, which, in effect, contributed further to their rising reputations. Enterprising theater impresarios plumbed such events for enormous financial gain.

Sophie Tuck's entrance into this dynamic theatrical milieu could not have been more fortuitous. Ethel Barrymore had been asked what contributed to becoming a successful actress. She replied that success derived from such characteristics as "temperament," "instinct," and "intelligence," totally frustrating reporters who sought a magic formula they could write about. Yet these abstractions could easily have applied to Sophie when she arrived in the big city, an awestruck and unschooled outsider. It was her unique combination of these features that gave Sophie the motivation by which to overcome the obstacles facing new aspirants to the acting profession. Sophie quickly understood it was going to be a hard road. Unhesitatingly, she took on the challenge and never flinched once.

Yet Sophie was faced with another critical issue when she entered the theatrical world. She was Jewish and had been raised in a very religious family. Only in recent years had Jews been openly accepted on the stage. Weber and Fields were the only famous popular entertainers known to be Jewish, but playing "Dutch" characters downplayed their own ethnic roots. In their well-known Music Hall skits, they always included a blatantly Hebrew character to distinguish themselves from the stereotypical Jew. Although many Tin Pan Alley companies were Jewish-owned and employed Jewish songwriters, the publication of American songs—ballads, topical, "coon," and patriotic—masked any Jewish identification. Yiddish Theater had its own adherents, performers, plays, and venues, and such plays as "Uncle Tom's Cabin" and "Cyrano de Bergerac" were often translated for the American Yiddish stage.

To a large extent, anti–Semitism still prevailed among theater managers and agents, and stories abounded about Jewish entertainers who had experienced rejections because of their ethnicity prior to reaching headliner status. In 1906, besides Weber and Fields, the only other popular Jewish performer was singer Nora Bayes, who, when she began her career, had changed her name from Goldberg. Fannie Brice, Al Jolson, the Howard Brothers, Al Shean, and the Four Marx Brothers had not yet arrived on Broadway.

When Sophie was first signed to appear on the popular stage, she was instructed to appear in blackface, not because she was considered fat (actually her body shape and size were very much in keeping with the preferences of the day), but because she was Jewish. Agents and managers of these "secondary market" theaters did not want her Jewishness to seem so obvious on stage.

It took another four years before Sophie could openly inject examples of Jewishness into her act and hear them applauded for their ethnicity. By that time, Jewish identity and popularity had become more commonplace, spearheaded by theater moguls like Abe Erlanger and the Shuberts, who owned most theaters and many performers, and Flo Ziegfeld, who blurred ethnic differences with beautiful girls and extravagant productions.

In the meantime, however, Sophie was required to maintain the persona of the blackface "coon" singer, and then, at the end of her act, to shock audiences by exposing her whiteness when she removed her wig and white gloves. Though these impositions may have bothered her, she realized that, to achieve stage success, she had to perform in a way that audiences (and theater managers) would find most comfortable and acceptable.

Sophie Tuck's arrival at Grand Central Station brought to popular theater a unique individual who truly exemplified a rags-to-riches story. Rarely in the history of English-language theater would audiences so clearly recognize and heartily applaud a young, ambitious, hard-working, orthodox Jewish immigrant woman, one who came to personify the American Dream and gain both domestic and international fame.

For Sophie, making a living on the stage had been an attractive lure compared to working in her family's restaurant. The stage obviously offered an escape from the poverty and limitations of home and family. The stage also offered high salaries, mobility, and independence. For a young Jewish woman, the repressive social environment allowed few other avenues. Although Sophie would have been hard pressed to define what independence meant, her departure from home to seek her fortune, leaving behind a husband, a young child, and strongly disapproving parents, was a rare act of courage for any woman during any era. This strength of character would become both a distinct advantage and sometime liability in her future life and career. Nonetheless, she neither shrank from the opportunities nor shirked the responsibilities that life's events brought her way.

As an entertainer, Sophie more than lived up to her billing. Charles Samuels, a journalist and theater historian, called Sophie "a force of nature." Another theater critic declared, "Miss Tucker can move an audience or a piano with equal address." A woman of verve and passion, she knew her audiences and gave fully of herself to them. According to critics, when Sophie came on stage, she "owned the place." What so endeared her to theater patrons and colleagues alike was that she was the same person whether on or off the stage.

For sixty years, Sophie Tucker (she changed her name from Tuck two years after arriving in New York) entertained a wide variety of audiences with astounding success. From the early years as the "World Renowned Coon Shouter" to her later career as the "Last of the Red-Hot Mamas," Sophie carefully honed her presentation to meet and satisfy the changing demands of theater patrons. Few early performers had been able to achieve that elusive goal. Sophie accomplished it with a defining charisma that projected itself to every remote corner of the theater, capturing audiences with her eagerness to please, singing directly to them, and only to them.

Called by many theater historians and critics the "First Lady of Show Business," Sophie Tucker was unequaled as an artist and distinctive as a woman.

1

Welcome to America

In 1881, the assassination of Tsar Alexander II of Russia and the accession to the throne of Alexander III became the catalyst that set in motion the mass emigration of Jews to the United States. Particularly devastated were the *shtetls* (Jewish villages), whose inhabitants overnight lost their ability to self-govern, had much of their property confiscated, and their lives threatened.[1]

During the latter part of 1885, the *shtetl* of Tulchin had been visited by Russian authorities as they made their systematic way through the prosperous farm country south of Kiev. Tulchin, a classic Hassidic *shtetl,* was located on a direct route almost midway between Kiev and Odessa, west of Uman, along the River Bug. Tulchin was one of seven villages, situated almost in a circle, surrounding the villagers' rich farmland.[2]

Not only was the existence of the village in danger, its inhabitants were menaced with the threat of expulsion, forced enlistment into the army for all males regardless of age, or death if they failed to comply with new government edicts.

Charles Polteil Kalish was born in Odessa, Russia in 1855. Jennie Linetsky, his wife-to-be, was born in Tulchin in 1850.[3] The difference in their ages and the common practice of arranged marriages suggests a union in which Charles, a tailor, came to join Jennie in Tulchin. Their marriage is believed to have taken place around 1880. Jennie suffered the death of several children in childbirth before Philip was born in January, 1884. On January 13, 1886, Sonya Kalish was born. It was shortly afterwards that the Kalishes hastily departed for the United States.[4]

To travel across Russia, Poland, and into Germany during the late winter and early spring of 1886 must have been a terrifying experience. Rutted dirt roads were often turned into quagmires during frequent rains. Finding shelter was problematic since, as Jews, the Kalishes were ostracized in many towns and villages. Food sources were few and far between. The threat of attack by highwaymen or Cossacks was ever present. Tending to the needs of two children, one of whom was newborn, made traveling that much more of a burden. Moreover, there were the serious doubts about obtaining space aboard a ship, yet unidentified, to a destination, yet unknown. Nevertheless, through a sheer, dogged determination to survive, the Kalishes at last arrived in Bremen, Germany, along with hundreds of other Jewish families likewise escaping Russian pogroms, all of them anxious to seek passage to America.

The Kalishes arrived in New York during the late spring of 1886. By virtue of an unspecified episode during their long and perilous journey to the United States, Charles Kalish identified himself to U.S. customs authorities as Charles Abuza. The name change likely occurred during the trek across Russia in order to protect the family against the rampant and open anti–Jewish hostility. Family lore suggests that Charles assumed the name and identity papers of an acquaintance named Abuza, who had conveniently died. Whatever the story, when Charles, Jennie, Philip, and Sonya arrived in New York and proceeded through U.S. immigration facilities at Castle Garden, they gave the family name of Abuza.

Upon passing through immigration, the Abuzas were given train fare to Boston, where they would reside. Jewish organizations concerned with placing immigrants in "appropriate" communities had recommended the Abuzas settle in Boston because the Jewish community in New York was already "overcrowded." The Abuzas also claimed to have relatives living in Boston. They received food and money to aid their relocation, at least until the Abuzas could support themselves, however minimally. The Abuzas were assigned an apartment on 22 Salem Street, in the heart of Boston's Jewish enclave. Since Charles was unable to establish himself as a tailor immediately, he obtained a job as a bartender in a neighborhood saloon. Jennie, in the traditionally expected manner, took over care of the household and children. Daily life was full of hardships, yet they were infinitely easier to overcome than those that would have challenged them in Russia.

Still, for people who had lived in the *shtetl*, urban America was certainly frightening—the noises of the street, the size of the buildings, and the constant pushing and shoving of everyday life seemed like chaos. When these people chose to flee their homeland, they were forced to leave behind a good part of their traditional culture, as well. To many immigrants, this new experience was a profound culture shock, an assault on their religious and moral convictions. Those wanting to remain faithful to Jewish traditions had to make a special effort. To many, this new country provoked spiritual confusion. Some became almost totally demoralized. It would take time to learn the roles one played in this urban miasma and how a Jewish person defined his existence.[5]

Life was improved, if at first confusing; but was it really better? In Boston's Jewish section, that part of it allotted to recent immigrants, families were packed together in rows of two- and three-story tenements. Crowded and unsanitary conditions were the norm. Plumbing was confined to closets, one to a floor. No electricity was available. One coal stove provided heat for the entire family. There was little ventilation, and no hot running water. Refrigeration consisted of blocks of ice, purchased each day from passing wagons.

At the same time, the streets were lined by and packed with wagon and pushcart peddlers selling everything from food and clothing to needles and hairpins. Veterans of the neighborhood had advanced their living conditions by using the front of their apartments as places of business. It had likely taken them years of saving and negotiation to secure such an apartment on the ground floor.

Jewish children were enrolled in public school at age six. In a typical classroom, one teacher oversaw at least fifty children from mixed ethnic backgrounds, while working in overcrowded conditions, with low budgets. Yet, as a distinctively American educational form, public schools became the springboard for immigrant children to learn and experience the new world.

After having attended public school, many of these children also attended a Hebrew School several hours each day to maintain their Jewish beliefs and heritage, as dictated by their parents. Older children were expected to help their parents, at businesses and at home. On Sundays, families walked the short distance to Boston Commons, a large park on the Charles River, where they could experience open spaces, tall trees, green grass, fresh breezes, and the young children could play near the water and eat ice cream. This brief yet poignant visit helped to buoy them for the rigors of the coming week.

The crowded streets were the only place where children could experience feelings of freedom and sociability. By its very dissonance, the streets were spontaneous and unpredictable, and they drew children "like a magnet." To children, the home, where the parents prevailed, signified a life of rules, rituals, and responsibilities. The streets, however, signified not only one's freedom, but one's future.

The Abuzas lived in Boston for more than seven years, then moved to Hartford, Connecticut. In the meantime, two more children were added to the family: Moses, born in December, 1889; and Anna, born in March, 1892. Both Philip and Sonya, now called Sophie by her friends, were enrolled in Brown Elementary School.

The Abuza's move to Hartford was likely aided by the Hebrew Immigrant Aid Society, responsible for the "removal," that is, dispersion, of families to small cities and towns where the Jewish population was small. With an already well-accepted Jewish community — where they shared space with Italians and Irish immigrants — Hartford was highly qualified as a settlement for "removed" families.

The Abuza family arrived in Hartford in 1895. They rented a second-floor apartment at 51 Morgan Street, around the corner from the neighborhood's main business section on Front Street, where Charles obtained a job as a bartender at a saloon. Front Street overlooked the thriving docks and wharves along the Connecticut River, in support of a vibrant river-based economy.[6]

Commercial life on Front Street seemed a scene of violent congestion, with noises, motions, and smells assaulting everyone. There was no space, and no privacy. In fact, privacy of any kind was at a premium within the entire community. The street was highlighted by a flourishing market of peddlers and pushcarts, which stretched for blocks in either direction. From dawn to dusk, the cries of peddlers hawking their wares virtually drowned out the cacophonies emanating from river commerce. On the street, everything was for sale — peaches at a penny a quart, "damaged" eggs,

Front Street, Hartford, Connecticut, was the heart of the Jewish commercial area, filled with small shops and hundreds of pushcarts. It was on Front Street that the Abuza restaurant was located.

eyeglasses for thirty-five cents, old coats for fifty cents. (Everything except pigs.) A good pushcart salesman could earn up to twenty dollars a week, enough to meet family needs in a comfortable home.

Front Street was also the location of small shops—restaurants, butcher shops, pharmacies, tobacco shops, and an endless array of second-hand storefronts—run by Jewish immigrants. By the turn of the century, Front Street had not only become the center of Jewish commercial and social life, it was a place where Jews would congregate to transact business or just meet for the sake of conversational exchange.

Nevertheless, sustaining life in the community remained an unending battle. There were no health safeguards for the chickens, produce, and meat sold by peddlers. Children played in the unpaved streets or around the river docks.

Interspersed among the shops were gambling dens and houses of prostitution. The nearest hospital was miles away; local doctors—or those who purported to be representatives of the medical profession—cared for the sick, many using familiar, old-world methods. Nearby were vaudeville theaters, pool halls, and saloons. A storefront usually housed the Yiddish theater performers from New York when they came to Hartford on their tour of New England cities. The actors were a welcome respite from the tedium of daily life.

Each spring, the Connecticut River threatened to overflow its banks, and when it did, water approached the doorsteps of Front Street shops, made the street itself a quagmire and a natural if unsanitary swimming pool for children. Due to a combination of these conditions, many residents did not survive to middle age.

Still, it was the rutted, hard-scrabble streets where the children played and learned. Generally, boys played with boys; and girls with girls, at least until sexuality became part of the game, which usually occurred at age twelve. Due to the myriad attractions of the street, parents struggled with their children, fearful of losing control over them and believing that the secular world would lead them to stray from the family's traditional religious beliefs.

Although parents determinedly fought the battle, deep down they suspected they were helpless to combat their children's urge for freedom. This confrontation was more than the usual parent-child conflict that occurred during adolescence. Parents literally saw their children leaving behind the "old ways" of their elders, striving to Americanize themselves. Given the freedom of the streets, these children could pursue their own interests and, at the same time, break from Jewish customs with little fear of retribution.[7]

In 1896, Charles and Jennie leased 189 Front Street and opened a kosher restaurant. They turned the second floor into living space for the family and, with some rooms to spare, also operated a rooming house. Jennie supervised the food preparation, Charles acted as host and cashier, Philip waited on tables, and ten-year-old Sophie helped her mother in the kitchen. The combination of appetizing, wholesome kosher food and reasonable prices soon attracted a faithful crowd of patrons to Abuza's Restaurant. The restaurant became a neighborhood fixture. Not only was it patronized by the local community; it also provided a welcome, homey way-station for dock workers, boat people, and touring theatrical performers, all of whom found the familial dining experience at once satisfying and cheap.

Monitoring family finances, however, proved quite a struggle. Charles was drawn to games of chance; and he more often lost than

A formal family portrait of the Abuza family, just after they arrived in Hartford. Left to right: Jennie; baby Moses; Sonya, four years old; Charles; and Phillip, six years old. (Museum of the City of New York)

won, although losing never prevented him from continuing to gamble. Jennie, on the other hand, worked hard to save money, and her efforts had been notably successful. Besides maintaining a comfortable home, she supported her children's schooling and gave generously to various Jewish groups, in several of which she was deeply involved. Jennie was president of the Ladies Hebrew Benevolent Association, as well as being one of the founders of the Hebrew Ladies Old People's Home and the Hebrew Women's Home for Children.

Initially, Sophie had been relegated to the kitchen. As business improved, however, and she grew older, she was promoted to waitress. It was during this period that she exhibited an interest in music, particularly singing popular songs. In school, singing lessons were her favorite subject. An excerpt from the Brown School Class of 1902 Almanac humorously acknowledged Sophie's singing.

During Christmas exercises in Room 22, Miss Clark presiding, voices were raised in rendering holiday carols. Miss Clark then called on Sophie to sing a solo. No Christmas carol that! In a strong and rhythmic fashion, Sophie sang the popular song of the moment, "Hello, My Baby!" Poor Miss Clark slumped in a state of near collapse. Still, according to the almanac writer, the song was a hit and was possibly Sophie's first public performance.

In addition, Sophie and her girl friends frequently attended local vaudeville theaters where she literally absorbed Tin Pan Alley's latest tunes. Five cents would get one a seat in the gallery. For another ten cents, copies of the latest sheet music were available in the lobby after the show.

Undoubtedly, Sophie would have been exposed to Yiddish theater and some of the most famous Yiddish actors and actresses who came to eat at the restaurant. Yet, Yiddish theater primarily put on serious plays that did not appeal to young people. On the other hand, vaudeville featured popular performers, including comics and soubrettes, female singers rendering the most popular songs of the day. It was to these performers that Sophie was immensely attracted.

Like many young people, Sophie learned all the latest songs being turned out by Tin Pan Alley tunesmiths; and she delighted in singing them in front of patrons of the restaurant whenever given the chance. The latest tear-jerker songs had restaurant patrons weeping as they ate their meal; the latest rag had them bouncing in their chairs. For Sophie, singing was obviously more enjoyable than waiting on customers and cleaning tables, until her parents forcefully reminded her of restaurant responsibilities.

Undeterred by parental admonitions, Sophie continued to learn the most popular tunes and, unashamed, sang them to restaurant customers, who often gave her a few pennies for her efforts. Encouraged by their response, and seeing performance as a way to avoid the drudgery of restaurant service, Sophie not only sang to patrons while they were eating, she frequently sang at the entrance of the restaurant to attract new customers. Although Charles would rather have seen Sophie work the tables, Jennie tended to support her daughter's musical interests by allowing her to take singing and piano lessons, although neither lasted for very long.

1. Welcome to America

It seemed that the confluence of a good voice, an excellent memory for songs, a responsive audience at the restaurant, and the fantasies of a young girl prompted Sophie to perform. Indeed, given the opportunity, she would rather have visited the local vaudeville house every day than work at her parents' restaurant.

Nevertheless, Jewish girls had special problems, burdens, and expectations, namely marriage and motherhood and a life that often meant social inferiority. Many faced the challenge of whether they would be allowed to define their lives at all. Still, brought up in urban areas, girls like Sophie were continually attracted to American ideas. The pleasures of the immediate moment and freedom from parental supervision gave them brief glimpses of a right to an autonomous self. Could they be bold and resolute enough to grasp the opportunity?

At age sixteen, in June, 1902, Sophie graduated from Brown Elementary School. She was now being

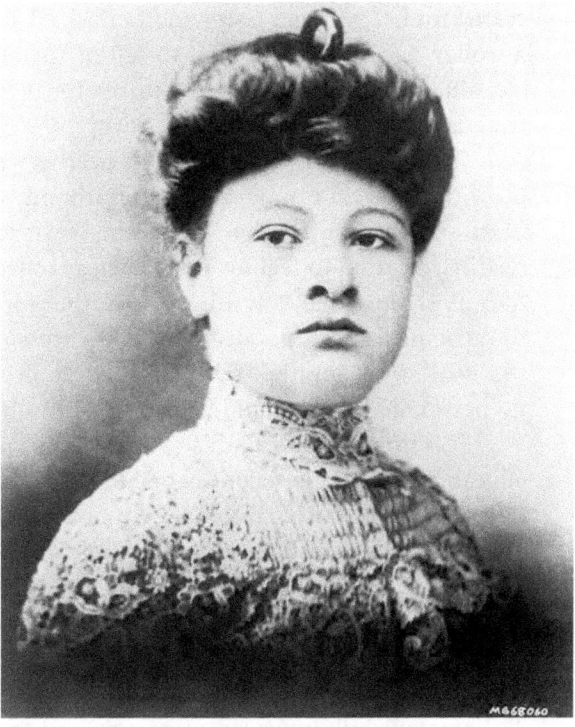

Sophie was sixteen years old and had completed one year of high school when she eloped with Louis Tuck. When told of their actions, her horrified parents forced them to live apart until a formal Jewish wedding had been celebrated. (Harry Ransom Humanities Research Center, University of Texas)

encouraged by the restaurant's customers with theatrical connections to make a career in theater; and she was excited by their encouragement.

"I was born with a quick and true ear," Sophie would say later. "It was the life I always wanted."

It was also a suggestion met with vigorous disapproval from her parents. To the orthodox Jewish family, popular theater was viewed as the work of the Devil; and those entering the profession would become sinners. These were strong warnings to any aspirant.

Although, along with other young women in the community, she accepted her situation, working hard and dealing with life's daily struggles, Sophie was, however, different from her peers and readily admitted her "separation" from the customs of the community. "I hated everything I did as a girl because I wasn't a normal child. I had no playmates. I had nothing," she confessed in her autobiography.

Examples from Sophie's eighth grade English essays reveal the mind of a lonely girl. Articulate, expressive with words, and candid in her feelings, Sophie disdained caring for her younger sister and fantasized about picnicking with friends. A trip on a trolley offered the occasion to tell of various experiences with fellow riders. The cleaning of an attic became a lament for being unable to share the event with girl friends or even family members.

Given the Jewish community's overbearing influences and miserable conditions growing up in an immigrant neighborhood, such feelings were not surprising coming from a young person seeking her own identity. In her autobiography, Sophie readily admitted to feeling alone, a clear reflection of her perceived role in the community: "More than anything else in the world, I wanted to be wanted." In the not too distant future, this deep-seated expression of loneliness would serve as strong motivation for Sophie to define and seek her own identity. One thing was certain: no personal identity could be found within her current restricted environment.

To lend Sophie's fantasies additional momentum, some of the more knowledgeable performers recommended she try out for an amateur nights appearance at Poli's Theater, the local vaudeville house. Most small town vaudeville houses set aside an evening, usually Friday, to hold amateur nights featuring local talent. Winners, based on audience response to the performer, received a plaque or trophy for their efforts and, if they truly entertained the audience, a notice in the local newspaper. Erstwhile performers were required to audition before the theater manager and musical director. If deemed satisfactory, they were included on the amateur bill. The amateur bill, however, was compared to the current vaudeville bill; so if a person happened to juggle and a juggler were already on the regular vaudeville bill, his or her appearance could be delayed for weeks until a juggler "opening" was available. For Sophie, the obstacles of her being chosen, let alone appearing on the bill, seemed monumental. To prepare for her audition, she taught herself the latest songs and, practicing in front of a mirror, worked up routines for each of them.

To her surprise and her parents' consternation, Sophie's first audition garnered her a spot on the next amateur bill. Her strong voice and ability to act out a popular coon-song won her the opportunity to appear. How Sophie learned to render coon-songs can only be guessed. It is likely, however, that the distinctive style had been picked up through her frequent visits to the vaudeville theater where she could observe and later practice such renditions. It was at this point that Sophie began seriously to consider entering show business.

Coon-songs were the rage of the day. Musically, coon-songs were Tin Pan Alley's interpretation of ragtime. As developed by black composers like Scott Joplin, ragtime was an instrumental style characterized by an up-tempo, but unhurried, syncopated melody. In the hands of Tin Pan Alley composers, the coon-song differed from ragtime more in spirit than musical style. What defined the coon-song were its lyrics—stereotypical plantation dialect and racial characterizations, usually dealing with love, loss, and heartbreak—which were almost always sung by whites. Coon-songs were one of the last vestiges of minstrelsy, another case of a black art form reconstituted by white sensibilities.

Sophie was reported to have done well at amateur night, although she did not win a trophy. Nevertheless, subsequent amateur-night performances served to encourage her even more about a possible career in theater. And she clearly excelled at executing popular coon-songs.

All the children in the Abuza family were expected to graduate from high school, with Philip and Moses destined for college. At age sixteen, a little old for a girl to finish her elementary education, Sophie entered high school in September. Her parents had great expectations for her.

Physically mature for her age, Sophie's appearance was in keeping with the voluptuous feminine ideal of the day, exemplified by such popular stage stars as Lillian Russell, Fay Templeton, Anna Held, and Eva Tanguay. Sophie was an attractive girl, with long brown hair. Her appeal was enhanced by a gregarious nature that tended to distinguish her from other, shyer Jewish girls. In spite of these attributes, she later admitted that she neither attended dances and picnics, nor attracted any boy friends.

Her mother now raised with Sophie the subject of marriage and motherhood. Young Jewish women were expected to marry in their late teens. By twenty, they were to have become accomplished homemakers and mothers, thus fulfilling their parents' aspirations and their role in Jewish community life. Sophie's mother was already looking for a suitable marriage prospect and, in keeping with tradition, had already set aside a dowry for her eldest daughter.

Yet Sophie had already demonstrated her disdain for the conventions established for young Jewish women. She had openly testified to her interest in the theater and, against her parents' wishes, participated in amateur-night contests. She would prove equally forthright in her relationships with men.

One such young man, Louis Tuck, age twenty, a bottler and earning fifteen dollars a week, good-looking, considered a sharp dresser, and from a respectable neighborhood family, expressed an interest in Sophie; and she in him. Tuck was viewed as an attractive "catch" by the eligible girls. That he chose Sophie to escort to a dance thrilled her beyond her fondest expectations. That he soon became her boyfriend likely attested to her friendly, outgoing personality and her desire to "break out" of the restrictive mold of traditional boy-girl relations.

The relationship between Sophie and Louis advanced rapidly. Within a short time, they discussed the possibility of marriage. They were both having fun, and the prospect of a future life together seemed mutually exciting. When Louis suggested to Sophie that they elope, such defiance of Jewish marriage rituals seemed to her a grand act of self-proclaimed independence. It also represented a personal statement in her attempt to formulate her own identity. With no hesitation, she agreed to Louis' bold proposal.

On May 14, 1903, telling her mother she was going to a matinee with a girlfriend, Sophie met Louis at the railway station for the short trip to Springfield, Massachusetts.[8] They planned to be married there and then return to Hartford later in the day. In Springfield, the couple was married by a Justice of the Peace. When they returned to Hartford to tell Sophie's parents the news, the young people found themselves confronted by the harsh realities of their deed.

Not surprisingly, Charles and Jennie were astounded. Surprise quickly turned to anger, and anger to shame as her parents faced the prospect of disgrace within the Jewish community. That Sophie had chosen to participate in a marriage ceremony outside the religion — even to another Jew — was a devastating disappointment for her parents. As far as Sophie's parents were concerned, such a scandalous episode could only be rectified by having the couple marry again, this time in the orthodox manner.

Sophie later related the story that her mother forbade her and Louis to reveal anything about the marriage. It was determined that Jennie would confer with Louis's parents to make wedding arrangements, and that the young couple would live separately until after the ceremony. In the meantime, Sophie would suffer family punishment — which usually meant no public appearances — for angering her parents, destroying their plans for her education, and flouting Jewish customs.

Nonetheless, with all of its ritual and colorful activities, the wedding was reported to have been a great success. All the parties involved evidently enjoyed the joyous event. Very likely, no one outside the family ever knew of the couple's trip to Springfield. The newlyweds rented an apartment on Park Street, which happened to be within easy walking distance of the restaurant. Once settled down, Sophie had time to assist her parents when the need arose. Thoughts about pursuing a theatrical career seem to have momentarily vanished.

A year later, however, Sophie found herself pregnant. Since the couple's budget was so meager, she asked her parents about their "going home to live with the folks." To pay for their room and board, Sophie returned to work in the restaurant. As the responsibilities of marriage grew, along with Sophie's swelling abdomen, Louis appeared to lose interest in her; and she in him. She claimed not to be able to abide his lack of initiative, especially in comparison to her own workload; and so she came to ignore him, as if he were no longer a member of the family. Others claimed Louis had been abusive to her.

Their child, Albert Tuck was born on February 5, 1905.[9] As the first grandchild, he was afforded all the attention that could be given a newborn. Now, Sophie wished to move into her own home again; but Louis complained they did not have sufficient money. The standoff continued for several months.

Working in the restaurant put Sophie back in touch with its theatrical patrons; and she was persuaded to sing popular songs, to the customers' delight. The requests reactivated her interest in show business. But how could she even contemplate such a goal in her present predicament?

Sophie confronted Louis about his obtaining a better job and devoting more time to helping her at home, promises he felt unable or unwilling to make. Since Louis thwarted her desires, she requested that he leave, since she wished to separate from him. That action itself would undoubtedly cause embarrassing neighborhood gossip; but Sophie was undaunted in her belief that she had to improve her situation, even if it might mean a dissolution of the marriage.

Living with the family allowed Sophie the flexibility to attend to baby Bert's care, assist her parents in the restaurant, and still have sufficient time to pursue her increasing interest in show business. Home was now located at 26 Morgan Street, where the Abuza family had moved to larger quarters. The entire living space above the restaurant had been converted into rental rooms, making the Abuzas not only restaurant owners, but landlords as well. The house was situated only a few doors from where they had originally lived after arriving in Hartford; but, in terms of space and amenities, the family situation was considerably improved. Sophie had a large room for herself and Bert; and when she worked in the restaurant, younger sister Anna cared for the child.

While Sophie marveled at how her mother had been able to arrange such a lavish wedding and, at the same time, prepare the boys for college, she did not realize that the Abuza family had become quite comfortable financially. The combination of a successful restaurant, now a community meeting place, rooms to rent, and Jennie's businesslike frugality seemed to have contributed to their financial stability. For Jewish children, that they should know so little of their parents' financial situations was not uncommon. In fact, many family matters, including such knowledge as people's ages, births, and divorces, were often kept from the children, not to mention the existence of relatives referred to only in whispers.

By rapidly learning the latest popular songs and frequently visiting local vaudeville houses, Sophie quickly regained her joy of singing and her desire to perform. At this point, however, her increasing attraction to the theater was tempered by her parents' trepidations, her role as a wife and mother, and the community's prejudicial beliefs regarding the wickedness of popular theater. These represented formidable barriers.

Nevertheless, with a hundred dollars in her purse, a set of dresses that she believed would be suitable for stage appearances, a list of Tin Pan Alley song publishers, and unmitigated bravery, Sophie believed she was ready to escape to New York, to launch her show business career.

She told her mother she planned to go to New Haven for a vacation. Louis now lived there, and Jennie likely assumed that Sophie was seeking reconciliation with him. Jennie and Anna would care for Bert in the meantime. Leaving her son was extremely difficult for Sophie, however, especially when he waved goodbye to her as she departed the house for the railway station. Yet Sophie convinced herself that she would not return until she had made good. Or, heaven forbid, run out of money. Or be told she had no talent for the stage.

For a young Jewish girl from Hartford, this New York adventure meant not only a new way of living, but a whole new way of life. It would prove to be far removed from the customs and traditions by which she had been raised.

At the time, vaudeville was highly popular, a major form of American popular entertainment. As Sophie had been told by the restaurant's theatrical patrons, vaudeville always needed and keenly sought new talent. The only question theater managers asked young aspirants was: "What can you do?" Sophie would try anything.

2

Breaking In

A week after arriving in New York, Sophie wrote to her parents. It was a letter bursting with bravery and bravado.

> Dearest folks:
>
> I have decided to go into show business. I have decided that I can do big things and have definitely made up my mind that you will never stand behind a stove and cook any more, and every comfort that I can bring you both, I am going to do, and I know I can do it, if you will let me alone. Don't come to take me back home. Take care of Son, and I will make you proud of me some of these days.
>
> Love to all, Sophie[1]

When Jennie and Charles received their daughter's resounding letter, they were understandably shocked and angered by what they viewed as her wanton desertion of family, custom, and tradition. They did not respond to her. What could they say? In what way could they communicate how they really felt about her unconscionable actions?

Instead, as befit wayward children, Sophie was ostracized from the family. The very mention of her name caused an outburst of epithets and pleas for God's forgiveness. In subsequent letters, Sophie promised to write every week and, she hoped, send money home as soon she could afford it. There are no indications that her parents responded.

The first week in New York had not been encouraging for Sophie. She had obtained a room in a cheap hotel near the train station. As suggested by Willie Howard back at Abuza's restaurant, she had begun her job quest by visiting the offices of Tin Pan Alley publishers. A meeting with Harry Von Tilzer, then one of the premier music publishers, netted a polite refusal. Visits to other music publishing houses elicited similar responses. As Sophie began to understand the employment situation, in order to promote their songs, publishers seemed to be seeking an impossible performer, one who was new and fresh but, somehow, already had some stage experience.

2. Breaking In

Nevertheless, to Sophie, the music publishing offices were exciting places. Piano music and singing voices were heard, seemingly from behind every closed door, all blending into a melodic montage that overwhelmed the senses. Phones rang constantly. Employees literally ran in and out of the main waiting room, as if every moment they hesitated threatened the livelihood of their employer. Amid this tumult sat others like herself, waiting anxiously to be recognized.

And yet, Sophie felt somewhat remote from the activity around her. How could she, an unknown from the hinterland, possibly "make it" in such a dynamic, turbulent environment? Her first week's experiences had gained her nothing but rejections, the majority of employers not even interested in hearing her sing. She was learning quickly that the process of selection was tough and an unknown talent was always the easiest to refuse.

Attempts to speak to agents were no more rewarding. Agents, indeed, were seeking new talent; but always at their time and bidding. Beginners, particularly young women, were usually summarily dismissed because so many of them crowded agents' offices.

Sophie was forced to move to a cheaper hotel. Two more weeks of attempts to sell herself to music publishers and agents proved utterly unfruitful, eliciting not even a reluctant suggestion to "come around later." By this time, regular meals were difficult to obtain. Well then, Sophie reasoned, why not try to get a job singing at a restaurant for meals? It was, after all, a familiar venue.

A number of "song pluggers" suggested that Sophie convince the owners of the Metropole Cafe on Eighth Street that they needed a singer, since one had recently quit. After the proprietor listened to her renditions of a number of popular songs—Sophie had practiced new songs each day since arriving in New York—she was hired. She would sing from 5:00 P.M. to 3:00 A.M. daily for six dollars a week and, of course, meals. For the time being, Sophie had been rescued from the embarrassments of unemployment.

Immediately upon receiving her first salary, she sent three dollars home, her first contribution to the family. In spite of the long hours, she found the working arrangement to her advantage; she had time to practice new songs and, at the same time, continue to look for better employment. Actually, the Metropole Cafe had already established itself as a place to begin one's career. A few years earlier, a young waiter named Irving Berlin had entertained patrons with his piano playing.

Sophie soon learned that opportunities for employment could also be found at the numerous beer gardens located in the theater district. Popular venues for both locals and theater people, beer gardens did not hesitate to hire aspirants, if at low salaries. Enticingly, they promised ambitious performers that, if they pleased the clientele, tips would likely more than double their salaries. Even more important, however, was the fact that agents looking for new talent were often sighted among beer garden patrons.

One of the most popular of beer gardens, The German Village, on Fortieth Street, off Broadway, was reported to be seeking entertainers. Sophie approached the proprietor for an audition, but was initially turned away. Friends persuaded her to return and, at least, request an opportunity to sing. After all, she had little to lose after searching for employment for almost six weeks. This time, the proprietor agreed to hear her and, afterwards, surprised Sophie by offering her a job at fifteen dollars a week. For her part, she would be singing from 4:00 P.M. until 2:00 A.M. daily, except Sunday. (New York City had a "blue" law forbidding theaters to charge admission on Sundays.) This, of course, meant Sophie would be required to sing dozens of popular songs each day, which, in turn, demanded frequent trips to music publishers to obtain the latest tunes. Once the songs were selected, she practiced them until they were ready to be publicly introduced. She was also required to dress for the role.

This latter requirement could be easily fulfilled. For one dollar, she could rent a different dress each week. Learning songs, however, required Sophie to practice each day with a pianist at the beer garden between visits to Tin Pan Alley to seek new material. It was not long before song pluggers became familiar with the friendly young woman who seemed to have an insatiable need for songs.

"Got something new, boys?" she asked at each visit. "Something new. That's what the customers like."[2]

After a few visits, some pluggers saved songs especially for her. "Try this, Soph. It's your stuff." Others offered to arrange a song to meet her style. "Try it like this," they suggested, and proceeded to pound out an alternative rhythm for her.

The German Village was an ornate three-story building, decked out in blinking electric lights and colorful banners. Each floor of the building had been designed to satisfy a different clientele, based on its decor, prices, and the quality of its entertainment. The top-level second floor, reserved for beginning performers, was Sophie's first assignment. The ground floor attracted a "better class of customers." The underground rathskeller, however, was reserved for the best clientele, which meant the well-to-do and theatrical patrons, particularly agents. Prices there were the highest, performers' tips the best; and talent on display the most high-class a beer garden could offer, in close competition with that presented at nearby vaudeville houses. It was well-known that many current vaudeville headliners had begun their careers as beer garden performers.

In her weekly letters home, Sophie wrote of her show business success, never mentioning, however, that she was singing in a beer garden, dressed in clothes "that would have turned Mama's hair white." Money accompanied the letters, with admonitions like, "hire some help in the restaurant," "have Papa go to the dentist," and most revealingly, "take five dollars out of this and bring the baby to New York for a day so I can see him."[3] During all of her first year in New York, there is no evidence to suggest she saw her child, let alone received encouragement from her parents.

Sophie's blooming performance skills soon got her promoted to the ground floor of The German Village, along with a salary increase — to twenty dollars a week — plus more substantial tips. A good week could net fifty dollars, a handsome sum that prompted her to move to a better hotel and rent dresses more frequently. Another new element to her singing, likely influenced by her song-plugging buddies, was the increasing inclusion of ragtime, still referred to as "coon songs."

Ragtime was not a new musical form. W.C. Handy, the pioneer of blues, had insisted that ragtime was nothing more than a pepped-up version of Negro spirituals. In contrast to Negro spirituals, however, ragtime was happy, funny, and sometimes sexually suggestive, thus departing from the domain of Negro music and entering the white man's lexicon. The outstanding feature of ragtime was syncopation, a dislocation of regular rhythmic accent. Among ragtime composers, it contributed to a move away from precise pitch and a special accenting of both words and music. For singers, ragtime became an aural instead of a notational expression. Each singer made the song what they wanted by dictating the beat, phrasing emphasis, and repetition of words.

Tin Pan Alley took these musical directions and simplified them so music lovers could play them on their upright pianos and sing them without having to be concerned with the subtle intricacies of melody. Still, few people found they could play or sing ragtime songs to any real degree. It took singing professionals to give ragtime its excitement, its jump and edge. In so doing, they identified themselves as unique interpreters of the style. Babies became "babes"; mothers became "mamas"; and the implications were obviously different, thus providing a "glow" to the meaning of the lyrics.

Rag could laugh at itself and could also laugh at the conventions of the day, containing in its lyrics social criticism, sexual innuendo, and the use of the interpolated vowel. Using Negro dialect lent itself well toward rendering such songs. Whereas, in elementary school, Sophie sang "Hello, My Baby" as it had been originally written, at the beer garden, she would sing "He-ge-dello, ma baby, He-ge-dello, ma ragtime girl," with an upbeat tempo. Ragtime interpretation seemed to come easy for Sophie and she turned syncopation into an art form that she could uniquely render. Audiences quickly began to take notice.

Sophie's popularity soon advanced her to The German Village's rathskeller, with all of its potential benefits. Patrons applauded her singing, shouted out for encores, and, when she had concluded, shouted the names of other songs they wished to hear her sing. For most of these requests, she was already prepared, which in itself astonished patrons. And when she was not yet familiar with a song, she told the clientele to "come back tomorrow, when I'll sing it for you."

Already, patrons were aware of her strong voice, one that could permeate every corner of the room. Yet, her vocal power did nothing to inhibit articulation or accent. Sophie was learning to "sell" a tune, song pluggers observed; and audiences were responding with obvious enthusiasm.

Still, her success at The German Village had not attracted agents anxious to sign Sophie for high-class vaudeville or even a tour of the "provinces." Instead, Sophie continued to haunt the offices of small-time agents, begging for a tryout. Though vaudeville salaries would be less than those she currently earned, such engagements gained considerably more exposure and prestige.

An agent who had been accosted by Sophie a number of times finally took pity and signed her to appear at a ten-cent vaudeville house in Harlem, the 125th Street Theater, near the corner of Third Avenue. Sophie had been unaware, however, of the arrangement made between the agent and the theater manager, Chris Brown, that she would have to audition at an amateur night before he agreed to have her appear on the bill. This being her first appearance on a vaudeville stage in New York, prior to going on, Sophie alternated between nervousness and outright fear. In fact, when she was announced, Brown actually had to push her onto the stage.

Ten-cent vaudeville audiences were tough on performers, just as apt to ruthlessly jeer someone off the stage as applaud her. Unsatisfactory performers would literally be "given the hook." Upon a signal from the manager in the wings, a stagehand would use a cane to snag the hapless performer and unceremoniously pull him or her off the stage. The dreaded "hook" was embarrassing, if not downright devastating, for any aspirant.

Yet, once Sophie came on stage and the pianist gave her cue, all fear vanished. Instinctively, she let loose with her first song, "Rosie, My Dusky Georgia Rosie," a new ragtime tune. The audience enjoyed her so much, she was asked to sing three more songs.

Sophie had passed the test. She was signed for the week, at a salary of twenty dollars. (One dollar—five percent—went to the agent; three dollars were sent home; one dollar went for a rented dress.) Even more important, the agent was so impressed with Sophie's performance and audience response to her stage presence, he asked if she were interested in a contract to appear on the Park circuit, a string of ten-cent vaudeville houses in New York and "surrounding territories" (a euphemism for any theater within 250 miles of New York that could be reached by overnight train). She would earn from fifteen to twenty dollars a week, depending on her position on the bill. Rooms would be paid for, but train fare and food were her responsibility. With no hesitation, Sophie eagerly embraced the engagement.

Only then did the agent inform her that she would be required to perform in blackface, explaining that, in blackface, she would be able to convey her dialect coon songs better in front of the less sophisticated audiences in small towns. In fact, the agent believed it would be better for her to be perceived as Negro than Jewish.

Sophie's first road date was in Meridian, Connecticut, where she gained her first experience at blacking-up. Even with assistance from fellow performers, the job was awkward and messy; and she quickly learned not to perform in a white dress. Banners announcing the vaudeville bill called Sophie the "World Renowned Coon Shouter," the usual advertising exaggeration given unknown performers in the "provinces," as agents called the small-town, small-time vaudeville circuits.

A month of week-long and three-day engagements in small New England towns (many such towns could only afford their theaters to be open three days a week) finally procured Sophie a return to New York City. On December 9, 1906, Sophie appeared on the bill at Wilson's Music Hall on 116th Street, a ten-cent vaudeville house that kept the neighborhood guessing when and if it would be open for business.

2. Breaking In

Sophie became a blackface "coon" singer while touring with the Gay Masqueraders, a burlesque company. She had begun as a member of the chorus, but soon became a featured performer because of her stage presence and clarion voice. To prove she was white, Sophie removed her gloves and wig at the end of the performance, which elicited both surprise and cheers from audiences. (Harry Ransom Humanities Research Center, University of Texas)

This time, the New York audience was friendly and relaxed and welcomed performers with enthusiasm.

By this time, Sophie had experienced a wide variety of audiences and had learned to accommodate herself to their idiosyncrasies. Her worst experience so far had been when a snowstorm reduced the audience to ten people. How does one perform to an empty space? Sophie asked her colleagues. Exactly the same way one performs to a full house, they replied. One pretends it is full. Orchestras were always helpful in these situations, loudly applauding the performer and banging on their instruments to add to the noise.

Sophie earned twenty dollars for the week at the 116th Street Theater. She appeared with seven other acts, from comic teams to acrobats to trained dogs. Third on the bill, she held an advantageous spot, directly before the headliner's appearance. When she gave too many encores, however, the headliner reminded her that she was occupying too much time on stage.

The following week, for the same salary, Sophie appeared at the Family Theater, this time in the sixth position, where she had been placed to allow for audience requests for encores. Sophie took full advantage by singing seven songs and remaining on stage for twenty-one minutes, an unprecedented time at such a theater. It was good to be back in New York.

Yet, in spite of those brief, exciting moments on stage, Sophie found touring to be a lonely existence, made even more difficult by the fact that she was one of the few performers who played solo. Further, unpredictable touring practices often made life on the road unpleasant. Sophie had to handle her own travel arrangements. Sometimes, train rides lasted more than a day. Arriving at a destination, she had to find a hotel or boardinghouse that catered to theater people. (In every city, there were still a few hotels and boardinghouses that refused to rent to actors, displaying signs that read "No dogs or actors allowed.") A boardinghouse usually provided meals. If one stayed at a hotel, recommendations from stage veterans provided the names of affordable restaurants.

Sophie quickly adjusted to the daily routine on the road. Actors slept late, then ate a large breakfast to fortify themselves for long morning rehearsals at the theater. After a light lunch, Sophie had the afternoon off to take care of personal business or just walk around seeing the sights, since most towns she visited were unfamiliar. She would often try to strike up conversations with locals, but it was difficult to find people who would stop to talk. Traveling variety performers were generally regarded with suspicion. Frequently, Sophie would visit music stores to look for the latest song releases. Those she found she immediately practiced on her own. At next day's rehearsals, she worked with the orchestra pianist to prepare for the song's introduction that evening. Rarely did Sophie "kill time" with other performers.

Being a solo performer also affected how colleagues and theater personnel responded to Sophie. For the most part, she was left alone. While respect for privacy was an unwritten law among performers, Sophie's apparent independence and self-sufficiency seemed to have intimidated colleagues to the point that they were hesitant to include her in group activities. Her actions both on and off the stage suggested to some that Sophie was a focused and "driven" person.

But it was the nights after the theater that troubled Sophie most. Though she was surrounded by friendly people and audiences showered her with accolades, Sophie, nevertheless, suffered from acute loneliness. During these uncomfortable moments, she wished she could see her family and felt remorse about having left them. Occasionally, she cried herself to sleep. The following morning, however, she awoke, even more resolved to prove herself, to herself and her parents, to "plug away and get to be a headliner," "to succeed, whatever it cost."[4]

One way Sophie discovered to earn additional money was to make herself available for one-time performances, at Sunday concerts, fraternal parties, conventions, and amusement park shows. Each week, newspapers listed upcoming events; and Sophie wrote to these people to offer her services. More often then not, she was able to earn an extra five or ten dollars a week by appearing at these events. Such activities also served to give her more public exposure. It was during this time that Sophie began to collect business cards, names and addresses, to include them in her scrapbook for possible future use. It became an activity she continued throughout her career.

Most important, the return to New York brought a visit by sister Anna and son Bert for a day. Visiting with her family certainly buoyed her spirits; but she had been away so long from her son, he was calling Anna his mother. The episode reminded Sophie that she still had a long way to go to be accepted by her family for who she was, all the more for who she aspired to be.

While in the city, Sophie hounded Tin Pan Alley offices and her song plugger friends for new material. When she lamented the lack of available material on the road, song pluggers pointed out that playing in a different town each week actually lessened her need for new songs. Yet, Sophie would not accept their thesis; she always wanted the latest songs if, for no other reason, to keep herself sharp and excited about performing.

Back on the road, Sophie was appearing in theaters where she had already played. To her delight, audiences remembered her blackface act, her powerful, expressive voice, and her repertoire of songs. Now, she was being billed late in the program to allow for encores and additional songs. Colleagues marveled at how Sophie could practice all morning and then belt out songs in the evening without affecting her vocal cords. Some gave her the nickname "iron lungs," an affectionate gesture of professional recognition. Still, the life of a single woman playing alone seemed to Sophie a liability; no question, she longed for more companionship.

When Sophie finished her engagement on the Park circuit and returned to New York in the fall of 1907, she had completed nine months on tour, in towns she had never seen before, let alone knew existed, and hoped she would never see again. Nevertheless, the experience had been an excellent training ground for her, an opportunity to perfect her act and add "business" that gained greater acceptance from audiences. One such educational episode occurred by chance when she caught a cold that affected her singing voice. Unable to sing, she "talked" the lyrics; and audiences responded favorably to the departure. It immediately became part of her song presentation.

What turned out to be a significant addition to her blackface routine came when a theater manager noticed that the audience had shown uneasiness about listening to a Negro singer. He suggested that, at the conclusion of her act, Sophie remove her wig and gloves to reveal to the audience her "whiteness." At first, the audience was in shock when she removed the props; but, after a poignant pause, as if to collect their collective breath, they broke out in cheers and applause due to the surprise. The stunt became a regular, triumphal ending for her blackface act.

Sophie was signed to appear at the 116th Street Theater, at Lenox Avenue, currently being operated by Loew, Zukor, and Schenck, partners and recent graduates from nickelodeon ownership.[5] Marcus Loew particularly admired Sophie's singing, and he promised to feature her at all of his theaters in the New York area. (He and his partners operated twelve at the time.) Her salary remained twenty dollars a week, but she had been promised bookings for several months.

Still, the assignment was a good deal more rigorous than she had realized, since it involved appearing in sixteen shows a day — eight during the daylight hours in blackface and eight more at night as a white. Since Sophie had so little time between shows, Loew would bring in food for her.

On the positive side, playing consistently in New York allowed Sophie to rent several gowns and change them each week, not to mention obtain new material from the music publishers. Of course, they were pleased to see her, knowing the songs she selected would be featured in her act that very night.

The 116th Street Theater closed—Loew sold it—but reopened in February 1, 1908, as a two-performance-a-day vaudeville house, with shows at 3:00 P.M. and 8:20 P.M. at higher prices, for that theater, a definite step up in class. During the new theater's opening week, Sophie was billed as one of the headliners, "Your Favorite Coon Shouter," for the magnificent salary of thirty-five dollars a week. She appeared fifth on a bill of ten acts. Although she came on immediately after intermission, she made the most of it, her performances so lively, and so long, those following her complained that she spent too much time on stage. The astute manager, however, told Sophie to take as much time as she wanted; and even then, audiences still seemed to feel they had not gotten enough of her. Sophie was held over for another week.

Word on Sophie had passed around by now: a powerful and expressive voice; an audience pleaser; an encore producer; a unique act, unlike any other currently found on the vaudeville stage. But she had yet to prove herself in high-class theaters.

For the aspiring performer, one was not really recognized unless he or she had appeared at Tony Pastor's Theater. In show business since the 1870s, Tony Pastor had popularized an entertainment he named "variety." His presentations became famous; and Pastor was recognized as the "Father of Vaudeville," although he publicly disliked the name. First to appeal to women and children, ban drinking and smoking in his theater, Pastor sought to present a high-class, "clean" production that satisfied patrons and made them eager to return again the following week, when a new bill would be playing. Pastor not only made his shows an enjoyable experience, he had also featured many of the top vaudeville headliners as they were beginning their stage careers.

A spot on a Pastor bill was prestigious. To perform at Pastor's Theater meant legitimacy, exposure, and the opportunity to launch a quality show business career. Familiar with Pastor's reputation, Sophie wrote him, asking that he consider her for an engagement. Pastor set up an audition, to which Sophie came armed with seven songs. She needed to sing only three of them to be signed to appear April 11, 1908, for a week, at thirty-five dollars.

For each performance at Pastor's Theater, Sophie wore a different gown and sang a different set of songs. Finding himself practicing new songs at rehearsals each morning, the piano accompanist admitted he had never encountered a singer such as she. Despite being identified as Sophie Taylor on the theater program, Sophie received her first New York reviews, one in the *New York Clipper*, the weekly theatrical newspaper that everyone connected with show business read zealously, and *Variety*, the *Clipper*'s young and aggressive competitor.

The *Clipper* review was short and to-the-point.

> Sophie Tucker, with her coon songs and melodies, her pleasing voice and manner, won applause.[6]

Variety embellished Sophie's act by pointing out the compelling affinity of her blackface performance.

12 minute act. She wisely appears in blackface and makes an attractive looking young woman. She is wise in making her appearance in darkey makeup as she strengthens her act by carrying out the coon impersonation to the strict letter. She sang three songs, took many bows, and had to return to sing an encore.[7]

Tony Pastor was old and tired, and he spoke openly of retiring. In fact, he sold his theater a month after Sophie appeared there. Three months later, the grand old man of vaudeville was dead.

Sophie's appearance at Pastor's gained her the attention of the proprietor of the Hathaway circuit, a group of eight (or ten, depending on the season) theaters operating in Connecticut, Rhode Island, and Massachusetts. Sophie agreed to play them for the summer, at a salary of thirty-five dollars a week. She would, however, have to do double-duty with Hathaway's touring stock company. Hathaway summer shows consisted of part melodrama, part olio; "something for everyone" was Phil Hathaway's motto. Sophie was to appear white in the melodrama portion. In the olio portion, however, Sophie would continue to sing in blackface.

Prior to beginning the engagement with Hathaway — Sophie had more than a month to fill — she appeared at The Auditorium in Lynn, Massachusetts, on a first-class vaudeville bill. Sharing the stage with her was Fred Zobedie, an Olympic gymnast, the first to use his games-winning fame in vaudeville, and W.C. Fields, identified in the program as "the world's greatest juggler." Hyperbole came easily to vaudeville theater programs. Sophie also filled her time with Sunday concerts in New York at Lyceum Hall, Periscolo Hall, Aswin Hall, the St. Paul's Club, and the Hotel Astor, which was sponsoring a railroad truck driver's dinner. Anything for a few extra dollars.

The summer tour helped Sophie to sharpen her acting abilities, thanks to the various roles she played in the melodramas. The stock company performed a new play every two weeks. She was also recognized through a number of reviews for her work: "best coon shouter ever heard"; "Sophie Tucker, coon shouter, is a real blackface comedienne and sings her southern ditties with a good deal of spirit and enthusiasm."[8]

Sophie's summer *tour de force,* however, came when the company appeared at Rock Springs Park in July. Sophie appeared on the street in a new fashion called the sheath skirt and came close to acquiring a police escort straight out of town. She was arrested for demonstrating to locals how easy the skirt made it to jump off curbs and step over puddles, in doing so, not only revealing her ankles but a portion of leg as well. Local newspapermen rescued Sophie and brought her to their offices, where she was interviewed about her revealing attire. That evening, at the theater, when Sophie came on stage, people in the audience shouted for her to wear the sheath while she performed. When the episode was reported to Phil Hathaway, he warned Sophie not to do anything that would defame his good name. "Confine your actions to the scripted stage," he cautioned.

The episode, reported in *Variety,* did not miss the alert eye of Gus Hill, who was at the moment in the process of hiring personnel for his touring burlesque company,

"The Gay Masqueraders." A former vaudeville headliner who had parlayed his success into the management of several traveling burlesque and vaudeville companies, Hill had the reputation of running a tightly-managed group, cheaply. For performer misdemeanors, Hill reduced the guilty party's weekly salary. He had bought boarding houses in many cities his company played; and he required members to stay there, at the same time charging them a fee. Yet Hill recognized talent and allowed his performers to change and freshen their acts frequently. Nor did he seem to mind if occasional "blue" material entered skits and song lyrics (depending on city laws governing "obscene" material).

Sophie was hired as a multifaceted performer: she would act in skits; participate in ensemble pieces; and sing in blackface in the olio portion of the program, all for forty dollars a week, plus rail fare. The company would open in New York, September 7, 1908, and play until May 15, 1909, a total of thirty-seven weeks. They would perform two shows a day, seven days a week in states that permitted Sunday shows. For Sophie, a continuous booking (and salary) such as this engagement was a daydream come true. Although burlesque was viewed as a step below vaudeville and was banned in some cities, its popularity was equally great. (Burlesque shows then featured farce-comedy, satire, and travesty, sometimes tinged with sexual innuendo. Scantily-clad "girlie" shows had not yet been invented.)

A letter home told of Sophie's new stage success, although she did not reveal being part of a burlesque company. She mentioned traveling for eight months to places she had never been—the Midwest, South, big cities—and the excitement it was to bring. She also mentioned she was sending home ten dollars a week, a handsome sum of money that she hoped would help prove her stage triumphs to a skeptical family. On the other hand, although she would be appearing in Boston, Springfield, and Holyoke during the season, all of them cities quite close to Hartford, Sophie carefully omitted any reference to her presence there.

A review of "The Gay Masqueraders" during its opening week in New York made a brief mention of Sophie's work.

> Although Miss Tucker confines herself to coon songs, and is found in the olio, she is an able songstress and actress. Her stage presence and powerful, mellow voice are well worthy of recognition.[9]

In fact, the more encores Sophie was asked to give and the more songs audiences wished her to sing, the better company management liked it. Further, they encouraged her to add new songs and new routines to her act. Sophie also learned to grace her singing with a slight touch of sexual insinuation—a movement of her eye, a significant pause on double-entendres, an exaggerated lyric—thanks to instruction given her by the company's stage manager, Harry Emerson, a veteran burlesque headliner. Audiences could not get enough of her performances. By the third week of the tour, Sophie was being advertised as the "Queen of Coon Shouters."

A visit to the Howard Theater, Boston, gained great praise for Sophie from a newspaper reviewer.

A top-notch coon shouter who has the chocolate dialect down as fine as the native. She'll warble the notes that land hard on the mark every time.[10]

In a Brockton, Massachusetts, review, Sophie was called "the sunny singer of Southern songs." The reviewer in Colwes, New York, wrote that Sophie was a "refined coon singer." He went on to state that she was "one of the few, and best, coon singers in vaudeville." Not all comments, however, were plaudits.

The program at the Olympic Park Theater identified her as Ethel Tucker; in Elizabeth, New Jersey, she was Sadie Woods. And an Albany reviewer called her songs "offensive."

The company's return to New York in November met with full houses and good reviews, although Sophie was not particularly singled out. She was, however, approached by the Atlas Advertising Company, a recent entry into the phonograph recording business, to make a record for them. Sophie was their first choice; the song chosen, "Rosie, My Dusky Georgia Rosie," the same song she had sung in audition before appearing at the 125th Theater two years earlier. Of course, Sophie was proud of her first recording. It was reported that she received twenty-five dollars for her efforts. An ad for the phonograph record was placed in various theatrical publications. Shortly thereafter, however, Atlas retired from the recording business; and Sophie's record quickly disappeared.

Sophie's first visit to Chicago evidently ended in triumph, although under singular circumstances. The city had passed strong laws governing theaters featuring

Thanks to the Atlas Advertising Company, in 1908, Sophie made her first phonograph record, "Rosie, My Dusky Georgia Rosie." Unfortunately, the record had a very short selling life because Atlas decided to quit the music distribution business.

burlesque. Those that did not conform to the laws were quickly closed by police. Not surprisingly, theater managers attempted various methods to circumvent being included in the suspect group playing "blue" or suggestive material. Euson's Theater had engaged "The Gay Masqueraders," and they were not about to have their theater closed down. To assure patrons of their respect for the law, they advertised the theater as a place to see "censored burlesque for ladies and gentlemen." The advertising ploy proved highly successful, filling the theater at every performance. The degree to which the performance actually adhered to the law was open to question.

Within moments of taking the stage on opening night at Euson's, Sophie captured the audience. Wearing a shimmering blue gown with dazzling jewelry (rented and fake), sporting a feathered hat, she talked to the audience, assuring them she would sing no "blue" songs. Still, she warned them she might sing songs that could be "taken another way," to which the audience responded "sing 'em." She asked them if they wanted her to appear in blackface, and they shouted for her to "stay white."

"You've got it," she replied, then launched into the rag "Naughty Eyes" while the audience cheered and stamped their feet in approval. "Shine On, Harvest Moon" had to be encored three times, the last time with the audience singing along. When she sang "I Want Someone to Call Me Dearie," each pause, each exaggerated phrase brought whistles and appreciative groans. She sang three more songs, and the audience shouted for more.

Business in Chicago had been so profitable, "The Gay Masqueraders" returned in early March, 1909, and two weeks later played at another theater in Chicago featuring "censured burlesque," The Star and Garter. As far as reviewers were concerned, Sophie was the primary reason the theaters were filled. She was no longer appearing in skits or with the ensemble. Rather, an extended block of time had been set aside for her spot; and it was not uncommon for Sophie to be on stage for half an hour. The combination of new songs, beautiful gowns, and stage presence primed audiences from the moment she appeared. Chicago would soon become one of Sophie's favorite cities. She returned often throughout her career, as, over the years, enthusiasm for her performance turned to adulation and, ultimately, worship.

"The Gay Masqueraders" planned to close the season in Boston in May; and Sophie decided to spend a few days with the Abuzas, hopefully to improve family relations. Still, she wondered, how could she prove to her family that she was really "making it" in show business?

The stop before Boston was Holyoke, Massachusetts, playing a small theater known for its noisy college clientele. One evening during the engagement, however, the audience buzzed with excitement due to the possible attendance of a well-known theater impresario. They proved to be correct in their anticipation.

Midway through the show, Flo Ziegfeld slipped into a box to watch the performance. It had been rumored that Ziegfeld was seeking acts for his Follies' new season. Sophie had not yet appeared on stage, and the knowledge that Ziegfeld was in the audience made her tremble. "Pretend like he isn't there," suggested Harry Emerson. "Just do what you usually do."

Immediately after the show, Sophie introduced herself to Ziegfeld and asked for an opportunity to audition for him. He suggested she write him to let him know the next time she planned to play in New York. From Boston, she wrote Ziegfeld that she was appearing in a Sunday benefit in two weeks. His written response was a simple "thank you."

Ziegfeld attended the benefit, saw Sophie perform, and signed her for an as yet unspecified role in the upcoming "Follies of 1909."

Sophie had been selected to appear in the Ziegfeld Follies! What, she thought, could be better than that?

When Sophie visited her family, she was greeted warmly, with affection. Yet they seemed sad. While they acknowledged her recent successes, especially her new employment with the Follies, they informed Sophie that the Jewish community continued to view her as a "bad woman" for having left her husband, child, and parents.

Sophie could see that the burden of these accusations had gravely aged them. When she went out on the streets to talk to people in the neighborhood, she was rebuffed. Women turned their backs on her; men stared; children hurled jibes at her. Even her sister Anna and son Bert were pointed at in derision. That night, overcome with regrets, Sophie promised herself and her parents that she would not come back to Hartford until "I'm a big success."[11]

3

The Mary Garden of Ragtime (1)

Displaying his well-known authoritarian and blunt demeanor, Ziegfeld Follies stage director Julian Mitchell presented Sophie with a large cloth bag. "Here is your costume." Then, waving some papers at her, he said, "And here is the song you will sing." Finally, he instructed her: "Learn it immediately, so we can begin blocking out the jungle scene."

Mitchell handed Sophie a faux leopard-skin suit, which obviously required alteration — "the seamstresses will shape it for you," Mitchell advised — and the music for "Moving Day in Jungle Town." Mitchell's ensemble scene called for twenty-three performers, ten men dressed as animals, eleven women dressed as jungle girls, and two white hunters.

Since Sophie had to finish her engagement with the "Gay Masqueraders" in Boston before joining the cast, she arrived in New York less than three weeks before the Follies was to open in Atlantic City. The cast had already been rehearsing for more than a month.

After producing two highly successful revues, Ziegfeld had decided to make these productions an annual event, each designed to be more elaborate than its predecessor. "The Follies of 1909" was directed by Herbert Gresham, with Ziegfeld constantly at his shoulder ready to veto material he did not believe sufficiently stageworthy. Following a series of Victor Herbert hits, among them "The Wizard of Oz" and "Babes in Toyland," Julian Mitchell was hired as the impresario's stage director. Harry B. Smith, a veteran of musical comedies, was responsible for the book and lyrics; and Maurice Levi wrote the music. Typical of revues, the Follies offered no plot, only a series of olio scenes, which were continually undergoing change. Throughout the production's run, the cast was required to learn new material every day. The changes could be as minor as additional dialogue, as major as the incorporation of entirely new scenes. The Follies opened with two acts and thirteen scenes. A month later, Act One contained nine scenes; Act Two eleven scenes.

Headliners for the 1909 version of the Follies included Nora Bayes, now at the height of her performing career and a holdover from the 1908 Follies; her singing and dancing husband, Jack Norworth; Lillian Lorraine, a beautiful Ziegfeld favorite, both on the stage and, if rumor could be believed, in the boudoir; Bessie Clayton, toe-dancer deluxe (who also happened to be Mitchell's former wife); Mae Murray, of future silent film fame; Gertrude Vanderbilt, an excellent dancer and actress when she was not importuning the orchestra to follow her beat; and Harry Kelley, a veteran comic song-and-dance man. Sophie was scheduled to appear in the middle of Act Two, after Bessie Clayton's dance and before Jack Norworth's song and dance to "Dear Old Father."

Although only six minutes in length, "Moving Day in Jungle Town" was probably the liveliest, most animated skit in a rather formulaic Act Two. The act and the production ended with a patriotic ensemble number, featuring Nora Bayes in a salute to the U.S. Navy.

Led by Sophie, in blackface, attired in a leopard-skin costume, ten assorted animals entered the stage singing "Moving Day in Jungle Town" and dancing to the rhythmic music. They were quickly followed by eleven scantily-clad jungle girls who began dancing with the animals. Enter Teddy Roosevelt and his gun bearer. The animals, in fear of the mighty hunter, ran away or climbed trees to hide. The jungle girls then lured a distracted Roosevelt off-stage. Both the animals and jungle girls returned to front stage to finish out the act with a happily sung flourish. Sophie, at the head of the animals, led the singing. She could easily be heard above all the rest.

The "Jungle Town" scene had been a late addition to the mix of olios, having been included by Ziegfeld to take advantage of Teddy Roosevelt's recent return from an African hunting expedition. Smith and Levi were instructed to write a song for the proposed skit, and Mitchell was directed to design the ensemble piece. Since Mitchell had only three weeks to get the scene in the kind of flawless shape he might be satisfied with, performers were rehearsed day and night. Until the skit had reached his level of perfection, Mitchell was unrelenting in his demands. At the same time, he supervised other scenes in much the same way, pushing performers almost to utter exhaustion. Sophie had never experienced such a taskmaster in her brief career, but the lessons Mitchell taught her about performance discipline never left her.

On June 7, 1909, the "Follies of 1909" opened at an Atlantic City theater to a house filled with celebrities and New York reviewers. The production received favorable comment, with the principles singled out for their individual efforts. None of the reviewers mentioned the "Jungle" scene or Sophie. The week in Atlantic City smoothed out the show and prepared it for the critical New York opening.

The production opened at the "Jardin de Paris," atop the roof of the New York Theater. Everyone who was anyone was in attendance to see Ziegfeld's new creation. Audiences and critics had already acknowledged that the Ziegfeld-originated revue was a new form of entertainment, particularly with its emphasis on beautiful girls posing in resplendent and elaborate costumes.

New York critics gave the Follies excellent reviews, praising especially the work

Broadway and Longacre Square (soon to be renamed Times Square) in 1909. On the right was the New York Theater, site of the Ziegfeld Follies of 1909, in which Sophie had a brief, starring role before she was unceremoniously dropped from the cast due to headliner Eva Tanguay's jealous complaints.

of Nora Bayes and Lillian Lorraine. The week in Atlantic City, they pointed out, had clearly improved the show, ridding it of "dead" material and sharpening the comedy. In one of the many reviews, Sophie happened to be mentioned, albeit briefly.

> Sophie Tucker's fine appearance and clear, powerful voice, made a success with "Moving Day in Jungle Town," assisted by counterfeits of various wild animals.[1]

Back stage, however, what had once been subtle tensions suddenly rose to the surface. Nora Bayes had not been entirely satisfied with her contract and now demanded a renegotiation. Ziegfeld refused; and after a series of angry confrontations, Bayes and Norworth abandoned the cast, leaving Ziegfeld without a headliner. A month later, Ziegfeld sued Bayes for breach of contract. She claimed that restaurant waiters loudly attending to patrons and the excessively bright lights of the stage had given her an attack of nervous prostration. Ziegfeld's lawyer countered the accusation by pointing out that her alleged condition had not prevented Bayes from attending the races and indulging in late-night suppers.

At the same time, Ziegfeld was having all too obvious problems with his wife, Anna Held. Ziegfeld had recently installed Lillian Lorraine in the same hotel where he and Anna lived, which only exacerbated Held's connubial distress. On stage, Julian Mitchell repeatedly argued with Ziegfeld about increased costs due to the constant adding of new scenes and revamping of old ones.

Yet, even though the Follies ran two weeks without a headliner, the theater was packed at every performance. After hasty negotiations, Ziegfeld hired the volatile, flamboyant, and imperious Eva Tanguay to headline the show. Her engagement was on a trial basis for two weeks, despite the fact that Gresham, Smith, and Mitchell had all tried to prevent it. The move created additional press attention but also murmurs of protest from some members of the cast who knew and had worked with Tanguay. Nonetheless, Tanguay took over Bayes's songs and performed creditably enough to gain favorable comments from reviewers.

After Tanguay's two-week trial period, Ziegfeld needed only favorable reviews to sign her for the duration of the season. Tanguay immediately made her own demands regarding the show. She would introduce a number of new songs; her skits would have to be lengthened, thus requiring the entire second act to be expanded; and she claimed the crowd-pleasing song, "Moving Day in Jungle Town," as her own. Up against it, Ziegfeld was forced to drop Sophie from the cast. Losing her sixty dollars a week salary, Sophie was suddenly out of a job, after performing successfully in the Follies for almost nine weeks.

It was during her engagement with the Follies that Sophie became friends with Lillian Lorraine's maid, Molly Elkins, herself a veteran of Negro vaudeville. A calm, stoic, and supportive woman, Elkins helped to soothe Sophie's profound disappointment when she was fired. Sophie, in turn, cherished the relationship; Mollie had been like a mother to her in her time of despair. Some years later, when Sophie could afford it, Elkins would become Sophie's maid and confidante, until her illness in the 1920s.

Meanwhile, at Sophie's lowest ebb, enter William Morris. Nee Wilhelm Moses, Morris was born in 1873 and came to the U.S. as a young man. One of the odd jobs he took to help support the family was acting; and he liked it so well, he decided to enter show business. In the 1890s, his initial attempt to become a theater owner failed. Instead, he chose to become a performer's agent. He quickly enjoyed success because clients considered him "a gentleman in a profession crowded with vultures." During the early 1900s, Morris again attempted to secure ownership of theaters, believing that combining ownership with representation of performers would prove a profitable endeavor.

Morris planned to pattern his theaters after the London Music Hall, in an attempt to create a cosmopolitan atmosphere to complement the talent on stage. Refreshments would be served at a buffet whenever the theater was open to the public, from 1:30 in the afternoon until the last patron left the evening performance.

During this time, beverages would also be available in the box seats. Smoking would be permitted in all parts of the theater during evening performances. During matinees, the first six rows in the center of the main floor would be nonsmoking sections reserved for women and children.

In late 1909, Morris was looking for actors he could represent to play at his theaters. When he discovered that Sophie had been "retired" from the Follies, he rushed to sign her, both as her agent and as booker for his own theaters, which, at the time, extended from New York west to Chicago and south to New Orleans.

Less than one week after Sophie's heartbreak with the Follies, she was signed by Morris. He promised her not only headliner status at his theaters, but also to advertise and promote her so vigorously that she would become "the talk of Broadway." Sophie embraced the offer, made even more agreeable by a starting salary of seventy-five dollars a week. Sophie's career was about to take an almost unbelievable leap into stardom.

William Morris was a popular actors' agent, considered a gentleman in a profession crowded with vultures. He recognized Sophie's potential and made her a vaudeville star in two years. The relationship between Sophie and the Morris agency lasted her entire career, more than half a century.

Immediately, Morris advertised Sophie's "triumphant" return to vaudeville. It was Sophie's first mention in the *New York Clipper*.

> Sophie Tucker, "that singer," recently prominent in the "Follies of 1909," is entering vaudeville on the Morris time, opening this week at the American Music Hall, Rockaway Beach, Long Island.[2]

The announcement in the newspapers was accompanied by pictures of Sophie. Posters were mounted within a five-mile radius of the theater.

The strategy worked admirably, generating full houses through the week to see Morris's new "find." Moreover, for the first time, Sophie was included in the vaudeville route list featured in all theatrical newspapers, a weekly alphabetical record of every performer and the date and place they were appearing.

The American Music Hall had nine acts and movies on the bill. Still, no doubt due to Morris's influence, Sophie was the only performer mentioned in the *Clipper's* review.

> Perhaps the most pronounced "hit" was made by Sophie Tucker, late of the Follies of 1909. Her songs were of the latest vintage, and the audience could not seem to get enough. Miss Tucker has a clear and powerful voice, with powers of expression that bring out all the 'meat' in her coon songs.[3]

The following week, Sophie helped open the season at the Lyric Theater, Newark. In successive weeks, she was featured at the Fulton Theater, Brooklyn, and the American Music Hall, Boston. Box office receipts were so profitable that Morris raised Sophie's salary to one hundred dollars a week. Her next engagement was to be at the American Music Hall in Chicago, with familiar, enthusiastic audiences awaiting her. Yet Morris made sure of Sophie's reception with a flood of advertising.

When Sophie opened her week-long engagement, SRO was the order of the day. Full houses continued throughout the week due, in large measure, to Morris's advertising campaign—a skillful and pervasive combination of newspapers, posters, and broadsides splashed across the downtown area. Joining Sophie were a number of high-class entertainers: Julian Eltinge, the stage's most popular female impersonator; Little Hip, a performing elephant; Violinsky, a violin virtuoso whose comic routines with his instrument awed audiences; and the Seven Perezoffs, an acrobatic crew, who in some of their antics, soared across the stage so recklessly that audiences gasped in fear.

It was Sophie's act, however, that captured the patrons. Enveloping the audience and immediately planting herself down-stage center, she remained quite still, except for a graphic wink, a glowing smile, and expressive eyes that wandered the expanse of the theater.

"What are we here for?" she shouted. "To hear you sing," they replied. "Then, let's go," she responded.

Armed with a completely new set of ragtime songs, Sophie had the audience tapping their feet and shaking their heads in unconscious accompaniment. When she paused, they paused with her; when she belted out a lyric, the audience leaned back in their seats as if the sheer power of her voice had overwhelmed them. When she ended the set with "The Wild Cherry Rag," which some critics had suggested contained double-entendre lyrics, the audience shouted for more. Sophie complied by singing three more songs, and still the audience begged for her to continue.

"Sorry, folks," she apologized. "I have to sing again in a few hours, and I have to save my voice for tonight's crowd." Still, cheers and applause resounded through the theater as she pranced off the stage. It was that way at every performance.

Amy Leslie, critic for the *Chicago Daily News,* having seen Sophie perform for the first time, called her act a noticeable "go" in an otherwise average bill.

> There is a young person of fair, fat and ample proportions who gives us something refreshing in the way of jaded ragtime singing. She is Sophie Tucker, a coon shouter. Her voice is big, resonant and brassy like an E flat horn and her twinkling eyes, tricky little pink fingers, charming smile and general breadth of displacement, physical and artistic, commend her as the only legitimate successor to May Irwin of fifty years ago. She is rather the relief on the American bill this week.[4]

Wrote the *Clipper:*

> Sophie Tucker scored a big hit at the American Music Hall last week, being obliged to do seven songs and twenty-eight minutes at every performance.[5]

After two SRO weeks in Toledo, Morris brought Sophie back to New York. The *Clipper* reviewer again singled her out as the bill's real headliner.

> The appearance of Sophie Tucker's name on the board caused lots of applause which she proceeded to justify by singing some of the best things in coon songs in her own characteristic manner. "My Sunny Southern Rose" and "My Husband's In the City" seemed to be the best liked of her selections.[6]

An article in the *New York Sunday Reviewer* acknowledged Sophie's sudden blossoming as a vaudeville headliner, calling her another Morris-inspired phenomenon.

> The real surprise of the bill was Sophie Tucker, a new arrival in the vaudeville field. Her style of coon singing is admirable. Her name is destined soon to be blazoned forth in electric bulbs, judging by the enthusiasm with which her offerings are received.[7]

Two weeks of full houses at the Plaza Theater generated even more accolades for Sophie's work.

> Sophie Tucker is making a hit of huge dimensions at every performance. Her personality is so likable, her humor so fetching, her manner so breezy and confidential that you are just glad to sit back and let her have her own way.[8]

As a father would with a precocious child, before Sophie headed for a Boston engagement, Morris took her aside to warn her of overconfidence, which he believed had "seeped in" during her recent appearances. "Keep your preparation as before," he advised. "But don't let the audience's enthusiasm cloud your presentation. And don't give them too much of yourself," he counseled. "Make them want more."

In addition, to temper her fervor, Morris placed Sophie as third headliner on the bill, behind Pauline, a hypnotist, and Williams and Walker, a popular Negro comedy song-and-dance team. A quick tour of Morris houses in New Orleans, Indianapolis, and Cincinnati—Sophie was wonder-struck by New Orleans and puzzled by the audience's polite restraint in response to her rousing songs—appeared to bring Sophie back to the hard realities of the touring life.

To open 1910, Morris brought Sophie back in New York to continue her orchestrated surge into high-class vaudeville. During the holidays, he featured Sophie in newspaper ads with a becoming photograph; in addition, he distributed colorful posters announcing her upcoming engagement.

In another move to publicize Sophie's career, Morris persuaded the Edison Phonograph Company to feature her in a number of recordings. Morris had already obtained agreement from the F.B. Haviland Publishing Company to distribute the recordings. When Sophie was notified about her new assignment, she could not have been more delighted.

In late April and early May, Sophie made three recordings: "That Lovin' Rag" (released in June); "My Husband's in the City" (released in July); and "That Lovin' Two-Step Man" (released in October). For her services, Sophie received one hundred dollars for each recording. Even more important, however, was a royalty of one penny for every record sold by Haviland.

For the March, 1910, issue, under the heading of "new talent," the Edison Phonograph Monthly spoke of Sophie as their "recording find." Material supplied by Morris explained Sophie's unique stage persona.

> There's a fine, buxom, happy-go-lucky girl for you, all dressed up in a greeny green skirt and a black-and-tan waist that goes with the cheerful voice. There's a lot of voice and there's a lot of the girl, both solid and substantial. When they come out on the stage together, everybody wakes up and takes notice. They're blustery, rollicking songs she sings, too. She gallops along over Negro ragtime melodies with the true Southern swing; then she sweeps into a grand "hugging" song with nothing on the stage to take advantage of it but a lone, gilt chair. From the moment she greets the audience with her cheerful "Ho" they are her friends.
>
> She is now an exclusive Edison artist, a statement which is made without reservation or fear of possible retraction.

No sooner had she finished with the recording sessions than Morris booked Sophie back at the American Music Hall in Chicago for a two-week engagement. To promote her, signed photographs and copies of her recordings were made available for sale in the theater lobby.

To full houses, Sophie was reported to be "at her best, singing some very catchy character songs." Still, the reviewer from the *Chicago Daily Tribune* wrote sarcastically about the risqué nature of her song selection. "Miss Sophie Tucker, having subjected her repertory of songs to a treatment of chloride de lime, may be listened to at the American this week without danger of infection."

As Sophie's local renown grew, so did reactions to the double-entendre songs she sang. Some critics found them offensive and excoriated Sophie for performing them in popular vaudeville houses in front of self-respecting men and women. More of them, however, supported her renditions, since, they said, the songs were treated inoffensively, with self-effacement and humor. The negative comments would not disappear, but they did not seem to bother Sophie. She was going to sing whatever pleased audiences, and nearly all of them demonstrated their enthusiasm for her choices.

So as not to overexpose Sophie at the theaters on his circuit, Morris signed her to appear at that primary west-coast Pantages chain for the remainder of the year. Strategically, he would have her finish the tour and the year in Chicago. The Pantages people found no problem in agreeing to Sophie's one hundred dollars a week salary, plus rail fare.

When her family was informed of Sophie's triumphs in Chicago and her upcoming tour of Western states—all letters continued to pass through Anna—they were

Sophie had quickly become a featured vaudeville performer. At her first appearance on Broadway, she wore jewels purchased on the installment plan and a rented dress. Her renditions of ragtime songs made her an immediate hit. (Museum of the City of New York)

taken aback by her obvious successes and equally impressed by the increased amounts of money she sent home. Brazenly, Sophie promised to buy her parents a new home and allow them to retire from the restaurant.

Sophie was paid every Sunday night. On Monday morning, she visited the post office to make out three money orders: one to her mother; one to brother Moe, studying law at New York University; one to "the boss" (Morris), his five percent commission. The sense of security that Sophie achieved simply by sending money only motivated her to work harder and sing better. In what seemed a relatively short time, William Morris had shrewdly made Sophie into a vaudeville headliner and turned her stage performances into unique, exuberant, and colorful events that attracted enthusiastic audiences.

Jack Lait, Morris's publicity man, first saw Sophie in Chicago. He had known little about her and had not yet been supplied with the material needed to promote her as a performer. After watching Sophie walk on stage, capture and hold an audience for half an hour, Lait wrote a "puff" piece for Chicago newspapers, advising readers to come to the theater "for a musical thrill," to hear "The Mary Garden of Ragtime," a sobriquet that became Sophie's public identity for several years.

Mary Garden was a famous international opera star who was born and raised in Scotland. After training in Paris, she became one of Europe's most sought-after performers. Her career had been made more colorful by a self-admitted dissolute personal life. Her frequent trips to the U.S. to appear at Hammerstein's Metropolitan

Opera courted much attention, not only for her outspoken views and outrageous behavior, but, as one opera composer reported: "You'd surely have to be wearing earplugs to enjoy the charm of her voice." Hence, Jack Lait's inspired phrase to identify Sophie. That a portion of Sophie's repertoire was "not for parlor use" only added further credence to Lait's ballyhooed title.

The train trip from Chicago to Seattle, where Sophie was to open on Pantages time, came as a revelation to her. Fertile Midwestern meadows sustaining placid cows, then suddenly sprouting giant rows of corn, gave way to deep blue lakes and dark green forests, then to long, flat, almost gray, desolate plains. The Rocky Mountains were so high and rugged — Sophie had never seen real mountains before — she wondered how the train could climb them. In her autobiography, Sophie marveled at the experience. "What a thrill to see my own U.S.A.; picturesque and historic spots I had read about; towns I had heard other performers talk about!"[9] Every city she visited was an enlightening revelation.

Over a five-month period, the tour took Sophie to Seattle; Vancouver, B.C.; Portland; San Francisco; Oakland; Los Angeles; Salt Lake City; Denver; and many small towns in between. Now publicly featured as "The Mary Garden of Ragtime"— there was some question about how many people in the West even knew who Mary Garden was— Sophie matched her name in lights with outstanding performances. In all of the cities visited, this was the first time audiences had seen Sophie; and they were curious about her extravagant billing. In most cases, they came away convinced that she was one of the most entertaining performers they had seen in years. An impressed Portland reviewer reported: "The accomplished singer creates enthusiasm with her inimitable renditions of funny songs. She is called back time after time in response to the applause of her hearers."

Watching Sophie for the first time at the Chutes Theater, San Francisco, a local critic professed that "Miss Tucker is without doubt the best interpreter of coon songs before the public, and she has reduced 'coon shouting' to an art."[10] Along with these reviews came full houses.

Will Rossiter of Chicago, one of the music publishers who had developed a friendship with Sophie, frequently sent her new songs to add to her repertoire, that is, if she believed audiences would enjoy them. Sophie had arranged a deal with Rossiter that for every song she featured, she would receive one penny for each music sheet sold. Although some in the industry considered such reciprocity illegal, it was a deal commonly struck between singers and music publishers who wished to promote their new songs. Singers often became identified with these songs, which, in turn, helped to sell music sheets and, at the same time, induced audiences to request these songs during the encore portion of every performance.

In July, Rossiter announced that, with some "sharp hustling,"— meaning they had outbid rival publishers— they had acquired a "coon lament" entitled "Some of These Days," by Sheldon Brooks, specifically for Sophie's use. In Rossiter's announcement, they indicated she would be the first to sing it as "it was bought with that understanding with her." The song became an immediate hit — the most popular number in 1910 — and, in a short while, more than twenty different performers had added the song to their acts. Among the singers following Sophie were Belle Baker, Eva Tanguay, and Fanny Brice. Sales of sheet music passed the million mark. Even today, the song remains one of the all time favorites.

Sheldon Brooks, a Negro, was born on May 4, 1886, in Amesbury, near Windsor, Ontario, across the river from Detroit. He spent his boyhood in Detroit, having learned at an early age to play on an old foot-pump organ. In his early teens, he began work as a pianist in Detroit cafes and graduated a few years later to the vaudeville stage. At age twenty-two, Brooks wrote both the words and music to "Some of These Days," which gained him many years of appearances on the Keith and Orpheum circuits. The song also opened the door for him to join Tin Pan Alley composers, a rare opportunity for a Negro at the time. Among the many songs he composed, two others became legendary hits: "Walking the Dog," in 1916, and "Darktown Strutter's Ball," in 1917.

Brooks had worked for weeks with a melody he believed might gain him entrance to music publishers; but as hard as he worked on the lyrics to the music, nothing seemed to fit. One afternoon, sitting in a restaurant, he overheard a young couple quarreling.

"Better not walk out on me, man," the girl declared. "For some of these days, you're gonna miss me, honey."

Inspired, Brooks quickly wrote out the lyrics for his song. That night, he sang it in his own act. Shortly thereafter, he sold the song to Will Rossiter. "Some of These Days" was soon blazing the trail of ragtime hits.

Sophie embraced the song with passion. Almost overnight, it became so associated with her act that, if she neglected to include it, audiences would demand it of her. In their advertising, Rossiter consistently mentioned Sophie as the foremost exponent of the song. In a matter of months, however, because so many other singers had appropriated the song for their own acts, Sophie's identity with it had all but disappeared. As other new songs became popular, Sophie always sought them out to keep her act fresh; "Some of These Days" was soon dropped from her repertoire. It would be another eleven years before Sophie reinstated the song in her act, at that time, forming an insoluble bond that lasted for more than forty-five years.

Sophie returned to Chicago in the middle of December for a two-week engagement at Morris's American Music Hall. Although the show was four hours long and consisted of twenty-two acts, SRO houses prevailed. Sophie was listed to appear eleventh, immediately before intermission, a headliner's position.

One of the first things Sophie did upon arriving in Chicago was to visit music publishers to try out new numbers. Most of the publishers were located in two adjacent buildings on Clark Street. Sophie would systematically move from floor to floor, examining material from each publisher in turn.

"When they saw me coming," she recalled, "they took out everything new. Instead of going to New York, I'd get my songs right here; and then I'd have the songs ready to sing when I got there."

"One of the song-pluggers would say, 'I've got a great hit, Miss Tucker,' and I would take it in the morning, learn it by the afternoon, and introduce it at the matinee." A Chicago critic claimed that Sophie knew more than 300 songs, and he was likely correct in his assessment. Often, at the conclusion of her act, Sophie asked the audience for requests. She almost always satisfied their demands, to their utmost delight.

4

The Mary Garden of Ragtime (2)

Although the Chicago engagement elicited accolades for her work, Sophie became the center of a controversy caused by singing a recently released rage, "The Angleworm Wiggle." She was arrested by police (though not until concluding her performance) and brought before the court to answer charges of obscenity.

The attorney representing Sophie requested that she be allowed to render the song in order that the court could decide whether it was sufficiently objectionable to warrant the arrest. The judge declined the offer for Sophie to perform, and he released her. At the same time, however, he denied an injunction against police interference, which prompted Sophie to drop the song from her act. As a result of the publicity, the episode served to raise the prices ticket scalpers were quoting to see her perform.

The entire issue of singing what the *Chicago Tribune* called "smut" songs became public debate when the paper published a series of articles featuring the opinions of clerics, teachers, politicians, and the police regarding "this offensive behavior" found in local theaters. They protested the spread of jingles by singers flouting decency, whilst flaunting their physical appeal. Although Sophie was not specifically identified, it was obvious from the articles that she had been singled out as an "enemy of youth."

The newspaper went on to describe Tin Pan Alley writers as possessing "degenerative habits" and composing songs to "pollute the minds of the young." Further, they produced lyrics that went "the limit." And where is police protection from these obscenities? the newspaper asked.

"Who puts smut songs on the market?" Song pluggers and singers, the articled answered. Singers got the song across "in a way that made the words even more suggestive than written." They wiggled their shoulders, bit their lip, and sighed, "putting on the stuff." The fact that such songs captivated audiences appalled the newspaper. That they got away with it spoke of police indifference.

A short time later, the Illinois vice commission initiated an inquiry inspired by the *Daily News* allegations. Three days of hearing concluded with no decisions. A number of investigators were sent out to interview a wide range of entertainment people to uncover "objectionable" behavior. Sophie was identified as a prime defendant to be interrogated, but she had already left Chicago for the East.

The issue raged on for several years. Hearings and testimony produced myriad accusations but no indictments nor changes in city policy. Song writers and singers continued to present "smut" songs to enthusiastic audiences. And Chicago was not the only city that wrestled with these issues. Although, in various cities, Sophie often faced such complaints about her song selections, she remained unaffected by them. She would sing what she believed audiences enjoyed, and she cared little for the threatened consequences, which themselves proved to be more moral posturing than a real exercise of the law.

The Chicago engagement also served to introduce Sophie to two well-known local newspaper critics, Ashton Stevens, of the *Chicago Examiner,* and Amy Leslie, of the *Chicago Daily News,* both of whom became long-term friends. Interestingly, both reviewers revealed trepidations about Sophie's song selections while, at the same time, acknowledging her success with audiences. It was when they met off-stage that the friendships, especially with Leslie, bloomed into mutual admiration. In later years, whenever Sophie visited Chicago, she and Leslie roomed together at the Hotel Sherman. When Leslie became ill, Sophie helped her financially. When Leslie died in 1939, Sophie mourned the loss of a dear friend.

It was becoming common for Sophie to make friends during every engagement, from fans and other admirers to theater people. She methodically collected their addresses and filled her scrapbook with their business cards. Whenever she planned to return to a city, Sophie would write letters (later, they became printed invitations) telling of the upcoming engagement and asking the recipient to "come around" again to visit her. Over the years, her mailing list grew to sizable proportions, as did the number of cards, letters, and telegrams she received from hundreds of well-wishers for every show opening. In turn, each Christmas, Sophie sent holiday greetings to all the people on her list. Near the end of her career, this amounted to more than 5,000 names. Only during her last years did she have other people assist her in addressing, sealing, and mailing the cards.

Morris brought Sophie back to New York at the beginning of 1912. As before, he advertised her appearance heavily, promising the public that she would appear in every Morris-operated theater (seven) in New York City and Brooklyn. Then, he added a bit of unsubstantiated, fanciful news that, after her New York appearances, Sophie would be going to Europe.

This claim was often used by agents to "prove" a performer's appeal and served as notice to booking agents that the headliner would be unavailable for engagements for a considerable time. More often than not, the strategy worked. In fact, Sophie had no intention of going to Europe. Instead, she was approached by Walter O. Lindsey, a veteran Chicago producer, to appear in a musical comedy. Lindsey had seen Sophie perform in local vaudeville houses and wanted her, and her obvious appeal to Chicago audiences, to headline his new show, scheduled to open in April.

In the meantime, Morris had raised Sophie's appearances in New York to headliner status. An article in the *New York Clipper* described Sophie as standing "in the front rank of coon shouters and rag singers." Likewise, the *New York Post* reviewer declared:

> This lady had no trouble at all in drawing applause, once she started with her coon and rag songs, and could have continued much longer, had she saw fit to.[1]

This was Sophie's first appearance on the cover of the *New York Clipper*, a place reserved for vaudeville headliners. She had already gained a reputation for wearing elegant costumes.

Throughout January and February, Sophie filled Morris houses. She even doubled her act one week in February, replacing Vesta Victoria at the Plaza Theater when the British entertainer became ill. Anything to help her mentor, William Morris. Sophie also spent January producing two more recordings for Edison, "Reuben Rag" and "Phoebe Jane," both of which she was featuring in her act. More recordings were planned for the summer.

"Merry Mary" opened at the Whitney Theater, April 15. Harry Sheldon White wrote the book, Jack Kenyon the lyrics, and Hilding Anderson the music. Sophie sang three songs: "I Am Married," in Act One; "Experience Will Teach You How," in Act Two, with an ensemble; and "Put Your Paws Around Me and Be My Bear," in Act Three. Both the first and last songs were construed by some critics "as not to be classified as polite."

Reviews of the production tended to be negative.

> Merry Mary, the latest of the local productions to see light, opened Saturday night. The critics who have seen the show voted it anything but merry as to book.[2]
> Merry Mary is scarcely in condition at present to withstand a cold calculation of its virtues and its lack of them, so extended comment concerning the entertainment will be deferred until promised amendments have been made in severaldepartments.[3]

Amy Leslie reported the play "a somewhat wild and woolly draft blowing in through the Whitney doors" but singled out Sophie for her exuberant yet "untamed" talent.

> If somebody could lasso Sophie Tucker and tame her enough to smooth the haremscarem edges flying about her performance, there would be an immense comedienne revealed, for Miss Tucker has splendid talents entirely undeveloped.[4]

Actually, except for Sophie's "boundless enthusiasm," the show would likely have folded in a week. Lindsey quickly hired new book and song writers to fix the production. As the show was being rewritten, which meant performers learning new lines, songs, and dances each rehearsal, the new material was introduced at each evening performance. By the fourth week, no one would have recognized the show except for its name and its star. Sophie was singing two new songs, "The Land of Bom-Ba-Loo," and a crooning Southern melody, "They Sent For Me," to replace the previously questionable tunes. Critics wrote that the show's changes "had been for the better" and predicted it would "run into the summer."

Nevertheless, Sophie continued to receive mixed reviews. On one hand, she was praised for her contributions in adding an "enlivening presence to the entertainment." In contrast, "her torrid ballads of the Negro underworld" were deemed unacceptable because they "described the amorous emotions of their characters." Even her rendition of a "respectable" quiet ballad met with criticism. Sophie's "armor plate throat" (hardly a compliment) had been so subdued, the critic said, that the audience "could distinctly hear the blare of the trombone and the first violin."

The production staggered through six weeks of continuing changes. Finally, because of the extremely hot weather, so the management claimed, the show had to be closed. In reality, "Merry Mary" had done so poorly at the box office, management was unable to pay for costume and scenery rentals. The performers received no salary for their sixth week of work and refused to play another week. The show closed down.

Critic Ashton Stevens summed up the demise of "Merry Mary" with his typical sarcasm. Upon being notified of the show's closing, Ashton wrote: "This isn't news as we see news in our opinionated way. News would have been the uninterrupted continuation of 'Merry Mary.'"

A week later, Sophie sued for $321.50 in back wages from Lindsey, alleged to be due for services at the rate of $250 a week. To no one's surprise, she never collected the money.

Morris quickly moved Sophie to an all-star bill at Sans Souci Park, Chicago, where she remained for several weeks while he arranged bookings for her in New York. Morris announced, that along with her appearances at New York theaters, Sophie would be making several more recordings for Edison. In addition, she had been signed to appear in another Chicago-based musical company, opening in September. Still smarting from her failure in "Merry Mary," Sophie had been reluctant to sign so quickly; Morris. however, reassured her the new show would fare much better; and her salary would be $300 a week.

Another busy summer prevented Sophie from visiting the family. Instead, she paid for their travel to come to New York. Usually, Anna made the trip with Bert, now a young boy of seven; this time, Sophie persuaded her mother to accompany them. Upon their arrival, Sophie dramatically announced that she had accumulated enough money to buy her parents a new home in Hartford. Nothing is known of their reaction to her surprise gift, but several months later the family moved into a duplex at 160 Barker Street, in a higher-class neighborhood within the Jewish community. Philip and his wife, Leah, lived next door, at 156 Barker Street. As she had originally promised, Sophie continued to send money home each week for her mother, for Moe, and for Anna and Bert. In fact, Sophie's contributions had become so substantial, her parents were seriously considering the sale of their restaurant.

Sophie recorded three songs for Edison: "That Lovin' Soul Kiss"; "Missouri Joe"; and "Some of These Days," at the time a hit among many vaudeville singers and a million-dollar seller of sheet music. At the various New York theaters where she appeared, Sophie introduced a number of new ragtime songs that were immediately taken up by other singers. These days, Sophie had become a full-fledged singer of ragtime songs; and she was so billed.

At the end of August, Sophie returned to Chicago to begin rehearsals for "Louisiana Lou." She was costarred with Alexander Carr. (Louise Dresser and Marie Dressler had declined the role because of its vocal demands.) The show also featured Bernard Granville, Eva Fallon, and Mary Quive. The book had been written by Addison Burkhardt and Frederick Donaghey, the music composed by Ben M. Jerome (an already renowned Tin Pan Alley writer), and staged by Frank Smithson, a veteran stage manager. According to critics, the entire production was, indeed, more professional than the ill-fated "Merry Mary."

Jacob Lidoffski (Alexander Carr), a rich New Orleans Jew, adopts a child and raises her as his daughter, Lou (Mary Quive). Man-about-town Nixon Holmes (Bernard Granville) wishes to marry her. Jacob, however, has decided that Lou should marry Jack Kondarney (William Riley Hatch), the son of an Irish political boss. But Lou and Kondarney do not love one another. With the assistance of Lou's chaperone, Jennie Wimp (Sophie Tucker), true love wins at the end. In retrospect, some critics later believed that "Louisiana Lou" had been the forerunner to the hit musical of 1922, "Abie's Irish Rose," which used a similar, ethnic plot juxtaposition.

For this production, Sophie had to make some concessions to appear in the cast. She had been reduced to third billing; she appeared on the stage only a limited time; and her role was that of a blackfaced nanny to Lou. She performed three songs: "Now Am de Time!," a solo in Act One; "What Do You Say," with Hatch and an ensemble in Act One; and a hoped for show-stopper, "The Puritan Prance," in which Sophie parodied a "foot-stomping spoof of negro dancing." When asked how she felt about returning to blackface, Sophie was undeniably disappointed.

The production opened at the La Salle Theater, September 3. The *Clipper* called the show "a splendid diversion of mirth and melody." And, in spite of the limitations of her role, Sophie gave a standout performance.

> Now Am de Time! Now Am de Time! shouts Sophie Tucker, and everybody seems to realize it. With two rousing darky songs to her liking, she storms the stage and envelops everybody with her singing. "Now Am de Time" is very catchy, and she roared it out in a manner exhilarating. In "The Puritan Prance," she dances and sings obligato to the chorus. The song assures a run for the piece if nothing else. Her clothes are picturesque caricatures, and she is at once enormously funny and attractive.[6]

Amy Leslie selected Sophie as the show's "streak of chain lightening."

> Shouting Sophie Tucker was out ripping the air with her rollicking voice of thrills and startles, and the audience greeted her as if she had been to war and had dropped in, home on a furlough or a stretcher. Sophie roars everything she has to say, bellows melodiously everything she has to sing and injects gimps, noise, enormous vivacity and a thousand irresponsible laughs in every torrent of voice she wastes. How she can sing a rathskeller rag![7]

Alex Carr was a veteran "Hebrew delineator," having played the part on the vaudeville circuit for years to great success. (Later, he and Barney Bernard would star in the long-running comedy farce "Potash and Perlmutter.") Carr played the Jew to perfection, and Sophie was quite taken with his mannerisms and singing renditions. During one rehearsal, Carr suggested to Sophie that, although there was no place for them in "Lou," she consider incorporating some of this "Jewishness" when she returned to the vaudeville stage. His suggestion and her agreement to interpolate something of her heritage was to become another successful addition to her stage presence. It was no longer onerous for Sophie to advertise her Jewishness on the stage. These days, Al Jolson and Fannie Brice were using it successfully in their acts. In the future, adding Jewish words and phrases to her act would prove even more effective in capturing audiences. (Of course, her use of Yiddish would be used selectively, since patrons in some cities might be confused by the insertion of a foreign language into her songs.)

"Louisiana Lou" was not only an overnight hit, but it appeared to "have legs," (longevity, in stage parlance). In its fifth week, the show was said to draw "crowded houses at every performance." By the tenth week, tickets were put on sale three weeks in advance, and the management's only handicap was not having a larger seating capacity. In the middle of November, "Lou" played its 100th performance; and plans were being made to send the production on tour. Abe Erlanger, one of popular theater's moguls, wanted to know when the production could come to New York, since "it seems to be the only new musical play of the season that is worthwhile." According to the press, Sophie and Alex Carr were now sharing headliner honors.

The year 1913 began with "Louisiana Lou" passing the 150th performance milestone, its cast the same, and its box-office success proving it to be one of the most prosperous shows in Chicago in many years. (Only David Henderson's fairytale extravaganzas back in the 1890s earned more money.) The production played for thirty-five weeks, closing on May 4; and plans were already underway for the show

Sophie's second appearance in a musical comedy, "Louisiana Lou," co-starred Bernard Granville (left) and Alex Carr (center). Carr persuaded Sophie that there was nothing wrong with her interpolating Yiddish phrases into her songs and identifying herself as Jewish.

to travel, beginning in early July. Management kept the cast together by raising everyone's salary; Sophie would be earning $350 a week for her part. When she informed her parents about the increase in salary, they remarked that the restaurant barely earned that amount of money in a month.

Taking advantage of Sophie's hiatus from "Lou" for two months, Morris booked her into the Majestic Theater, Chicago, as well as a number of other houses in the Midwest. It was at the Majestic that Sophie first publicly revealed being a Jew and inserted a number of Yiddish expressions into her song lyrics. The audiences cheered her on for more of the same.

Coming on stage, Sophie introduced herself as a "Jewish girl from Hartford, Connecticut, who began her career singing in my parents' kosher restaurant." The audience applauded. "I've come to entertain you with a selection of popular ragtime songs." The audience applauded again. "I hope you like them," she continued; and the audience broke out in sustained cheers and foot-stomping. When she began with a new song, "You Can't Expect Kisses From Me," the audience demanded that she encore it several times. In one of the encores, she added a number of Yiddish phrases, to the listener's delight. With the help of her audience, Sophie's new act was taking shape.

Amy Leslie, the *Chicago Daily News* stylish theater critic (and friend), reported on Sophie's "hurricane" reentry into vaudeville.

> Sophie Tucker romps on with a hurricane atmosphere about her and a whole lot of extraordinary clothes and rollicking songs. She is the biggest kind of a favorite, and her local celebrity almost excuses her assuming the title "The Mary Garden of Vaudeville" without immediate effects. Mary never could dream of shouting a bearcat rag with the Yiddish fury of Tucker nor fight the frog in her divine throat with the humorous abandon of the ragtime Sophie.[8]

At another Chicago engagement, a benefit matinee performance at the Shriner's Circus, Sophie was featured along with George M. Cohan, George Primrose (of minstrel show fame), and the Howard Brothers, Willie and Eugene. Besides singing several songs, Sophie and the Howards improvised a comic turn. It was the first time they had shared the stage together since, at the Abuza restaurant six years earlier, Willie had persuaded Sophie to go to New York to seek a career in vaudeville.

A special train took the "Louisiana Lou" company to San Francisco to open at the Columbia Theater, July 4. Unfortunately, a number of railroad-related mishaps delayed the trip, causing the company to arrive only hours before the opening, thus denying them any opportunity to rehearse on the theater stage. Instead, bits and pieces of the show were practiced in the dining car each time the train stopped at a station to refuel. At one stop, locals crowded around the train to listen to the performers, although they were unable to see who was doing the singing. Upon arrival in San Francisco, backstage personnel rushed the scenery and costumes to the theater along with the orchestra, who hastily practiced the music as best they could under the circumstances. Actors and actresses began applying their makeup even before arriving at the theater.

"Louisiana Lou" was well-received by San Francisco audiences, even though it took the company a full week to return the production to its previous fluency. Local newspapers remarked that the show's raggedness had been due to the company's late arrival but praised the entertainment it provided. Although she continued to play a limited role, Sophie was featured as costar. Her "Puritan Prance" stopped the show at every performance, just as it had the previous season.

The planned tour took the company through the Pacific Northwest, across Canada to St. Paul, Minnesota, stopped in Indianapolis, Kansas City, and Cincinnati, and arrived in Philadelphia the middle of October, where a two-week engagement was extended to four weeks due to box-office demand. The press acknowledged the full houses.

> Louisiana Lou continues to be popularly received and last week's audiences were as large as the preceding week. Alex Carr, Sophie Tucker and their associates are a merry bunch of entertainers and score hits nightly.[9]

From Philadelphia, the tour took an irregular route, typical of a production near the end of its run, with booking agents working hard to fill dates as best they could. The company played a one-night stand in Chattanooga; two days in Williamsport; a week in Baltimore and Washington, D.C.; then another one-night stand in Hamilton, Ohio. Except for the week-long engagements, only portions of the scenery were unloaded. When the manager announced to the company that their next stop would be Denver, a four-day jump, their strained groans reflected the increasing fatigue of the tour and the hoped-for conclusion of the show. It finally came in Omaha, on February 1, 1913. All in all, "Louisiana Lou" had been performed 512 times. Sophie had never missed any of the performances, although several times she had risen from a sickbed to perform.

Within a week, thanks again to William Morris, Sophie appeared at the Hippodrome, St. Louis, breaking all box-office records. Returning to Chicago, she spent two weeks at the Willard Theater, regaling audiences with new ragtime songs: "All Night Long"; "Oh, You Georgia Rose"; "Can't Get Enough Of It" (which almost got her arrested again); and "Down Home Rag."

Accompanying Sophie on stage, at the piano, was Frank Westphal, an accomplished musician, though only twenty-one years old. Sophie had discovered him on a vaudeville bill early in the Chicago engagement. They discussed working together and soon were seen in tandem as much off the stage as on.

While Sophie's personal life appeared to have suddenly improved — "Sophie has a man," her colleagues whispered — her relationship with William Morris was jeopardized by a number of significant financial losses that he suffered, causing him to sell his theaters and relinquish his agency operations as well. Sophie was now forced to book engagements for herself, and that became part of Frank Westphal's job as well, at least until another agent was selected.

Sophie appeared in various Chicago theaters for seven weeks, a number of them in outlying areas of the city, where lower admissions were charged, which, of course, meant a reduced salary.

Frank had moved into the Sherman Hotel with Sophie, and gossips spoke of an impending marriage. Under questioning by the press, both denied the rumors and reiterated that their friendship was entirely a business arrangement. Yet, unknown to the press (until three months later), on March 21, Sophie had filed for and secured a divorce from Louis Tuck. Then the newspapers revealed that Sophie had an eight-year-old son from the marriage. When the judge asked Sophie if she could support him, she answered that she made a living singing "in vaudeville shows."

Newspapers also reported that Sophie was soon to leave for England for an extended engagement at U.K. vaudeville houses. Who planted the information is unknown, but it garnered her extensive coverage for almost two months.

Of course, Sophie had no intention of traveling to England; but as a public-relations stratagem, the news attracted offers from several East Coast agents. Sophie and Frank soon found that the job of booking was filled with behind-the-scenes negotiations and hidden deals. Morris had warned her about handling her own business, suggesting, instead, that an old friend and colleague, Max Hart, should assist her.

Hart was a grizzled veteran of the booking wars and Syndicate intrigues and had a reputation for representing only the best actors in vaudeville. He was a hard bargainer, but was said to have a soft heart for performers in distress. Hart possessed an additional formidable advantage: for many years, he had cultivated a close relationship with

B.F. Keith and E.A. Albee, proprietors of the extensive Keith circuit. When he recommended an actor to them, they invariably signed on the dotted line.

As good as Hart was in dealing professionally with performers and theater managers, his constant marital problems often generated newspaper headlines. His wife sued him for divorce a number of times, accusing him of consorting with actresses he represented, only to drop charges and presumably return to a normal married life. Along with her periodic accusations came threats to "put him out of business." One such threat made headlines a year after Hart had become Sophie's agent; his wife accused him of an affair with Sophie. The entire issue became a laughing matter when it was revealed that Sophie had been playing thousands of miles away at the time. (In 1920, however, Hart's wife obtained a divorce; and her demands did in fact all but put him out of business. He died several years later, a broken man.)

Sophie and Max Hart did become good friends, for business purposes only; and he helped promote her as much as William Morris had. The results proved equally gratifying.

Before returning to the East, Sophie's final appearance in Chicago was an engagement at White City, a combination amusement park (during the day) and cabaret (at night). It happened to be Sophie's first experience with the cabaret form of entertainment, and she quickly realized its advantages.

Unlike vaudeville, cabaret was more intimate. Audiences were not only seated close to performers, but they could interact with them if they chose. Cabarets were much more informal venues; and performers had more freedom to boost songs, some of them taboo for vaudeville audiences. With the opportunity for long engagements, less need for constant booking and frequent travel, and the potential for higher salaries, certain performers came to believe that cabaret performance was ideal for them. Sophie's initial experience made her feel that she and cabaret were made for one another.

Frank Westphal had now become Sophie's recognized accompanist and receiving billing with her, although in smaller type. When Hart obtained engagements for Sophie in New York, Westphal was always included. Hart had also negotiated a role for Sophie in a Joe Howard musical comedy, destined for Chicago; but negotiations broke down due to a debate about her and Westphal's salary. Howard refused Sophie's demand for $1,000 a week.

On her return to New York, Sophie and Frank played at Hammerstein's Victoria Theater. Since Tony Pastor's death, it had become the premier vaudeville house in the city. They played to SRO audiences.

> She is the same Sophie Tucker, with the same great voice and the right idea of putting over the syncopated melody. Her selections are of the popular rag order, and the audience didn't seem to get enough of her, as she had to sing seven songs before she could bow off. Frank Westphal accompanied her on the piano.
>
> "Floating Down the River" was a fine opener. "Moonlight on the Mississippi" was another standard. "Somebody's Coming to My House," "Swing, Swing, Swing," Irving Berlin's medley, and "Carnival Time" were her selections."[10]

In 1913, the *New York Clipper* published another picture of Sophie, having reached vaudeville stardom. This was unique for a performer, particularly a woman playing a solo act. No longer a "coon shouter," Sophie was now being billed as "the Mary Garden of Ragtime."

Sophie added a few Yiddish expressions to the Berlin song. The audience, including a sizable number of Jewish patrons, applauded her interpolations enthusiastically.

"The Mary Garden of Ragtime" had become a headliner now, and mention of her name meant full houses and substantial box-office receipts. Reviewers and critics marveled at how quickly Sophie had become one of Broadway's biggest hits. In lengthy essays, they attempted to explain her rapid success.

Meanwhile, sitting quietly in his New York office, plotting new strategies for his revamped organization, William Morris smiled with satisfaction at his protege's rise to stardom. He had believed in her talent, and her work ethic had been exemplary. If he had anything more to say about it, Sophie Tucker would shine on Broadway even more brightly than she did currently.

When Hart informed Sophie that she had been signed by the Keith circuit, she was ecstatic. When he told her that she had been booked into Poli's Theater in Hartford, she knew the day that she had hoped and longed for had finally arrived. It had been seven years since she left home and swore to her parents that she would return only as a headliner. Sophie could barely contain her excitement about returning to her "old home town" in triumph.

5

Vaudeville Stardom

In grandiose terms, the *Hartford Daily Courant* reported Sophie's opening at Poli's Theater, saluting her as the "The Pride of Hartford."

> Perhaps no announcement that the Poli management might make would be received with greater enthusiasm or interest than that Sophie Tucker, formerly of Hartford, will be the headliner this week.[1]

The front-page feature extolled the virtues Sophie had displayed while starring in vaudeville and musical comedy and noted that "only a few years ago Miss Tucker left Hartford to go on stage."

> On Monday afternoon, Miss Tucker will make her first appearance in Hartford since she became a star, and the large advance sale of seats shows that she will be heartily welcomed.[2]

As the train pulled into the Hartford station, Sophie found herself full of conflicting emotions. Would anyone be at the station to meet her? How would the Jewish community respond to her recent successes? How would she perform before townsfolk? It was personally gratifying to return home; but, at the same time, a potentially frightening experience.

Glancing out the window, Sophie saw crowds of people on the platform, welcoming her, some carrying colorful banners. She saw her entire family awaiting her arrival—father, mother, Phil and his wife, Moe, Anna, and Bert, brought home from boarding school to see his mother. She saw friends and neighbors, among them several who had previously shunned her. She saw a band playing tunes she had sung on stage, Poli's theater manager and his staff dressed in their theater best, and a host of reporters, some having traveled from as far away as New Haven.

As she jumped from the train, Sophie was met with cheers from the crowd, hugs and kisses from the family. Her apprehension quickly disappeared, replaced by warm feelings of tender devotion, even adoration. While the crowd's reactions were a surprise to Sophie, she embraced the welcome with sincerity and honesty. It was, indeed, a moment for thankfulness.

As she was escorted home, Sophie's spirits were elevated even more, noting the many banners and broadsides announcing her return to Hartford: Sophie Tucker, the Idol of Hartford; Hartford's Own; and the now familiar sobriquet, The Mary Garden of Ragtime. She had been invited to stay at the city's best hotel by Poli's manager; but Sophie replied, "Sorry. I'm going home with my family."[3]

For the first time entering the home she had purchased for her parents, Sophie found the familiar surroundings of her childhood. An elaborate meal, served with the entire family gathered around the old dining room table, reminded Sophie of her affinity to the family. She was a daughter of her parents, a sister to her siblings; the role of vaudeville star seemed a distant memory at that moment. Although the fact remained unstated, the visit was all the more gratifying given that she had been unconditionally embraced by her parents. When her mother announced that she and Charles were about to give up the restaurant and retire, Sophie glowed with validation.

A huge banner welcoming Sophie hung across the facade outside Poli's Theater. Colorful posters in the lobby displayed full-length photos of Sophie in her best finery. A becoming photograph appeared in the week's program. Stagehands spoke to Sophie in hushed tones of reverence. Looking out at the theater from the wings, Sophie observed that the house was full, the audience abuzz in anticipation of her entrance. A family box had been set aside for the Abuzas; except for Anna, it would be the first time the family had seen Sophie perform. Her old elementary school principal was there, along with the mayor and his family. Seated up front, looking like a jury in judgment, were all of her mother's synagogue lady friends, though few of them could understand English. The reviewer from the *Hartford Courant* described Sophie's first appearance as a "right royal welcome."

> Immense audiences gathered at Poli's Theater to greet Sophie Tucker on her first appearance in this her native city. Her many old friends and acquaintances took advantage of every opportunity to make her feel that they were glad to see and hear her in the profession in which she has made a splendid name for herself.[4]

The *Courant* went on to report the "tremendous outbursts of applause" at the end of each number. "That she pleased the audience," the reviewer went on to note, "goes without saying, and she showed her appreciation by singing encore after encore, so many, in fact, that it looked for a time as if she was going to sing all night."

At the conclusion of her act, Sophie was presented with several large bouquets of flowers. In response to calls for a speech, she attempted to speak but was overcome with emotion. While drying her tears, she bowed and gave the audience a heartfelt, simple, "Thank you." Hoping she might return, they continued to cheer and applaud her for many minutes after she left the stage.

Sophie had put even more energy into her normally exuberant act, and the effort seemed to have paid off. That she had been received so wholeheartedly as a professional performer convinced Sophie that her trip to Hartford had, indeed, been a personal victory.

Sophie played to full houses the entire week, providing excellent box-office receipts; and she could have stayed longer had her schedule been more flexible. (The Keith circuit rarely allowed even the most popular performer more than one week in a city.) Yet, for Sophie, "it was the windup of the most wonderful week of my life."[5]

Each night, after the show, Sophie returned home to be served a late supper, a special meal set out by her mother. Not only had Sophie been forgiven by her parents, but respect and good wishes had also come from many members of the Jewish community. It seemed as if Sophie's theater successes superseded any memories of past transgressions.

This was also the moment that Phil persuaded his sister that she needed help to oversee her finances. Although Sophie had been earning an excellent salary, a good deal of her money went for elegant dresses and hats, new songs, and the usual travel expenses. Acknowledging her need for more fiscal discipline, she promised to send Phil every dollar she could spare to invest "for a rainy day." Although Sophie occasionally strayed from Phil's budget — she enjoyed playing poker and the horses — he did a reasonably good job of amassing an estate for her until his untimely death in 1945, at which time Moe took over as her business manager.

Frank Westphal had accompanied Sophie to Hartford but stayed at a hotel during the engagement. There is no evidence that Sophie spoke of Frank to her family, nor does it appear that he associated with any of the Abuzas. He did, however, receive mention in the newspaper for his support of Sophie's act. When speaking of the many songs Sophie had to memorize, they reported that "Frank C. Westphal, who is Miss Tucker's pianist, is also obliged to memorize the music for them." His relative invisibility was a situation to which Frank was becoming accustomed.

Appearing in Boston the week after her "heady" engagement in Hartford, Sophie was uncharacteristically billed as third headliner; but for good reason. In Boston, she followed Olga Nethersole, a renowned dramatic actress who had been lured into vaudeville by a substantial salary for minimal work, and the Three Keatons, with little Buster already a star in his own right. She was acknowledged, however, for her ragtime renditions. Sophie's father came to visit her in New Haven, at which time she introduced him to life backstage. Life behind the scenes seemed a hodgepodge of activity, highlighted with actor's behavior that, in Charles's eyes, bordered on the irreverent.

Sophie attempted to explain to her father something of the real life of actors and other performers. Her explanation seemed as much a self-analysis as it was a performer's credo. William Morris would have been proud of Sophie.

> Backstage everyone learns self-control and discipline. You have to learn how to take it on the chin, and to smile while taking it. You learn never to be late. Never to be caught unprepared. Above all, never to think you are the whole show.[6]

Back in New York, Sophie appeared at the Bronx Theater and at Hammerstein's Victoria, playing to the usual full houses. She introduced two new songs, "The International Rag" and "I Wonder Where My Easy Rider's Gone," the latter generating comments from a number of reviewers about its "suggestive" lyrics, a complaint not usually expressed by New York critics. It is possible they were more upset because Sophie departed from wearing her usual elegant gown; instead, when she sang "Easy Rider," she wore trousers. Audiences in Providence, however, cheered her change of costume and shouted for encores. Comments about her performances did not deter the *New York Clipper* from featuring Sophie on the front page of their November 29 issue, her first photo appearance in that publication. Their biography, although brief, told of Sophie's rapid rise to stardom and the audience's ardent reaction to her ragtime renditions.

Thus began an eighteen-week tour on the Keith circuit, every engagement in high-class theaters with full orchestras, supported by extensive advertising and promotion. Sophie did not disappoint theater managers, attracting generous box-office receipts. Of course, Keith did not depend on one or two headliners to draw large audiences. In fact, the Keith circuit lineup had been one of the best in many years, offering headliners like Eddie Foy and the Seven Little Foys, Mae West, Will Rogers, Sam Bernard, the Three Keatons, Trixie Friganza, and James J. Corbett. Theaters on the circuit had at least one of these people appearing on the bill every week.

During the tour, Sophie and Frank continued to enhance their stage routine. Frank became more involved in the act, ad-libbing with Sophie between songs. The success of these exchanges persuaded them to build their patter into the act, and the result turned out to be quite amusing to audiences. Normally, the interchange was used to introduce the next song; sometimes, it was topical humor solely for audience enjoyment. By the end of the tour, Frank and Sophie had so perfected the routine that it seemed more a skit with songs than a simple singing performance. At the beginning of every performance, Sophie inserted her admission to being "a poor Jewish girl from Hartford who grew up working in her parent's kosher restaurant"; and at least one song included Yiddish expressions. Whatever the audience, at this point, Sophie used her "Jewishness" with open confidence.

After some years of "under-the-table" payoffs to singers by music publishers, a major legal battle went public when a number of singers and music publishing houses brought suit against a group of other publishers accused of giving "royalties" to singers "selling" their songs. Rossiter was one of the groups being sued, since they had made "special financial arrangements" with singers, including Sophie. A number of singers were subpoenaed to testify, Sophie one of a group because of her ties to Rossiter. Before any testimony could be obtained, however, the case was supposedly settled out of court. The result: no more "royalties" to singers. Nonetheless, according to the judge, singers could still receive "dividends" for the sheet music they sold by promoting songs. Legal experts quickly questioned how such sales could be documented and reported. In the end, the arrangement between publishers and singers continued, although handled in a more discreet way. The "payoff" system proceeded for several more years, until the federal government entered the argument. Due to the adverse publicity, Rossiter's business suffered; and Sophie had to look to other music publishers for new material.

Sophie's tour came to an end almost simultaneously with the death of B.F. Keith, April 4, 1914. All Keith houses were closed for two days, and the routing system disrupted. Rather than continuing on an unpredictable, week-to-week basis, Sophie closed in Montreal and returned to New York. The next week, Max Hart had her headline Hammerstein's Victoria. The bill included fifteen acts, from a team of monkeys to comedy cyclists to female impersonators. In the program, Sophie was labeled "a singing comedienne." There was no mention of Frank, although he played an important part in the act.

The following week, however, among seventeen acts, Sophie was headlined; and the *Clipper* identified her as "the hit of the bill." Her recent successes, as well as Hart's influence, won Sophie a coveted engagement at the Palace Theater, her first (of many) at the city's most prestigious vaudeville house.

The Palace had been opened seventeen months earlier but was only now beginning to be appraised as the finest and most luxurious venue for first-class vaudeville. The theater's early months of operation had been problematic; audiences were sparse, not entirely comfortable with the prices nor the quality of entertainment. Some critics were openly betting that the theater would soon close. Successive bills featuring Ethel Barrymore and Sarah Bernhardt, however, filled the theater; and its future success was assured.

Sophie's first engagement at the Palace was both gratifying and frustrating. Marion Spitzer, author of *The Palace,* called Sophie's appearance "a force of nature."[7] The *Clipper* reported she "showed her caliber as a Broadway favorite from start to finish of her presentation. She sang eight songs and owned the place."[8] Frank was mentioned as doing "good work on the piano."

At the first matinee, however, when Sophie sung "Who Paid the Rent for Mrs. Rip Van Winkle When Rip Van Winkle Was Away?," E.A. Albee (now owner and manager of the Keith circuit) demanded she drop the song from her act because, he believed, it offended the audience.

For many years, Albee had been obsessed with the belief that vaudeville must be meticulously "clean" (by his definition); and, to prove his point, he posted signs backstage threatening performers with expulsion if they swore or engaged in any questionable behavior. Sophie was given a choice: drop the song or leave the theater. She was not about to close prematurely her first appearance at the Palace.

Although Hart had booked Sophie for the Loew circuit to begin the new season, she opted to take a month off after the arduous Keith tour, a decision that could only be taken by a genuine headliner. It was her first vacation in six years, and she chose to spend it with Frank at the beach in Atlantic City.

Loew planned to advertise Sophie as "The Queen of Ragtime," their literary invention designed to counter the title previously used by the Keith circuit. Actually, Sophie had been feeling somewhat confined due to her longtime association with

In 1914, Sophie made her first appearance at the Palace Theater. With her repertoire of ragtime, ballads, and racy songs, audiences would not let her leave the stage. However, E.A. Albee, owner of the Palace, warned Sophie not to sing "double entendre" songs, or he would drop her from the bill. (Museum of the City of New York)

ragtime; and the new title bothered her. Throughout the last tour, she had observed that ragtime songs were losing their popularity, likely because so many of them during the past few years had been written for and employed by dozens of singers. In addition, it seemed that the war in Europe had become a significant influence on Tin Pan Alley composers; they were producing fewer ragtime songs, replacing them with sentimental ballads and war songs.

Sophie, herself, had been altering her delivery. Routines had become smoother and more modulated. Along with the beautiful gowns, she was incorporating stage props to enhance the dramatics of the act. Sophie openly expressed dislike for war songs and adamantly refused to sing them, but she took up ballads and interspersed them with rag. Having recognized the apparent decline of ragtime, she had begun to look for alternatives. Her plan was to pay particular attention to audiences during the Loew tour to observe how their tastes were changing.

Unfortunately, Sophie's appearance in Chicago was marred by two events, one affecting all performers, the other stemming from a confrontation with theater management. After much rancorous debate — theater people lobbied vigorously against its adoption — Congress passed the War Tax Bill, by which all theaters would be required to pay to the government ten percent of their gross box-office receipts. The ultimate affect of the bill meant performers would have to take a reduction in salaries, since theater managers were not about to add the fee to the price of tickets. Under the guise of patriotism, performers quietly accepted the new law, although they were very displeased with its impact on their incomes. No one suggested that salaries might be returned to their previous levels after the war emergency had passed.

When Sophie was about to open at the McVicker's Theater, she discovered that management had not billed her as the week's headliner. After three weeks of generating full houses at other Chicago theaters, she was not going to appear on the McVicker's stage without top billing. Sophie challenged the theater manager; when no decision seemed forthcoming, she contacted Marcus Loew, who immediately commanded that Sophie be featured as the headliner. He followed up his decision by distributing posters promoting Sophie's appearance at the McVicker's. Her billing, having become a public issue, the *Clipper* reported on the impasse.

> Sophie Tucker refused to appear this week, account of poor billing. She is too big a star for headline honors to be shared with another act, and brought the Loew people to realize this.[9]

Marcus Loew, embarrassed by the episode, ordered all theaters on the circuit to adhere to his instructions and sent copies of posters for them to use when Sophie was to appear. Thus began Sophie's western tour on the Loew circuit, to be plagued by mishaps and further misunderstandings. Visits to St. Paul, Minnesota, and Billings and Butte, Montana, had to compete with cold and snow; more frequently than not, the weather won.

Engagements in Seattle, Portland, Sacramento, and San Francisco attracted full houses and excellent receipts. At the beginning of her second week at the Empress Theater in San Francisco, however, Sophie found that her billing had again been reduced. The situation was similar to that in Chicago. This time, however, Marcus Loew was not involved, because he had recently sold a number of west coast theaters, allowing local managers to dictate their own terms. The San Francisco manager declared he did not care for Sophie's "suggestive" song selections; Sophie let him know she would not accept second billing.

Claiming to suffer a severe cold and temporary loss of voice — in a statement for press consumption — Sophie abruptly canceled her time on the Loew circuit and returned to New York. Her purpose, to meet with Marcus Loew and renegotiate a contract to appear in his theaters only. The negotiations took several weeks because west coast managers, no longer under Loew's supervision, demanded that their contracts be fulfilled and threatened possible legal action. A month later, Loew announced that Sophie was returning to complete her tour agreement.

> Sophie Tucker has returned to the West to complete her tour of the Marcus Loew circuit, opening in Sacramento, April 19, and will play Eastward.[10]

After Sacramento, Sophie took another long jump to Chicago, to appear there and in Milwaukee for several weeks. To everyone's surprise, and to the consternation of performers playing the circuit, Loew sold the remainder of his Western houses to Sullivan and Considine, as of May 1. Fortunately for Sophie, she was heading East anyway and looked forward to a smooth return to friendly New York audiences. Instead, family tragedy intervened and nearly persuaded Sophie to end her theatrical career.

While she was playing in Chicago, Sophie received a frantic telegram from Anna. "Father dying. Please return home as quickly as you can." After a period of mild ailments, Charles Abuza had suffered a severe heart attack. Doctors reported he had only a short time to live. Sophie departed Chicago immediately after her last show and arrived in Hartford two days later, joining an already grief-stricken household.

Partially paralyzed, unable to talk, Charles lay helplessly in bed, attended by Jennie and Anna. The doctor visited Charles daily to check on his condition, although his visits seemed more a courtesy to the family than a medical intervention. The rabbi also visited daily, primarily to console family members. Charles was rapidly failing; he had days, a week at most, to live.

Sophie's mother was distraught; Moe and Anna seemed too young to deal with

The Abuza family in 1915, shortly before Charles, Sophie's father, died. Sitting, left to right: Charles, Jennie, and Sophie; above them, sister Anna and a friend; sitting below Sophie, her son, Bert; standing, Philip; the other children sitting on the steps are likely Philip's children. When Charles died, Sophie was not sure she wanted to continue performing. William Morris came to Hartford to convince her of a bright future in show business. (Harry Ransom Humanities Research Center, University of Texas)

the situation; and Phil had his own family to care for. Upon her arrival, Sophie took over, attending to the needs of her father, as well as those of her family. Daily visits by the doctor, rabbi, synagogue and business friends required a decorum unfamiliar to the family. Although under distressful circumstances, Sophie carefully managed the many obligatory activities.

On May 24, 1915, Charles Abuza, fifty-nine years old, died in his sleep. In accordance with Jewish custom, Charles's body was laid in state, in anticipation of a funeral and burial two days later. "Sitting Shiva," the family would mourn and engage in prayer for seven days, a group of men from the synagogue coming each day to conduct services. Family members were not allowed to cook or serve food; friends brought meals for the family and snacks for the many visitors who came by the house to pay their respects.

During this time, Sophie tenderly cared for her fragile mother, who was greatly depressed by her husband's death, as well as for her siblings. (Son Bert remained at boarding school.)

Jewish law declared that immediate family members, spouses and children, were not allowed to partake of any celebrations or entertainment for an entire year. The edict presented Sophie with a difficult dilemma. Would she forgo returning to her profession for a year? Could she afford to, since her income strongly affected the wellbeing of her family? The law did allow mourners to return to work, but was entertainment considered work? It seemed a decision for Talmudic scholars. Sophie's decision was further complicated by the fact that many in the Jewish community still regarded the theater as "evil and seductive."

Max Hart came to Hartford to pay his respects and to find out when she might return to the stage. To his surprise, Sophie told him she planned to remain home indefinitely and she could not say when, or if, she would return. When a concerned Hart met with William Morris, he repeated Sophie's comments and, under Morris's questioning, offered his observations about Sophie's state of mind. It seemed obvious to Hart that Sophie had been deeply affected by the death of her father and was personally conflicted about continuing her career.

A month later, a determined William Morris visited Sophie, primarily to plead for her return to the stage. The meeting was a family affair, involving Philip, Moe, and Anna. Sophie's mother had already made her feelings known by deferring to Sophie in the decision. Morris did not need to use Sophie's successes as a persuasive tool; rather, he spoke of what accomplishments and contributions she could make in the future and the opportunity for her to command even more generous salaries. Sophie's siblings supported Morris and promised they could handle family affairs and care for their mother.

Although reluctant at first, Sophie finally agreed to perform again. "When would you like to start?" Morris asked. Sophie expressed a wish to delay her return for another month, because she had doubts about her ability to perform with the same degree of enthusiasm as in the past. Morris agreed to a trial period and offered his personal assistance if Sophie felt the need for professional guidance and support. It was a gesture of friendship that Sophie never forgot.

Max Hart got Sophie back on the Keith circuit as soon as possible. Her initial appearance was slated for Detroit, at the Temple Theater, August 23, more than three months after her father's death. The long train trip to Detroit was a lonely one for Sophie, similar to those she had endured during the early years of her career. Frank Westphal could not join her for several weeks, because he was appearing on another vaudeville circuit. Sophie played to full houses in Detroit—these days, just the mention of her name generated crowds—but both she and the reviewers noted her less-than-expansive performances. After successive weeks in Cleveland and Indianapolis, Sophie asked for a week off; she felt unable to perform acceptably for audiences. An appearance in Cincinnati precipitated another week off, as Sophie continued to battle her demons.

On November 8, Sophie opened an engagement at the Palace Theater, Chicago. Frank had joined her, and William Morris was in attendance at the Monday matinee. When Sophie walked on stage, she was met with a standing ovation that lasted five minutes. Welcoming her back, the audience's reaction served as an antidote to her personal insecurities. She smiled and bowed repeated times; and when she prepared to sing, as Frank began the piano introduction, Morris observed the familiar twinkle in her eyes. Sophie was back. Morris recognized it; the audience recognized it; and Sophie felt it. In reporting her "return to the stage," the *Clipper* marveled at her extended act but worried whether she could keep up such efforts.

> Sophie Tucker, at the Palace Theater, Chicago, last Monday at the opening show, probably made a record there that will stand for some time. She sang 16 songs and was on the stage for fully 38 minutes. It's a wonderful test of Sophie's vaudeville powers, but we doubt very much if the performance doesn't do her personal injury. Very few singers can get away with as many songs as she did and do justice to herself at the next shows.[11]

Sophie took their advice. During the remaining performances, she sang only nine songs and remained on stage for only twenty-two minutes. The encouraging events in Chicago helped to launch a more confident and assured Sophie on another successful tour of the Keith circuit in the Midwest and East. Still, as she traveled the circuit, she noticed subtle changes in the vaudeville milieu.

Many of the old, familiar headliners had been replaced by newcomers, people like Fred and Adele Astaire, Hugh Herbert, Amelia Stone, and Joseph Santley, some of them veterans of musical comedy, because in vaudeville they could make more money for less work. Songs were increasingly identified with the war, although the U.S. itself was still quite removed from European battlefields. And a new form of music was finding its way into vaudeville acts and audience awareness. Tin Pan Alley referred to it as jazz. They had co-opted the music of Negroes, cleaned up its suggestive implications, and made it more commercially appealing. The music was not really jazz as played by its Negro originators in New Orleans and Chicago, but rather a more syncopated version of it, to replace the familiar, timeworn ragtime melodies. Still, the music's beat, melody, and lyrics appealed to Sophie. Obviously, it was something to explore as she worked to keep her act fresh.

During Christmas, at the Majestic Theater, Chicago, a review of Sophie's act revealed significant changes in her song selection.

> Sophie Tucker showed she could sing a ballad, featuring "Mother," "Mollie, Dear," "Old Home Town of Mine," "Dancing Shoes," and songs she used with an upbeat, including "It's All Your Fault," "Araby," and "Suffering Suffragette."[12]

Since Sophie believed that audiences were no longer "into my act," she made time to discuss the situation with William Morris. Morris suggested she do something that took into consideration audience interest in the new jazz sound, an idea she was already contemplating. Yet another reason for her concern about the act had to do with Frank Westphal. She liked Frank very much and believed he was an excellent pianist and straight man. Personally, she did not want to lose him. But because Sophie was the headliner and earned more money, Frank had been showing increasing unease with his secondary role. Frank's feelings seemed obvious to Morris, as well; and he likely discussed possible alternatives with Sophie.

It was during this time that Max Hart was faced with another publicity-driven divorce suit brought by his wife. This time, he was accused of having an affair with Sophie. Under the circumstances, Hart and Sophie agreed it would be better for them to discontinue their business arrangement. And since William Morris had recently reopened a booking agency, Sophie was delighted to renew her business ties with him. When Morris booked her into the Palace, New York, he renamed her "The Empress of Songs," an obvious attempt to distance her from her previous ragtime identity. Posters and broadsides headlined with the new title announced Sophie's triumphant return.

During Sophie's opening matinee, however, an unfortunate episode so unnerved her that she cut short the act, much to the disappointment of the audience. She had already sung eight songs when a huge bouquet of roses was passed over the footlights. While the audience called for their favorite songs, a loud voice boomed from the balcony requesting that Sophie sing "Louisville," adding that he had sent her the flowers.

The *Clipper* reported that "one particular music firm" normally bought up a block of seats whenever a performer was to sing one of their songs and, when it was sung, would respond loudly in recognition. Then, the *Clipper* revealed, the next edition "of a certain theatrical paper" (it could only have been *Variety*) would come out with a report that the song was "the hit of the performance." The blatant request from the balcony had come from an employee of just such a music firm, interestingly, one that had initiated the law suit implicating Sophie with Rossiter.

Sophie was so upset by the intrusion, she cut the evening performance to only four songs, none of them from the offending music publisher. After the show, Sophie spoke to reporters about the episode. "For the good of vaudeville, this thing should be stopped. That a song-boosting stunt by a bunch of 'pick-ups' from this certain publishing house could break up a show at the Palace should never again occur."

The remainder of the week went smoothly, but Sophie carefully selected the songs she sang, rather than allow the audience to choose them. The *Clipper* acknowledged her limited act with courtesy.

> Sophie was in splendid voice. "Ballin' the Jack" was her first song, followed by "Morning, Noon, and Night," the latter song being heard for the first time here. Somebody has at last struck something original in songs, and if the reception accorded Sophie is a criterion, some lucky publisher is due for a big, juicy hit. "Mollie, Dear, It's You I'm After" was her third song, and after singing a verse and chorus a drop was lowered with the music and chorus printed so the audience could join in. It went over big. "Back Home" was her fourth and last number."[13]

A week at the nearby Royal Theater was highly successful, with Morris continuing the publicity campaign to promote Sophie as "The Empress of Songs." Morris also announced to the press that Sophie was considering a tour of Australian variety houses in the near future, but it was very likely another public relations scheme. Actually, Sophie still had five more cities to play before returning to New York for an extended stay. While on the road, Sophie was subpoenaed to appear before the New York court, again investigating music publisher payoffs to singers. Since she was on tour, she was excused from testimony. The publisher Rossiter, however, was indicted for their massive payoffs to singers. Sophie now made an increased effort to select songs from a wide range of publishers.

While appearing in Chicago, Sophie introduced two tunes that not only displayed her unique talents, but also demonstrated her independence from increasing public pressure to include patriotic songs. Tin Pan Alley houses had been hard at work churning out war-related songs and were promoting them heavily.

A collaboration between Sophie and Negro composer Chris Smith brought his dance song, "Ballin' the Jack," to public attention. The song was a swinging example of the current dance craze being led, at the time, by such luminaries as Vernon and Irene Castle, Maurice and Walton, and Mae Murray and Clifton Webb. Sophie lent her own interpretation to the song, with facial and body movements, as well as lyric emphasis, that suggested a more thoroughly sensual experience. "Ballin' the Jack" became a classic dance number and was performed by dance bands into the 1950s.

"Nat'an, For What Are You Waitin', Nat'an?" was a character song that Sophie sang almost entirely in Yiddish, the first time she had presented a song in that manner. Still, coupled with her facial expressions and brief breaks into English to emphasize a lyric, audiences could easily understand her. Other singers quickly picked up the song; and it soon became a national hit, albeit of brief duration. No one, however, could put the song across like Sophie.

At the same time, theater managers cajoled Sophie to sing the big patriotic hit, "Wake Up America"; but she refused. Her constant demurrals elicited jeers about her lack of patriotism, along with some anti–Semitic remarks, not to mention disappointment from song publishers that Sophie would not champion their war songs. Sophie's answer was simple: she did not sing patriotic songs because they were already being used by dozens of other performers. Yet, the friction did not entirely disappear. Several months later, when the Shuberts offered Sophie a role in one of their revues, they requested that she sing "Wake Up America." She refused the request and the role.

The Chicago visit also offered the opportunity for Sophie and William Morris to discuss changing her act. Audiences seemed less enthusiastic about the routine, Sophie observed; and Frank had become disgruntled with the arrangement. Morris believed that Sophie could no longer operate as a single. Together they came up with the idea for Sophie to work with an as yet unidentified group, in addition to adding sets designed to "romance" the songs. Morris also suggested that Sophie feature more upbeat melodies—jazzy music, in his words—and drop Frank from the act.

"Loaf for a while," he advised. "You haven't done that for a long time. It will do you good. Get out and see what's around town. You'll get an idea."

Frank had already discussed his secondary role with Sophie and wished to terminate it, maybe even get out of vaudeville altogether. Conversations with Philip generated an idea for Frank to run an automobile garage, since he had a long-term interest in racing cars. Consequently, during the early summer of 1916, the Sophie Tucker Garage was opened, with Frank as proprietor. Sophie was now free to pursue the formation of a new act.

The emphasis was to be on jazz, or at least the use of the jazz framework in the music performed. With the assistance of Morris, Sophie gathered five young men from various vaudeville and night club sources to form a band. Their versatile talents would allow them to play music from ballads to actual jazz works. Their primary responsibility would be to back Sophie; but they also had the opportunity to perform, on their own, popular jazz music. The combination also gave Sophie and band members the freedom for comic banter between songs, as well as during their introduction.

After three weeks of hard rehearsals, the new act, called "Sophie Tucker and her Five Kings of Syncopation," opened at the Royal Theater, New York, June 26. They were an immediate hit.

> Many vaudeville women are gifted with temperament — whatever that may be — and very little else. Sophie Tucker is not one of those women, as the capacity audiences yesterday will agree readily. Headlining an entertaining bill, Miss Tucker and her five aides — styled "kings" of syncopation — offer a diverting lot of music and rhythm. There is little better in vaudeville than Sophie Tucker's broad A's and silent R's, unless it is her ability to be just a little ahead of the snappiest ragtime that our contemporary music writers offer.[14]
>
> The hit of the program was easily captured by Sophie Tucker and her band of syncopation. Not to be outdone by the many dancing acts carrying their own band, Miss Tucker's has put together as fine a band of five pieces as has ever played here. The audience just simply couldn't get enough of Sophie's singing; she was a little short of a riot.[15]

To begin the new season, Morris signed Sophie and the group to play the Orpheum circuit — a Canadian and west coast trip again — for twenty-four weeks. Sophie would be earning $1,000 a week, but that included musician's salaries, sets, costumes, and travel expenses. When Phil was informed of the contract, he chided Sophie for leaving so little for herself. Phil also had less pleasant news to share with

Sophie and Frank Westphal, her piano accompanist, were a couple for several years before they married in 1917. After their marriage, Frank complained about his second billing and small salary. First, Sophie bought an auto repair business for him. When that closed, she divorced him, claiming desertion. (Harry Ransom Humanities Research Center, University of Texas)

Sophie: Frank was a failure running the garage, and Phil was taking over the obligation until it could be sold. Because of her deep feelings for Frank — she had sincerely missed him — Sophie had him signed on the Orpheum circuit as a separate act, on the same bill she and the band played. They were together again, and the new arrangement seemed to rekindle their intimacy.

The group's opening in Minneapolis featured Sophie's rendition of Sheldon Brooks's new song, "Walkin' the Dog." She planned to promote the song throughout the tour; but it gained attention so quickly that other singers appropriated it. These days, many singers, some of them well-known, carefully watched Sophie's featured selections; once Sophie gained acceptance for a song, the others incorporated it into their own acts. This forced Sophie to drop the pilfered songs — in spite of audience requests — in favor of presenting new material.

Sophie, the "boys" (as they were being referred to), and Frank played engagements across Canada and down the west coast before turning East. Stops in the Midwest preceded a return to New York in the middle of March, 1917. Reports about the tour were slim, but those published indicated a resounding success for Sophie's new act. The highlight of the trip, however, occurred in Los Angeles when Sophie ostentatiously called together the press to announce her engagement to Frank Westphal. The *Clipper* reported the news, as if in wonder.

> Sophie Tucker, the "Mary Garden of Ragtime," is engaged to be married! All the details to be gained up-to-date are that he has lovely eyes and is worth a million. The wedding will not be solemnized until next season.[16]

Interestingly, as news, the startling announcement disappeared as abruptly as it had appeared. Most people in the theatrical business knew Frank, knew about his relationship with Sophie; and he surely did not fit the *Clipper's* description.

Nevertheless, Sophie believed she was in love. If she did not want to split with him, marriage seemed the only alternative. No matter that Frank was six years younger and not Jewish.

Yet, when Sophie completed the tour and visited her family, Frank did not accompany her. How Sophie's mother really felt about the impending wedding is unknown. The actual marriage did not take place until October 13, 1917, in Chicago, in a quiet, private ceremony, conducted by a justice-of-the-peace, ten months after the announcement.

Sophie and the band's success on the Orpheum circuit had caught the eye of the ever enterprising Shuberts as they were in the process of preparing a new "Passing Show" production, their own slim version of the Follies. When the Shubert rep approached Sophie, she set her price at $850 a week. Reporting to J.J. Shubert, the

As Sophie moved from ragtime to jazz-inspired songs, she built an act comprised of the "Five Kings of Syncopation." They backed her on songs that reflected her interpretations of the jazz rhythms and, while she changed costumes, entertained audiences with jazz melodies.

rep said, "I told her she was a lunatic, and reminded her that she had no railroad fares to pay or no other expenses."[17] Sophie instructed the rep to go see William Morris.

Morris refused the offer and reiterated Sophie's fee. The rep again conferred with J.J. Shubert. "Her band cost her $250 a week, although she originally lied to me and told me the five men cost her $65 each. She pays in commission to Morris and the U.B.O. $115 a week."[18] J.J. responded by telling the rep to offer Sophie $650. The rep doubted she would consider such a salary.

When the rep visited one of Sophie's performances, he raved to J.J. about her appeal. "There is no doubt that she is one of the biggest hits ever in Chicago. All in all, I think she would be a corking good addition to 'The Passing Show,' especially for this town."[19] J.J. replied, "No more than $700 a week."

Morris and J.J. exchanged letters negotiating Sophie's salary, but neither changed his position. J.J. broke off the negotiations by suggesting that Sophie "cannot afford the crazy things that she did," thereby offending her. At the same time, however, Sophie had no other engagements lined up for the future. For the moment, at least, Sophie and her boys were unemployed.

6

Celebrating Cabarets

When the Shubert's engagement failed to materialize, William Morris cabled Sophie: "For the time being, would you be interested in appearing at a cabaret? The salary would be at least equal to what you earn in vaudeville, and the venue is high-class." Without hesitation, Sophie accepted the assignment. For some time, she had wanted to play at cabarets because she believed they were "my kind of place."

In Western Europe, during the later part of the nineteenth century, cabarets had flourished as irreverent places of amusement, where the well-to-do could "slum" and be entertained by populist artists spouting social and political diatribes against the establishment, reciting provocative poetry, and presenting shadow-theater allegories ridiculing royalty. Cabarets had become infamous outlets for satire, travesty, and populist themes that attracted crowds of patrons looking to laugh at the foibles of society and government, as well as themselves, and to do so safely. Cabaret was also an environment in which soon-to-be famous artists could showcase their wares and build their careers. Many craftsmen of the period, including Strindberg, Satie, Massenet, Delibes, Dumas, Degas, Verne, and Zola had their beginnings in cabaret venues. The richness and inventiveness of this milieu continued in Europe through the turn of the century.[1]

Predictably, the phenomenon took another decade to reach the United States. Typical of American popular entertainment, cabarets shaped their own style, giving expression to the particular interests and desires of their audiences. Historians believe cabaret night life began in New York in 1911, when the Brothers Bustanody offered dancing along with supper for their customers. They were so successful with the innovation, restaurants like Rector's, Shanley's, and Reisenweber's quickly copied them. Ziegfeld further Americanized the cabaret by presenting his summer Follies productions on the roof of the New York Theater, where drinking and dining accompanied the show. Such a venue offered additional financial benefit for theater managers. Urban theaters usually closed for the summer because of the heat. Outside performances allowed shows to be put on the entire summer season. Ziegfeld continued to give summer shows for several years until competitors invaded the territory with their own versions of roof entertainment. Enter vaudeville, burlesque, and revues with their assortment of acts and actors.

When the fad declined — impresarios soon found that the costs of producing such shows were prohibitive — popular restaurants stepped in as the purveyors of night entertainment, often running well after theaters normally closed. For Broadway's night-life denizens, this new venue was very appealing, for social as well as amusement reasons. It quickly became fashionable to be seen at these spots, and performers just as quickly discovered that cabarets offered distinct advantages over the usual theater engagements.[2]

In the years before World War I, cabarets offered a unique combination of features: familiar and well-liked personalities; intimate, exclusive venues; dining and drinking accompanied by entertainment; and an unabashed freedom in the material presented. The war years and the onset of Prohibition only increased cabaret's appeal. While everything about the cabaret was presented in a high-class manner, liquor was readily available "under the table"; and prostitution was discreetly practiced.

Still, not every performer could be successful within the cabaret environment. As free and easy as it may have seemed to the general observer, there were heavy demands placed on actors to establish an intimate rapport with patrons and entertain them in the manner they had come to expect when visiting a cabaret. Many entertainers tried; most failed. In contrast, Sophie believed cabarets to be her particular venue; and audiences surely agreed.

Only strong, high-profile performers were able to make a name for themselves in cabarets. The cabaret setting, by means of its physical layout and social informality, brought patrons and performers into close proximity, so close they could converse and touch. Unlike in the usual theater environment, cabaret performers had to reach out to involve audiences, to seduce them and hold their attention. The most successful performers were those who could readily interpret and understand patrons' needs and desires and manipulate those feelings to their own ends.

Obviously, the performer who attracted the largest crowds most often played the longest engagements. Cabarets had decided advantages over traditional popular theaters and vaudeville circuits, since performers could remain at one venue for an extended period of time. This enabled performers to build a substantial following among cabaretgoers and help build identity for the house itself. Such engagements eliminated touring and the insecurities of serial bookings. For the successful cabaret performer, the reduction of these constant stresses was exhilarating.

Always looking for ways to promote their songs, music publishers found the cabaret an excellent source for song boosting. If a performer embraced a new song — although supposedly illegal in theaters, payoffs to singers continued in cabarets — the intimacy between patrons and singer proved an excellent vehicle to popularity. No question, it was much easier to remember the lyrics and more entertaining to listen to songs sung in a cabaret than in a theater.

Top headliners—those who gained acceptance in cabarets—also enjoyed the benefit of negotiating better contracts. Based on their ability to attract and retain crowds, performers could receive not only their salaries, but also a percentage of gross receipts over the minimum. The arrangement could generate hundreds of dollars more each week.

Adding to the informality and intimacy of the setting, performers often acted as hosts to patrons, a familiarity that could not be achieved in theaters. Such actors became known as "friendly entertainers." They might greet customers at the door and seat them. They might engage in casual conversation. For returning patrons, "how's the family" was the usual conversation opener. If celebrities happened to be in the audience, performers would introduce them. The celebs would bow (or wave) and might even perform a number. The physical proximity between patrons and performers added a sense of freedom and improvisation to the entire proceedings. Actually, cabaret promoted an "unscheduled nature of entertainment," since it promoted a sense of conviviality and lent an aura of unexpected excitement to the experience. If patrons came to believe they were a part of the performance, they enjoyed it even more thoroughly.

As the popularity of cabarets grew, they became celebrity gathering places. By attracting more and more people from the theatrical business, cabarets also became places where business would be consummated and gossip exchanged. The usual result was added publicity for the participants. Later, when cabarets became a haunt for reporters and columnists, much of the information they wrote—whether truthful or rumor—came from cabaret attendance. The careers of Walter Winchell and Hedda Hopper were built on such visits.

Cabarets also created another boon for performers—"doubling." Performers could handle two engagements at one time, working first at a vaudeville house and then appearing at a cabaret later that same night. It was a demanding, hectic life, but highly profitable. If Sophie did not invent the idea, she at least established its legitimacy and the fact that it could actually be accomplished.

Still, it was not all celebration and profit for cabarets. From the beginning, the press continually accused them of being elitist; admittedly, their prices for food, drink, and entertainment were very high. They were frequently accused of tacitly condoning, if not promoting, prostitution; and some cabarets were repeatedly raided and shut down, albeit temporarily, due to these charges. Yet, public perceptions resulting from these accusations lent the cabaret an added aura of sexuality that, naturally, increased patronage.

The content of cabaret acts were under particular scrutiny by both self-appointed moral arbiters and the police. Cabarets were often blamed for presenting suggestive material, which was likely true. Already known for their rigorous attention to "indecent" behavior in vaudeville houses, Chicago police frequently shut down cabarets accused of presenting "obscene acts." Even in Chicago, however, the typical cabaret owner would pay a fine and reopen two days later. Periodically, citizen crusaders demanded cabarets be shut down because of their "corruptive influences." "But corruptive of whom?" critics asked, since cabaret attendance was selective, voluntary, and for adults only. Actually, "the veneer of respectability," as Erenberg called it, gave even conservative people a reason to visit cabarets. When Prohibition went into effect, cabarets became a familiar outlet for illegal liquor. Everyone knew it; but few did anything about it, until some citizen-led or politically motivated incident forced police to shut the cabaret. Within the week, however, the offending venue would reopen for business.

Although Prohibition made it problematic for many cabarets to operate profitably, they stayed in full bloom through the mid–1920s. During this period, nightclubs—a variation on the cabaret theme—came into prominence. Nightclubs were venues that emphasized entertainment over food and presented suggestive material that surpassed even the limits of cabaret propriety. Not surprisingly, the increasing success of nightclubs eroded business at cabarets and sent them into decline. (The depression badly injured cabarets, and the end of Prohibition killed them.) Led by such crowd-pleasing venues as the Martz, the Deauville, and Fay's Follies (with hostess Texas Guinan, greeting customers with her cheery "Hello, sucker"), nightclub attendance flourished.

When criminals insinuated their way into the nightclub business, the genre was taken to its most flamboyant level. Such venues as The Bath Club, Ciro's, the Trocadero, the Crillon, and Club Alabam' represented New York's effulgent era, the degree of decency varying with performers' material and police indulgence. The period also promoted the mainstreaming of African-American entertainment by white managers. Bamville, the Nest, and the Cotton Club, where white patrons enthused over Negro music and dancing, were led by newcomers like Cab Calloway and Duke Ellington. More sophisticated than cabaret audiences, the patrons of nightclubs sought more risqué shows, liquor, and no curfew; and they paid dearly for what they received. For her part, Sophie refused to appear in these nightclubs because of their suspect management.

William Morris had booked Sophie and the band into the Islesworth Hotel, Atlantic City, New Jersey, June 26, for an eight-week engagement. The hotel's cabaret was relatively small, holding no more than 150 patrons if all tables were occupied; for Sophie's appearance, however, they allowed standing room. Two shows a night were presented, at 10:00 P.M. and midnight. Each show normally lasted forty-five minutes; but with audiences begging Sophie for encores, shows often lasted for more than an hour.

Given the cabaret format, Sophie and the Five Kings of Syncopation began the act by performing a few ballads, followed by a regular ragtime tune. While Sophie went off to change, the band played a number of jazz melodies, featuring each of the individual performers. When Sophie reentered, she began with a song lamenting the loss of a lover, launched into a tune touting women's independence from men, and ended the set with a rousing and sexually suggestive song that had audiences tapping their feet and clapping their hands. Encores were usually familiar ragtime songs done in Sophie's inimitable fashion. To keep the act fresh, Sophie changed her song

6. Celebrating Cabarets

All of Sophie's costumes featured hats covered with feathers and flowers. Audiences often applauded the costumes even before her act began. Sophie claimed that no costume was worn more than twice, the discarded gowns given to other performers or clothing stores. (Museum of the City of New York)

selections every few days, since she had discovered that cabaret audiences returned often.

According to the press, Sophie and the band played to full houses the entire eight-week period and were commended for their ever changing material. Observers noted that Sophie's personality and presentation were ideally suited to the cabaret milieu, that she was, indeed, the epitome of the "friendly entertainer" and the consummate cabaret performer.

When the fall season opened, Sophie and the band were signed by the Orpheum circuit for a twenty-six week tour. Although not a part of Sophie's act, Frank Westphal had a spot on the bill, thanks to Sophie's insistence. Frank's garage had been a failure, but now they could travel together. On opening night at the Orpheum Theater, Memphis, Tennessee, Sophie introduced two new songs: "Nobody Much," a tear-producing ballad, and "I'm a Real Kind Mama Lookin' For a Lovin' Man," which enthused audiences but received disapproving remarks from reviewers because of what they considered to be the lyric's questionable meanings. Such disparaging comments, however, did nothing to deter full houses; in fact, they likely encouraged more people to see Sophie.

While in New Orleans, Sophie and Frank came up with an idea to hold a benefit to purchase cigarettes for soldiers. The first benefit garnered only a modest amount of money; but newspapers and tobacco companies quickly grabbed the promotion and, with Sophie's agreement, set up similar benefits in a score of cities in which she was to appear. Each benefit collected more money and publicity; and by the time Sophie returned to New York, special benefits were planned for "Sophie Tucker's Tobacco Fund," which, ultimately, collected thousands of dollars to purchase "smokes" for the soldiers.

Sophie's appearance at the Majestic Theater, Chicago, brought her together with the Four Marx Brothers. The mayhem they created on stage not only obtained rave reviews, but guaranteed sellouts at every performance. Running on and off the stage, breaking into each other's acts, the performers found their regular business turned into improvisational skits full of zany comedy and group singing that delighted audiences, often extending shows an hour longer than usual. Two of the Marx Brothers, Chico and Harpo, played in Sophie's band, to mixed but decidedly funny effect. While Sophie sang, the Marx Brothers danced behind her irreverently. When Frank Westphal pushed his piano on stage to begin his act — he was dressed in a hat, overcoat, and galoshes — the Marx Brothers shoved the piano into a far corner of the stage. They stole his costume and put on his clothing. When Sophie came to Frank's rescue, they put the costume on her over her gown. After the show, the performers' activities consisted of all-night poker games. Martin Beck, the Orpheum circuit owner, was so pleased by the box-office receipts generated by these performances, he canceled a Milwaukee visit so that the two acts reappeared in Chicago in tandem to continue the hilarity a few weeks later.

On October 13, 1917, while playing in Chicago, Sophie and Frank were married in a brief ceremony by a Justice of the Peace; the boys from the band the only witnesses. A supper party, honoring the bride and groom, was held at the Restaurant Royale. Friends and colleagues were invited to this party, which continued through the night until the newlyweds were forced to rush to the station to catch a train to Winnipeg, Ontario, their next professional engagement. Sophie wrote a letter to the family telling them of her marriage to Frank, but she included few details.

The tour took them across Canada and down the West Coast, a trip highlighted by a two-week engagement in San Francisco. It was here that Sophie introduced Sheldon Brooks's new song, "The Darktown Strutters Ball," which quickly became a nationwide hit. Walter Anthony, critic of the *San Francisco Chronicle*, both praised and panned Sophie; it had become an increasingly frequent reviewer's response to her act. They could not deny her talent and ability to entertain; but they were disturbed by her song lyrics and stage antics.

> The popularity of Sophie Tucker is perennial. It follows her like dialect follows the "coon shouter," nor do the years seem to affect the hold she has on her audiences. Her songs are not notable for their deftness nor for any subtle, hidden wit. A spade with Sophie is no implement wherewith to overturn the soil. It's a spade. Her manipulation of her lyrical material is graced as ever with an equal amount of energy involved in digging a sewer, into which most of her verse might be consigned, so far as I'm concerned, without regret. But they like Sophie and her song about Pop, her yearnings for someone to love her, etc., etc., and her Jazz band's antics — descendants

straight from the hysteria of a Georgia camp meeting in Darktown — remain a gigantic hit.[3]

When Sophie and the band visited Salt Lake City during the Christmas holidays, she was warned by the Orpheum people to temper her song selections. Performers were quite familiar with the city's reputation. Police were not hesitant to close a show on the slightest pretext. Yet, audiences requested she sing her new hit, "I'm a Real Kind Mama Lookin' For a Lovin' Man," several times. Sophie sang the song straight, carefully leaving out any actions or gestures that might be interpreted as provocative. In turn, she was given "stellar honors" by the local reviewer.

The early part of 1918 found Sophie and the band gradually working their way East — Denver, Omaha, Kansas City, Des Moines, Minneapolis, and St. Paul — to continued box-office success. With the war and patriotism now occupying all aspects of people's lives, theater managers used the mood of the public to proclaim that they were determined to eliminate all smut and "morale-breaking" songs and that they planned to send to all vaudeville houses an order forbidding the use of indecent materials. Their stated reasons: such songs "break down the morale of the people of this country, and also sow the seeds of doubt in the minds of soldiers abroad." The order was really just another in ongoing attempts by theater managers to control actors.

Following the lead of Martin Beck and E.A. Albee, the self-proclaimed arbiters of vaudeville morals, most theater people complied with the order. A few reluctant music publishers, however, were accused of using the war as an opportunity for profiteering and were requested to remove their offending songs from the market. Not surprisingly, pressure was being applied against Sophie to comply with the new rules. Voicing the argument that she never sang war songs anyway, she maintained that the edict, therefore, did not apply to her. A patron in St. Paul, however, questioned Sophie's patriotism so vigorously that the issue became front-page news in all the theatrical papers.[4]

The episode began innocently enough. During her act, Sophie noticed a woman, sitting in an orchestra seat knitting. Sophie requested that she stop until the act was finished. St. Paul newspapers took up the issue and panned Sophie mercilessly, alleging that her attempted interference with the patriotic knitter — the woman claimed she had been knitting sweaters for the boys overseas — inclined them to the belief that Sophie was lacking in patriotism.

In response, Sophie replied that she had worked diligently to raise thousands of dollars for Liberty Bonds and had appeared at several benefits for soldiers and sailors. The newspapers printed her rebuttal, and they seemed satisfied. The issue, however, did not go away. Newspapers in other cities — those where Sophie planned to be playing in the future — continued to repeat the story, not necessarily in an accusatory vein, but still framing it in a sarcastic tone. Sophie, of course, remained very upset by the accusation. In fact, she was so disturbed that Frank wrote a letter to the *New York Clipper* explaining Sophie's numerous Armed Forces benefits and the many letters she received defending her actions.[5] It was later rumored that the St. Paul reviewer who initiated this accusation against Sophie believed that Jews had brought the U.S. into the war. Whatever the reasons for the attacks, no theater people doubted Sophie's patriotism. Maybe, the press speculated, the problem had more to do with Sophie's frequent brushes with Beck and Albee's "moral song" code.

A few weeks later, Sophie placed an ad in the *New York Clipper* expressing her views about using war songs. As before, Sophie refused to sing them, not out of lack of patriotism, she said, but rather because they were not her type of song. Sophie had obviously been stung by the accusation. Indeed, she had a number of war-related events in which she participated particularly publicized, evidently to defend her integrity.

No sooner had Sophie and the band arrived in New York than it was announced that Frank had been drafted into the Army. Sophie told reporters that, when Frank went to France, she would go with him to sing for the boys. William Morris immediately followed with an announcement that Sophie and the band would soon leave the States to entertain the troops. Planted notes in theatrical papers capitalized on Sophie's proposed visit.

> When Sophie Tucker gets to France the boches will think the Yanks are coming, for fair.
> Just wait till those boches hear Sophie Tucker's band. She will be able to put up a barrage that will break down any Hun advance.[6]

Nonetheless, Sophie never went to Europe. Previously committed engagements and the war's end were her excuses. The publicity she received (administered by the Morris office) could very well have been simply another way to prove her patriotic spirit. A large benefit sponsored by Sophie for the Tobacco Fund, at the Hotel Claridge, New York, seemed to serve as an additional example of her patriotism. As reported in the newspapers, had it not been for Sophie, the event would never have happened.

> The record-breaking Claridge party not only was Sophie Tucker's, it came very nearly being Sophie Tucker herself. The idea was hers. She fixed the date and sent out announcements, telling the fund about it afterwards. She was the stage manager, the director, the master of ceremonies, the prompter, the auctioneer-in-chief, the collector, the treasurer, and all the other factors that go to make up a notably successful dramatic, musical and financial enterprise.[7]

The combination of all the Tobacco Fund benefits held across the country had raised more than $10,000 for soldiers. "Thanks to Miss Tucker's patriotic interest in the work of the tobacco fund," the article concluded, "the show was the best program ever seen or heard in a hotel show."

But what of Frank? He had supposedly been drafted and was now set to enter the air force as a cadet. Yet, he continued to appear at all of Sophie's New York engagements. First, it was reported that his induction had been delayed. Then it was rumored he had been rejected by the Army; although that was denied by Frank himself. A month later, vaudeville "word-of-mouth" suggested that Sophie and Frank had separated, insiders reporting that their arguments could be heard plainly backstage. For ten weeks they had appeared together at New York's high-class vaudeville houses. When Sophie next played the Palace Theater, however, Frank was no longer on the bill. A month later, Frank was reported to have appeared at a Chicago theater, performing his old vaudeville act. For the next month, Sophie and the band continued to play various New York theaters, no one seeming to know why Frank had so abruptly left town. The couple had, indeed, separated.

In the meantime, Sophie and William Morris had begun negotiations for her to appear at Reisenweber's Restaurant (and cabaret), to open sometime in June. Reisenweber's was one of the best restaurant-cabarets in town. A successful engagement there would clearly confirm Sophie's reputation as the city's premier cabaret entertainer, and she was not about to lose the opportunity.

The Reisenweber family had been in the restaurant business for more than thirty years and their restaurant, like Rector's, Shanley's, and Delmonico's, had acquired a reputation as being one of the high-class eateries in the theater district. The family's real interest remained elegant dining, but as other restaurants began to include entertainment, Reisenweber's followed. The popularity of dining and entertainment together soon turned the restaurant toward various amusements, one room dedicated exclusively to cabaret performance.

Housed in a tall, ornate building at Eighth Avenue and Columbus Circle, Reisenweber's had four floors set aside for customers. The main (street) floor was the restaurant; the second and third floors were devoted to dancing and, during these years of frequent dance crazes, provided a haven for young people; the fourth floor, called the 400 Club Room in reference to the elite 400 of New York society, offered cabaret entertainment. Like other high-class cabarets, Reisenweber's was subject to police monitoring due to rumors that the management tolerated prostitution. (Actually, prostitutes arrived at the restaurant with escorts and never solicited on the premises.) After Prohibition, frequent police raids attested to the gossip that liquor was readily available at the restaurant, which, of course, was true.

Sophie and her Five Kings of Syncopation opened their engagement at Reisenweber's on June 13, 1918, and were booked to appear in the 400 Club Room until the end of July. Their typical performance included two daily shows. Each show consisted of Sophie's singing eight songs and the boys' playing three instrumental jazz pieces plus the usual encores, primarily, audience requests. Each show lasted for about an hour. Sophie wore a different gown each time she appeared on stage, and her song selections differed, as well. As had become characteristic of Sophie, she introduced new songs every few days. Similarly, the Morris office claimed, she never wore a gown more than twice, the "old" gowns reportedly given away to needy actresses; or so the story went. After two weeks at Reisenweber's, a brief note in the *Clipper* reported that "she is working like a Trojan, and things look very promising for a smashing engagement. She is playing her second tremendous week and is a perfect riot."[8]

Sophie frequently made publicity photos while she traveled the vaudeville circuits, especially when she played at cabarets. These signed photos were given out to patrons as a souvenir for attending the shows.

Indeed, Sophie and the band were instant hits; and show tickets were sold out days in advance. What had originally been planned as a six-week engagement turned into ten month's of employment. Along with her fixed salary, Sophie shared in a percentage of the *couvert* charges. She was said to be averaging more than $2,000 a week.

While appearing at Reisenweber's, Sophie and the band participated in a series of Sunday benefits and visited several military camps. Collaborating with Sophie were such stage luminaries as Fritzi Scheff, Bessie Wynn, the Dolly Sisters, Will Rogers, Blanche Ring, Houdini, and Eddie Dowling. The fact that the news media now included Sophie together with these outstanding performers further validated her Broadway reputation. A benefit at the Palace Theater for the Salvation Army netted close to $200,000, with Sophie and the band featured entertainers. The annual National Vaudeville Association (N.V.A.) benefit at the Hippodrome attracted 6,000 people and raised $75,000 for destitute artists. Sophie sang a number of old-time coon songs to the delight of the audience and the *Clipper* reviewer, who reported: "She has lost none of her ability as a coon shouter. The only trouble was that she left too soon."

At the same time that Sophie and the boys were regaling Reisenweber patrons, they read in the newspapers of a virulent strain of influenza, soon discovered to be highly contagious and fatal, that had recently spread from military camps to the general populace. Almost immediately, the New York Health Department warned of possible closures of all public places, which, of course, included theaters, if the "Spanish flu" became a certified epidemic. Indeed, within two weeks, the Health Department shut down all theaters; and no one had any idea when they might reopen. The city's theatrical season had abruptly come to a halt, freezing touring companies, aborting show rehearsals, and putting thousands of performers temporarily out of work.

Nonetheless, all places of entertainment did not close when the Health Department announced its edict. Cabarets remained open as long as they could attract audiences. However, even with Sophie's ability to pull in the crowds, attendance at Reisenweber's dwindled. After two weeks of sparse attendance, the restaurant had to shut down due to the prohibitive costs of operation. Never one to miss an opportunity, Sophie and the band turned the "down time" into a complete restructuring of their act, rehearsing every day to perfect it. Fortunately, neither Sophie nor any of the band members became ill.

Reisenweber's reopened September 10, and the 400 Club Room had been renamed The Sophie Tucker Room. In addition, Sophie had negotiated a new contract with management: her band would now be paid directly by the owners; and, along with fifty percent of the *couvert* charges, she would receive ten percent of the gross receipts. From the September reopening to the following April, The Sophie Tucker Room was filled each night, sold out weeks in advance. Occasionally, the restaurant had to close for a day or two due to police invasions; but those infrequent events only attracted more patrons.

During the early months of 1919, while they were playing at Reisenweber's, Sophie and the band continued to make themselves available for benefits and military camp appearances, all of which were duly noted in the newspapers, and a few of which were notable events. One Sunday benefit at the Winter Garden, Sophie and the band were co-featured with Frank Westphal. No mention, however, was made of Sophie's marital estrangement from Frank.

In March, Sophie appeared at a Purim carnival for the benefit of a Jewish congregation, her first work for a Jewish organization. Another benefit performance, a week later, found Sophie collecting a Passover Fund for Jewish inmates in New York jails.

William Morris then announced that Sophie would begin rehearsals for a new comedy, with music. The show had been written for her by Jack Lait—former publicity director for the Morris organization, now a musical comedy writer — and would open in the near future. Was the announcement real or strategic? Coincidentally, a week later, Sophie's contract with Reisenweber's was extended until June. Shortly after, it was reported that Sophie would not appear in the proposed comedy due to the play's similarity to a current hit. Instead, Morris said, after the conclusion of her engagement at Reisenweber's, Sophie would appear in an as yet unnamed musical play that he was producing. Astute reviewers doubted the news, pointing out that the usual salary for a play would be much less than Sophie was currently earning at Reisenweber's.

What neither Morris nor Sophie revealed was an increasingly contentious behind-the-scenes argument with the band, its members threatening to "go on their own" if they did not receive a raise in salary. The argument continued for several weeks, although no one seemed to notice any tension during the performances. Then,

Sophie abruptly announced she was taking a four-day hiatus from "my endeavors to entertain the guests of the Sophie Tucker room at Reisenweber's."

The entire band was summarily fired. New musicians were selected; new songs rehearsed; additions made to the act. Sophie mailed out hundreds of invitations to friends and colleagues announcing her new show. This was the first time she had used such a notification for an opening, and its evident success ultimately made it a required exercise for every opening of her future shows.

The *Clipper* reported on the cabaret's reopening, supposedly to play through the summer, after July 1, Prohibition permitting.

> The room was opened at 10:30, and after a little speech of welcome in which she alluded to the success she had achieved since she temporarily forsook the stage and came to Reisenweber's; Miss Tucker then went into the special program of songs she had arranged for the evening.[9]

Along with the new jazz band—comprising a pianist, clarinetist, cornetist, drummer, and violinist—Sophie had hired three young Negro women to back her on a number of songs and perform several dance routines of their own. It was an experiment to see how audiences would respond to the new approach. The women had come from a recently closed Chicago show where they had leaned "the shimmy" dance from its inventor, Gilda Gray. Sophie gambled that by her introducing the new dance—considered by many to be obscene—New York audiences would accept it with little complaint. To publicize Sophie's new act, Reisenweber's ads now called her the "Queen of Jazz."

At the same time that Sophie was scoring a hit with her new act, the Federal Trade Commission opened an investigation of the Vaudeville Managers Association (Keith, Orpheum, Loew, and Fox circuits) and the N.V.A. The investigation was a result of charges filed against these organizations, stemming from their long-term control of actors and booking. It seemed to observers that the old Syndicate was "alive and well," keeping actors under their tight domination. As everyone expected, management interests mounted a sizable legal defense of their business practices; but public testimony clearly revealed the extent of their control. As a witness to management practices, Sophie was requested to appear at one of the hearings, to which she willingly agreed.

Some time previously, Sophie had come to New York with three Rossiter (then a V.M.A. nonmember) songs that she planned to sing. She testified that when the theater manager (a Keith employee under E.A. Albee) had been made aware of her choices, he advised her that she could not sing these songs in Keith theaters. She was told frankly that, if she persisted in singing the songs, her time would be canceled. Sophie contacted Rossiter; and, rather than having her lose bookings, Rossiter joined the organization. Sophie believed the Keith actions to be "unprincipled."

While the investigation turned up little to indict V.M.A. members for monopolistic activities, a side result of the suit dealt specifically with the use of the "suggestive" song. (Sophie was never called to testify when hearings about these songs

6. Celebrating Cabarets

Sophie had recorded more than thirty songs by 1920. All of them appeared as sheet music, as well, earning her a penny for every unit sold. Many of the songs she recorded became national hits, like "Oh! Papa, Oh! Papa." Lyrics for the records and sheet music were tame compared to the interpolations she lent these songs when performing at cabarets.

were held.) Although no general orders were given regarding use of the songs, instructive letters were sent to theater managers, making it dangerous for any singer (like Sophie) to attempt to perform these songs in vaudeville houses. Songs had already been ordered out of the repertoire of several singers. In two additional cases, choruses in big musicals had also been barred from singing a number of "questionable" songs. Scrutiny by managers to eliminate anything "that would offend the most critical" was believed by performers to be blatant censorship; and they blamed the V.M.A. and E.A. Albee for attempting to retain control. For the actors' union, the issue added yet another dispute to an increasingly hostile confrontation with managers. Up to this time, Sophie had been apolitical. Now, however, realizing the need to press for actors' rights, she joined the actors' union.

Sophie herself had little worry about the ban, since she was spending all of her time performing in cabarets, where such rules did not apply; for the V.M.A. had no authority over cabarets. She continued to sing what she wanted and, these days, rarely encountered reviewers questioning the propriety of her song selections. But what might happen when she returned to vaudeville? Sophie wondered. Moreover, due to the impact of prohibition, how long would cabarets be able to stay in business? Her second question was quickly answered when Reisenweber's closed at the end of July because of the increasingly strict ban on alcohol sales. The impact on Reisenweber's had been so devastating, the family decided to put the restaurant up for sale. Sophie and the band found themselves out of a job.

The Shuberts, the only theatrical organization not a member of the V.M.A., soon came to Sophie's rescue, if anything the Shuberts did for actors could be considered a rescue. Unfazed by previous failed negotiations and the exchanges of acrimonious words between themselves and Sophie, the ubiquitous Shuberts tried again to enlist her to appear in a new revue. At this juncture, their timing was fortuitous.

The revue, called "Hello, Alexander," featured veteran blackface performers McIntyre and Heath in a series of their old vaudeville skits. Sophie and her band would appear in olio interludes quite distinct from the play itself, an obvious attempt by the Shuberts to capitalize on her public appeal. They even acceded to her demand for $1,000 a week salary, to begin when the show opened in the middle of August. Typical of the usual Shubert show-opening schedule, rehearsals were slated to begin July 29, meaning there would be only two weeks of preparation. Against William Morris's judgment, Sophie signed a contract to appear in the revue, since she and the band needed employment.

Her hasty decision would quickly prove a failure, both in timing and in show selection. At that very moment, a group of theater owners and union representatives were engaged in a contentious debate about actors' rights. A strike seemed imminent.

7

Risky Business

In spite of a steady, uncomfortable, light rain, the umbrella-covered crowd lining Broadway enthusiastically cheered and applauded the parading actors, many of them carrying banners and posters demanding their union rights. Much to everyone's surprise, particularly the theater managers', actors had actually gone on strike. Whereupon, theaters went dark; and so did the immediate future for show business.

As part of their negotiating demands, actors pressed for a maximum of eight performances a week, all salaries to be paid on Saturday, layoffs to be paid at one-half salary, and company layoffs during holidays to be compensated with one-half salary if actors continued to rehearse. On the surface, these requests did not seem like issues of major contention; but one had to be aware of the severe constraints and punishments actors had long suffered under domination by theater managers.

Initially, theater managers were defiant and ridiculed actors for their inability to unite. When the actors' union — Actors Equity Association — realized full support from the American Federation of Labor, they not only received a significant infusion of money but also benefited from a dramatic increase in membership. For the first time, actors believed they had obtained full union support.

An early meeting between the opposing sides ended in a flurry of accusations and threats, with the actors walking out in revolt. The actors immediately called for a strike to begin August 7, 1919. Francis Wilson, head of the A.E.A., declared, "We will win! As for yielding to the managers, you can tell them to go to hell." Dramatically, theater managers shot back: "We will never deal with the A.E.A."

Not only was the parade down Broadway the first to inform New Yorkers about the actor's plight, it was the first of many attempts to collect funds for their cause. Sophie and the band were part of this parade, waving to onlookers and occasionally breaking into song, with the crowd happily joining in. At various theaters—those not owned by the V.M.A.—benefits were held to obtain funds; and Sophie participated in each one of them. Newspapers tended to favor the acting profession but also pointed out that both sides "have already suffered grave and irreparable losses." Theater patrons also sided with the actors, but they wanted the disagreement to be settled quickly so they could resume enjoying one of their favorite pastimes.

After four weeks of literally no progress, theater managers cracked first. Losses in gross receipts had already amounted to more than $245,000 a week in New York and total losses to theater managers had mounted to more than $2,000,000. On August 31, managers called for a meeting with the actors' negotiating team to discuss a settlement. Long hours of discussion and debate culminated in a contract that closely resembled A.E.A.'s original demands. When news of the agreement was announced, cheering and singing could be heard in all the bars and restaurants along Broadway, as actors and theater patrons celebrated the victory. It was a decided milestone in the years-long confrontation between management and actors, although not the last in an ongoing battle for supremacy. Yet, for the first time, actors had won important rights; and they were relieved to be earning a salary once more. Theaters reopened and were quickly filled with customers, happy to see their favorites performing again.

Sophie usually rehearsed in "casual" clothing, the only time she would be seen in public wearing such garb. She rehearsed new songs daily, for several hours at a time, so she could introduce them at her evening performances. Sophie claimed that, at any point in time, she could sing more than 300 songs. (Harry Ransom Humanities Research Center, University of Texas)

The Shuberts called for rehearsals to begin September 10 for a late month's opening. Sophie, having been out of work for a month, chose to double — rehearse "Hello, Alexander" by day and play at Reisenweber's (under new management) by night, during the entire rehearsal period. "Hello, Alexander" opened in Wilmington, Delaware, September 26, for one week. The Shuberts were already angry about Sophie's extracurricular activities, but they became infuriated when she announced she would reopen at Reisenweber's when "Hello, Alexander" returned to New York.

"Hello, Alexander" received an excellent review from the Wilmington critic.

> Hello, Alexander is a fast, clever, tuneful show. It scored here and will do the same anywhere.[1]

In the review, Sophie received more attention than the show itself.

> Sophie Tucker, who has established herself on Broadway as an ever welcome variety actress, and a recognized "big-time single" was among the headliners of the new piece. The "Queen of Jazz," as she is known, with her Seven Kings of Syncopation brim-full of jazz and pep presented a new line of songs that stopped the show. She was encored many times as the result of "Yazoo Rag," "Wild, Wild, Women," and other songs of the jazz variety.

Regrettably, the show did not fare nearly as well in New York, receiving negative reviews from critics, who called the production simplistic, tame, disjointed, and old-fashioned, "of the vintage of 1906." To no one's surprise, the show closed in three weeks; but the Shuberts still had Sophie under contract for several weeks more. Publicly, they used the excuse that Sophie's appearances at Reisenweber's had been one of the reasons for the show's demise. Harsh words were again exchanged between Sophie and J.J. Shubert.

Due to the failure of "Hello, Alexander," the Shuberts hastily put together another revue, this one called the "Gaieties of 1919." A mixture of olio acts that made full use of Sophie and the band, it was to open November 1, in Boston. The new venue effectively separated Sophie from Reisenweber's, or so the Shuberts thought. In response to the new assignment, Sophie boldly announced that, as long as the "Gaieties" played in Boston, she would return to New York each Sunday and appear at Reisenweber's with the band. She would call these special engagements "Sophie Tucker Nights," and they would be advertised as such. Not surprisingly, the Shuberts were extremely upset with Sophie's bravado; but, because she was the headliner in "Gaieties," they could not fire her for fear of being forced to close the show. The continuing disagreement became a war of attrition.

The Shuberts purposely placed Sophie both early and late on the bill, rather than the usual headliner positions. Sophie wrote J.J. Shubert to complain about the positioning: "Either arrange the show so that I can do what I know will be for the betterment, or I will have to leave."[2]

J.J. chose not to respond to her letter. Then, in their desire to reduce the costs of an already terminal show, the Shuberts fired a number of musicians and placed Sophie's band in the pit, a decision that further angered her. Another decision that must have disturbed Sophie was the Shuberts' announcement that they were planning to hire Frank Westphal to join the cast.

A week later, a report in the *New York Clipper* revealed that Sophie was leaving the cast of the "Gaieties" when its Boston engagement ended. "She will not travel with the show," as she announced, "preferring to return to New York for a few weeks rest." When William Morris met with Sophie, she expressed considerable relief of having rid herself of the Shuberts' vindictive control.

> After taking a rest, she expects to begin a vaudeville engagement, playing in houses around New York, so that she may be enabled to continue holding forth in the Sophie Tucker Room at Reisenweber's, a most lucrative engagement for her.[3]

Morris had been waiting for Sophie to return to New York so he could sign her for an extended stay in local theaters; and Reisenweber's owners were delighted to have her back, as well.

Sophie's return to vaudeville and her opening at the Colonial Theater were treated like a homecoming.

> Sophie Tucker and her new jazz band opened in vaudeville after a year's absence and scored a hit. Miss Tucker took two encores and stopped the show. Although intermission was next, the audience stayed to hear her put over one of her old numbers. The buxom Sophie now has a better act than she has ever been using.[4]

Sophie and the band appeared on stage for twenty-five minutes. The setting for the act was the living room of an apartment. As the curtain rose, the band was discussing the lack of riches they had acquired while playing for Miss Tucker. They decided they were underpaid and would no longer play for her. On Sophie's entrance, they told her of their decision, whereupon she began humming a jazz tune. One by one, the band succumbed to the melody and joined her in music and song. The reviewer of the act was particularly taken with Sophie's gown: "a silvery shining butterfly evening gown is breathtaking, because of its splendor."

The early months of 1920 found Sophie and the band doubling at vaudeville theaters and Reisenweber's, and the stress of playing at two venues for an extended period of time was taking its toll. A number of reviewers complained that portions of the act had become "old" and the band seemed "in need of rehearsals." Were the performers just tired from the pressure of doubling? Or had Broadway itself begun to feel the urgency of maintaining its business after two years of almost euphoric growth and profitable box office receipts?

Show biz problems were now attracting the public's attention. Theater managers agreed that business had been on the decline but admitted the reasons for this decrease were, at present, elusive. Production costs for shows had substantially increased and had to be compensated by higher ticket prices. Were patrons balking at the increased prices? Were the shows being produced inferior to what more sophisticated audiences expected? Or were audiences exhibiting a general malaise due to the first signs of a softening economy?

In recent years, many Broadway stars had been "stolen" by movie makers. Actors found that, in the cinematic medium, they could make more money and work less; and the almost instant national exposure through movie appearances definitely enhanced their careers.

The jazz band craze had supposedly declined, with managers now claiming that audiences had grown tired of it. The cabaret business had evolved into a risky enterprise, hounded by civic do-gooders and the police, forcing owners to spend an inordinate amount of time and money just trying to stay open. Nightclubs threatened to replace cabarets, with an ownership resembling a rogue's gallery of "shady" businessmen. Moreover, the entertainment offered there pushed the parameters of propriety, well beyond what anyone would have imagined a few years previously.

"Girlie shows" were finding success in the theater district; and, according to their owners, the business showed great promise. Several years of dance crazes had created an interest in and desire for professional dance orchestras. Responding to the public's heightened interest in dance orchestras, the *New York Clipper* published a special page for news about them. Orchestra leaders like Paul Whiteman, Vincent Lopez, and Art Hickman were fast becoming familiar names in popular entertainment. Tin Pan Alley's primary production was now concentrated on love ballads and danceable songs. Meanwhile, the music publishing business continued to expand, thanks to the increasing popularity of cheap phonograph records.

Vaudeville remained entertainment's most popular leisure time activity, but vaudeville theaters now had to incorporate the showing of movies to maintain their business. Already, movie studios were talking of expanding their distribution by building theaters exclusively for motion pictures. Experiments with a new "talking device" called radio had experts boasting about a new, flexible, in-home, and free form of entertainment.

Popular theater appeared to be in transition, and no one had any sure idea of its future direction. The changes, however, were opening doors for a whole new group of young and talented writers, composers, and actors.

Was Sophie aware of the changes taking place in show business? Actually, she had already been in the process of changing her act. Sophie had added a jazz band; modified her song selection; included additional performers in the act; made phonograph records; played in musical comedy; and explored new venues, like cabarets, which lent themselves so well to her style of performance. In fact, it was her versatility that kept the act fresh; and her decision to continually incorporate new material that kept it original. Sophie worked hard to achieve these goals; and her success in attaining them attested not only to her having become a smart performer, but also to her sensitive understanding of changing audience moods and expectations. The spring of 1920 signaled another change of direction.

Herman Timberg, actor, composer, and sometime producer, had taken one of his vaudeville skits and expanded it into a musical comedy called "Tick, Tack, Toe." In March, he optimistically opened the production with great fanfare, only to see it become an immediate flop. When Timberg announced he was going to rewrite the piece and reopen the show in a few weeks, critics doubted he would be successful. A number of them even suggested he should not waste his time.

Timberg surprised everyone by hiring Sophie and the band to headline the new show. Sophie was also announced as one of the producing managers—there were three—which meant she had invested in the production. Quitting her vaudeville appearances, much to William Morris's concern, Sophie began rehearsals and quickly discovered that the show was, just as critics had pointed out, of dubious quality. Still, she believed her presence in the cast would make the show successful; and she even hoped for a profitable enterprise, since she had already invested several thousand dollars in it. Unfortunately, she had miscalculated her ability to rescue what was already viewed as an obvious debacle. To her dismay, Sophie soon learned that good people in bad shows never succeeded.

The revised "Tick, Tack, Toe" opened at the Columbia Theater, Far Rockaway, New York, April 23. In spite of heavy promotion for the show, the theater was far from full; and less than $1,500 had been deposited in the box office. Reviewers of the show suggested that "there was still plenty of work for the play doctors," which was an oblique way of saying the show remained a failure.

Sophie appeared in six of the ten scenes that comprised the two acts. She told jokes; she sang; she danced; the band played jazz tunes; she and the band presented a skit at the show's finale. "This last scene is the only hit that would fall under the conventional category," reported a critic. "The other nine scenes are totally void of coordination or plot." The only bright moment of the play, according to the critic, was when "Miss Tucker pulled the scene through by singing a rag ballad in her characteristic style."

Sophie was thoroughly embarrassed by the entire episode, along with suffering the shamefaced loss of several thousand dollars. She later admitted that investing in other people's shows was bad business, and she would never again commit to such a decision.

Amazingly, the show played four weeks before it finally closed. The excuse given was that no theater at which it could appear was available in Chicago. The critics knew better. The cast had played the final two weeks without salary, and theater attendance was so sparse, that free tickets were being given out to passersby. To make the show's demise even more demoralizing, Timberg sued the investors, including Sophie, for not remanding him the money he had supposedly spent on reworking the show. The suit was never submitted to the court; but publicity about it exposed Sophie as a bereft investor, hardly the kind of image she was seeking.

Thanks to some quick work by William Morris, after "Tick, Tack, Toe" closed, Sophie and her band opened at the Moulin Rouge Cafe (a cabaret), in Atlantic City on June 7. Their engagement was to continue until the middle of September. A local critic called Sophie "a sure-fire personality who is one of the most interesting and vividly active of cafe entertainers." Interest in Sophie's exploits were further heightened when police raided the cafe and entered her apartment, where they discovered a case of wine and five gallons of gin. "The goods are my own private stock," Sophie protested, as police hauled away the alcohol.

At the conclusion of her engagement at the Moulin Rouge, Sophie was signed to appear at the Edelweiss Gardens, Chicago, for which she was said to be earning $2,000 a week. The Gardens held a unique place in Chicago entertainment history.

In 1913, the renowned architect, Frank Lloyd Wright had been commissioned to design a pleasure garden and bandshell. He was given the impression that he was working with an unlimited budget. Nonetheless, an examination of frequently revised plans in 1913 and 1914 showed constant budget restrictions. Called Midway Gardens, the group of structures was to comprise a locus for food and entertainment. A symphony orchestra was hired to play at the opening festivities and attracted an overflow crowd to the elegant surroundings. Unfortunately, Wright's designs for the restaurant, murals, and sculptures had never been completed. A personal disaster at his home at Taliesin, Illinois, brought Wright's involvement in the project to an abrupt end.

Debts plagued Midway Gardens from its inception. To stay open, the owners offered a wide mix of entertainment, from symphonies and ballet to vaudeville. However, by the fall of 1915, law suits were rapidly accumulating; and, six months later, the owners filed for bankruptcy. The Schoenhofer Brewery bought the property as an outlet for their Edelweiss Beer. They changed the name to the Edelweiss Gardens and booked vaudeville entertainers to appear there. The Garden's popularity hit a new high when Sophie was signed "to offer new and daring perspectives."

According to Edelweiss management, Sophie would be the best known performer the Gardens had ever featured. Actually, playing at the Gardens had become quite risky, since its questionable reputation as a cabaret made it a target frequently raided by police. Sophie and the band opened at Edelweiss Gardens on October 4, for a scheduled fifteen-week run. Yet Sophie also had more personal matters to attend to while in Chicago.

It was rumored that she was about to initiate divorce proceedings against Frank Westphal, and Sophie readily verified the report. Other than admitting to the divorce action against Frank, however, she had nothing else to say to a press eager for a high-profile story. Frank was found to be living in a small hotel on the north side of town, and he also refused to discuss the report. He would only say: "If there is any news forthcoming, you will have to see Miss Tucker."

Still, the press did discover that Sophie was suing Frank for desertion and she planned to remain in Chicago until the divorce had been finalized, which usually took several months. Hearing the news, theater managers flocked to Sophie's suite at the Hotel Sherman to offer her enticing deals to appear at their theaters in coming weeks, at attractive salaries. It really all depended on how long Sophie could play uninterruptedly at the Edelweiss Gardens. After receiving rave notices for her work at the Gardens—"She is proving a great drawing card"—Sophie and the band were reported to be receiving a weekly salary of $3,500. The claim was grossly inflated, but it kept competing venues from bidding for her time. Meanwhile, reporters questioned Sophie every day regarding the divorce. Her only comment was to the effect that anyone who married in the profession was foolish.

Sophie had officially applied for a divorce decree from the Superior Court of Cook County on October 5, 1920. Depositions leading to the decree were collected two weeks later, on October 21. In the deposition, Sophie claimed that Frank had deserted her on April 26, 1918, "without any reasonable cause," although she had conducted herself "in a manner well becoming a good, true, chaste and affectionate wife." At the time, desertion was the most commonly used excuse for divorce.

Frank, in turn, denied that he had deserted Sophie and also denied that she had conducted herself as a "chaste and affectionate wife." Frank, however, never pressed charges regarding this specific declaration.

During the judge's interview with Sophie, he pointedly asked her how she had treated her husband when they lived together. "Oh, that's a silly question," Sophie replied. "It may be silly," the judge responded, "but it is necessary."

"Oh, I treated him all right," she said. "As a mother treats a baby. How is that answer?"

"How did he treat you?" the judge asked. "Not so good," Sophie answered.

Property adjustments had already been agreed upon. Frank received nothing from Sophie; nor did Sophie ask for any alimony. When asked if any children were involved, Sophie said none. "Just a couple of syncopated songs, your honor."[5]

In support of her suit, Sophie supplied two witnesses, Gertrude Bennett, who claimed to have performed with Sophie for two years, and Hogan Simous, a theatrical agent who happened to live at the Hotel Sherman. Bennett testified that she had not seen Westphal during the two years of their separation. Simous confirmed that Sophie's residence had been at the Hotel Sherman, Chicago, for the past several years.

Having chosen not to attend the deposition, Frank hired a lawyer to represent him at the hearings. The lawyer explained to the judge that Frank did not intend to live with Sophie any longer and claimed himself "to be the man who made Sophie's fortune." In return for his extensive efforts, the lawyer explained, Frank received only $100 a week, while Sophie received $3,500 a week. Despite the opportunity to make counterclaims, Frank contested nothing more.

The divorce decree was granted on October 27, 1920. It would not take effect for six weeks, however, forcing Sophie to remain in Chicago for that period of time.

A number of statements made in the deposition were of a decidedly questionable nature. Sophie claimed Chicago as her residence though her actual residence was New York. Since they had been married in Chicago, she had to claim that city as her residence. Nor had Miss Bennett appeared with Sophie for two years; a short stint in New York was her only professional association with Sophie.

The matter of desertion could have been heatedly contested by Frank. He had been appearing with Sophie as recently as six months earlier on a vaudeville tour. Indeed, he was her accompanist at Reisenweber's only three months prior to the divorce proceedings, though whether he was actually living with her during that time is unknown. The only formal separation between the two occurred when the Sophie Tucker garage in Freeport, Long Island, had been opened, with Frank as proprietor. The business had lasted only six months. and Frank then returned to his role with Sophie in vaudeville.

Frank's claim to be "the man who made Sophie's fortune" was, to an extent, true. From the time they became a duet, Sophie's vaudeville career soared; and her success was more than a coincidence. The combination of Frank's combined abilities as piano accompanist, comedian, and straight man to Sophie had caused their act to be viewed as unique and his presence undoubtedly added "class" to the routine. Frank's musical and comic timing abilities certainly enhanced the act. In reality, only William Morris might be said to have "made Sophie's fortune," but Frank did contribute to a considerable extent. Nonetheless, like many of Sophie's endeavors, the act got "old" and had to be replaced. Frank was excised from her life, both on and off the stage.

Meanwhile, the process of waiting for divorce papers to pass through Chicago courts seemed to move so slowly that Sophie became nervous about the loss of potentially good contracts and the drain on her personal finances. To the consternation of the Edelweiss Gardens management, Sophie decided to double again, signing to appear at a number of vaudeville houses while, at the same time, continuing to play at the Gardens. It was the first time in the history of Chicago vaudeville that a headliner appeared in two venues at the same time, a fact that caused considerable comment in the theatrical profession. Not surprisingly, the Gardens immediately saw their attendance decline.

Palace Theater management raised ticket prices to $1.50 when Sophie appeared, but the theater filled to SRO anyway.

> At the Palace last night, she was like a wonderful dessert after a nine-course meal, a dessert the customers couldn't get enough of. Tucker packed them in, and when they got there they waited only for Tucker.[6]

Sophie's opening at the Majestic Theater continued to demonstrate her universal appeal to Chicago audiences, notwithstanding the press's outlandish reports about her divorce.

> Doggone, they just don't seem to get enough of that woman, Sophie Tucker. One thing, Sophie is never stingy. She is doing an almost new act with entirely new numbers. She packed them in.
> See what the intrepid and energetic Sophie Tucker did for this captured town of cabaret and vaudeville. Miss Tucker, whose industry is amazing, whose physical magnificence is no less than her ragtime talent, has never stopped working night and day since last September. She arrives with a wardrobe ready to make any fashion show fade away and quit kidding. She brings an entire new repertoire of fuzzy, tricksome and whistly ragtime melodies and to her usual dashing comedy, risqué to a turn and full of laughs.[7]

On November 29, police raided all of Chicago's cabarets, including Edelweiss Gardens, and closed them down. Specifically, Edelweiss Gardens was accused of the illicit trafficking of liquor. They reopened two days later, but patrons were hesitant to visit the cabaret. The Gardens never recovered; and when Sophie quit to play at another cabaret, the Marigold Gardens, in December, the future of Edelweiss Gardens was in jeopardy. A month later, the Gardens went into bankruptcy.

The divorce issue heated up again when a newspaper headlined: "Is Sophie Tucker to be married to George White?" White was a veteran vaudevillian on tour. An intrepid reporter had found them together in Sophie's room at the Hotel Sherman.

MOSS & FRYE   KANE & HERMAN
Hildegarde Lachmann & Her Pal Florence
Resista   Buch Bros.   Frank Gaby   Bono
Photoplay—Exclusive Showing
"HALF A CHANCE"
with MAHLON HAMILTON & LILLIAN RICH

MATS.	EVES.	Sat. Sun. Hol.
31c-45c	36c-50c	36c-54c

EDELWEISS GARDENS
Cottage Grove and Midway
EVERY NIGHT
SOPHIE TUCKER
EXTRA ATTRACTION
RAJAH JOVEDAH The Master Mystic
Every Wednesday—BOHEMIAN NIGHT
Dancing from 7 P. M. Till Closing
Music by Sophie Tucker's 5 Jazz Kings
and George Mallon's Orchestra

WOODS
CHICAGO'S
UTMOST
THEATER
HAPPINESS MEANS periods or marking posts in our journey along life's road. An evening with DONALD, PEGGY and RALPH in "BUDDIES" will help keep you in continuous state of joy and happiness. "BUD" Matinee to-morrow.

Jones, Linick & Schaefer's
RIALTO   CONTINUOUS VAUDEVILLE
11 A. M. to 11 P. M.—COME ANY TIME
WELLER   O'DONNELL
& WESTFIELD
Three Famous Melody Monarchs
5 AVALLONS   MURRAY & LANE
COOK & HAMILTON   JIMMY GALLON
4—GINGER SNAPS—4
8—BIG ACTS ALWAYS—8

CORT   EVES at 8:20   MAT. TO-MORROW at 2:20
ORDER SEATS TWO WEEKS AHEAD
FOR PROTECTION
THE SELWYNS Present
JANE COWL in "Smilin' Through"
NO ONE SEATED DURING THE PROLOGUE

SHUBERT
GARRICK   MATINEE TO-MORROW
A. H. WOODS Presents
THEDA BARA

BY ZOE AKINS
The play in which Ethel Barrymore has met with a triumph unparalleled in the history of the American stage.
Owing to the unprecedented demand, it will be impossible to receive telephone orders during Miss Barrymore's engagement

LA SALLE   —7TH WEEK—
Madison, near Clark   EVENINGS AT 8:10   MAT. TO-MOR.
F. Ray Comstock and Morris Gest's
Sparkling Comedy Success
ADAM and EVA
with
MOLLY McINTYRE
One Solid Year, Longacre, N. Y.

The Premier Dancing Club of Chicago
Dancing Parties
Every Saturday Evening
Stevens Main Restaurant, 8th Floor
Stevens Bldg., 16 N. Wabash Ave.
ADMISSION 50c
Most Charming Spot in the Loop
SUPERB ORCHESTRA   Mgmt. John Oddy

COLONIAL   NEXT MATINEE TO-MORROW
A. L. Erlanger and Harry J. Powers, Mgrs.
THE SENSATIONAL MUSICAL REVUE
GEORGE WHITE'S SCANDALS OF 1920
with ANN PENNINGTON
GOOD SEATS AT PRICES TO SUIT EVERY-BODY—TWO BOX OFFICES OPEN
SEATS NOW SELLING FOR
THANKSGIVING MATINEE AND NIGHT

Supreme Vaudeville   POPULAR PRICES MATINEE DAILY
MAJESTIC   Phone CENTRAL 6480
Orpheum Circuit
SOPHIE TUCKER
KENNY & HOLLIS   JAMES H. CULLEN
NELLIE V. NICHOLS
Elisabeth Nelson and the Barry Boys
"RUBEVILLE"
Eckoms—Everest's Novelty Circus—Kinograms
BRONSON & BALDWIN

SHUBERT
CENTRAL   MATINEE TO-MORROW
Steinway Hall Bldg., Van Buren, Nr. Michigan
Seats for All Performances.
Last Time Nov. 18

NANCE O'NEIL

Was she really serious? Sophie said yes, but George did not stay long enough to confirm or deny the rumor. Later, when a *New York Clipper* representative telephoned Sophie, a man answered the phone. When asked to verify the rumor, the man hesitated and informed Sophie of the phone call. Although refusing to divulge his name, the man told the representative, "Miss Tucker will confirm the rumor. Then he hung up. The hotel desk had stated that "Miss Tucker was indisposed and had denied herself all callers." George White was also reported to be registered at the hotel but not found in his room. Later, tracked down at the Majestic Theater, he claimed to have nothing to say. The press reported that, some time before, White had announced his engagement to Ann Pennington. "So what is going on?" they asked.

To extend her stay in Chicago, Sophie announced that, for the next six weeks, she would be appearing in the smaller vaudeville houses throughout Chicago. Apparently, the continuing divorce proceedings were the cause of this extension. George White left town to meet his vaudeville obligations. No mention of the supposed relationship between Sophie and White ever surfaced again.

January, 1921, found Sophie appearing at outlying vaudeville theaters in the Chicago area, playing to full houses but at reduced salaries. Final divorce hearings were announced for the third week in January. At the same time, it was reported that Frank Westphal was engaged to marry Dorothy Dickinson, a local actress. Yet, none of the rumors that swirled around the divorce were ever verified.

Feeling relieved of the divorce pressure and her extended stay in Chicago, Sophie consented to an interview by old friend Ashton Stevens of the *Chicago Examiner*. Considering everything she had been through, Stevens wanted to know how she had been able to manage all of her stage commitments. The interview provided a revealing insight into how Sophie conducted herself on stage.

> I reconstruct everything I touch. I get wonderful ideas and reconstruct to fit myself. It was hard at first. It took brains, but it's natural with me now. I've gotten classical and personal with my work. Me, myself, Sophie Tucker. I put myself into the words, into the story, of every song I sing. I dramatize myself. I'm my own heroine.[8]

Not forgetting her deep devotion toward her father, Sophie traveled overnight to Hartford to appear at a synagogue program in his memory. No one in the family questioned Sophie about the confusing events surrounding her recent Chicago divorce. In fact, these days, no one in the family any longer questioned Sophie about anything she did.

As she was finishing her engagements in Chicago, Sophie received a visit from

Opposite: **In many cities, Sophie often appeared at two venues simultaneously. She would play at a vaudeville theater early in the evening and at a cabaret for late shows. An ad from the amusement section of a Chicago newspaper shows Sophie appearing at the Majestic Theater (vaudeville) and the Edelweiss Gardens (cabaret). Sophie's dual appearances coined the show biz phrase, "doubling."**

Sophie and her son, Bert, age twelve. Throughout her life, she felt guilty about their long separations. (Museum of the City of New York)

John Wagner, one of the new owners of Reisenweber's, who had traveled from New York to persuade her to return and "revive the Sophie Tucker Room." For two month's work, he promised her a guarantee of $2,000 weekly, fifty percent of the cover charges, and twenty-five percent of all checks at the 6:30 to 10:30 dinner service. Moreover, if she desired, she could play in vaudeville during that time. How could Sophie refuse? Actually, she could not have departed Chicago at a better time; theater managers were complaining that they were suffering from one of the worst business slumps in years.

In addition to playing at Reisenweber's, Sophie (and William Morris) announced that she was about to open her own music publishing company. The first song to be published was one she had written herself, in collaboration with two band members, Jimmy Buffano and Jimmy Steiger, called "Learning." A fox trot, Sophie featured the song at Reisenweber's with a drop showing the words of the chorus to the patrons. Several other songs were published by this fledgling company, but none became hits. Some months later, the company closed down, having spent much more than they had earned. The venture represented another of Sophie's attempts to diversify her career, but she failed again. Nevertheless, the failure would not deter her in any way from pursuing other entrepreneurial endeavors.

The New York engagement at Reisenweber's also allowed Sophie to make a number of benefit performances during the spring and early summer, appearances that were becoming common practice for her. She and the band played at a fundraiser for the Sisterhood of Mt. Zion synagogue. At a benefit for the Adirondacks Fund for Tuberculosis, held at the Lexington Opera House, Sophie, Rooney and Bent, Belle Baker, Van and Schenck, Willie and Eugene Howard, and Vincent Lopez's Orchestra, collected thousands of dollars. One Sunday night, Sophie and the band even entertained prisoners at Sing Sing.

In June, Sophie moved to the Sherbourne Hotel, Brighton Beach, then to the Le Marne, Atlantic City, for a July to September run; anything to avoid having to play in vaudeville. The protestations coming from theater managers across the country echoed a substantial downturn in the economy. Managers bemoaned the fact that business was bad, which affected all types of entertainment — even movie studios were grumbling — and many theaters were near to closing indefinitely. To stay in business, managers claimed, performer's salaries would have to be reduced. This was always the first action that managers threatened when box office receipts lagged. It was reported that unemployed chorus girls filled New York streets around theaters and crowded agents' offices. Even Reisenweber's reported poor attendance since Sophie had left and admitted to owing actors' salaries. They found themselves in further trouble when police alleged that hostesses were ordered to mingle with patrons and sit with them at tables in full makeup and costume. The remarks were really subtle references to the unlawful act of soliciting for prostitution.

Nevertheless, when the new season was about to begin, William Morris persuaded Sophie to sign an eighteen-week contract with the Orpheum circuit, at a guaranteed $2,000 a week. Morris believed it was time for Sophie to remind the rest of the country who she was. He promised, however, if Sophie could not fill theaters in other cities, he would bring her back to New York. Since the first eight weeks of the tour were in East Coast cities, Sophie would still be close to home.

At the same time that combination houses (theaters that offered both vaudeville and movies) were switching entirely to movies and *Variety* claimed more than 5,000 actors were idle as a result of the countrywide slump, Sophie and the band opened their tour at the Maryland Theater, Baltimore. Reviews were good, and reports indicated she did excellent business.

> Sophie Tucker, back from the cabarets, was surrounded by a field of class but won the blue ribbon with no difference of opinion. Miss Tucker took the number 7 position, remaining for 38 minutes to splendidly entertain with a range of songs that alone is a credit to her.[9]

At the time, the Orpheum circuit had systematically cornered the best in vaudeville entertainment, with such headliners as Eddie Leonard, George Jessel, Gallagher and Shean, Trixi Friganza, Van and Corbett, Lew Dockstater, Jack Benny, Eddie Foy, Sheldon Brooks, the Four Marx Brothers, Marie Dressler, and Helen Keller. (Yes! Helen Keller in vaudeville.) The performers represented a mixture of old-timers and newcomers, mostly new comedians, a quarter of them Jewish. Orpheum was spending a great deal of money to take advantage of the highly competitive situation during a mediocre season, hoping to increase their position in vaudeville by keeping all of their theaters open and featuring certified headliners. Judging from the audiences attracted, their strategy proved successful.

Sophie modified her act once again. It now included not only the jazz band, but also a man and woman duo for background dance bits. When Sophie sang a plaintiff "mother" song, she was on her knees, crooning to a white-haired old lady specifically brought on stage for the scene. Signs on the stage indicated that she and the band were celebrating their third year together, which entailed a mixture of old and new songs, some of them Sophie's specialties, like the rouser, "When They Get Too Wild for Everyone Else — Perfect for Me." Another unique feature was Sophie's rendition of the Jewish hymn, "Eli, Eli," with the band offering its own jazz interpolation. She ended the act with a song about a woman who "aired" her boyfriend since she had "Another Male Hitched in Your Stable." A thirty-eight-minute performance on stage went well beyond the time that any other entertainer in vaudeville was allowed.

In early November, William Morris announced that Sophie and the band had been booked for a tour of the Moss houses in England the following spring. Unlike previous self-promoting declarations, this one was authentic. No sooner did Sophie begin to talk about the upcoming trip, however, than the band members demanded higher salaries. If she did not agree to their demand, they would leave her and go out "on their own." Sophie's compromise offer did not please the boys; and, in the middle of the tour, they abruptly quit the act, stranding Sophie with no backup. It occurred a week before she was to play a three-day engagement in Hartford, her "second coming," so to speak.

With William Morris's help, Sophie quickly recruited pianist Al Siegal in place of the Five Kings of Syncopation. Siegal had a superb reputation as a backup pianist but was viewed as a temperamental performer whose resume revealed a long series of short-term associations. Siegal had been the former partner and husband of Bee Palmer, the shimmy queen, and was currently suing her for divorce, naming Jack Dempsey, the boxer, as her companion. Still, Sophie needed an accompanist; and three days of rehearsals with Siegal assured her of a respectable showing in her home town.

No crowds or colorful banners greeted her when Sophie arrived in Hartford this time. Only the mayor and theater manager were there to welcome her home.

Together, the three of them walked the main street from Union Station to her mother's home to show her how the city had changed since she last performed there in 1913. Sophie observed that the "old haunts" had been replaced by "large structures of brick and steel." Except for a few old buildings that were still standing in the Jewish section, there had been a decided change in the city's architecture. As if overnight — actually eight years— Hartford had become a modern city.

The Jewish community had grown as well: a new synagogue; a home for the aged, and a children's home (thanks in part to Jennie's years of effort). The pushcarts and peddlers had disappeared from the streets, replaced by modern stores. Public transportation rumbled down Front Street. Where Abuza's restaurant had once stood, Sophie now found several retail businesses with varicolored awnings.

Sophie's mother and Anna lived together in the old home, although Anna, now engaged to be married, would soon be moving out. Phil, his wife, and children lived next door, close enough to their aged mother in case of need. Moe was now living in New York. But it was the interior of the family home that deeply affected Sophie. The old place was quiet, dark, timeworn, and in some disarray. So much had changed since her father died.

Sophie's engagement at the Palace Theater (Poli's no longer existed) filled the house; and audiences loved every minute she spent with them. Her act, too, seemed to have taken on a different dimension. The piano accompaniment created a more intimate atmosphere; her presentation was more relaxed, seemingly more spontaneous; and her songs captured the audience's emotions more easily.

Prior to the show, Sophie welcomed two visitors to her dressing room. By coincidence, Willie and Eugene Howard were appearing at Parson's Theater in the "Passing Show of 1921." Together, they all reminisced about old times, Sophie's days before she went to New York, her meteoric rise to fame, and her current headliner status. "We knew that the theater was the place for you," the Howard Brothers declared, "and look what you've done." Between staying with the family and meeting the Howards, Sophie returned to New York somewhat abashed by the experience.

Just to make sure her income would not be interrupted by any setbacks on the Orpheum circuit, Sophie returned to Reisenweber's just prior to the Christmas holidays. She was doubling again, and the press marveled at her strength and stamina. Newspapers told of the past year's show failures—only sixteen hits out of 104 opened—and future prospects appeared no better. Even during the holiday season, box office receipts were down. The upcoming trip to London had to be better than this, Sophie believed.

On January 2, 1922, when Sophie opened at the prestigious Palace Theater, New York, she had changed her act once again. Although it was a significant departure from the jazz-band format, the *Variety* reviewer called her act "many times better than her former vehicle."

> The first half was closed by Sophie Tucker and it was a winner all the way. With Al Siegal at the piano, she sang a variety of numbers, most of them not so spicy as some she sang in the past. After a few numbers, she was joined by a youth in uniform of a private military academy whom she introduced as her son, and followed with some mother and son stuff that was natural, and, undoubtedly many in the audience still believe it really is her son. After a solo by Siegal, and, later, a violin solo by the boy, more songs by Miss Tucker, and old Granny was ushered in and "Granny" was sung by Miss Tucker, the act closing with a sort of fireside scene, and an encore of course.[10]

Indeed, the boy was not Sophie's son; but rather a talented young actor Sophie had taken under her tutelage. The Granny, an older Negro woman, was said to have been Sophie's longtime maid, Mollie Elkins. The audience did not seem to care that Sophie's "Granny" was a Negro. The addition of these people into the act certainly created a diversion, with initially positive results.

A review of Sophie's appearance at the Alhambra Theater two weeks later called her act "the best work of her career." A number of additional bits had been included; the act ran for thirty-six minutes.

To take the place of her famous jazz band, she has a boy announced as her son, an elderly woman to typify her grandmother and a dancing demon of Ethiopian extraction to add to the hurrah. Siegal and Tucker had recent divorces and talked about it humorously. Sophie talked about the breakup with the band and how it affected her.[11]

She added real heart-interest numbers, delivered with such consummate artistry and showmanship that they appeal equally to the gallery god and the dress suit contingent in the orchestra boxes. A woman who can have them laughing and swaying in their seats one moment, and pulling out their handkerchiefs the next, is an ARTIST with capital letters. Miss Tucker combines them both and melds them together with a smoothness and an artistry that makes you want more.[12]

Reports verified that Sophie had perfected the act to elicit a wide variety of emotions with such ease and aplomb that audiences appeared to have been mesmerized throughout her performance. Yet at the same time she was tugging at heartstrings in the vaudeville houses, Sophie was blasting Reisenweber's roof with suggestive jazz-style songs. Notwithstanding her recent successes, she still was not satisfied with her presentation. She had become quite comfortable with the piano accompaniment approach, but not with Siegal's offstage antics. (He was making passes at all the women backstage.) Siegal was soon fired. In his place, Sophie hired two young pianists, Ted Shapiro and John Carroll, not only to back her up at local theaters, but also to accompany her to London. (Ted Shapiro would remain Sophie's accompanist for the rest of her career, traveling where she traveled and appearing in every medium in which she appeared.)

After she fired the "Five Kings of Syncopation," Sophie hired two pianists, Ted Shapiro and Jack Carroll, to accompany her on her first trip to London in 1922. Carroll left two years later to get married. Ted Shapiro remained Sophie's accompanist for the remainder of her career, more than forty-three years. (Museum of the City of New York)

As had been predicted, the radio craze stormed the country, sales of the new apparatus mounting by thousands each month. More than one hundred radio stations were now in operation; and, much to music publishers' consternation, these stations featured popular music. Sophie was one of the first singers to be signed to appear on radio; and she regaled listeners with her broad repertoire of (clean) ragtime songs.

A debate raged in the industry over whether the popularity of radio would drive down the sales of sheet music and phonograph records, causing great concern among publishers and distributors. Instead, they quickly found that radio stimulated sales and expanded the market for both industries, because of the enormously increased exposure to songs and singers.

Shortly after Sophie's first appearance on radio, it was announced that she had been signed by the General Phonograph Company, producers of Okeh Records, to produce eight discs. The Okeh declaration boasted of having signed Sophie to an exclusive contract.

> As Miss Tucker has a style of singing all her own and is well known throughout the country by way of her vaudeville engagements, the announcement of being signed by a mechanical company is expected to greatly increase Okeh record sales and prestige.[13]

Sophie promised Okeh that she would make all the records before leaving for London, which meant she had only two weeks to complete the assignment. Nonetheless, her characteristic work ethic met the challenge with ease. Not so easy for Shapiro and Carroll; their fingertips were often so raw at the end of rehearsals, they had to soak them in salts each night.

At the same time that managers refused to book companies for the coming season, actors feared salary reductions; and the industry complained of poor theater attendance, Sophie and her pianists were preparing to invade London with an act British audiences had never before experienced. Debate was wide-ranging as to whether Sophie would "fly" or "flop" in front of mercurial London audiences.

On March 18, Sophie, her maid, Mollie; Shapiro and Carroll; and sister Anna sailed out of New York harbor on the newly commissioned *S.S. Homeric* bound for Liverpool. Sophie had asked Anna to accompany her as a present to honor her forthcoming wedding.

To the press, Sophie boasted she was ready to take on London. The press wondered, however, how London audiences would take to her style of entertaining.

8

At the Top of Her Game

William Morris, Sr., his wife, and his son, William Morris, Jr., now assisting in his father's business, sailed for London a month before Sophie. Along with seeking new acts to bring to the U.S., they were there to insure that Sophie would receive suitable publicity for her planned appearances. Senior expressed considerable worry that Sophie's style of performance might be met with typical English coolness, a reaction London audiences had frequently demonstrated toward American actors. Nor was Senior confident that Sophie could adjust to the idiosyncrasies of English audience behavior and distinctive entertainment expectations. He promised to work hard to make her introduction a successful one, but he could accomplish only so much. Sophie had to assume full responsibility for selling herself.

When Sophie and her entourage arrived in London, she was met at the train station by representatives of the sponsoring Moss theater group, publicity people, newspaper reporters, and the Morrises. Eager to find out more about this unfamiliar American headliner, the press took numerous photographs, while quotes were given freely, although few were actually offered by Sophie, other than those expressing her pleasure at being in England. Questions related to her act, her career, and her life were parried by Morris, who explained to the press that they had to see Sophie on stage to best gauge her talent. An anonymous taxi ride to the Picadilly Hotel and a ritualized greeting from hotel employees suggested they knew little about their American visitor. Of course, Morris was quite correct in his observations; few people knew anything about the American popular singer, one Sophie Tucker.

The very evening of her arrival, Morris took Sophie to attend the "Midnight Frolics" revue at a popular cabaret, so she could observe English performers and audience behavior. When, during the course of the performance, her name was shouted out — the crowd looked around curiously to see whom the emcee had singled out — Sophie stood up and moved to the stage, ready to perform. Backed by her two piano accompanists, who always seemed to be with her, she exploded with a jazzy ragtime song that gave her the opportunity to demonstrate the full range of her singing abilities.

8. At the Top of Her Game

At first, the audience sat stunned, then, after a pause, gave her pleasant applause. Her second number had the audience swaying their bodies and clapping in time with the music; and, at its conclusion, Sophie received an enthusiastic burst of applause. Her third, and final, number was laced with suggestive material, at which the audience went wild over her rendition, applauding and shouting for more. In a matter of three songs sung to an audience previously unfamiliar with her, Sophie captured London.

An ebullient report by the *London Times* of her impromptu performance further enlightened London audiences concerning this "overnight sensation from America."

> Almost plain, with nothing much of a voice, and with a figure against her, she is a genius. She sang three songs to a tumult of enthusiasm. She laughed at herself in melody; she made fun of her own limitations, and the audience rocked itself in a frenzy of appreciation. She made the midnight revelers sing with her, like Lauder does; and they encored her until the small hours of the morning. She is now the Yvette Guilbert of ragtime.[1]

Several visits to other theaters during the next few days were sufficient to convince Sophie of the differences between English and American popular theater. Sophie admitted that she had a lot to learn about English theater decorum and tastes; "but I'm a fast learner," she assured the reporters.

In the typical English music hall, patrons were allowed to smoke, including pipes and cigars. Sophie noted that, by the middle of the show, it was often difficult for performers to see the audience due to the heavy layers of smoke in the air. A large bar was located at the back of the theater and patrons felt free to wander there at any time during the performance. This was especially true between acts—there were pauses of several minutes—and at the beginning of new acts, not exactly advantageous to a performer playing a new routine and attempting to gain the audience's attention.

Top headliners were featured on the marquee; but secondary performers were listed in small, almost indistinguishable print. This was also found to be true in the programs. Unlike in American theaters, the pit seats (next to the orchestra) were cheaper, causing patrons to line up for blocks in front of the theater to obtain them. Insistent hawkers worked these long lines selling sandwiches and hot tea. Street musicians also entertained the waiting crowd to earn a few pence. Sometimes the entertainment outside the theater was more enjoyable than that held inside.

Seats in the theater were quite comfortable, large enough for patrons to wear coats and hats since many of the theaters were underheated (a holdover from wartime restrictions). The stage curtains were quite elegant, hung in rich velvet, the theater's gold embroidered coat-of-arms emblazoned in its center. The English used three spot lights to highlight performers—only one was used in the U.S.—which gave a pronounced view of the performers but tended to blind them as well.

Regarding the show itself: twenty or more acts were presented at one performance, many more than in the U.S.; and all were no more than ten minutes in length. Clearly, this would not have fit a Sophie Tucker performance. Male performers wore comic clothing whether they were comics or not and, in Sophie's eyes, female performers looked "dumpy." How would Sophie's audience respond when she entered the stage wearing a dazzling sequined gown and a finely feathered hat?

The variety show featured the usual assortment of acts: acrobats, dancers, comedians, jugglers, monologist, animal acts, and sketches; and then the headliners appeared. Nevertheless, audiences appeared to enjoy the eclectic festivities.

Two items of importance caught Sophie's attention. First, she discovered that the stage sloped downward toward the footlights and striding the boards with a long gown could be hazardous. Second, Sophie realized she was unable to understand what many of the performers were saying or singing. How, then, would they be able to understand her?

Quickly, she gathered together her pianists and local song- and script-writers for the sole purpose of modifying her act so that audiences could understand her. Lyrics were changed by substituting English words for American, and she slowed down the tempo of her songs so that the lyrics could be more easily understood.

Word of Sophie's preparations quickly passed through the theatrical community. When she was ready to open at the Finsbury Park Empire Theater, tickets had already been sold out for the first week. Critics wondered: Who is this Sophie Tucker? And what does she do to entertain audiences so well? After days of heavy advertising and merchandising, theatergoers also were anxious to find out for themselves. Morris was making sure the public would be familiar with Sophie and how she entertained. In anticipation, the theater was packed. Upon completion of her set, audiences shouted "Core! Core!" (encore) and "wouldn't let her leave the stage." One other important lesson Sophie quickly learned about English audiences: they loved to hear songs with suggestive lyrics.

> Sophie Tucker has scored a great success at the Finsbury Park Empire in song-monologues, half sung and half recited to syncopated times; but one song of the "don't-cry-mother" type made me weep with laughter. Sophie brings on her very old "mother," real or borrowed, kneels down beside her, and puts the sob stuff right across.[2]

After a week at the Finsbury Park, Sophie was signed to play at the Hippodrome, in a George Robey play already in progress, called "Round in Fifty," a musical version of Jules Verne's book, "Around the World in Eighty Days." Now being labeled by the press, "Everybody's Pal," Sophie sang several songs in the production, each of which literally stopped the show, with audiences shouting to have the songs repeated numerous times. "Her addition to the cast strengthens what was already a strong entertainment," one reviewer reported.

Likewise, Sophie's daytime activities were akin to staged publicity events. The press followed her wherever she went, snapping photos and getting quotes about all the sites she was seeing for the first time. As was her habit, Sophie talked to everyone she met; and they all came away liking this gregarious and amusing American woman. All of her visits were published in the press, giving her exposure far beyond what mere posters would have accomplished. When she came across a group in need, she promised to perform and raise money for them; and it was reported that she kept every promise.

During the middle of May, Sophie introduced another feature of her unique performance persona by announcing she was going to double—continue to play in "Round in Fifty" and also make late-night appearances at the Metropole cabaret. London audiences could not have been more delighted with her capers. The new arrangement required her to make additional daytime excursions to dress shops so she could be "properly attired" for the engagements. On such days, not only did the press follow her; but dozens of women trailed behind, anxious to see the kinds of gowns she purchased. Each day's trip was amply reported in the newspapers, often with photographs of Sophie showing off her acquisitions.

Reports of Sophie's triumphs multiplied. *The Daily Mail* boldly boasted she had "the largest voice in London."

> Plump, golden-haired, good-humoured and with the largest voice in London, Sophie Tucker steps briskly on the stage of the London Hippodrome and conquers the audience in three minutes.[3]

Reviews of her appearances in "Round in Fifty" were equally matchless.

> Sophie Tucker has joined the cast of "Round in Fifty" and opened to great success. She is doing four numbers, which were part of the music hall act, and appears in the cabaret scene in the second half of the show. Her two pianists are with her, and her speed, humor, and forceful manner of getting her personality across the footlights has made "Round in Fifty" more attractive than ever.[4]

Sophie found the Metropole much like Reisenweber's, with high prices and friendly, well-attired patrons, all of whom loved a risqué song. Regarding her Metropole performances, "her songs and her manner of delivery have especially delighted the critics, one of whom called her a 'seriodiseme.' Miss Tucker is certainly a character."[5]

At the Metropole appearances, Sophie found that the in-house orchestra could not adequately integrate her new songs fast enough, so she relied totally on her pianists to back her; and the arrangement turned out surprisingly well. So well, in fact, that she decided to continue it. With the piano, Sophie sang the songs more slowly and toned down the strength of her voice, to excellent effect. It offered her greater expression for the tear-jerker songs, enhancing their effectiveness with audiences even more.

Yet, it was her appearances at benefits that garnered even more attention from the press. These were "for those who are unable to go to theaters," she explained. She sang for a group of blind soldiers at St. Dunstan's Hospital, sang and danced at other military hospitals, and arranged parties to take large numbers of children into the country on full-day picnics.

Likewise, Sophie was invited to many dinner parties, where she had the opportunity to meet lords and ladies, royalty, and the country's richest businessmen and most eligible bachelors. Not only was she treated with the utmost courtesy, her attendance was met with royal acclaim.

From London, Sophie traveled to Manchester, Liverpool, and Glasgow in successive weeks, to full houses and cheering audiences. The press preceded her; and demands for her time, both on and off the stage, far exceeded her ability to satisfy everyone's wishes. Not surprisingly, wherever she went, rumors followed about possible romantic liaisons. One such report had her about to marry an English lord. She had met him at a party in London, and he accompanied her wherever she traveled. Sophie took to teasing the hungry press ever seeking information. "I don't know where you heard that," referring to the rumor. "It may be true, and it may not be. You know one can never tell just what I am going to do." The story died as quickly as it had risen.

Prior to introducing one of her songs, its topic to highlight a "prince's" activities, censors informed her that she could not use the song because it would offend the Prince of Wales. Sophie refused to drop the song; but when she sang it, she omitted the "prince" reference, to the delight of audiences and the exasperation of the censors. Near the end of her engagement in London, Sophie was invited to a royal dinner at which the Prince was in attendance. When Sophie asked the attendees for requests, The Prince requested the song in question, including its entire lyrics, which command, of course, Sophie obeyed. Everyone stood behind the Prince with bated breath. When Sophie began the song, an observer reported hearing gasps of discomfort and unease when she mentioned the prince in the lyrics. However, when he laughed heartily at the song, everyone followed in unison. Some newspapers reported how Sophie had so handily captured the Prince of Wales's sense of humor. Others commented about Sophie's lack of respect for royalty. Still others applauded her on her American "guile."

Sophie's last week in London was highlighted by an engagement at the Rivoli Theater, located in a primarily Jewish section of the city. With a large banner hanging from the front of the theater—"Welcome Sophie Tucker, America's Foremost Jewish Actress"—crowds jammed the theater at every performance. Sophie used all the Jewish songs she knew, and each received an overwhelmingly favorable reception. When she visited nearby restaurants, she was mobbed for autographs and photographs. She complied with every request. It was a long way from Abuza's restaurant on Front Street, she mused to reporters.

The final night of her London appearance turned into an evening-long party both for performers and for an audience that had paid double the usual ticket prices to attend the event. London's *New York Clipper* representative detailed the happening.

> Probably no American artist playing in a West End theater has ever before been given such a send-off as was accorded Sophie Tucker last Saturday night.[6]

No question, in the course of several months, Sophie had endeared herself to the London theatrical community. When the final curtain fell, George Robey, on behalf of the company, presented her with an old–English silver casket, a rare gift for anyone, let alone a performer. "Sophie," said George, "I want to give you something from the boys and girls. Also, come here. Give me a kiss. Now you've got to say something."

Overwhelmed by the emotion of the moment, Sophie sobbed: "I just can't." So everyone kissed Sophie, instead. Afterwards, there was a gathering in Sophie's dressing room that last until "the wee sma' hours."

The stage had been covered with floral tributes from friends and admirers, highlighted by a gigantic display given by R.H. Gillespie, the managing director of the Hippodrome. William Morris, standing in the wings, quietly observed the clamor around him. Not only had Sophie become an almost immediate hit, her unique talent had made her London's favorite American entertainer.

"Sophie has just been one of the boys," said George Robey later, "and we shall miss her." When Sophie replied that she would soon return to London, cheers echoed throughout the theater. Sophie left the city in almost total exhaustion; in turn, London seemed even more exhausted, thanks to her propulsive and tireless stay.

On August 23, 1922, Sophie and her group sailed triumphantly for home. Any rest she might accumulate would have to take place at sea; she was already booked to open a tour on Keith time immediately upon her arrival in the States, beginning August 31. She was reported to be "armed" for the engagement.

> In addition to a complete wardrobe, which she will use when she opens her tour on the Keith time at Atlantic City, Miss Tucker brought along a specially designed cyclorama which was designed and made up for her in London.[7]

Sophie's extravagant spending exploits had been well documented in London newspapers. She had spent more than $10,000 on the cyclorama; each of her dresses cost $250–300. According to the press, new dresses, shoes, and jewelry were purchased each week; and, within a few weeks time, all the dresses were discarded for new ones. Sophie was reported to have purchased twenty pairs of shoes at one time, the used ones donated to needy groups. The money she spent on benefits was unaccountable. Brother Phil, in his unenviable capacity as Sophie's manager, attempted to persuade her to restrict her profligate spending. The trip to England, where she spent at least as much as she earned, had greatly depleted her reserves.

Sophie's new act was the most scripted and complicated she had ever presented. With Ted and John accompanying her on the pianos, Sophie began with "Homesick"—"I'm Glad to Be Back Home"—followed by "Lovin' Sam, Sheik of Alabam," a typical ragtime-jazz number. A special tune, both recited and sung, "That's What Keeps Me Broke," told the history of her career, divorces, jazz band experiences, and her refusal of a marriage offer to a lord while in England.

"Lost, A Wonderful Man," began with a few brief lines, when Sophie abruptly left the stage. The pianists (now given dialogue) speculated what she had lost backstage. From a corner of the stage, arranged as the interior of a newspaper office, Sophie pleaded with a newspaper man to frame an advertisement for her, regarding the loss of her man. Then, while she was making a change in attire, Shapiro and Carroll played a medley of popular jazz numbers.

"Do I?" was Sophie's next number, followed by "Bluebird Blues," which she performed first as Sophie would render it, then as a Jewish cantor would sing it. A brief conversation with the boys led into a rousing and suggestive ragtime tune, "There's More Music in a Grand Baby Than There Is in a Baby Grand."

Sophie performed two encores: "Where Does My Daddy Go?" and, finally, another rouser, "Bad Little Boys Aren't Goody-Good to the Goody-Good Little Girls," first sung in English and then in Yiddish. Sophie claimed the number was an old Jewish ditty her mother had taught her when she was a child.

The *Clipper* noted that "Sophie Tucker is doing a more effective act than she has ever done."[8] *Variety* wrote: "The entire act is sure-fire. It's Sophie Tucker at her best. What more could one want?"[9]

One astute reviewer mentioned that Sophie appeared to have taken off "quite a good deal of weight (pardon the frankness) and looks more youthful now than she has in years." Sophie responded to the compliment by revealing she was in love. His name, Al Lackey (Lackeyman), a New York merchant. She explained that they had met at Reisenweber's several years earlier, where she had danced with him. He returned night after night, and she danced with him each time. They began going out together after the shows. Although Al was revealed to be eight years younger than Sophie—that would make him twenty-seven—"in spite of the difference in age it was love right from the start," according to Sophie.[10]

When Sophie went to London, Al followed her but obviously kept a low profile. When she began the Keith tour, Al was her companion. His real occupation was uncertain, and it was doubtful he earned a reasonable living. Sophie hoped that his getting a steady job would put them in a position to marry. In fact, one observed that Al seemed little different in personality than Louis Tuck and Frank Westphal. But at least he was Jewish.

After four weeks of packed houses at various New York theaters, Sophie made her grand entrance at the Palace Theater for an unprecedented two-week engagement. It was her first appearance since returning from abroad.

> Practically all the patrons look upon Miss Tucker as being an entertainment institution that never disappoints, but always makes good with a good act, put over in her own particular style.[11]

For the entire engagement, the Palace was filled at every performance. So many floral bouquets were offered to Sophie, some nights she found it difficult to navigate the stage without bumping into them. Unlike other performers, Sophie wanted all the bouquets she received to remain on stage with her, so she could publicly identify from whom they were received.

At the Riverside Theater, two weeks later, Sophie topped the bill. "She came though with a repertoire of songs," the *Clipper* reviewer wrote, "that consisted of everything that is anything in the shape of zippy melodies."[12]

Three ragtime songs ended with "Who'll Take My Place," a ballad in which she worked an extra mother chorus that brought tears to the eyes of her audience. Shapiro and Carroll then entertained with a medley of jazz tunes. Sophie returned, in a new dazzling gown, with her now familiar comedy song, "That's What Keeps Me Broke," mention of her marital history causing considerable laughter from the audience. She ended with the stage door hit, "Who Cares." "Sophie was in excellent voice," noted the *Variety* reviewer, "and sold her stuff like a veteran."

Three more successful weeks in New York; and then the tour carried her to Jersey City, Baltimore, and Milwaukee. During her Milwaukee appearance, Sophie persuaded her mother and Anna to visit. It was Jennie's first experience on a long distance sleeper and the first time since Hartford that she had seen her daughter perform. A pleasant family reunion, including Sophie's introduction of Al, was crammed between her usual jam-packed rehearsal and performance schedule. The Chicago Palace Theater was next; Sophie would be heading the bill for two weeks. Already sold out shows suggested a gala reunion with all of her "Windy City" friends and admirers.

"Sophie Tucker comes to the Palace Music hall tomorrow," reported the *Chicago Daily News*, "for the first time since she added London laurels to those she had worn for so long in America." The newspaper also revealed that Sophie came to the Palace "thin." "That's an awful blow to hefty art, but it becomes the ragtime empress of watch-your-step balladry."[13]

Newspaper ads were now calling Sophie "the International Comedienne, direct from her London triumphs." Heading the bill for a two-week engagement, Sophie unquestionably scored a tremendous hit.

> Last night the packed house clapped until its hands were sore, and then came the whistles from the gallery — gods we thought had passed into the great beyond — and encore followed encore — and they were genuine, those demands for more, and yet more.[14]

Not only her performances were congratulated, but newspapers were filled with articles about Sophie's "reduction in girth" and how she was filling out her Parisian gowns with style and reserve. How did she slim down, they asked, and yet retain her robust voice? "The voice remains the same," she answered. "Hard work and 'stepping on the gas' takes care of the body."

In fact, the *Herald Examiner* featured a drawing of Sophie's costumes worn at the Palace, and they were described in detail in an accompanying article. That they were Parisian purchases from the ateliers of the great costumiers came as no surprise to the reporter. In addition, no gown was complete without the appropriate shoes and earrings. "That's Sophie Tucker," wrote the reporter. "Now I know there will be a grand rush for the stores."

Even more stirring was Sophie's second week at the Palace.

> Sophie Tucker dawns upon the Palace bill with stunning new frocks, new box-shaped scenes, capital new songs and irresistible comedy.[15]

Writing about her old friend, Amy Leslie asked the rhetorical question: why was Sophie so popular. "It seems to derive from her general attitude and accessibility, as well as her stage presence," Leslie commented. But even more telling were her follow-up observations.

> There may be a more cautiously reticent comedienne but no more sunny, brave, honest, or industrious slave to their public. The consequence is she grows closer and more beloved as her years pile up in hard work in an easy, delightfully candid, dutiful way.[16]

Thanks to Leslie, Sophie's commitments to her audiences and career could not have been more accurately expressed.

The euphoria of successes continued through her tour of Midwestern cities, as she worked her way back to New York, where she planned to appear at a number of theaters. Another engagement at the famed Palace during the Easter holiday season (a normally slow week) turned people away from the box-office.

Sophie stayed on the stage double the allotted time, entertaining with new songs, "hot as only Miss Tucker could use and keep from being burnt." She opened the act by arriving on stage in a new touring car, with chauffeur, singing "You've Got to See Mamma Every Night (or you can't see Mamma at all)," which contained some "potent punch lines." She ended the set with "When the Leaves Come Tumbling Down," staged with a place-drop with actual falling leaves. The enthusiastic *Clipper* reviewer concluded that "Sophie is one of those stagefolk who look younger and knock 'em colder at each successive performance."

No sooner had Sophie captured New York audiences than William Morris announced that she would leave vaudeville "temporarily" to appear in a stock-company production. West Coast producers, Ackerman and Harris, had prepared a musical revue to be featured at the new Century Theater in San Francisco. Sophie, and her two pianists, would headline the show, to be called the "Pepper Box Revue."

The show opened April 14, 1923, to an enthusiastic first-night audience.

> Sophie Tucker, who is headlined and featured, received an ovation equal to any Grand Opera prima donna, and deservedly so, for she more than pleased and entertained with her specialties, and found it difficult to retire, only after promising to appear later on the program.[17]

The production was staged by Fanchon and Marco, the book was by George Le Maire (the performer who had supposedly taught Sophie how to apply blackface makeup), and the music and lyrics was by Fanchon and Marco. An exception was made for Sophie, who had a pair of her old tunesmiths from Chicago, Ager and Yellen, prepare her songs. There were nine separate stage scenes, each with its own plot, songs, and dances, not too dissimilar from the tabloid shows produced years earlier by Lew Fields and Gus Hill. George Le Maire not only wrote the book, he was co-headliner with Sophie and an accomplished song-and-dance man. With the price of seats at $1.50 top, critics believed the show would have "good business."

Upon her return to San Francisco, the *Call* reporter cornered Sophie to obtain a brief interview on her feelings about having become a headliner since her last appearance in the city. He quickly found that Sophie's commitment to the profession was, indeed, compelling.

"I love this life," she enthused. "I live when I'm in the theater. The theater that is unreal to other people is the realest thing in life to us who know it." She went on. "If I had my life to live over, I'd do it again. I couldn't help it. It's fascinating."

"Oh, it's so hard," she admitted, "but the thrill! Why, I'd do anything in the world for an audience. I'd play to them till I dropped. There's nothing I can't do for them."[18] Not surprisingly, the *Call* published a full page feature on Sophie in their Sunday edition, publishing her views.

"The Pepper Box Revue" received good reviews, "the interesting production is one of the nattiest, snappiest, fastest show seen in many a long day." Of course, Sophie's appearance was "bright and shining."

> The buxom Sophie queens it gallantly with her songfest, set like a crown on the first act, each particular song a polished gem, given charm and brilliance by the act of Miss Tucker. She has come back to the Coast after an absence of six years a sublimated replica of her old self.[19]

Nonetheless, in spite of the scintillating reports, the show was equally panned for Sophie's use of "obscene" lyrics. "New York and Chicago may demand this type of filth," pontificated the *Chronicle*, "but the West is still clean-minded enough to reject it." Le Maire quickly had Sophie change the offending lines in the songs, if, for no other reason, to save the show from faltering at the box office.

"The Pepper Box Revue" played to full houses for four weeks. Nonetheless, when McIntyre and Heath opened at the Curran Theater in "The Red Pepper," audience attendance for "Pepper Box" dropped precipitously. Whether it was a new show — San Francisco audiences were always attracted to new shows — the confusion of show names, or just the fact that "Pepper Box" had run its course, the producers decided to close the show and move it to Los Angeles. The show made an immediate hit in that city, as did Sophie.

> Good old Sophie, or perhaps in view of her glittering blond wig, good young Sophie. She stepped out to the footlights and the evening's entertainment really commenced. Miss Tucker can make those complaining, wailing tunes have a character that is as rare as southern honeysuckle. She can make you see the old roughneck glare of the old cafe days come to life again, and she can make you hear all the wild pal-ly sal-ly melodies, as she sends a zingy line across about the man who's too wild for anybody else, is the man just perfect for me! She's a peach — even yet.[20]

"Due to the hot weather" (a theatrical euphemism for poor ticket sales), "The Pepper Box Revue" played only two weeks in Los Angeles and headed back to San Francisco to an undetermined fate. Sophie, however, decided to remain in Los Angeles for a rest. She was joined by Amy Leslie, recuperating from a disabling illness;

and, together, they lived in a cottage, rented by Leslie's newspaper, in the heart of the moviemaking district. Prompted by Amy, Sophie attempted to get into the film business. A few screen tests, however, convinced her that she was not ready for movies, if they would ever be ready for her. Al came out to stay with Sophie; and for two months she did not perform, although she continued to practice each day with her two pianists. This period of time was the longest she had not publicly performed since the beginning of her career, and she admitted to enjoying the "time off." Nevertheless, "time off" to Sophie meant she was involved in a number of business arrangements. Her earnings had allowed her to make various investments, some of which failed, like investments in "Tick, Tack, Toe" and the Sophie Tucker garage, and some which thrived. Brother Phil was handling most of Sophie's business details, but he made none of the decisions and often was informed of a transaction after the fact.

Sophie had purchased a number of apartment houses in Brooklyn; she had underwritten a "smart" cafe in Atlantic City; and she had purchased property on Long Island, upon which homes were to be built. These seemingly viable transactions kept Phil busy. Unfortunately, a deal with a builder in San Diego ended in a loss for Sophie, in spite of the use of her name on the enterprise. She had been persuaded to purchase a piece of property upon which a group of "Sophie Tucker Homes" would be built. Some properties were sold, but the builder failed to fulfill his part of the deal. Litigation regarding restitution was settled out of court but cost Sophie a good deal of money. At the same time, Sophie was negotiating to take over a failed cabaret in Cleveland; she would finalize the arrangement when she visited that city on her way back to New York. All of these schemes were designed to increase her estate beyond the entertainment income, which she recognized was irregular; but her ability to select those with a reasonable chance of success was problematic. There would be more such problems to come.

When Sophie told William Morris she was ready to go back to work, he obtained a contract from Martin Beck, at $2,000 a week, to play on the Orpheum circuit. Back in vaudeville, Sophie opened at the Orpheum Theater, Los Angeles, October 7, 1923. "Miss Tucker still has Ted Shapiro and Jack Carroll with her," reported the *Los Angeles Times* reviewer, "a new line of songs, new frocks, but the same blond winsomeness and infectious smile. She was a sensational success." For this show, Sophie drove out on the stage in an old Ford, which fit her opening number, "Rattling to New York." The number where she pled with a publisher to accept a song that her sweetheart turned down and a dressing-room ballad, brought out her emotional talents, as well as tears to the audience's eyes. The spicy numbers were there as usual (Los Angeles had no uneasiness about her lyrics); and "It Takes A Good Girl to Do That" and "Cross-Eyed Papa Look Straight At Me" were well received. Her act lasted twenty-seven minutes; but Sophie added another fourteen minutes, encoring a number of the audience's old favorites.

This engagement was followed by a two-week run at the Golden Gate Theater, San Francisco, where her return to that city was treated like the reestablishment of royalty, from the moment she arrived on the train to her first appearance on stage. "Sophie at the Orpheum, blond and blooming," was all the newspapers said.

Five weeks on the road brought Sophie back to the friendly confines of the Palace Theater, Chicago, for the Christmas holidays. Still being billed as the International Comedienne, Sophie and her pianists opened the engagement with a new repertoire of songs. The house was packed at each performance.

> She is looking fair and in rollicking spirits, wears strange and costly garb jubilantly, and yesterday was greeted with hurrahs and a stampede of applause, which broke into her best songs and least veiled innuendoes.[21]

New songs and new routines were added for the second week of the engagement. Leading off with "That Old Gang of Mine," Sophie sang it like no other singer had rendered it, to the delight of the audience. "Kiss 'Em and Run, Girls!" and "Somebody's Wrong" were greeted with enthusiastic shouts of approval.

Changing pace and manner, Sophie introduced the next number with a lecture addressed to "giddy young flappers" who led too fast a life. The song, "You're the Kind of a Girl Men Forget," was sung seriously and with a touch of motherliness, the audience shaking their heads in agreement with her plaint. Then, abruptly, she donned a Mandarin jacket and pitched into a riotous jazz piece that rocked the theater.

When the crowd shouted for a speech at the end of her set, Sophie asked them if, instead, she could introduce her mother "to her friends out front." The crowd shouted "Yes" in unison. "A gentle little Russian woman in costly furs and plain black," as she was described by the *Daily News,* "without alarm, stood up in a stage box when her daughter told her to and bowed when directed so to do, with no airs nor any other than simple courtesy."

Newspapers claimed that Sophie's mother had never before seen her daughter on stage before — which elicited extended applause — and marveled at the adulation she received. Actually, Jennie had seen Sophie perform before; but the announcement was always a great crown pleaser.

During her Chicago visit, Sophie also introduced a new song, written by Jack Yellen, that was destined to become her theme song for the remainder of her career. The song was called "I'm the Last of the Red Hot Mamma's," and it was so well received by the audience that she had to encore it several times at each show.

Jack Yellen was born in Poland on July 6, 1892.[22] His parents emigrated to the U.S. in 1897, to settle in Buffalo, New York. Yellen attended the University of Michigan, where he started writing songs, receiving up to five dollars a tune, if he was lucky. In 1913, after graduation, he got a job as a reporter for the *Buffalo Courier,* but continued to write songs in collaboration with a local music teacher, George Cobb. His first hit was "Are You from Dixie?" After a brief period in the army, he moved to New York to seek a composing career. He helped found the publishing firm of Ager, Yellen, and Bornstein.

Ager and Yellen compositions became featured in Sophie's act because they were able to compose songs that seemed tailor-made for her style of singing. Soon, she hired them to prepare most of her musical material. Sophie sang "I'm the Last of the Red Hot Mamas" her entire career. For his part, Jack Yellen wrote songs exclusively for Sophie for as long as she wanted them. Shortly after its introduction, "Red Hot Mamma" was produced by Okeh records.

Visits to Kansas City and New Orleans preceded the planned stop in Cleveland, where Sophie took over negotiations to own and operate a cabaret in that city. Renaming the club "Tucker Terrace," Sophie planned to headline the bill indefinitely. Instead, she appeared there for only two weeks, to moderate success, not enough to cover her expenses. Deciding to keep the cabaret open, against Phil's advice, Sophie returned to the Orpheum circuit for a tour of the West.

At the Orpheum Theater, San Francisco, Sophie "had a lot of new songs" and sang them with that "fine combination of nature and art that made her an international favorite." Accompanying Sophie on this trip was Amy Leslie who, after recovering from a severe illness, expressed a desire to revisit the West Coast. Sophie and Amy decided to make the trip together.

While in San Francisco, Phil informed Sophie that the Cleveland cabaret was about to shut down due to poor business ever since she left town. Disappointed, Sophie had no choice but to shutter the business. This failed enterprise cost her more than $10,000. A somewhat chastened Sophie admitted failure, although she was not really able to explain to Phil "what went wrong."

George Warren, a feature writer for the *San Francisco Chronicle*, obtained an exclusive interview with Sophie (he was reported to be a friend of Leslie), to better explain "the fire, pep, and vigor" in her act. Instead, to his surprise, he found a tired actress, a weariness in her voice, a bit of lassitude in her usually blithe self. Under these circumstances, Warren obtained a more intimate portrait of the "working" Sophie, one that uncovered many personal thoughts previously unexpressed.

"I work mighty hard," she said, "because my people out there in front expect something new from me all the time; and I never disappoint them. Why, I didn't go to bed until six o'clock this morning, getting my new songs ready for next week and fixing up the act so it will be fresh and crisp.

"And because of all that," she sighed, "I am tired. But I gotta work on."

According to Warren, Sophie showed great pride in her family. She spoke of brother Moe: "I put him through college. He was the one others didn't have much faith in; but I did, and I stood back of him." She showed a wire from him telling that he had just bought a $13,000 house and an electric brougham for their mother. He had said: "It's your home, Sophie. Come here and rest yourself. It's for mother, and you and sister." Warren reported tears in Sophie's eyes when she spoke of the family.

Two photographs lay on the dressing table, one of Sophie and her mother and one of Sophie and her son, Bert, at age fourteen. "He's twenty-years-old now," Sophie explained. "And he's going to be an actor. Oh, yes, at a little start from me, he's going on the stage."

Then she pointed to her mother's picture. "Isn't she sweet?" she asked. "See the diamond pendant hanging on her breast. I hope, when I am as old, I will be as fine as she is."

Warren came away from the interview hesitant to print the details; but Sophie urged him to do so, so people could get some idea of her family and personal life. An hour later, sporting a new hair bob and an elegant gown, Sophie headlined her act, leading off with "Red Hot Mamma."

"She becomes our warm-hearted pal," wrote Warren. "She is our same old Sophie."

In June, Sophie returned to the Palace, Chicago, for another two-week engagement. Any time she wanted or needed encouragement, Chicago was the place to play. Amy Leslie was always available for a rousing review.

> Just Miss Tucker, like a blazing comet of relief from the age and decrepitude of the world of western amusement. Sophie is a tremendous, universal, national pet and seems imperishable in voice, strapping vitality and wholesome good fellowship for the world. Miss Tucker is thinner, handsomer, younger, more tempestuously animated and sleek than ever.[23]

The houses were packed; both weeks were sold out, and at advanced prices. Her second week featured new songs and new gowns. At each performance, Sophie was showered with bouquets and shouted pleas to speak. Even a bad cold did not prevent her from entertaining "her armies and hosts of admirers." The only holdovers from the first week's work were a "mother" song and "Red Hot Mamma."

Upon Sophie's return East, in preparation for a tour on the Keith circuit, E. A. Albee, in what he considered a stroke of genius, decided to publicize her as "Madame Sophie Tucker," a title that quickly elicited a good deal of sarcasm and debate, much of it to Sophie's embarrassment. When informed of the title, Sophie refused to accept it. When informed that it had already been printed on posters and programs, Sophie threatened to withdraw from the Keith tour. At the same time, New York newspapers were enjoying the use of the title in numerous ways: cartoons of Sophie dressed as a "Madame"; the name colorfully emblazoned on theater marquees; photographs with "Madame" signed at the bottom. In the process of making fun of Albee's selection, the jokes also offended Sophie.

Sophie complained to William Morris, for she believed the title demeaning; and she refused to be identified with it. Morris pointed out that the damage had already been done. Why not use the title for publicity and joke about it in her act, as a way to diffuse its importance and take advantage of its humorous possibilities. Everyone knew who Sophie was, he reminded her. Use it for your own purposes.

Sophie demurred but reluctantly agreed to Morris's advice. Still, it took some time before she became comfortable with the ill-starred Albee title. In contrast, the Keith people were pleased and excited with the publicity and planned to wrap all of Sophie's tour appearances around the title.

At the Alhambra Theater, Madame Sophie Tucker entertained the entire first half of the bill, reported the Keith publicity people. The *New York Times* declared "The Madame rang up an individual bulls-eye with her song cycle." It was fast becoming a Broadway gag.

In addition to her songs, Sophie engaged in a number of burlesques, which included a mind-reading stunt, a room-and-board routine, and playing the bass drum in a clown band. Through all of these skits, Sophie was referred to as "Madame," its use eliciting considerable laughter. Then a reviewer raised an interesting question with his readers.

> If Sophie ever should be sitting in a party, and a nice party, all nice people Sophie mixes with in her travels, and some gay guy busts in saying, "How do you do, Madame?," what will the party think?[24]

This sarcastic comment was followed by an appeal to Sophie from Albee, requesting that, before she appeared at the Palace again, she moderate her material and eliminate a number of catch lines that might be considered risqué. Her response to Albee was unprintable, but the songs were dropped. When Sophie came on stage to open her engagement, everyone in the audience greeted her as "Madame." Had it not been for her promise to Morris, Sophie would have abruptly walked off the stage.

When Morris announced that Sophie had signed a contract to appear in a new version of Earl Carroll's Vanities, the "Madame" issue was quickly defused. Carroll promised not to use the title, although a number of newspapers continued to use it with some frequency for several weeks. Carroll also told the press that Sophie would contribute her own specialties and would "be woven into a number of non-singing skits." The show was scheduled to open at the Music Box Theater, September 10. Sophie was reported to be receiving $1,500 weekly in the production.

The opening of the show was delayed twice. In a break with the usual pre-opening rehearsals, visitors were permitted to watch them. While the performance took place, messengers passed among the audience stating that a fund was being collected for the chorus. "Any amount would be acceptable, and five or ten dollars most agreeable." The total amount would be equally divided among all the chorus girls. In reality, the girls would have had to been paid a salary by Carroll because he had demanded the extra rehearsals.

Sophie also provided an additional incentive for the show. As she had been doing for some years, she sent out printed announcements to her friends about the opening of the Vanities. The announcement stated that she would not feel confident on the stage unless her friends were in front. Enclosed were two first-night tickets at $11 each.

Earl Carroll's Vanities featured Sophie, comedian Joe Cook, and ninety-seven girls. Carroll was credited for both the lyrics and music (except on Sophie's songs, which had been written by Ager and Yellen). Sammy Lee staged the dances and ensembles. Reviewers responded to the show with disfavor.

> The new "Vanities" must get over upon the strength of its production and girls. It has little else.

8. At the Top of Her Game

Sophie was excused for a poor showing by the limited use of her talent.

> Soph could have walked out with her two piano players and tied the show up at any given point, but didn't. The continuity confines her to spasmodic song insertions, some of which were prolonged with brief lines by others in the cast.[25]

Sophie was frustrated. In spite of the extended rehearsals, the chorus was "woefully lacking." The comedy was not funny. And Carroll was irate at the reviews. During the production's first week, he fired and hired at will, demanded more late-night rehearsals, and was reported to be "engaged in violent combat with practically everyone."

In anger, Carroll told the cast that "none was a world-beater" and "anyone caring to hand in his notice, he would receive it with open arms."[26] Both Cook and Sophie took particular exception to Carroll's condescending remarks. Cook handed in his verbal notice on the spot. Sophie left the cast after the week's performance to return to vaudeville. A week later, she opened at the Orpheum Theater, Brooklyn, with an entirely new act. Included were, besides her two pianists, new songs, a small orchestra, eleven Negro dancers, a violin soloist, and a singer from a cabaret. *Variety* quickly recognized her efforts. "Sophie Tucker is of vaudeville. What it takes to make a vaudeville audience stand up she has."[27] The "Madame" title had almost entirely disappeared.

The following week, Sophie's appearance at the Palace Theater lasted for a record forty-two minutes.

> Sophie slung a new act together on short notice, and before she left the stage, she had stopped the show with her own specialties. Anyone in the vicinity of Broadway and 42nd Street at 11:10 Monday night could have told that Sophie had returned to her first love.[28]

For the remainder of the year, Sophie played at various New York houses, to record-breaking box-office receipts. As a surprise to everyone, particularly her family, Sophie made a quick trip to Hartford to attend the Abuza family's first night of Hanukah. At the dinner, Bert revealed to his mother that he was going to be in Chicago in January, the same time that his mother was appearing at the Palace, to begin his own vaudeville career. Sophie expressed pleasure that Bert had obtained a billing, but she was disconcerted that he was going to appear simultaneously with her. Moreover, she was not pleased that he had decided to use the Tucker name for the stage (instead of Tuck, his real last name). It was an interesting dilemma that she could do little about, except to applaud Bert's success at getting into vaudeville, no matter her personal feelings about the event.

Sophie opened at the Palace, Chicago, January 12, 1925, using almost no stage props and only her two pianists, Shapiro and Carroll, to help introduce her new songs. For reasons unknown, Bert's entry into vaudeville had been postponed indefinitely. In competition with Sophie at the time were George White's Scandal's; Charlot's Review of 1924; "Rose Marie," "No, No, Nanette," Ethel Barrymore; Anna

In 1910, when "Some of These Days" first became a hit, the song's popularity was relatively short-lived because so many performers used it and new releases relegated it to the list of "used" songs. Thirteen years later, Sophie revived the song, and it again became a national hit. From that time on, Sophie and "Some of These Days" were inseparable.

8. At the Top of Her Game

Pavlova; and the Shuberts' "Passing Show." Nevertheless, Sophie reigned successfully for a record-breaking performance at the Palace. She did so well, in fact, that her engagement was extended to the middle of February. The Chicago amusement scene had become increasingly competitive in recent years since producers realized its financial importance, now second only to New York. These days, many shows opened in Chicago and, if they appeared to be successful, moved to New York.

As a special feature, Sophie used the Lady Godiva entrance to begin her act. On horseback, she was fully clothed in a long flannel nightgown—which itself contributed to the humor of the situation—and allowed her long blond hair to trail around her. Reliable Amy Leslie again regaled Sophie in elegant prose.

> Sophie's voice has an eternal youth within its almost baritone quality, and she has such distinct utterance, such charm of good heart and love of her listeners, that her popularity is even more eternal than her splendid voice and her lovely hair.[29]

During her last week at the Palace, Sophie put on a "mamma" show, persuading the other actors on the bill to sing or dance to "mamma" songs. Among those participating were comedians J.C. Flippen and Olson and Johnson. It was akin to a giant sing-along, with an audience that took it upon themselves to participate in every song that was presented. Of course, Sophie's rendition of "Red Hot Mamma" won the blue ribbon; and she was asked to encore the song repeatedly.

The spring was spent in a tour of Midwestern and Eastern cities, before a return to New York venues with, as usual, an engagement at the Palace. In her act, she included a young violinist—her find, she claimed—named Milton Spiro; a Negro dancer negotiating recent jazz numbers (or from a local burlesque down the street, wrote one reviewer); and quite a bit of repartee from Shapiro and Carroll to introduce each of her songs. The feature of the evening, however, was the introduction of a new song, written for her by Jack Yellen, called "Yiddishe Mamma."

With lights dimmed, a single warm spot focused on Sophie. Standing very still but pulling on her long handkerchief to effect, she sang the song with deep feeling, at times tearfully, in both English and Yiddish. While repeating it in Yiddish, she broke off occasionally to speak of her old mother, to whom the song was dedicated. The audience, likewise, were soon in tears as she rendered the song. Its popularity was so instantaneous, Sophie was requested to sing the song, not only at every Palace performance, but at every other New York theater she played as well. "Yiddishe Mamma" quickly became another of those signature songs that lasted her lifetime, requested by audiences again and again thirty-five years after she had introduced it. Interestingly, Okeh records declined to record the song (no reasons given); but Columbia recorded it several years later with excellent results.

May brought Sophie back to Chicago at the behest of Balaban and Katz, local vaudeville and movie impresarios who already owned four theaters and were in the process of constructing a cinematic empire. Sophie jammed the theaters and caused people to be standing in front of the theaters hustling for tickets. Balaban and Katz promised patrons that Sophie would be back in the near future, "to take up where she left off."

After the engagement in Chicago, Sophie, her pianists, and Al traveled to Miami Beach for a short holiday prior to their planned trip to London. Like all of Sophie's holidays, most of the time was spent on rehearsing new material for the numerous London engagements, a schedule that promised to be demanding, even for Sophie. Photos of Sophie and Al found their way into New York papers with headlines like "What? Sophie on Vacation?"

Sophie, Anna, and Ted Shapiro departed on the *Acquitania* for London on August 18, 1925. Shortly after, Al Lackey arrived, to accompany Sophie during her tour of English theaters. Jack Carroll had abruptly abandoned the ensemble when he got married, leaving Sophie with a one-piano act to which she and Ted Shapiro easily became adjusted. Up to the day of her departure, Sophie received hundreds of cards, telegrams, and personal notes wishing her well from colleagues, friends, and admirers. Every one of the missives she not only placed in her scrapbook, but also answered as well.

Sophie was booked to appear at various venues through the spring of 1927. This time, William Morris did not have to prepare English audiences for her arrival, Sophie's reputation having already been established. He was confident she would do even better than she had in 1922.

Sophie opened at the Kit Kat Club (a cabaret) on August 30; she was scheduled for a ten-week engagement at 400 pounds a week (equivalent to about $2,000 in American money). The club was by membership only; but fees were reasonable, making it a popular place for American tourists. The club building was spacious, with a large staircase, dance floor, and balcony, situated in such a way that everyone in the audience could easily see the stage. In turn, Sophie could just as easily see the audience. Patrons choosing to use the dance floor were required to wear dinner clothes; those in the balcony were permitted more casual attire. Still, entrance fees were charged (similar to American cabaret couvert charges). These fees ran more than five pounds for men, three pounds for women, and almost three pounds for foreigners; they were all subject to change "at any moment," if the management so desired.

Sophie appeared at two shows, 10:30 P.M. and 12:30 P.M., to sing five or six songs. Typical of her appearances, however, encores often extended the act for another half hour. With Sophie now billed by the London press as the "Queen of Vaudeville," the Kit Kat Club was filled at every show. Sophie had simplified her act somewhat, keeping in mind what she had previously learned about London audiences. Songs tended to be ballads, tear-jerkers, and suggestive, all with a jazz beat, backed by Shapiro's expressive piano-playing. When she changed gowns—which she did at every performance—Ted entertained with a series of jazz pieces. She used no props except for the long handkerchief she held, used strategically to emphasize lyrics and create emotion. *The Encore* reported on her initial success at the club.

> Sophie Tucker is great! Her forceful personality, strong voice, general good humour, and excellent material combined to enable her to twist the audience right around her little finger. All her items were splendid.[30]

At one point in the engagement, Sophie reintroduced the "prince" song; but management again advised her to drop the song. The two songs that she had recently become intimately associated with, "Last of the Red-Hot Mamas" and "Yiddishe Mamma," were requested at every show. The latter song she sang in both English and Yiddish; and audiences openly cried as they were rendered by her, although many could not understand the lyrics. In fact, audiences requested more tear-jerkers than any other songs in her repertoire.

Five weeks later—instead of the ten weeks promised at the Kit Kat Club—Sophie cheerfully gave up a portion of her engagement to Paul Whiteman and his band because of a booking conflict. She opened at the Alhambra Theater to tremendous ovations and box-office records. (All the theaters raised their ticket prices when Sophie appeared.) The Alhambra was a two-a-day vaudeville house, requiring Sophie to extend her singing time considerably longer at each performance; and the stress on her voice finally took its toll.

Midway though the Alhambra run, Sophie caught a bad cold, which affected her voice and her stamina. Refusing to abandon her audiences, Sophie talked her way through the songs. Finally, a physician ordered her to bed with the threat that her voice could be permanently damaged if she continued. Her condition was so serious, Sophie canceled all dates for a month. Doctors reported that Sophie's voice was gone and she was "physically worn out." Her illness, however, did not prevent hoards of visitors, hundreds of get-well cards, and bouquets of flowers delivered to her room every day, nor a daily scorecard in *The Encore* reporting on her recovery. During the last week of her confinement, with a piano wheeled into her room, Sophie and Ted practiced new songs they intended to introduce when they returned to the stage.

A week at the Kit Kat Club—to get warmed up, Sophie said—preceded her November 30 opening at the Picadilly Hotel cabaret, for a proposed eight-week engagement. Now claiming to be healthy again, Sophie also participated in a number of benefits and dinners that, according to the doctors, threatened to put her back in bed. One of the highlights of Sophie's visit was an appearance at a dinner given by the Price of Wales, at which she entertained him with several songs. Other benefits included Sophie's attending several Jewish Hanukah gatherings where her mere appearance substantially increased fund-raising activities.

Sophie was rumored to be liking London so much that she intended to stay there indefinitely, but the news was attributed to several William Morris press releases suggesting how much Sophie appreciated English hospitality. Another rumor suggested she was going to star in a revue, but no additional news corroborated the report. Still, newspapers had plenty of material to write about regarding Sophie's activities, shopping jaunts, dinner parties with royalty, and celebrations during the Christmas holidays. "Sophie was one big party," said a reviewer, who also readily admitted fatigue in his attempt to follow her around each day.

Anna had returned to Hartford a few weeks earlier, having received a cable from Phil that Jennie had become quite ill. While Sophie was deeply concerned about her mother's health, she still had weeks of commitments to fulfill before she could

Sophie and her mother, Jennie, shortly before Jennie's death in 1926. Over the years, Sophie's attachment to her mother's memory increased and exerted a significant influence on Sophie's philanthropic activities, both in the U.S. and Israel. (Universal Music)

reasonably return home. Nonetheless, a cable she received from Phil on December 16 was the message she had dreaded but knew would be arriving any day: "Make first boat home." The news seemed to shock London almost as much as it shocked Sophie.

Immediately and without hesitation, Sophie canceled all of her future engagements, reported by the press to be worth many thousands of dollars. "I'll play only to January 15 and then head for home," she told reporters. When told of Sophie's plans, Phil responded by advising his sister that Jennie had but a short time to live. Sophie promised to leave London on January 19. During her final weeks in London, audiences seemed in sympathy with Sophie, knowing she was performing her best with the burden of a leaden heart and accorded their heartfelt sympathy.

When questioned by the press about her actions, Sophie responded: "What is money when your mother is concerned? All I think about now is her welfare. Little have people thought that when I came on and entertained them, I have really felt like crying." In this, Sophie was mistaken. Her audiences were crying with and for her, this woman who had given her all for them.

9

Burning Up the Boards

On January 15, Sophie hastily departed from London on board the *Leviathan*, bound for New York. She already was cognizant that her return would be a race against her mother's imminent death.

Jennie died in her sleep on January 16, 1926. She was seventy-six years old. To spare Sophie's feelings, the family decided not to inform her of the death until she arrived in New York. In spite of Jewish Orthodox beliefs that burial should take place no later than two days after death, in a final deposition, Jennie made the rabbi and her family agree not to hold the funeral and burial until Sophie had arrived home.

Due to unusually bad weather, the Atlantic crossing of the *Leviathan* was delayed several days. Phil and Moe then decided to cable Sophie and reveal Jennie's death. Ironically, on board, that very day, Sophie had agreed to perform at an evening entertainment. Prior to the beginning of her act, fellow passenger Rudolph Valentino delivered the cable to Sophie. It read, simply: "Heartfelt sympathy." Since the cable came from her brothers, Sophie knew her mother had died. With bravery and resoluteness, since the show must always go on, Sophie performed all her familiar signature songs before an audience who had no idea of the deep grief she endured. After her gallant performance, Sophie quickly excused herself, returned to her suite, and mourned her mother's passing with prayers and tears.

The following day, news of the event quickly passed through the ship, bringing condolences from many of the passengers, particularly those who had attended the show. Valentino, Al Lackey, and Ted Shapiro were on hand to provide for Sophie's needs. A number of British peers on board—the Duchess of Norfolk and her daughter, as well as Lord and Lady Camoys—saw to it that Sophie received adequate assistance for the remainder of the trip.

On January 25, the *Leviathan* arrived in New York at 3:30 P.M. Phil and Moe were there to escort Sophie home. Although large numbers of the press had stationed themselves at dockside to interview Sophie, they were bypassed in favor of a quick exit.

When Sophie arrived at home, she found many members of the synagogue and various ladies' societies standing in front of the house openly mourning the loss of their dear friend and benefactress. Rushing upstairs to view her mother's body, Sophie, in tears, knelt before the casket. Knowing that her mother had set aside Jewish customs to accommodate her daughter, Sophie declared in her autobiography: "There was nothing she could have done that would have [better] showed me how much she loved me and how well she understood my love for her."[1] Jennie's handwritten will revealed the thoughts of a knowing and understanding parent. She had given her jewelry to Anna; the fine bed clothes were divided between Anna and Phil; her own clothing and mink coat went to a dear friend; "and to my daughter, Sophie, who gave me everything, nothing, because she don't need anything."[2]

On January 26, at 1:00 P.M., a private funeral was held at home. Rabbi Silverman, from the synagogue, officiated. Later, funeral rites were held at the Hebrew Ladies Old People's Home, of which Jennie had been a founder. The burial, with Rabbi Hurewitz officiating, was held at Zion Hill Cemetery, where Jennie was laid to rest next to her husband Charles.

The week of "sitting shiva" was filled with visitations from many members of the Jewish community, especially those people who, at some point in their lives, had been helped by Jennie or had benefited from her generosity. During this period, Sophie spent much of her time in seclusion, wondering whether she had the desire and strength to return to the stage.

When William Morris visited the Abuza family to pay his respects, he used the meeting not to argue whether Sophie should or should not perform again, but rather to discuss her future stage alternatives. He assumed correctly that, given an appropriate amount of time, Sophie would return to the stage. Understanding Sophie as well as he did, he believed that, to convince her, she only needed reassurance of her stardom and renewed confidence in her ability to capture audiences. Morris spoke only of possible engagements; it was up to Sophie to decide which one she wanted. Contracts were waiting for her from various vaudeville circuits; London wanted her to return; and nightclubs and cabarets vied for her attention. "Which one would you like to pursue? Morris asked.

After a short rest in Atlantic City with Al and Anna, Sophie appeared ready to make a decision regarding, what she called, the next phase of her career. Nonetheless, still shaky and not altogether comfortable facing audiences, she expressed the desire to stay "close to home" (i.e., New York City) and possibly to operate and perform at her own venue, a decision which came as a complete surprise to all. Coincidentally, a former mob-owned nightclub on 52nd and Seventh Avenue, the Trocadero, had been shuttered and was up for sale. Purchasing the nightclub would give her the benefits (and liabilities) of ownership, as well as the opportunity for performance on her own terms.

Within a week, and with the aid of Morris, Sophie negotiated an agreement to purchase the Trocadero. By early March, the news was out about Sophie's surprising acquisition. Reaction from the press was mixed: some believed she was taking on a shady operation whose already questionable existence would be short; others felt it was just the kind of venue Sophie needed to regain her star power. She announced the nightclub's new name to be "Sophie Tucker's Playground," where she would act as both hostess and principal entertainer. The club would open on March 10, with just herself and Ted Shapiro slated. For dance music, she hired Eddie Elkins and his orchestra.

While her first week was a total sellout — she was reported to have cleared about $6,000 — Sophie admitted to Morris that she still was feeling uneasy on stage. As her mentor and "boss" (Sophie called him that frequently), Morris assured her that the more she played the better she would feel. As usual, he was correct. Within a few days, Sophie had regained her familiar stage persona. According to *Variety*, "Sophie had the greatest cabaret premiere ever." Yet, they also worried about whether Sophie could maintain this success. "Plenty of competition nowadays among entertainers on the night-life belt. Soph is about the only one trying it single-handed."

More than 500 attempted to get into a club that seated only 275. The cover charge was high, five dollars; but the cost seemed incidental. As fast as a table emptied, new customers grabbed it. Music publishers and song pluggers visited every night, hoping that Sophie had selected one of their songs to feature. Each night, she wore a different gown, each one catching the breath of women (and men) in the audience; "all very Parisienne," *Variety* reported.

The "Playground" prospered through July, when the summer heat finally began shrinking attendance. Many patrons were turning to the picture houses, some of which were promoting a new technology called "air-cooling," rather than to cabarets and nightclubs. Concerned friends suggested that Sophie turn the "Playground" into a picture house, but she refused. Texas Guinan, current owner of a similar nightclub, proposed that she and Sophie team up to run a picture house during the summer, maybe even appear together on stage; but Sophie expressed more interest in other ventures.

After four months of rigorous effort, although highly successful, Sophie was tiring of the exertion required to run a business and prepare the newest in entertainment for each performance. "If you're tired of nightclub work," Morris queried, "how about appearing in a revue? Less effort, as much money, and no administrative labor."

"What have you got?" Sophie asked the "boss."

Sophie returned to the Palace Theater for a two-week engagement, billed as her first U.S. appearance in vaudeville since returning from London. In the meantime, she shut down the "Playground" (and later sold it) but, at the same time, purchased property in New Jersey to subdivide and sell for home construction. Laying out the lots and streets, Sophie opted to name the streets after the people buying homes. If they left, the street name would be changed to recognize the next buyer. The system broke down quickly when lot purchasers began arguing about name rights and lots remained unsold.

The second week at the Palace, Sophie collided with the equally celebrated Nora Bayes. At this encounter, Sophie won the confrontation.

COSTUMES OF SOPHIE TUCKER AT THE PALACE

Sketched by Florence Walsh; described by Madame Rose.

PURPLE GOWN—Royal purple chiffon made on long straight lines. Length of chiffon crosses back, reaching to lower part of skirt in front. Fullness held in at this point by a knot. Front of waist plain, held by narrow straps. Unusual girdle of purple berries and roses. Similar band in hair. Purple kid shoes. Sheer flesh hose. Purple earrings.

GREEN GOWN—Bright emerald green chiffon. Straight foundation. Long waist line, bateau neck. Two long floats of chiffon. Egyptian flowers of leather on sides hold long fringe of wooden beads. Black Gainsborough patent leather hat. Brim slashed, trimmed with green ostrich. Green kid slippers. Long green earrings.

Sophie's gowns became so famous, one New York newspaper ran a feature in its women's section describing her latest attire. Often, in reviews, description of her gowns received as much space as coverage of her performance.

E.A. Albee had billed Sophie and Bayes together. That particular week, Sophie was in the process of closing down the "Playground" and asked management if she could appear early on the program to fulfill her other obligations. When Bayes discovered that Sophie would appear before her, she objected strenuously to Albee and gave him an ultimatum. Attempting to keep the peace between Bayes and Sophie, Albee promised Bayes she could begin the second half of the show and additionally appear in a "surprise bit" if she agreed to the schedule. Bayes refused and objected strongly to his so-called "arrangement." Albee could not force Sophie to change her appearance. After having the scenery hung for her act, Bayes walked out of the theater, as well as the engagement. *Variety* offered an amusing account of the Tucker/Bayes encounter.

> Sophie Tucker never looked better than when she stepped out on the Palace stage Monday afternoon. When Nora Bayes got one flash at Sophie she laid down and then passed out. A murmur of disappointment went through the large audience when Bob Keane made the announcement that "our Nora" refused to follow Sophie. "Our Sophie," instead, will be here for the rest of the week.[3]

Morris then released a statement to the press telling them that Sophie (and Ted) would be appearing in a new revue called "Le Maire's Affairs," to open in Chicago the end of July. Her co-stars were to be Ted Lewis and his band and Lester Allen, a veteran vaudeville comedian. A week in Milwaukee to get the show in shape preceded the show's official opening at the Woods Theater, July 31.

Rufus Le Maire was the producer; Martin Broones wrote the music; Ballard Macdonald the lyrics; and the dances were staged by Bobby Connolly. Max Steiner was music director; and Bud Murray, stage director.

Life and love were the themes of the revue, split into thirty scenes, each labeled an "affair," each telling a different story of love and lost love. A number of the "affairs" were satires of already existing plays, like "Dangerous Dan McGrew," "The Dove," "Minstrel Days," and "Gentlemen Prefer Blondes." Sophie was scheduled to appear in six of the "affairs": a set of songs backed by Ted Shapiro, written by Jack Yellen, Irving Berlin, Herman Ruby, and Jack Mills; a travesty on "The Dove," in which Sophie played The Dove in an outrageous feather costume; "Minstrel Days" with Ted Lewis and Lester Allen, a skit in which Sophie wore blackface; a skit on "Movie Land," in which Sophie played a leading lady who could not remember her lines; and a travesty on "Gentlemen Prefer Blondes," in which Sophie played Lorelei; and a suggestive love interest, with Lewis and Allen again supporting Sophie in a series of songs such as she normally sang in cabarets. In the credits, Sophie's gowns were said to have been designed by an exclusive London clothier.

The show's first week in Milwaukee exceeded expectation. "Le Maire's Affairs" was hailed as "a tremendously beautiful and magnificent spectacle which ran four hours." That meant the show would have to be cut down to three hours at most, which eliminated a number of scenes. None of Sophie's "affairs" were dropped, which forced the producers to limit the number of encores she could sing. The Woods

Theater reported "extravagant" reservations for the first week of the show, and they suggested that "Affairs" could last all summer. Main floor seat prices were $3.85 on weeknights and $4.40 on Saturday nights. With the success of the show, ticket scalpers were selling the tickets for $5.50 and $6.50 respectively. Because of complaints from theatergoers, the City Council threatened to put the brokers out of business. Instead, theater owners promised to treat the public fairly by dividing the good seats between the box-office and brokers, and the brokers would charge only fifty cents more than box-office prices. There was no way theater owners wanted to inhibit the scalpers business, since their activities helped promote the show.

Neither critics nor patrons were disappointed with "Le Maire's Affairs," the show playing to full capacity at every performance (eight shows a week, matinees on Wednesday and Saturday). The *Variety* reviewer claimed "Affairs" was nothing short of a great show.

> It has everything. Scintillating stars, good principals, beautiful settings, effective lights, song, dance, comedy, drama and satire. Above all, satire. It pokes fun at reformers, Y.M.C.A. secretaries and other Comstockians, yet it has subtlety that allows no comeback.

Sophie was singled out as the star of "Affairs."

> The years have dealt kindly with Sophie Tucker. Though she still is the same blasé Sophie, a change has come over her. An air of refinement about her. More polished, more artistic than ever, yet, underneath it all, the same Soph. She comes near tying up the show more than once.[4]

An interesting sidelight was the special interest the Shuberts had about "Affairs," partly to determine its affect on their own productions in Chicago, but also to "spy" on the show's inner workings, particularly the relationship between Le Maire and his principals. Sam Gerson, head of the Shubert Chicago office, wrote a series of reports to J.J. Shubert assessing the success of "Affairs" during its first month, his sources unknown.

On July 14, his first letter told J.J. "Affairs" would definitely affect their own shows. At the first show, however, Gerson reported that, although it was a sellout, both Le Maire and Sophie had bought so many tickets between them that gross sales were down considerably. (As was her habit, Sophie gave tickets away to friends whom she invited to attend opening night.) "With a capacity of barely $30,000 for a week and equally high expenses, I don't see what chance he has of breaking even," wrote Gerson.[5]

Three days later, Gerson reported the that theater was not full at successive shows, that Sophie had reportedly advanced money to help out Le Maire, and that Sophie, Allen, and Lewis were "fighting among themselves."[6]

The following letters became even more conspiratorial. Bad weather killed the business; brokers were stuck with tickets that could not be returned; Lewis had complained he did not receive his salary on time. Regarding Sophie and Le Maire, Gerson declared: "She is not very friendly with Le Maire, and it would not surprise me a bit to see her leave the show soon." Gerson also revealed that Sophie had a clause in her contract permitting her to play at cabarets after the show had been playing in Chicago for a month.[7]

In contrast to Gerson's information, *Variety,* a usually reliable source for box-office information, kept reporting weekly sellouts for the show and no broker unhappiness.

On July 23, Gerson spoke to J.J. of a conversation he had with Sophie: "She told me she is getting a straight salary of $1,500 a week and five percent of the gross over $25,000 a week." According to Gerson, she also told him she was going to remain with the show to September, at which time she would return to New York and her nightclub. "She is not a bit hopeful about the show," Gerson said, "nor is she fooling herself about it."

His last letter, on July 26, claimed that Le Maire's financial condition was in jeopardy and the show was near to closing.

Whether Gerson actually perceived these events and interpreted the conversations correctly or whether he was giving J.J. a story he knew his boss would accept is difficult to determine. In spite of his dire predictions, "Affairs" continued to play at the Woods to full houses through August, September, and October, with Sophie, Ted Lewis, and Lester Allen continuing to head the cast.

Only critic Ashton Stevens had tart comments about Sophie's repertoire. "The revue is as big as Sophie Tucker," but he found the lyrics of some of her songs "reprehensible."

> If you don't believe that Sophie Tucker, whose "coon-shouting" used to flicker the incandescents and lift the carpet, has become an artist, just listen to her sing 'em without calling out the constabulary. "I'm a later-on momma," she warns her swain in number one: "don't you right-away me." While as a ditty rich with the retrospect of childhood, she sings: If they babied me now as they babied me then, oh how I'd like to be a baby again.[8]

Nevertheless, audiences loved everything Sophie could give them. The show, now going on two months, had advanced sales sufficient to carry it for another month.

Unknown to Sophie at the time, family, in the form of her son Bert, was about to invade the Chicago stage and create an episode filled with complicated and mixed emotions. Down the street, at the Oriental Theater, veteran Chicago producer Paul Ash was putting on a series of vaudeville revues called "Paul Ash's All Star Jazz Show," in which he featured both old-time stars and newcomers in conjunction with first-run motion pictures. At twenty-five cents a seat, it was truly bargain entertainment.

Apparently, in an attempt to take advantage of Sophie's huge popularity in Chicago and her current stage success, Ash booked Bert Tucker to make his debut in vaudeville. Bert had somehow, someplace learned to tap dance and had appeared in a number of amateur shows back East. When Sophie was informed of Bert's introduction to the professional stage, she publicly expressed great excitement; privately, there was trepidation. To watch Bert's first appearance, Amy Leslie and Sophie went to the Oriental. Indeed, Sophie seemed excited at the prospect of seeing her son perform.

When Ash came on stage after Bert had performed, he announced to the audience: "This young fellow is a grand little dancer; and besides, he had a great mother, one of the biggest stars in the business, playing around the corner — Sophie Tucker." At her name, the crowd applauded enthusiastically and a spotlight was focused on where she was sitting.

Sophie was seen to be both laughing and crying, talking out loud to anyone who might listen, and waving her white-gloved hands in the air. "Look at him," she exclaimed, "how nervous he is." In the meantime, Bert was smiling and bowing, while Ash urged him toward the footlights to address the audience.

"Gee, I'm glad you liked my little dance," he said hesitatingly. "My mother said she would come to see my first show." Then, looking earnestly into the audience, he called plaintively: "Ma? Ma, where are you?"

Sophie literally leapt out of the box and ran down the aisle, calling, "Here I am, son. I'm coming." And, speaking to everyone in the audience, as she approached the stage, she exclaimed, "Listen to him calling his Ma!"

The audience loved it all, stamping, shouting, and whistling its approval. The three, Sophie, Paul, and Bert, arm-in-arm, bowed to the audience. Then, with no apparent prompting (although Ash likely planned it), the orchestra struck up Sophie's song, "Some of These Days," and the audience shouted to have her sing it.

Bert played at the Oriental for two weeks. The first week, the newspapers billed him as "Sophie's son"; the second week they were calling him "Sophie Tucker's son and heir to her genius." In a *Daily News* interview, Bert said he vaguely remembered his father, who had died when he was a child, that he had lived a sheltered life under the eyes of his grandmother and aunt, and that he had been educated at military school. He admitted to trying out several jobs and having done many kinds of work since leaving Stamford Military Academy. Earning "real money" for his first act on stage, Bert believed he was now on "the main highway." Bert also got a photo and brief mention in the *Daily News* for donating a week's salary to the newspaper's Fresh Air Fund.[9]

Amy Leslie gave Bert a good review: "He has a fine voice and can dance like an inspired young demon." Ashton Stevens was less enthusiastic: "Sophie Tucker's cute son, Bert, dancing so well and singing so-so."

At the end of his engagement, Sophie took Bert to the train to return East. Answering reporter's questions about her son's stage debut, she simply replied, "I like my boy's work." She then returned to the hotel, where Al was waiting (he had not met Bert), to share a quick meal before going to the theater for her evening performance.

Even after ten weeks of crowded theaters and continued accolades for "Le Maire's Affairs," Ashton Stevens could not refrain from grumbling about Sophie's song lyrics. "Sophie remains unchanged from the old nights when her singing shamed the trombone and made the footlights flicker." As usual, Sophie did not respond to Stevens's caustic remarks. Instead, she sent him a ticket for the "Affairs'" 100th performance, at which advanced prices were charged. Stevens found himself completely surrounded by enthusiastic fans who especially cheered her suggestive lyrics.

In late September, when "Affairs" began to weaken at the box-office, Sophie announced she planned to double at the Rendezvous nightclub, beginning in a few weeks. For weeks, Rendezvous management had been negotiating with Sophie for the limited engagement. Finally, at a salary said to be the highest ever paid to a performer in any cafe' in the U.S., Sophie signed a limited contract, which was quickly announced to the public.

Le Maire was furious about her public announcement, but he could do little but fume. It was, after all, in her contract. Sophie attempted to placate him by promising to play at the Rendezvous for only two weeks, but Le Maire remained in a pique. To defend his show and to reassure audiences that Sophie was still with "Affairs," Le Maire took out a number of newspaper ads stating that "Miss Tucker is still one of the international stars at the Woods Theater." A week later, under her name in the ad for the show, he claimed that Sophie would "positively appear at every performance." The ads disappeared once Sophie concluded her engagement at the Rendezvous, but Le Maire's feelings about Sophie had definitely soured. The show finally closed at the Woods on November 27 (after 127 performances) to begin a tour of cities that was to culminate in a New York engagement.

> Le Maire's Affairs, at its departure, will have broken all records for length of run made by revues of its kind.[10]

Sophie, Ted Lewis, and Lester Allen remained the show's headliners.

Abe Erlanger had gained the right to book "Le Maire's Affairs" by bidding over a Shubert office. The Shuberts were reported to be "burned up," claiming that Le Maire still owed them money and therefore should have favored them with the booking. Erlanger's reaction to the Shubert claim suggested "they were desperately in need of attractions for their theaters" and would say anything to gain attention. Although it had been more than twenty years since Erlanger and Shubert vigorously competed with one another for shows and performers, the animosity between them remained. Erlanger had since shed his alliance with Marc Klaw and attempted to improve his reputation by booking the best, or most appealing, of theatrical productions, both popular and legitimate. Shubert, on the other hand, continued to maintain tight control over the family theatrical empire. Yet, movies, radio, phonograph records, and the lavish productions of Ziegfeld ("Showboat") and Lew Fields (Rodgers and Hart productions like "Connecticut Yankee"), were bringing unprecedented changes to popular entertainment, and the Shubert empire suffered sizable defections and financial stresses. Actually, the Shuberts were but a few years away from bankruptcy and collapse.

"Le Maire's Affairs" played well in St. Louis, Cincinnati, and Pittsburgh, with a plan to open in New York the middle of March. While box-office returns remained satisfactory, Le Maire's penchant for backstage intrigue continued. Frequent changes in the cast contributed to a more ragged show. Its length — the number of "affairs" presented — was reduced, making Sophie's appearances an even more important part of the presentation. For that, Sophie's salary was raised slightly, though not enough to satisfy her.

In February, when Le Maire discovered that the William Morris agency was negotiating on Sophie's behalf with two vaudeville circuits— a salary of $5,000 a week was rumored for Sophie's services— Le Maire "blew up." He demanded Sophie deny the rumors, which she refused to do. He wanted her to promise she would play the show in New York, a commitment she refused to make. In anger, Le Maire took Sophie's name off the marquee, apparently to humiliate her. In response to Le Maire's actions, Sophie informed him she was leaving the show before it reached New York, effectively scuttling it for Broadway. Le Maire fired Sophie and hired Charlotte Greenwood to replace her. Regarding her firing, Sophie told the press it was a matter of billing that had led to her decision. The real reason for the breakup was likely Le Maire's agitation regarding Sophie's lack of commitment to the show. Rumors suggested that he had "had it in for Sophie" since her appearances at the Rendezvous the previous September.

Morris talked with representatives of the Keith and Orpheum circuits about signing Sophie but was met with the usual salary snags. He was asking $5,000 a week for Sophie, and they were unwilling to take on the load due to the decline in all vaudeville box-office receipts. Vaudeville's primary competition these days was motion-picture houses, offering their newly constructed ornate palaces, featuring first-run movies, comfortable seating, reasonable prices, and one or two stage headliners to attract patrons. For the past several years, the old vaudeville houses had been feeling the effects of these new elegant theaters with flowing staircases, elaborately hung draperies, deep-piled carpets throughout, and ventilation that offered controlled comfort throughout the year. The increasing interest in motion pictures shown in such stylish surroundings increasingly seduced audiences away from vaudeville.

Indeed, Morris had already advised Sophie to make the move to picture houses over vaudeville. They paid higher salaries because they hired only one or two actors to fill the "live" part of their program.

So it was not surprising that Morris soon announced that Sophie had signed with the Pantages circuit for the requisite salary of $5,000 a week. She was to open in Minneapolis in March. (Incidentally, "Le Maire's Affairs" opened in New York to mixed reviews and closed in four weeks.) No sooner had Sophie appeared in Minneapolis and Detroit, however, than she was called back to New York to open in a show that had already been going on for sixteen weeks and needed "new blood." The "never-give-up" Shuberts had contacted Morris with an offer to start Sophie at $5,000 a week plus a percentage of the gross (likely a first for the Shuberts) to appear in "Gay Paree," a revue currently playing at the Winter Garden. Morris called Alexander Pantages and asked him to delay Sophie's tour until she completed the Shubert assignment. Pantages agreed; but he stipulated that Sophie had to return to the tour by

May 14, giving her two months with "Gay Paree." Not surprisingly, the Shuberts were not told of this conditional agreement.

"Gay Paree's" business had fallen below $25,000 a week, well below what the Shuberts considered a break-even point. When newly hired Sophie and Ben Bernie's band went on stage March 30, Lee Shubert was said to have watched the show "with his finger nails badly damaged by his teeth." He became particularly annoyed when Sophie, during a closing speech, introduced some guests from the audience, namely Ted Lewis and Lester Allen from "Le Maire's Affairs." When the audience expressed their enthusiasm for Sophie's performance, however, Shubert was said to be relieved. Included in the revised show was comedian Chic Sale, an old vaudeville star, and two newcomers to the stage: Oscar Levant played piano in Bernie's band; and George Raft did a Charleston number in one of the acts.

On May 15, the 1927 summer version of "Gay Paree" opened at the Garrick Theater in Chicago, with Sophie heading the cast. The show's openly suggestive elements caused some reviews of it to be laced with sarcasm and ridicule.

> Nude is the watchword of this Winter Garden revue, and nude are the songs of its featured singing woman, the impassioned Sophie Tucker. The show had the nudest scenes that Messrs. Shubert have ever staged. Sophie sang straight from the chest as of yore; she hit hard and was a hard hit.[11]

Obviously, some critics were appalled at the show's sensationalism, although their comments did not seem to deter record box-office sales.

In contrast, the formidable Amy Leslie scribed her usual lavish prose in support of Sophie and the show.

> There's lots of fun, lots of beauty, lots of just Sophie Tucker in 'Gay Paree'; and it is a splendid show through and through, even when it is rough and raw at the edges, because it is all well done.
> She (Sophie) is immense in several bits and has a half-dozen capital songs and as many scenes. Her costumes are studies of loveliness and she is in great fettle, singing better than she has in two years and having Ted Shapiro at the piano to help her, and he always seems her inspiration.[12]

Not to be outdone, the ubiquitous Ashton Stevens continued his sniping at Sophie and the show, "at their nakedest." He was disappointed he could not censor Sophie's lines of "undraped ballads of the chocolate half-life." Stevens sarcastically observed that Sophie had a way of singing such songs that was at once sincere, humorous, and vulgar. "I mean honestly and unaffectedly vulgar. Although she is certainly the heart and lungs of the show," he declared, "she may be depended upon to make vulgarity funny."[13]

Interestingly enough, in contrast to previous Chicago police actions against "obscene" shows, "Gay Paree" was never disturbed by the police; nor did it arouse any negative outcries from the city's moral arbiters. Moral indignation over theater presentations had certainly mellowed during the past few years.

"Gay Paree" played to such good audiences, the Shuberts persuaded Pantages to delay Sophie's departure from the show until September. Because of theater booking conflicts, "Gay Paree" was moved to the Four Cohans Theater the middle of June. The change of venues, however, caused some problems with the principal performers. In their original contracts, it had been stipulated that the principals would be afforded large type on the marquee. Unfortunately, the Four Cohans' marquee was small, limiting both the size and quantity of type available. Unavoidably, the names of a number of performers were omitted. They threatened legal action to compel compliance with their contracts, and the debate was quickly tied up in court. To avoid confrontation, the Shuberts asked for continuance after continuance.

To add to the confusion, William Morris, Jr., visited Sophie to remind her of the Pantages agreement, now scheduled to begin in September. He also announced that Sophie was going to play in England in the fall, which sent theatrical heads spinning. At first, there was no answer from Morris as to how Sophie could keep her date with Pantages and go to England at the same time. Finally, under pressure, Morris stated that Sophie would likely leave for Europe after her "Gay Paree" engagement, which, to no one's surprise, caused Pantages to accuse Sophie of breaking her contract with his circuit.

In late August, "Gay Paree" was moved back to the Garrick Theater; and the impending lawsuits about marquee name size disappeared. This time, the Shuberts could not persuade Sophie to remain with the show. Instead, the Pantages people had been assured that Sophie would perform for them as scheduled; and the European trip was indefinitely postponed, if it had ever really been booked. During Sophie's last official week with the show, even with increased ticket prices, crowds jammed the theater. Her final performance literally did away with the show's script. She remained on stage during the entire time; she played in every scene; she danced with the "naked" chorus; and she added a number of familiar songs to the array, urging the audience to sing along with her. Finally, amid a panoply of floral bouquets and cast members, Sophie gave a brief farewell speech that had everyone in the theater crying. She bowed, kissed everyone around her, and, to the audience, said, "I'll be back soon." Ardent cheers and applause followed her offstage.

On September 17, 1927, Sophie's Pantages tour finally returned to the boards, opening in Spokane, Washington. Two weeks later, she visited San Francisco, to the delight of full houses. Interestingly, Frisco newspapers labeled Sophie a "blues champion," based on her selection of songs. "The audience liked Sophie," the *Chronicle* reported, "and there could be no doubt about that." Sophie's engagement in Los Angeles was equally successful; the press there also referred to her as a blues singer.

> Capturing all honors for recent receptions at the Pantages Theater was Sophie Tucker. Her ballads were lovely, and there is no disputing the fact that she is in a class of her own when it comes to singing blues.[14]

With new songs and new gowns, Sophie and Ted entertained for a second week in Los Angeles. While in town, Sophie was approached to appear in a Lon Chaney picture currently being shot, but her high salary demands precluded any deal. Tod

Browning had sent a representative to see Sophie, and he came back with the $5,000 figure. Instead, the studio got a character actress from central casting to take the role. At the same time, Sophie participated in a Halloween actors' benefit at the Mayan Theater with an assortment of Hollywood movie stars. It was also revealed that she was negotiating to purchase the Montmartre Club in Hollywood. Both Morris and Phil quickly warned her of the problems of running a nightclub as an absentee landlord.

Sophie's next engagement demanded a long jump to Chicago for a three-week run at Balaban and Katz picture houses (some of the most sumptuous built at the time) for a reported salary of $5,500 a week. Again, she was taken by surprise to find that Bert was going to appear on stage in Chicago at the same time, moreover, at one of the theaters she was scheduled to play. *Variety* covered the mother/son bill attentively.

> She's so different, so vivacious, such an utter knockout, Sophie Tucker has traveled from the pinnacle of vaude to the uppermost heights of the picture house field, showing and proving that anyone can do the same without injuring prestige. Tucker has not changed her routine or mannerisms in the least. She continues to fire a fast string of inimitable numbers. She skimmed through half a dozen, wowed after each, then encored as many.[15]

Of Bert and Sophie, *Variety* reported:

> Local arrangements of Miss Tucker were accompanied by no little sentiment. Bert, her son, is with her, though as a single. He's a very much improved youngster and he needed his mother more then than now. But she still comes in quite handy.[16]

10

Honky Tonk

Unfortunately, the ebullient accolades Sophie received from Chicago's ardent admirers lent only short-lived euphoria to what was to become a turbulent year. It began auspiciously enough for Sophie when, in early 1928, she cheerfully announced to the always eager press that she and Ted Lewis had bought the Vernon Country Club in Los Angeles. The club had been in business for several years but, under various managements, had produced unsatisfactory results. Sophie and Ted planned to convert the venue into a nightclub and run it themselves during the summer, but they immediately ran into city zoning laws prohibiting late closings. Lawyers found they could do little about the zoning laws other than obtain an OK from the city to provide entertainment. Meanwhile, a considerable amount of Sophie's money was tied up in the purchase and ensuing litigation, a fact that would soon have negative impact on her finances.

Sophie had to return to New York to fulfill an engagement at the Paramount Theater (leased by Pantages). There, she found, to her astonishment, that Bert was to appear on the same bill. Even William Morris had not known about the billing; but when he discovered the situation, he immediately contacted the Pantages booking people to change the arrangement. His argument was that, by billing the Tuckers together, both would be hurt by audience reactions to their acts. Even more importantly, Morris did not want Sophie upstaged by her son. Yet, not only was his request refused, the Paramount manager purposely promoted the mother-son combination in their ads. Moreover, he planned to have Bert introduce his mother's act.

When Sophie was told of the arrangement, she became so bothered she threatened to walk out of the engagement. Morris interceded. "Think what this would signify to the audience," he cautioned. "Are you afraid of being upstaged? Don't you care about your son's career?"

Reluctantly, Sophie agreed to perform; but the painful history of Bert's care and upbringing surfaced again and preyed on her emotions. Did she really want Bert to succeed or not? Or was it guilt for having abandoned Bert that really troubled her?

Even before she could deal with these issues, *Variety* added another dimension to her conflicted reasoning.

> There's a doubt if the audience wants to know that Sophie Tucker has a grown-up son; and even if they don't care, the son should not be his mother's advance agent on the same stage.[1]

It is very likely that all of these factors played a role in Sophie's emotional turmoil, but the age factor appeared the most obvious to audiences. In an attempt to offset possible perceptions of competition between them, they appeared together in one number, Sophie singing, Bert dancing, which was reported to have delighted audiences. Nonetheless, *Variety* continued its appraisal of the situation by pointing out that Bert was as tall as his mother, "and everyone around was asking, 'How old is she?'"

To Sophie and Morris's further consternation, they discovered that Bert was also booked to appear on the same bill in Newark and Philadelphia. Hastily, Morris had Sophie's contract modified so that the two would not appear together again on the tour. In fact, there is no evidence to suggest that Bert continued to appear on the Pantages circuit after Philadelphia. Had someone been responsible for the "coincidence?"

No sooner had the engagement with Bert been "handled," than Sophie suffered another shock when Phil informed her that, due to her recent purchase of the nightclub in Los Angeles and her long-standing financial losses from the closed Cleveland cabaret, her current liabilities were greater than her assets. Sophie had inadvertently overextended her finances or, more likely, had paid little attention to them for some time.

Big, bold headlines in New York newspapers proclaimed: "Sophie Tucker bankrupt!" Then, with no real evidence, the newspapers went on to speculate why it had happened "to our Soph." The more knowledgeable *Variety* suggested that the Cleveland cabaret misadventure had been the primary reason for her bankruptcy. Other newspapers were not so kind, some claiming her profligate spending on gowns and jewelry had led to her undoing. Not surprisingly, a moralistic reporter in Chicago blamed Sophie's stage deportment as the probable cause of her financial demise. A bit of anti–Semitism also crept in when it was mentioned by a reviewer that Jews in theater often found it hard to manage their new-found money.

As much as the story made headlines for several days, within a week it had disappeared from the newspapers. Between Sophie's bookings, at $5,000 a week, and Morris's behind the scenes efforts, no one any longer seemed to be worried about her liabilities, whatever they happened to be. Still, Sophie was ashamed about the episode and its public exposure; and she swore never again to suffer from such an embarrassment.

At her stage appearance the following week, the audience stood up and applauded her entrance and shouted for a speech. Ironically, the *Variety* reviewer dedicated most of his report to Sophie's new gown. So much for Sophie's bankruptcy.

Any embarrassments and personal discomforts were quickly dispelled for both Sophie and her admirers when William Morris announced that Sophie was booked to appear in London at the end of April, for appearances at the Kit Kat Club and possible doubling at the Coliseum. In addition, Sophie publicly announced sister Anna's wedding and promised the "grandest wedding any girl ever had." In her autobiography, Sophie said she had promised her mother she would give a sumptuous wedding for the sister who had raised her son. "Now I would make good on that promise."[2] A newspaper wag asked where the money was coming from to pay for Anna's wedding and the London trip, but he was quickly admonished by Sophie's admirers to "get lost."

Anna's March 31st wedding was a three-story affair, held at the Challes Hall on 57th Street in New York City. Leaving all their coats and wraps on the ground floor, the men and boys provided yarmulkes, guests ascended to the second floor. As she sat at the head table overseeing the activities, Sophie kept pointing at the about soon-to-be newlyweds and repeating: "I'm not the bride. There she is, over there. That's my sister, Annie." Anna was married to Julius Aronson, a businessman from Auburn, New York. After the ceremony, they moved to the back of the hall to receive congratulations and considerable kisses. From more than two hundred guests, many of whom had not seen one another for decades, kissing and weeping commingled uninhibitedly.

Up another flight of stairs, in the dining room, Sophie took over. She told family stories and joked with Lillian Shaw, who acted as emcee; but she was prevented from singing by the entire family, who, instead, had Eddie Elkin's orchestra play dance music. Still, Sophie received a loud vote of thanks from the revelers. The party ran late; the champagne flowed freely; and no police bothered the happy scene. The ever-present *Variety* covered the wedding and gave an award of merit to Sophie for having hosted so splendid an affair.

Sophie wore clothing like this when she played London. She literally stopped traffic, and dozens of women followed her to see what she bought when she went shopping.

If you're lucky enough to be invited to anything staged by Sophie, don't miss it. Whether it's a Christmas tree, a birthday party, or a wedding that is "under the personal direction of Sophie," it always means S.R.O. She put on real Hippodrome stuff. There was no crying at this wedding, only love, life, and laughter. It was an intimate affair of a few hundred relatives and closest friends. Enough wit and talent to build a revue. Jack Yellin insists it was the first time he ever met Sophie when she hadn't asked him for an opening song. And Sophie stoutly denies that the RSVP on the wedding invitations meant "Remember Send Vedding Presents."[3]

Two weeks later, Sophie, Ted, and the entourage embarked for London on the *Aquitania*. London knew she was coming. Met at the train station by hoards of admirers, led by a motorcade to her hotel, and greeted by a brass band at the entrance to the Savoy, Sophie was made to feel right at home. It was reported that she had been accorded the warmest welcome ever extended to an artist returning to London.

At the Kit Kat Club, Sophie performed for forty minutes, fifteen minutes of new songs and twenty-five minutes of old, familiar ones. During the familiar songs, Sophie simply stood, while the entire audience sang them for her. With flowers and speeches overwhelming the stage, "if Sophie hadn't begged off the audience, she would still be there." At the end of the show, many kisses passed between Sophie and London theater people; yet she wondered why no one noticed that she had bobbed her hair.

In a brief, recitative speech, Sophie responded to the welcome by adapting to the occasion the verse and chorus of "Last of the Red Hot Mamas"; and the audience roared its approval. Her speech was filled with topical allusions, enhanced by Sophie's usual dramatic expressions.

Verse

It may sound like a platitude,
But I must express my gratitude
For the welcome that's accorded me so clearly.
For I am so glad to be here,
And the way you've greeted me here,
I can only say I thank you most sincerely;
It's all my fault, and I did wrong
In staying away from you so long.
Look what's happened while I was gone.
How the boys on the flagships have been carrying on;
Affairs in Egypt haven't been so well;
And look at the Rubber Market — all shot to hell.
And if I'd been here, I'm telling you
I'd have put some pep into that Oxford crew.
And look at the King of Afghanistan,
What a predicament for a red-hot man!
He brought his own wife to England — dear, oh, dear!
He wouldn't have had to if I'd been here.

> Sorry I missed Mr. Churchill's budget, gee,
> He'd never have put a tax on petrol if he'd met me!
> Still, cheer up you men,
> Remember, the more babies you have, the less you pay;
> And if I can help you at all, why ring me up any day.
> Well, anyway, I'm back again
> To educate the women and entertain the men.
> Sweet sugar-papas, cast me that lovin' eye
> And treat your Sophie pretty; let me tell you why:
>
> Chorus
> 'Cause I'm the last of the red-hot mamas,
> They've all cooled down but me,
> Those red-hot, flamin' mamas that were once reputed
> For liquid-fire lovin' that was undiluted,
> All these modern flappers,
> They're just whippersnappers,
> They can't compare with me.
> They pet and kiss and hug and don't know what it's all about.
> When I kiss men, they feel they've had their tonsils taken out.
> And I'm the last of the red-hot mamas
> Gettin' hotter, hotter all the time![4]

Sophie's stay at the Kit Kat Club was a complete sellout. Moving to the larger Winter Garden, results were similar, with the added benefit of the attendance of society people and royalty in the theater audience, eager to make Sophie's acquaintance. Newspaper coverage of Sophie was as lengthy in the social columns as in the theater pages. Sir Oswald Stoll, longtime arbiter of British theatrical morals, was questioned as to why he had not warned Sophie about using certain forbidden words on stage. A reporter jokingly attributed the oversight to Sir Oswald's selective deafness. Lady Louis Mountbatten went three nights in succession to see Sophie. At one performance, even the Earl of Birkenhead was seen at the theater with the Lord Chancellor's stepson. According to the *Variety* correspondent, "Sophie seems to be having a fat time."[5]

But all was not glowing for Sophie. A visit by the income-tax man — England now levied taxes on foreigners who earned money in the country — made Sophie ill enough to spend a weekend at Margate to recuperate. Nevertheless, she was followed by the tax man wherever she performed, the determined official collecting all that was owed to the Crown.

Back in London, Sophie continued her appearances at the Alhambra Theater, after which she was scheduled to tour the "provinces." Instead, she moved to the Victoria Palace for a week and then took a week's vacation (with Al) in Deauville, France. There she was besieged by agents wishing to sign her for French engagements. Sophie's

10. Honky Tonk

response, however, was that they offered her "peanuts and popcorn" to sing. Instead, she offered her services to charity; and the Belgian resort of Ostend quickly took her up on it for a weekend gala benefit.

Returning to England, Sophie began her tour of the country, which included weeks in Leeds, Manchester, and Glasgow, before coming back to appear at the Holborn Empire, London, prior to her departure for the U.S. Before leaving, however, she and the tax man again had a serious get-together.

William Morris met Sophie at the dock in New York, partly to congratulate her on another successful British tour and partly to inform her that Warner Brothers had expressed interest in featuring her in a talking, and singing, motion picture. Would she be interested? Sophie asked only: "When do I start?"

On September 4, 1928, Sophie signed her first movie contract to appear in Warner Brothers' "Honky Tonk." She was expected to report on the set in early 1929. Her contract called for a salary of $5,750 a week for six weeks work, with an option for another picture. *Variety* dropped a short note that the "Red Hot Mamma" of stage had been signed for a moving picture.

To no one's surprise, Sophie's first U.S. appearance was at the Palace Theater. Billed now as the "Last of the Red-Hot Mamas" (William Morris, Jr.'s, idea), Sophie appeared on stage for twenty-two minutes, a relatively short turn for her. *Variety* bemoaned her brief outing by lamenting that "vaudeville needs her dynamic personality." For this opening, Sophie performed skits and vignettes as introductions to the songs she sang.

"Last of the Red-Hot Mamas" was recited in the same manner she had introduced it to English audiences, although

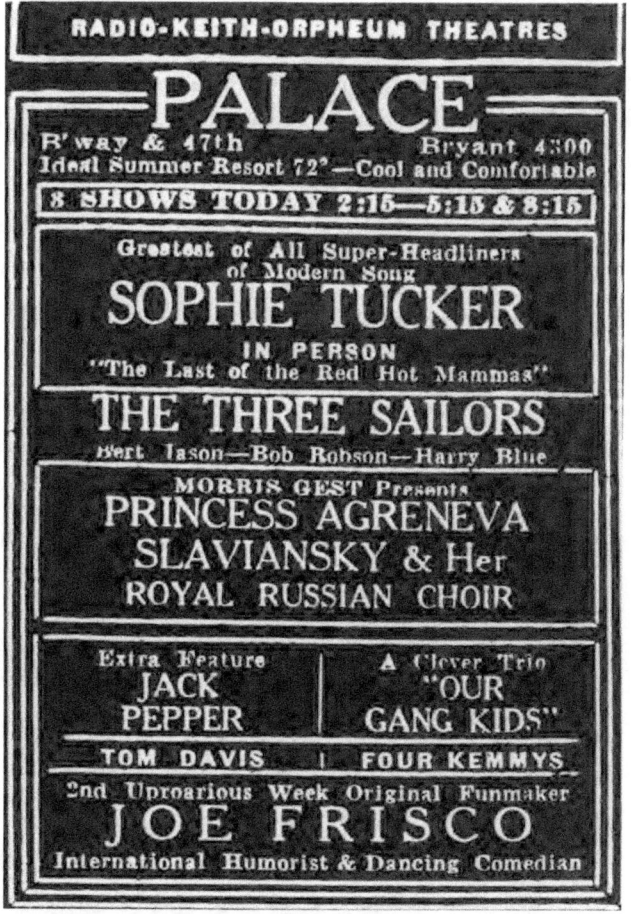

By the late 1920s, Sophie had acquired the sobriquet "The Last of the Red Hot Mamas." The Palace Theater bill also called her the "greatest of all super-headliners," at a time when a dying vaudeville needed all the star-power superlatives it could invent.

now substituting American topical issues. Interspersed with the lyrics were comments on her trip, her joy at being back topping the Palace bill, and her opinion that a woman should be President. Her second number, "Pleasure Man," told of a man who kept house and washed the dishes for her. Between songs, she and Ted kidded eager song pluggers and the present mania among music publishers to sell theme songs for motion pictures. One joke was about seeing a song plugger with a sack of oats taking Tom Mix's horse for a ride.

She regaled the audience with tales of how she had rehearsed her present act. Next, a young married woman came to visit and told of her date with a "Sleeky Greek Romeo." Sophie sang "Forgetting Vows": and the young woman left, weeping, to seek reconciliation with her husband. Then, Sophie ended the set with a series of familiar numbers, including "Some of These Days." The use of vignettes and dialogue to introduce songs was becoming an increasingly familiar device, and audiences seemed to enjoy the stories and informal repartee between Sophie and Ted.

Before leaving for a Chicago engagement in early November, Sophie recorded "Yiddishe Mama" for Columbia, in both English and Yiddish. The song became an immediate hit. Like "Red Hot Mamma," this song soon became a standard encore and crowd-pleaser.

The *Chicago Herald and Examiner* reported "the largest advance sale in the history of the Palace Theater" for Sophie's return visit.

> Sophie came home to the Palace yesterday and chanted her rapture to the adoring crowd, when she sang:
>
>> When I and many others who
>> struggled up the hill
>> Learned the thrill of triumph — to
>> play to a Palace bill![6]

"She was just a great big Jazz Queen giving the crowd just what it wanted," said the newspaper. "There is only one Sophie Tucker."

Sophie's longtime spokeswoman, Amy Leslie, called her audience "noisily affectionate," noting that they had been howling, clapping, and stamping their feet for her entire act. In her review, Leslie concluded:

> Sophie Tucker is one of the greatest comediennes and rough-and-tumble singers this country or any other ever produced, and she is at the height of her singularly triumphant career.[7]

Sophie packed the Palace to such an overpowering capacity, she was held over for a second sold-out week. Newspapers called her "Chicago's favorite; a queen."

To everyone's surprise, Sophie and Al were married on the way from Chicago to Boston. As Sophie reported the singular event in her autobiography, the marriage seemed to resemble her previous forays into matrimony. "We had waited and put it off, hoping for a time when he would be established in some business of his own, but it seemed as though that time would never come. We loved each other very much and wanted to be together, so I said to myself, even though it was against my better judgment, why wait?"[8]

Finding Newport, Kentucky, the nearest location for quick marriages, they drove there and, on December 14, 1928, were wed by a Justice of the Peace. Al Lackey was described as a New York dress merchant, age thirty-eight (?), living at the Park Central Hotel in New York City, although he had been Sophie's constant companion for the past three years. Sophie claimed she had Al acting as her personal manager because "he was smart about show business." Yet it was questionable what more he could have contributed to Sophie's success beyond what the Morris agency already offered. Sophie chose not to reveal their marriage until January, when the couple arrived in Los Angeles, where Sophie was to begin her film for Warners.

At the same time, she also admitted to a "few alterations" to her face. "Just a little fat and loose skin off the face," she explained. "That galvanizing of fat and loose skin is strictly business. After all," she stated, "I have to look younger for pictures."[9]

Reviewing the events of the past year at their New Year's Eve party, Sophie and Al's first social event since arriving in Los Angeles, Sophie held the opinion that the year had been one of the most emotionally unsettling she had experienced since her early days in the theater — from the embarrassing lows of bankruptcy to the euphoric highs of consorting with British royalty, from the discomfort of sharing the stage with Bert (am I really getting that old?) to the exhilaration of Anna's wedding (as her parents would have wanted it), and finally her own wedding (against her better judgment).

Now an established and veteran headliner, the "Last of the Red-Hot Mamas" (she liked the phrase, she admitted), Sophie considered where her future career might take her. Vaudeville, as one had known it, was nearly dead. Cabarets and nightclubs had been struggling. Many old-time stars had passed on. Stage work had been taking on different dimensions with the increasing popularity of more sophisticated musical comedy. Movies appeared to be in the process of overwhelming all the rest of popular entertainment. Whither Sophie? she wondered.

With some trepidation, Sophie reported to Warner Brothers to begin her movie career. Friends had already warned her of the long, boring waits between scenes; the repeated takes until the director convinced himself he had captured the proper scene; the constant, daily changes in script material; and the long hours of shooting. No sooner had she arrived at the studio than she was shunted off to be made-up, clutching a script she was to memorize prior to her first screen test.

When Sophie was presented with the picture's proposed musical numbers, she rejected them, feeling that none of them made sufficient use of her persona and gift for putting across a song. Instead, she requested that Ager and Yellin be hired to write her songs. Since the Warners had not featured singing in previous films, they were dubious. "All of this fuss over a couple of song writers," they groused. "Let 'em stay home." In response to the brothers' apparent indifference to her request, Sophie declared that she wouldn't "talk to a mike without her boys to write for it." After a brief discussion, Ager and Yellin were hired to write Sophie's music. Out they came

A lobby poster featuring Sophie in her first movie, "Honky Tonk." The movie was considered average, but Sophie's singing was praised by critics. Still, Sophie was not pleased with her performance, nor the way the studio treated her.

to Los Angeles to assist Sophie for six weeks, at $8,500 a week, more than what Sophie herself was earning. Sophie also called for William Morris, Jr., to be available to negotiate any disagreements.

Actual shooting of "Honky Tonk" began the second week of January, and Sophie quickly discovered that elements of the plot could have paralleled portions of her own life. She was even given the film name of Sophie, an obvious attempt by the studio to capitalize on her audience appeal. Sophie's singing numbers went well — "Last of the Red-Hot Mamas" was included after some argument — but the talking scenes frustrated her. Not used to following a script, Sophie found it confining to meet the rigid requirements dictated by the director. Lloyd Bacon was a veteran director, but he had never worked with a performer like Sophie. They were reported to have a respectful relationship, but long discussions regarding her acting caused Sophie chagrin and disappointment at her own inability to conform to the "rules of acting." Though her part in the film was completed by the end of February, as the schedule demanded, Sophie was not entirely pleased with the picture, nor with her role in it.

An interesting factor resulting from the hiring of outside composers for "Honky Tonk" was an announcement by Warner Brothers that they were putting under contract eight Tin Pan Alley writers for a song-writing department that would supply theme-song material for all upcoming productions. Writers hired included such

Broadway figures as Ray Perkins, Harry Akst, Al Dubin, and Herman Ruby. Another event of note was the report that one of the national magazines was planning to publish Sophie's life story, likely an attempt to tie in with the movie.

A week after completing her movie assignment, Sophie returned to the stage, opening at the Orpheum Theater in San Francisco. Both she and the audience seemed glad of her return to the more spontaneous medium.

> Her first stage entrance was hailed with thunderous applause, and her exit by a veritable shower of gorgeous flowers, from which it may be gleaned that Sophie's friends and admirers were present among the audience in numbers. Or else, that in audiences which greet Sophie Tucker may always be found a host of those who like her lusty songs and her forthright comments on life.[10]

Two weeks later, at the Orpheum in Los Angeles, Sophie was likewise met with enthusiastic crowds and prosperous box offices.

> Closing the first part, Sophie Tucker in person, surrounded by Ted Shapiro, turned in one of the best turns she has ever permitted Milt Ager and Jack Yellin to write. Sophie credited everyone and plugged "Glad Rag Doll" in a nifty scene. She also plugged her Warner picture, "Honky Tonk," that they say at the studio is OK.
> Soph was an easy panic for 45 minutes. Her current act intact should be waltzed right into the Palaces, New York and Chicago.[11]

Before returning to New York, Sophie spent another week in San Francisco and Los Angeles to great success; then she made intermediate stops in Minneapolis and Chicago. The Minneapolis reviewer called her forty-minute act "dazzling."

> Miss Tucker made it manifest that her sole occupancy of the feverish feminine spotlight has not dampened her proclivity for gingery song and patter. In a silver shimmery gown and with very blond hair, this "red hot mama" made quite a dazzling appearance. Applause returns immense.[12]

At the Chicago Orpheum, Sophie shared the billing with her old friends the Howard Brothers; the event became a week-long reunion, filled with old stories, familiar songs, and plenty of nostalgia.

> If Pulitzer awards were given for vaud acts living up to their billing, Sophie Tucker would be first in line. All around it is Sophie, "last of the red hot mamas," charging into a lyrical conquest of males with her voice in a barrel and sex appeal in a showcase. She's a department of show business, complete in itself.[13]

As old friend Amy Leslie described Sophie's act: "When Sophie arrived on stage, she seemed to bring an intimacy with each individual in the audience. She told a story and made them believe it, and that is one of her many fascinations. She is a magnificent saleslady, and she has more to sell than any entertainer before the public."[14]

Chicago's audiences loved her songs, from the new ones, like the ballads "I'm

Funny That Way" and "If I Had You," to the familiar "Red Hot Mamma" and her usual encore, "Some of These Days." Her promises to the crowd had turned to fulfillment, said the *Daily News,* and the audience embraced her with heartfelt adoration.

Sophie and "Honky Tonk" arrived in New York simultaneously.

"Honky Tonk" was classified as an all-dialogue film with songs. It was directed by Lloyd Bacon, with story by Leslie S. Barrows. Five songs were featured: "I'm the Last of the Red Hot Mamas"; "I'm Doin' What I'm Doin' for Love"; "He's a Good Man to Have Around"; "I'm Feathering a Nest for a Little Bluebird"; and "I Don't Want to Get Thin." All of the songs were written by Ager and Yellin. Larry Ceballos was dance director.

Sophie Leonard (Sophie Tucker), singer of "hot mamma" songs in a New York nightclub, says she is retiring. Her daughter, Beth (Lila Lee), returns from Europe unaware of her mother's occupation. She arrives in a limousine with a school chum, Jean Gilmore (Audrey Ferris), who also is the sister of Freddie Gilmore (George Duryea). Beth is shocked at the condition of her mother's home. In turn, Sophie reprimands her daughter for attending wild parties with Freddie. In a change of heart, Sophie tells Jim (Mahlon Hamilton) that, while she dislikes cafe' life, she will remain at her nightclub job. Freddie takes Beth to the nightclub; and, surprised to see her mother working there, Beth renounces her and moves out of the house. Thanks to Jim's intervention, Freddie asks Sophie's permission to marry Beth. He then persuades Beth that she has treated her mother cruelly, causing Beth to change her opinion. Sophie agrees to Freddie and Beth's wedding plans; and, a year later, Sophie is a grandmother.

Sime, of *Variety,* believed Sophie had done a good job as a first-time actor, although the picture itself was bad.

> Sophie Tucker is "Honky Tonk" and because of that, with her songs, must draw in the regular picture houses. Warners picked Sophie because she can sing songs. It was Harry Warner who did the picking. Soph is given a simple, idiotic story, but one she can play as a first-timer. It's better for Soph and the Warners to be simple and idiotic the first time than a flop for all time. This picture is bad, but the judgment and Soph great.[15]

Sime also pointed out that all of Sophie's lines in the picture had been specially written by Jack Yellin (as opposed to the rest of the script); and, as was characteristic with veteran performers, all of the other actors had deferred to Sophie during the shooting.

The *New York Times* critic was not quite as generous, citing Sophie for playing the role as well as could be expected, given the poor script, but calling the acting trite and some of the scenes questionable.

> Miss Tucker, as Sophie Leonard, plays her role with vehemence, pathos and a little fun, but she is handicapped by some lines in the dialogue. It is a picture of which one might say that those with whom Miss Tucker has found favor probably will appreciate it.[16]

According to *Variety*'s weekly box-office results, "Honky Tonk" played to good audiences. A six-month comparison of expenses to gross income showed that "Honky Tonk" had cost $250,000 to produce and had grossed more than $450,000 domestically. Yet, a month after "Honky Tonk" was released, Sophie's option for a second picture was not renewed. No reasons were given for the decision. Nevertheless, the picture gave Sophie a great deal of publicity for her continued stage appearances.

A return to the Palace assured the public that Sophie still loved to entertain audiences there.

> In her current turn, Soph is saying: "Rome wasn't built in a day; Tucker wasn't made in a night." That's a typical Tuckerism. No one else could say it the way Soph does and make them think its funny. Almost every notice begins by stating Sophie is back with brand new songs. And that's more important than anything—perhaps Sophie Tucker's most notable feat. It has never been surpassed by anyone, not even tied. When Soph stops coming back with a new act, she will have stopped being Sophie Tucker.[17]

To tie in her stage appearances with the movie, a full-page advertisement appeared in *Variety* July 3, promoting the songs that Ager and Yellen had written for her and featuring several positive reviews from New York critics, as well as a list of retail locations where records of these songs could be purchased. According to record retailers, the ad was an excellent selling device.

"Honky Tonk" played in theaters in large cities across the country through October. After sold-out stage performances in New York and Boston theaters, Sophie quit the Keith tour in Atlantic City when the manager, an Albee employee, objected to the lyrics of a song she was singing.

Sophie was playing at the Palace, Chicago, when the stock market collapse shocked the country. Within hours, theater attendance declined; some theaters closed; and touring company visits were abruptly canceled. Sophie switched her appearances to the Green Mill, a nightclub in Chicago, to attract larger crowds. Nonetheless, as in the rest of the country, local theater business plummeted into paralysis.

11

Escape to London

Sophie was in her second day of the engagement at the Palace, Chicago, when the stock market crashed — Black Tuesday historians would call it. Whereas her Monday appearance had generated a house full of enthusiastic patrons, Tuesday evening found the theater less than half-full. Meager applause did little to inspire the performers. The theater manager and cast knew of the event — radio and newspapers headlined the stock market debacle in their evening editions — but no one had any idea how the news would affect theater attendance. They quickly found out.

By the end of the week, the Palace reported its worst box-office receipts since the theater had opened. The attendance Tuesday proved to be no oddity; attendance for the rest of the week was barely able to duplicate Tuesday's result. Through it all, Sophie played as if she had a full house but later admitted that "one could hear all the echoes." Like a number of other theaters in Chicago, the Palace decided to shut down for a week to see what was going to happen.

Cognizant of the event's implications for popular theater performers — no performance meant no pay — Sophie agreed to play at the Green Mill restaurant (actually a nightclub), on Chicago's North Side for a four-week engagement. She had to agree to a salary below what she normally received because the owners were apprehensive about anyone's, even Sophie's, ability to attract crowded houses. Sophie felt that the four-week run would give her a better idea of what might happen to show biz. At the same time, William Morris was hard at work finding bookings for Sophie for the remainder of the year. At the moment, no thought was being given to what 1930 might bring.

The Green Mill owner wanted Sophie to stay longer, but she claimed to have commitments in Florida and England. Actually, the trip to Florida was to see Al, who was recovering from pneumonia, which had seriously threatened his life. Although he was now almost fully recovered, doctors suggested that he remain in Florida for several months more. After a short visit, Sophie returned to New York to begin a short tour on the struggling Loew circuit. A proposed trip to London in March had been delayed until June.

There was no question that, among the many headliners affected by recent economic events, Sophie's reputation helped her in obtaining future engagements. After finishing at the Green Mill, Morris got her a two-week appearance at the Mounds Country Club, East St. Louis, Illinois, and a return to Chicago at the Oriental Theater. After the beginning of the new year, Morris had made a deal with the Loew circuit, the only one at the time booking tours, to play Sophie in its theaters until the end of May, at her current weekly salary. Everyone recognized it was not going to be an easy route, what with all the uncertainties in the business. With theaters closing, touring companies stalled, and many actors dropped from already contracted jobs, who knew what the next several weeks might portend for Sophie?

When Sophie appeared at the Oriental in Chicago in January, she received the usual excellent notices; but the theater itself was almost empty at every performance. To supplement her income, Morris got Sophie to appear on a radio program — on station KYW, owned by Balaban and Katz. She was to sing four songs, all familiar old-timers. She shared the hour-long program with a saxophone soloist and Spitalny's Chicago Theater orchestra. For this appearance, Sophie received $1,250.

She then moved on to the Marbro Theater to headline a revue called "Hello Sophie," accompanied by a Vitaphone movie. During her second performance, she became ill — a severe toothache was reported — and was taken to a hospital for treatment. Two teeth were removed, and Sophie spent the remainder of the week recuperating at the Hotel Sherman. Visiting Sophie, Amy Leslie informed her that Bert was playing in small-time vaudeville houses, with a modicum of success.

While she was in Chicago, Sophie and William Morris met to discuss her future plans. Both believed the opportunities had become limited and would likely diminish. The situation appeared grim, especially for headliners, since no one was willing to pay their high salaries. Agreeing that the theater business would be faced with difficult times for several months, if not years, they decided that an escape to London for an extended period of time would likely be the best solution for Sophie's near-term finances. Morris knew from past experience that London audiences would undoubtedly greet Sophie with warmth, approval, and good box-office receipts.

With the stock market crash of October 24, 1929, the Great Depression had begun, although its real impact would not be felt nationally until the middle of 1930. Popular theater, however, was severely damaged by financial loss and actor unemployment almost immediately.

Theaters had already noticed their attendance declining in August and September, although it was then believed that the demise of vaudeville was the primary reason. Movie houses, however, also reported a decline. After the crash, theaters fought the low attendance by introducing gimmicks to attract patrons—certificates for hair care, free magazines, and discounts in women's apparel shops— but nothing seemed to increase interest. After a mediocre Christmas season, theater managers realized that they were in for hard times.

Vaudeville was already on its deathbed, and the Depression effectively killed it. No new routes were scheduled by booking companies, and no long-term contracts were offered. Salaries were substantially reduced. Headliners sought other venues in which to perform and many actors said they were leaving the business altogether. The gloom on Broadway was pervasive. Of eighteen theaters on the Great White Way, all but one were now playing movies. Only the Palace remained a vaudeville house.

By the mid 1930s, Broadway hotels reported a seventy percent vacancy rate. Between Forty-second Street and Fifty-ninth Street, there were fifty-four vacant stores. There were reported to be 4,500 apple vendors on the street. One enterprising vendor was selling two apples for five cents, but pressure from rival vendors forced him to return to competitive pricing. Pawn shops were doing a good business, and it seemed pawning had become the new national pastime.

Actor's Equity announced that half of its members were unemployed; in New York City, only twenty percent had jobs, although their particular assignments were not identified. Actors who had previously earned $250-$500 a week were working for $25-$50. Those making the rounds of agencies and booking agents went out daily seeking work. They checked the agencies in the morning, the booking agents in the afternoon, and the agencies again in the evening. Top stars lucky enough to be on stage were getting half the salary they normally received. No theater would accept a performer unless salary cuts were agreed upon beforehand, and the lower rates extended to backstage and pit (orchestra) people as well.

In October, 1930, *Variety* reported that there were 25,000 idle stage actors, cutting across both legitimate and popular theater. Actors were so hungry that they would "take anything," according to *Variety*. "Half an hour spent in the agency offices will bring out many real life heart throbs. The stories told are sad. Sometimes the faces behind them are sadder."[1] The newspaper itself cut prices from twenty-five cents to fifteen cents.

The Palace was losing $4,000 a week putting on the one remaining vaudeville show in town. When, in the summer of 1930, the theater was wired for sound, it helped signal the death of Palace vaudeville.

The film business fared no better. Picture house attendance had declined forty percent, the public contending that the movies being produced were "lemons." This was not surprising, since studios were turning out movies "on a shoestring" and distribution was spotty. Even though ninety percent of the theaters now had sound, people stayed away. Free coffee and tableware giveaways did little to increase attendance.

Broadway's only nightlife consisted of numerous Chinese restaurants offering a floor show and dinner for ninety cents. Penny-a-dance ballrooms opened and provided temporary employment for out-of-work chorus girls.

The Loew circuit finally dropped vaudeville in 1931. The Shuberts went into receivership the same year. A.H. Woods and Arthur Hammerstein, two of New York's well-known producers, claimed bankruptcy. Banks assumed ownership of Erlanger and Dillingham theaters, likely hastening the deaths of both longtime impresarios.

In 1932, death took E.A. Albee, Abe Erlanger, David Belasco, and Flo Ziegfeld. These former captains of show business passed on simultaneously with the rise of entertainment's new directions, with movies and radio now supplanting the stage as the dominant public amusements.

During early 1930, Sophie spent five months buoying the sinking Loew circuit, appearing at second-tier theaters—Akron, Syracuse, and Rochester—where she continued to receive rave reviews and mediocre box-office receipts. Her weekly salary was $3,700, well below her normal $5,500. To keep down expenses, she shed all of her act support except Ted, even reducing the number of gowns and shoes she normally purchased. Reviewers complimented her on her new "svelte" look—she had lost more than thirty pounds—but they attributed the loss more to her playing four shows a day than to any diet regimen. At the end of her Loew tour, Sophie appeared at the State Theater, New York. Although her shows no longer played to packed houses, she was reported to still "give them everything."

> A half-packed house at the second performance gave Soph a reception befitting a Queen, and she gave them plenty in return. They wanted more, but the four-show schedule interfered. Miss Tucker, with Ted Shapiro manipulating the ivories, came and conquered with her songs and wisecracks.[2]

To the press, Morris announced that Sophie was leaving for London on June 2 for an extended stay. Milt Ager and Jack Yellin, along with Ted Shapiro, would be the only people accompanying her. "Sophie's husband, Al Lackey, will not be going along," reported *Variety*. "Neither will either of the wives of Ager and Yellin. No suspicion," said *Variety*. "Just being careful about the funds," Sophie explained.

As scheduled, on June 2, Sophie and the boys departed for England on the *Ile de France,* along with the usual assortment of vacationers, who found Europe's cheap prices a welcome change from America's dreary economic downturn. Of course, Sophie concertized on board, much to the delight of the passengers.

Sophie had been signed to appear in the musical comedy, "Follow a Star," written by Douglas Furber and Dion Titherage, with music by Vivian Ellis. Ager and Yellin were along to write Sophie's songs and assist with her dialogue. Jack Hulbert, a comedian, was Sophie's co-star; Paul Murray served as stage director and supervised the entire show. Sophie played the wife of the world's worst conjurer, who discovers in a New York cabaret that he is an English baronet. As a result, Sophie enters English society as Lady Bohum. The action parodied various events typical of the English peerage, but all played in Sophie's inimitable fashion. Despite suffering from snobbery, excessive decorum, and a plethora of unspoken social faux-pas, the down-to-earth Sophie shone through as "the most womanly of women."[3]

Ager and Yellin wrote three songs for Sophie: "I Can Never Think of the Words"; "That's Where the South Begins"; and "If Your Kisses Can't Hold the Man You Love." Two other songs were added to the show later: "I Don't Want to Get Thin" and "I Can't Go Wrong Except with the Right Man," both holdovers from "Honky Tonk."

Sophie quickly discovered the rehearsal pattern in London to be quite different than that utilized for Broadway shows. First, rehearsals began months before a show's opening, giving everyone ample time to learn their parts. This also gave Sophie plenty of opportunity to pursue recreational interests, such as visiting friends, watching tennis matches with local nobility, and attending the theater. Visiting popular theater venues, however, had its "moments." For example, one evening when she and Jack Yellin went to see Gracie Fields perform, Sophie was spotted. With the entire crowd cheering her to step up and perform, Sophie climbed on stage and sang "Some of These Days" (without accompaniment, since Ted was not along). From that time on, Sophie took care to focus her visits on legitimate theater.

The long rehearsal period also created its own uncertainties. There were frequent changes in the cast, usually minor players, but nevertheless new actors who had to be integrated into the play. Equally as often, there were changes in the script, with skits rewritten and the blocking of entire scenes redone. On the very eve of opening, a new character was added to the piece, opposite Sophie, for an afternoon tea skit. Last minute changes meant additional rehearsals and, of course, the usual late hours.

More typical of U.S. productions, initial appearances were scheduled for the "provinces," Manchester in particular, to smooth out the show. On August 11, "Follow a Star" debuted to a full house and was quickly labeled a "great success." Successive engagements in Glasgow and Liverpool preceded its London opening, on September 17, at the Winter Garden. As with U.S. shows, changes in script and cast continued right up to the London opening and were, according to Sophie, seldom for the better.

Still, "Follow a Star" had a grand opening and a box-office record-breaking first week. It was hailed by London critics as "splendid entertainment." London's most acerbic critic, Hannan Swaffer, proclaimed that Sophie had "scored an enormous personal triumph." James Agate, theater critic of the *Sunday Times*, was even more eloquent, citing Euclid, Hamlet, Fouquet, and Salome as he divined Sophie's attributes.

> It occurs to me that the key to this artist is to be found in the use she makes of her vocal resources, the method being to spill them all at once. So generous is the spilling that it seems impossible exhaustion should not be reached.
> Every moment of her performance is an orgy of expense like that banquet which Fouquet offered to his royal master. And, indeed, you might liken her to an engine getting up steam, full pressure being attained at the fall of the curtain and not a second before.
> This artist has, too, that other attribute which always goes with genius, that of never appearing to do wrong. Sophie defies competition, and lo! even her peers are not.[4]

Box-office receipts for the production's second week topped all London theaters at $23,000. Advance bookings of seats were extremely heavy, at least until it was announced that Sophie was to reopen the Kit Kat Club in late November, while continuing to appear in "Follow a Star." Three matinees were being run each week, and Sophie begged Murray to reduce it to two to give her "overworked" vocal cords a rest. Because the show was doing so well, they acceded to her wishes.

Variety's report of Sophie's success was simply stated: "Sophie Tucker in 'Follow a Star' at the Winter Garden is in!" They then went on to speak of the stunningly elegant gowns she wore in the show, noting that "it made it hard to take your eyes off her to appraise the gems of the chorines."[5]

With the combination of a successful musical comedy, appearances at the Kit Kat Club, and heavy bookings for charity events, Sophie leased a house at Waybridge, figuring on an extended stay. No sooner had she established herself, however, than "Follow a Star" producers announced what they called "a reorganization of the salary list, due mainly to the effects of the business depression spreading across England." The entire cast was asked to accept a salary reduction so the show could continue. The production's box-office receipts had abruptly declined to $14,500 a week; and with expenses of $14,000, this left little if any profit.

With no argument, the entire cast, including Sophie, agreed to the salary cut, although, personally, Sophie was not pleased with the abruptness of the edict. Then, a week later, the producers announced that "Follow a Star" would close for two weeks to refurbish the show. They also announced that Maisie Gay would be replacing Sophie in the show.

When questioned by inquisitive reporters, Sophie told them that she would open in vaudeville, starting at the Palladium. In the meantime, Sophie continued her appearances at the Kit Kat Club.

"Did your change in acts have anything to do with money?" reporters asked. "Not at all," she replied, with a sly smile. It was later reported that Sophie's musical comedy contract had guaranteed her $2,500 weekly, with a fifty percent split on all gross over $20,000. The declining attendance had definitely affected Sophie's earnings. Meanwhile, even as she was playing the vaudeville theaters, the Kit Kat Club extended Sophie's engagement for another two months, to the end of the year, the arrangement seemingly agreeable to all concerned.

As if to provide a reminder that Bert still touched his mother's career, even as far away as London, *Variety* reported that he had been sued by the Claridge Hotel, New York, due to the passing of a "bad check." Sophie contacted William Morris, who dispatched a lawyer to resolve the matter. The hotel then reduced its claim to a balance of sixty dollars due for a room, and Sophie agreed to "make good" on her son's bills. Sophie also heard that Bert had temporarily quit dancing because his feet had swollen up. Instead, he had obtained a job at the Ansonia Bootery on Broadway. Did he plan to return to the stage? For the moment, Bert was unable to answer the question.

Now fully recovered, Al joined Sophie during the Christmas holidays, which, for Sophie, were even busier than usual with a plethora of benefits for worthy causes, generally for Jewish or children's organizations. She and Al took a quick trip to Paris to visit the Dolly Sisters, now retired. While the Dollys had never really reached stardom in the U.S.— the general consensus was that their charms and beauty could not offset their mediocre talent — they had become pronounced hits in Europe and were now living on the benefits of their success. Sophie talked to them about an offer she had received from the Empire Theater in Paris. She had demanded a large salary for two weeks work yet had strong doubts about playing before Parisian audiences, since they had developed a reputation for heckling English-speaking performers, especially those who could not speak French.

During January, 1931, Sophie played at various vaudeville houses, including the Trocadero, London's largest cinema, and established a record by appearing before more than 17,000 people. Due to the economic malaise on the continent, however, Sophie decided against an extended tour. Instead, she would restrict her visits to Paris only, where she planned to open February 20 for two weeks, then return to London.

Forewarned about the temperament of French audiences, Sophie developed special routines, including the addition of French choruses to some songs. She also hired a Negro orchestra to accompany her, instead of using the theater's orchestra, since they had no familiarity with her music. Even with these additions, the press wondered, could Sophie win over a French audience?

Ted Shapiro worked for days with the new orchestra to teach them contemporary nuances of American jazz and syncopated music. Sophie chose to use only melody and rhythm songs. She also planned to sing "Some of These Days" in French, requiring her to memorize the lyrics in a foreign language, which, of course, the words did not rhyme.

Opening night at the Empire, Paris; and Sophie was admittedly scared. The backstage people had received her with respect, as had all the other theater employees. When she took the stage, she immediately noticed the Americans sitting in the front boxes. The rest of the theater, however, was jammed with French patrons anxious to appraise this "unusual" American performer.

Sophie sang with her familiar flair and expressiveness. When she sang the chorus of "Some of These Days" in French, the audience broke out in tremendous applause. Overall, however, her songs were met with only polite clapping, a disappointing response. *Variety* reported that Sophie "had a tough time of it" and that it appeared she had been fighting with the audience to win them over.

After the first performance, Sophie changed her numbers and added more French songs and French lyrics to American songs. At her second show, she received a more enthusiastic response; and when she sang "Some of These Days" entirely in French, the audience went wild. After two weeks of sold-out performances, *Variety* declared that Sophie had "won out" in Paris, with the exception of one notable episode.

After several requests to sing "Yiddishe Mama," Sophie decided to sing the song and precipitated a shouting match that threatened to turn into a riot. When she announced her selection, boos broke out in the house, met by a large group of Jewish patrons who yelled at the booers to keep quiet. Nevertheless, the boos continued, louder now and with greater passion. As Sophie was about to begin the song, she realized the mood of the crowd and signaled Ted to switch songs, a seamless segue that, once begun, calmed the audience. Some sensational New York newspapers headlined that Sophie had been "hissed off the stage." While a gross exaggeration, it demonstrated the difficulty Sophie had playing to Parisian audiences. It was to be the only time that Sophie performed in Paris.

Back at the Palladium in London, Sophie offered five new numbers, sported several Parisian gowns—which one newspaper accused her of smuggling into England—and, as a special encore feature, sang a ditty in French, which had the audience in howls. After playing the Palladium for several weeks, she visited the "provinces"—Stratford, Glasgow, Edinburgh, Liverpool, and Nottingham. A syndicate of financiers approached Sophie to take over the Kit Kat Club, but she kindly declined the offer; this was not the time to invest in cabarets. Instead, she continued visiting the outlying theaters, with excellent box-office results.

June, 1931, brought new incidents with which Sophie had to contend. Ted Shapiro had fallen ill; doctors called it a "London cold." Yet when his tonsils became infected, he was hospitalized. Sophie canceled her engagements at seaside resorts to be with Ted. Unfortunately, his condition worsened and it was decided that he should return to New York. Sophie had to put together a makeshift band to accompany her for the remainder of her stay in England.

A week later, Sophie received a cable from Bert, informing his mother that he had just wed.

Was married today to a fine Jewish girl. Love, son.[6]

The unexpected message did not even name the bride nor the date of the marriage. Of course, Sophie wished she could have attended Bert's wedding, but how was this event different from previous encounters with her son? She would have to wait for her return to New York to meet the bride and find out what Bert was doing to earn a living.

Instead of continuing her British tour, Sophie and Al decided to take a vacation for a month, visiting Switzerland, Vienna, Prague, Budapest, and Venice. For once, Sophie was anonymous, just another American tourist.

Returning to England at the end of July, Sophie launched her tour of resort towns, having simplified her act to straight songs and instrumental interludes. Most of these engagements were two- or three-night stands over weekends to take advantage of the large resort crowds. Upon arriving in London, she announced her return to the States. She had been in England for more than a year, enjoying just the kind of success she and Morris had anticipated, both in terms of recognition and at the box-office. Her rewards were substantially better than what she would have received playing U.S. theaters.

Since Sophie had left the country, the theater situation in New York had deteriorated even further. Broadway's losses the past season on musical shows had exceeded $1,500,000. Every show operated on a cut-salary basis just to stay open a few weeks. Ziegfeld's "Smiles" alone dropped more than $200,000. The list of losers included Arthur Hammerstein, Lew Leslie (with his "Blackbirds" revue at the Cotton Club), Lyle Andrews, and Lew Fields. Musical producers delayed plans for future shows because their losses were so substantial that they had no collateral to fund new productions. Nearly all the vaudeville houses had been converted to picture houses and live stage entertainment was at a minimum. Many of the top entertainers had flocked to Hollywood, which itself was suffering from poor box-office receipts. When Sophie landed in New York on September 3, she had no specific plans. A large ad in *Variety* announced that Sophie, Tucker, "The International Favorite," had returned from a thirteen-month engagement in England and was available for new bookings.

Three weeks later, Sophie and George Jessel were signed to appear at the Paramount Theater, New York, at advanced prices. Screen support came from the premiere of Paramount's "The Road to Reno."

> Miss Tucker, with her experience and show wisdom, balances the entertainment with a couple of dramatic songs, new and special, and a couple of laugh-provoking tunes. In between, she does repartee with Jessel and Shapiro and also a blackout. One episode with the entire unit is a show stopper, but when Miss Tucker pulls her headshake as she delivers a hot number, the audiences fall over her.[7]

Sophie received $4,000 for the week and duplicated her effort the following week at the Paramount in Brooklyn. Horace Heidt's orchestra and Kate Smith shared the bill with Sophie.

Balaban and Katz then called Sophie back to Chicago to appear at their various picture houses, starting with the Oriental. The *Herald Examiner* noted that Sophie "holds the repeat record" for all those in show business—which meant that she had played more theaters more times than anyone else before the footlights. Besides the movies, there were three acts on stage: a tight-wire performer, an acrobatic dancer, and Sophie.

> Miss Tucker couldn't get off the stage. She probably didn't want to. She gagged and black-outed and sang. She sang songs that ran into the blue. This midwest town isn't accustomed to some of those punch lines; but this audience whistled for more. "Dance Hall Doll" was produced excellently and blew this audience up in dynamite, as Miss Tucker closed the show.[8]

Usually, when the curtain came down, audiences simply walked out of the theater. After Sophie's show, however, no one moved. They sat and applauded until Sophie came back out to sing "Some of These Days," and the audience applauded again. Still no one walked out. The house lights went off again; and Sophie made a speech. The audience stamped and whistled, then finally consented to leave.

While in Chicago, Sophie assisted Ben Bernie with his opening night at the College Inn. Soon, a note from Bert indicated that he had "renounced" the stage and had obtained a job at the I. Miller shoe store. In her autobiography, Sophie made no mention of visiting Bert and his bride upon her return to the U.S., nor any other family members, for that matter. Ironically, during the Christmas holidays, Sophie received a Christmas card from Bert, the first he had ever sent her. A *Christmas* card?

Sophie then appeared on NBC radio in a half-hour show sponsored by Nestle, in which she sang a number of old favorites. She was paid $1,250 for the thirty minutes. Although this was a single-engagement contract, Morris was busy arranging for Sophie to appear on the show several times.

Variety gave kudos for Sophie's radio debut, calling her "a natural" who "understands the invisible audience as well as she does those she faces in the theater."

> Her voice comes over like a million dollars and she radiates warmth and personality. Her voice is strong, impinging, effective, and apparently better than it has been in some time.[9]

An engagement at the Palace Theater followed, featuring both Sophie and Katharine Hepburn (movie) during the Christmas holidays. At every performance, Sophie closed the show with encores and a speech before audiences would depart from the theater. On Christmas Eve, she and the audience sang Christmas carols, to everyone's delight.

For the next two years, 1932 and 1933, Sophie performed almost full-time at picture houses and nightclubs around the country. Although the theater business was only now rebuilding, Sophie continued to attract crowds wherever she played. Her songs were new; and she changed her act and her gowns frequently, almost for every performance. But the old, familiar Sophie, the Sophie that captured audiences and sent them home happy, remained.

In February, 1932, she appeared at the Palace Theater, New York, a favorite haunt of Sophie's. It was a ten-act show that offered little except Sophie and she came on second-to-last.

> Sophie Tucker proved the climax of the afternoon two from closing, and was welcomed with a storm of greetings. She did 14 minutes, singing the numbers in her own style — "Something to Be Thankful For," with a gag in every other line, "Tears Won't Bring Him Back," and "Lord, You Made the Night Too Long." For an encore, she did her own paraphrase of "Extraordinary Gal," with some sizzling lyrical cracks, but delivered with the characteristic aplomb of the Madame that robs them of offense.[10]

The Palace was on the verge of change — undecided on four shows a day or movies only. With E.A. Albee now dead, it was believed that the Palace, like all the other old vaudeville houses, would turn entirely to movies. Actors now played the Palace as if it were their final appearance there.

One evening, while Sophie was performing on stage, she noticed a crowd gathering in the wings and the stage manager frantically waving at her. Sophie continued her act. When the backstage people, now quite agitated, pointed to the stage flies, Sophie looked up and saw flames. She abruptly stopped singing and moved to the front of the stage, telling the audience, "Take it easy, folks. Don't run. Give everyone a chance to get out." By this time, the audience had noticed the smoke, but Sophie's admonitions helped to effect a calm departure from the stage. Besides talking to the crowd, Sophie continued singing. Finally, out came the property boy, who dragged Sophie off the stage and dropped the fire curtain. No one was injured, but the theater suffered extensive damage to its overhead structure. The event signaled the end of Palace vaudeville. Newspapers jocularly headlined "Red-Hot Mamma Burns Up Palace Theater!" No mention was made that the fire likely represented the grand finale of an illustrious and exciting era of Palace entertainment.

Another jolt for Sophie came when R-K-O booked her into the Capitol Theater, New York, billed below a couple of Hollywood stars. Sophie was quite upset at having her headline status degraded, even though she was making more money, $3,500 a week, than any other performer. A month before, Sophie had made $4,500 at the Capitol; but with the large bill, she had to take less. Sophie was about to quit the engagement when the theater manager pleaded that he needed her on the bill. In a dilemma about what to do, Sophie called Morris, who was already working on angles to retain her headline status, unfortunately, to no avail. Jack Yellin suggested that she sing her signature songs, which would stop the show. "Grab your dough and forget the billing," he advised.[11] The show played in three different theaters on three successive weeks and drew record-breaking business. Even without her headline status, when Sophie appeared on stage, the show prospered. Yet show business was undoubtedly changing, Sophie observed; and she had to change with it.

Alternating between picture houses and roadhouses—the new outlet for old vaudeville entertainers—Sophie performed with continued success. Soon, she was summoned back to Chicago for the summer months to experience another first for her in this new era of show business; she was asked to substitute for the movie actress Norma Talmadge in a revue with George Jessel.

The Delles roadhouse, in Morton Grove, Illinois, seemed better suited to Sophie's act than were most picture houses; and she played to full houses in the Chicago suburb for four weeks. She acted as "Mistress of Ceremonies," introducing and performing with Gus Arnheim's orchestra, the Collette Sisters, Jules and Josie Walton, and the Marie Peterson dancers, the show strongly resembling an old vaudeville olio. She even claimed Gus Arnheim as her protege.

William Morris had obtained a six-month tour on what remained of the Loew circuit, all stops on the East Coast. No skits; no dancers or comedians; no orchestra; just Sophie and Ted. Along with these engagements in Boston and New York, Sophie doubled at the Paramount Grill (cabaret). Unfortunately, that appearance lasted only one week; the operators were unable to produce Sophie's agreed-upon salary. She then jumped to the Valencia in Jamaica, New York, where she played a week, before returning to New York's Paramount Theater, teaming with Ted Lewis and his orchestra. Familiar territory; familiar audiences; same box-office success.

> Lewis is prominent in the first half, virtually using up all his routines; Miss Tucker coming on about the middle and taking charge from then on.
> Looking fine and in her best form, Miss Tucker opened with "That's Something to Be Thankful For," a number which she does exceeding well and which practically places the audience in her lap. After introducing Teddy Shapiro to the audience,

something Miss Tucker never forgets, she does "Stay At Home Papa," a hotcha special and a number on the return of prosperity.[12]

While playing cards with several friends at the Friars Club during the early hours of November 2, 1932, William Morris, Sr., suffered a severe heart attack and was pronounced dead at the scene by an attending doctor. At age fifty-nine, the man considered the greatest of vaudeville agents died abruptly and painlessly in the theatrical environment he most dearly loved.

To the performers he represented, particularly Sophie, his death was as great a blow as that of a family member. For Sophie, he had served as mentor and father-confessor. "To me," said Sophie, "there never was anyone to equal him, or even to stand beside him."[13] Sophie and Morris had worked together since 1910, when he discovered her and helped make her a vaudeville headliner.

Telegrams of sympathy from thousands of persons prominent in the theatrical profession poured into his home and his business office. William Morris, Jr., flew in from California. Morris's second-in-command, Abe Lastfogel, arranged the funeral and took over operation of the agency.

Funeral services for William Morris were held in Temple Rodeph Shalom on West Eighty-third Street. More than 2.000 people were present. Burial took place in Mount Hope Cemetery, Westchester County. As much as she wished to participate in the services, Sophie could not, due to Jewish law; but she spent the entire time in tears for her "Boss." Honorary pallbearers represented more than fifty years worth of theater celebrities, many of whom Morris had inspired to stardom: Eddie Cantor, Martin Beck, Joe Weber, Lew Fields, Adolph Zukor, Gene Buck, Sime Silverman, Irving Berlin, Sam H. Harris, and Arthur Hammerstein.

Dr. Wise, leading the funeral services, summed up Morris's life in one word: "Faithfulness." He had, indeed, been more than faithful to Sophie. It took her months to realize that "the Boss" was no longer around to advise her.

Sophie began 1933 by appearing at the Chez Paree cabaret, New York. Cabarets had changed considerably in the years since Sophie first performed in these venues. During the Depression, moving picture stars had gained employment in nightclubs and cabarets to make money and help boost their movie careers. They were usually flops, however, because they had no stage experience; nor did they know what to do to entertain audiences. Still, people flocked to see their movie favorites "in the flesh." The rules on liquor were now more rigorously enforced, and "shady" cabaret owners had been put out of business. At the same time, Congress was working to repeal Prohibition; and chances looked good that liquor would be legally reintroduced into the nightclub scene. The shows at cabarets resembled vaudeville bills, with six or seven acts appearing, from jugglers to headliners.

Cafe's were rapidly becoming competitors to cabarets. They were smaller, less formal, cheaper, and featured only one or two acts. For a performer like Sophie, however, they demanded greater effort to develop new material, since cafe's' catered to repeat business.

Competition was fierce for cafe' dates. Large bands were booked, thanks to their popularity on radio, which had now become a formidable entertainment alternative. Radio crooners, too, found cafe's a good outlet for their talents. Sophie (and the Morris agency) had found that no radio sponsors expressed interest in her, likely due to her salary demands and her reputation for suggestive songs.

The Chez Paree was a perfect venue for Sophie, and the experience strongly suggested to her and the Morris agency that the cabaret/cafe' scene represented the outlets of greatest opportunity. When the Chicago World's Fair opened, Sophie was engaged to play the 225 Club for an extended stay in the Windy City. It was a small club of 125 seats, but Sophie was the featured star and received a good deal of newspaper publicity. She appeared there through the end of August and admitted to having had a great time with great audiences.

There was, however, an exception to her enjoyment: it was reported by the newspapers that Sophie was seeking a divorce in a Chicago court from Al Lackey, her third husband. The newspapers also revealed that the divorce had been precipitated by Al, who was accused of having slapped Sophie when she refused him money. The case was pending.

Publix, one of the new vaudeville booking houses, offered Sophie a lucrative contract to play their circuit in the Midwest. They had developed sizable strength in "tank towns"—small towns with one vaudeville theater—which they exploited by featuring well-known headliners and relying on considerable local publicity (posterboarding a town like the old circuses used to do) to attract large crowds. Aware that this could be her last fling on a vaudeville circuit, Sophie took the job and spent a month visiting towns like Peoria and Springfield, Illinois. In these towns, practically everybody in the telephone book got a call to inform them that Sophie was in town. In addition, an invitation from Sophie appeared in everyone's mailbox and in all the hotels. The note read: "Called but you were out. Drop in and see me at the _____ Theater. Yours, Sophie Tucker."

Judging from reports, these promotional activities helped to fill the theaters throughout her short tour. Publix wanted more of Sophie's time; but she chose to return to the Palace, Chicago, for a Labor Day weekend that attracted admirers from hundreds of miles around. Extra shows were scheduled to handle the overwhelming demand. The event turned into a Sophie Tucker reunion.

> It was one of those sentimental occurrences in show business that had Miss Tucker acting almost bashful as she tried to speech herself away. Couldn't be done, and came back for a second encore. There were posies, too. New acts, but though she may change and add to her material, its still the same Sophie Tucker act.[14]

Instead of a salary—actual salaries were hard to negotiate these days—Sophie played the Palace on a percentage, which garnered her around $5,000. Sophie spent $300 of her own money to publicize the show in newspapers. She did the same in Detroit and St. Louis, with similar results. The arrangement was so successful that Abe Lastfogel booked Sophie into a number of West Coast picture houses for the next several months.

Sophie's appearance at the Warfield Theater, San Francisco, coincided with a national event of great significance to the entertainment industry, indeed the entire country. It was the one action that might put popular stage theater back on the track of success and profit. Congress had passed the Twenty-first Amendment to the Constitution, which repealed the Eighteenth Amendment and ended Prohibition. That evening, Sophie's appearance was filled with drinking songs, while the audience passed around bottles and the city celebrated its "emancipation." After the show, Sophie entertained Press Club members to celebrate Prohibition's end.

Despite a mediocre bill, Sophie filled the Warfield at every performance.

> Unseen here since the old Orph days, Soph gave 'em the kind of songs Frisco likes and goes for, trimmed with the perennial "Some of These Days."[15]

From San Francisco, Sophie moved to the Hollywood Restaurant/nightclub in Los Angeles. Women patrons there voted Sophie "best dressed woman of the week." All her admirers cheered, "Sophie is home again." Holiday season crowds at the restaurant were elated both by Sophie and the novel availability of drink, and her evening appearances often extended into the early morning hours.

At the same time, Abe Lastfogel was in Los Angeles seeing what he could do to put Sophie back in the movies. He obtained a number of verbal commitments but no contracts. A short film with Leon Errol was a possibility. An appearance as herself in a picture for Majestic (an independent studio) seemed agreeable. A role in "Murder at the Vanities," for Paramount, appeared to be the most promising.

After the Hollywood Restaurant engagement closed on January 17, 1934, Sophie had to travel from Los Angeles to Hollywood, Florida, to appear for a week at the Hollywood Club. Show business engagements during the Depression years certainly kept one busy traveling. Any prospects for a movie meant that Sophie would have to return to California following the Florida engagement. Meanwhile, however, with the rapid growth of the Miami area, fueled by long winter vacations taken by East Coast Jews, the venue was becoming increasingly attractive for Jewish entertainers. Heading the list of popular stars sought by local managers was Sophie, and she and Lastfogel planned to take full advantage of the opportunities.

At the Hollywood Club, Sophie sang all her familiar, signature songs by popular demand, ending every show with "Some of These Days" and "Yiddishe Mama." The evening of February 13, Sophie celebrated her forty-seventh birthday with a big party, attended by hundreds of friends and admirers. The evening was filled with nostalgia, old songs, and old stories. Yet Sophie was surely aware that one recognizes her age in show business when nostalgia becomes the primary theme of the celebration.

Soon, it was back to Hollywood, California, to see about picture contracts. *Variety* listed two pictures for which Sophie was being considered, "Murder at the Vanities," and "Husband Hunters." The newspaper's talk of "fulfilling picture contracts" sounded as if the contracts had already been signed. Not so; both deals were brusquely scratched.

"Vanities" was being co-written by Earl Carroll from a play of the same name he had produced a year earlier. Carroll remembered the arguments he had had with Sophie several years before and refused to have her participate in the picture. "Husband Hunters" never got past the Breen Office for the censorship of movies.

Having been turned down by the studios, Sophie met with Lastfogel and Morris, Jr., to discuss her future engagements. "Book me to London, Abe," Sophie implored. "I'm stale. Can't do business here."[16]

The intrepid Morris operatives quickly got Sophie booked at a London cabaret, with an agreement that allowed her to double at theaters there. Before she left for London, they also obtained appearances for her in Baltimore, Boston, and New York. Even more important, however, was a request from the Hartford synagogue to help in a fund-raiser for their old folks home. Sophie would not only assist them, she would plan and produce the entire benefit.

Several years earlier, Sophie had promised officers of the home that, when she had an open date, she would visit Hartford and do a benefit for them. Her mother had been one of its founders, and Sophie herself had made many donations to the group. Although it was to be a benefit for a Jewish organization, the entire town enthusiastically planned to celebrate Sophie's return. The date was set for April 22 at Poli's Capitol Theater. The theater had been donated by its owners; stage hands and the orchestra offered their services free of charge; and *Hartford Courant* advertising was also free. For two weeks prior to the event, the *Courant* advertised: "Hartford's Own, Sophie Tucker, Famous International Singer, With Professional All Star Cast."

For the benefit, Sophie recruited Belle Baker, a singer of renown who shared many of Sophie's songs since they had begun together in New York; Lester Allen, a comedian who had played with Sophie in musical comedy; Bill "Bojangles" Robinson, the outstanding Negro tap dancer; and several other lesser acts. At the benefit, Sophie not only served as mistress of ceremonies, she sang several of her favorite songs and took part in a series of skits with Baker and Robinson.

"Gaiety and laughter were the keynote of the show," reported the *Courant*.

"In holiday mood, the performers romped through their routine, 'ad libbing' freely to the delight of the audience."

Wearing a striking gown set off by sequins of purple and green that flashed under the spotlights, Sophie was introduced as mistress of ceremonies. Greeted with a roar of applause, she spoke briefly, telling the audience she was glad to be in Hartford and to do her part in the work of the Hebrew Ladies Old People's Home, as her mother had done. Sophie was immediately rewarded with resounding applause and showered with bouquets of flowers.

Belle Baker sang a number of her characteristic songs, like "Carioca" and "This Little Pig Went to Market" but begged off requests for "Yiddishe Mama," telling the audience, "That's Sophie's song." Lester Allen told a series of crazy, comic stories, some of them involving Sophie when they had appeared together. Bill Robinson went through his routine with amazing speed, rhythm, and grace, flashing bits of his intricate tap dancing.

Robinson, Baker, and Sophie performed a couple of comic skits that left the audience howling with laughter. Baker and Sophie sang "Some of These Days" as a duet. Sophie closed the show with two songs, one dealing with matrimony—"I'm unfortunate as can be when it comes to matrimony"—and then segued to motherhood, singing "My Yiddishe Mama" in both English and Yiddish.

With telling effect, she gripped the audience with the song, which tells of the virtues and self-sacrifice of the Jewish mother. Tears flowed freely in the audience, and some patrons sobbed audibly. Her own eyes moist, Sophie concluded amid thunderous applause.

"I feel better now," she told the audience through her tears. "I missed my mother today."

That evening, Sophie and her troupe headed back to New York. The old folks home committee reported that the benefit netted $1,200. Yet missing throughout the entire event, from planning to conclusion, was any mention of the Abuza families.

On April 26, Sophie sailed for London, looking forward to her annual round of cafe' and theater appearances. On the voyage, she wrote hundreds of cards and invitations to friends and admirers announcing her return to the London stage.

12

Looking Back Over Her Shoulder

At the behest of the King and Queen of England, three days after her arrival in London, Sophie appeared at the Palladium as part of a Command Variety Performance. The annual event was given to aid the Variety Artists' Benevolent Fund. Sophie was included in the typically English benefit because of her popularity in the country.

On the evening of the event, crowds thronged the street in front of the theater to see the King and Queen arrive in the royal carriage. Cheers and applause greeted them as they mounted the stairs to the theater entrance, where they were met by the directors of the General Theater Corporation and led into the foyer, as the royal band played a stirring salute.

When the King and Queen entered their flower-decked box, the audience rose and, after singing the National Anthem, broke into prolonged, polite applause.

The program was made up of comedy skits, led by the popular George Robey, a one-act play by Sir Cedric Hardwicke, a circus act, a dance troupe, and a burlesque of a romantic drama. Completing the bill, Sophie and Violet Loraine sang their familiar signature songs. For Sophie, it was an exciting adventure to have been chosen to play before royalty. She was the only American selected.

> At the end of the performance which seemed to have spread enjoyment through every part of the house, not excepting the Royal box, the National Anthem was played, and the King and Queen were heartily cheered as they left the theater.[1]

Notwithstanding the honor of her inclusion on the bill, Sophie had doubts she would be able to appear at the Command Performance. Just a week before, on her transatlantic voyage, she had developed laryngitis and was unable even to talk her lyrics at a show given on board. Doctors dictated "mouth rest" to assist the ailing Sophie, a regimen that, by itself, was no small accomplishment for her.

Actually, the brief affliction reawakened Sophie's recent concerns about the state of her singing voice. She had recently celebrated her fiftieth birthday, an event that also marked more than a quarter of a century of her belting out ragtime, blues, and ballads. There was no question in her mind that her voice was showing the inevitable signs of decline: a slight loss of quality; a loss of strength; and occasional cracking in the upper registers. To relieve these "tired" vocal cords, Sophie often opted to "talk" her lyrics. She had also been selecting songs that made fewer and lesser demands on her voice, substituting, instead, more repartee with Ted. She had been warned by doctors that a fifty-year-old voice such as hers required more tender care. Yet, she continued to sing with as much gusto as before, if not quite as loudly. Nevertheless, it was a problem to which Sophie would need to pay particular attention during the next several years.

Upon her arrival in London, Sophie rushed to honor two commitments she and the Morris agency had agreed upon. First, she had a date to record six of her recent hits; second, she had lines to learn for a film being produced by British Lion studios. When asked by reporters what her schedule was to be in England, she ran off a list of activities that overwhelmed them: making records; appearing in a movie; touring the "provinces" and seaside resorts, as well as the usual London theater dates; "and don't forget the benefits I agreed to do," she added.

Completing the recordings came first, a task that she accomplished in a matter of days. Backed by Ted, the songs included "That's Something to Be Thankful For"; "Sophisticated Lady"; "Stay at Home Papa"; "Lawd, You Made the Night Too Long"; "Louisville Lady"; and "My Extraordinary Man." Although these songs were hits in the U.S., she never recorded them there. They represent some of Sophie's most memorable numbers, yet they were relegated to a British recording company. Consequently, these records are quite rare today.

Sophie opened her tour at the Empire, Finsbury Park, to record-breaking crowds, and duplicated the feat at the Empire in Holborn. In between, she played a one-night stand for a benefit at the Winter Garden and, on a supposed day of rest, appeared at Sherry's Dance Hall in front of 1,700 people. The month of June had been set aside for Sophie to shoot the movie, "Gay Love"; but she also traveled to the "provinces" for weekend shows.

The movie, "Gay Love," was an adaptation of Audrey and Waveney Casten's play. It had originally been planned as a vehicle for Florence Desmond, a well-known English mimic; but the studio decided to add Sophie to tap into the American market, or so it hoped.

The story told of two performers, friends, who were nearing the end of their careers. Sophie played Sophie; she had few lines and few songs, some of which she had just recorded. The movie was previewed at the Prince Edward Theater on August 21, literally days after final production. The reviewer seemed rather bored with the result, as did the audience.

> Everything about the story of Gay Love is good — it always is good — it always will be good. To recapitulate the plot would be just a waste of time. Production is designed to exploit the mimicry of Florence Desmond and magnetism of Sophie

Tucker. Both do their specialties and comment thereon would be superfluous. Intricate, self-sacrificing love story, backstage scenes of rehearsals, etc. New Year's Eve charity ball is designed for the production flash.[2]

The movie appeared in English theaters for only a short time. A revival several years later flopped. It never reached the U.S. Sophie had been paid $2,000 to appear. It became a quickly forgotten experience.

Much more exciting was the newspaper coverage Sophie received when she aided a child who had darted into traffic on a busy street. When a woman screamed, Sophie ran out into the street and shoved the child out of the path of a speeding driver. The *London Citizen* headlined, "Sophie Tucker Risks Life to Protect Child." They reported Sophie as the "heroine of a street accident, when she risked her life to save a child under the wheels of an automobile." She described her role as "spontaneous action." Although her leg was slightly injured, it did not prevent her from appearing on stage that evening.

While playing the seaside resorts, Sophie also filled some benefit dates, attended a civic reception for the Lord Mayor of Leeds, and appeared on a radio program. Bookings for Sophie were so heavy, she was persuaded to delay her English departure from the middle of August to the end of October. Her only interlude was a brief vacation on the continent with friends.

Because economic conditions in England were deteriorating as rapidly as they had in the U.S., Sophie agreed to play at a number of London theaters for a fifty-fifty split of gross ticket sales, rather than an agreed upon salary of $2,500 a week. The arrangement paid off handsomely, giving her nearly $5,000 a week for each of these engagements. It was sufficient for Sophie to afford a luxurious vacation, visiting Paris, Vienna, Venice, and Switzerland, all in the space of three weeks.

When she returned to London to begin an engagement at the Alhambra, she refused to play the opening date because it fell on Yom Kippur, the most solemn of Jewish holy days. Management was so disturbed by her refusal that they threatened to close her engagement altogether. Nonetheless, cooler heads prevailed and newspaper articles suggesting the management's insensitivity made them back off. Her opening performance was typical Sophie. Who in the audience cared that it had been delayed a day?

> Starting with an introductory number, Soph next gave them "Louisville Lady," followed it up with "Some of These Days," the opening bars being met with a salvo of applause. As an encore, she obliged with her classic "Yiddishe Mamma," and begged off with a speech.
> House was jammed to suffocation, and the "last of the Red-Hot Mamas" was accorded a royal reception.[3]

Sophie departed London October 20, to cheering crowds shouting for her to return soon, which she promised to do. When she arrived in New York harbor on November 1, she was met by a gayly decorated tug, with a brass band aboard. Taken off the ship, she was individually transported to the shore. At the pier, a fleet of fifteen cars carrying banners were waiting; and she was escorted by a squad of motorcycle policemen to her home. The only event worth noting on her return trip was a black eye she received when a waiter inadvertently bumped her with an elbow on a swaying deck. At her next engagement, she used the black eye as an amusing gambit to introduce a new song about "wandering papas."

Before leaving for a Chicago engagement, Sophie was feted by members of the American Federation of Actors for her longtime vaudeville work. Eddie Cantor, president of the AFA, emceed the festivities, backed by Joe Laurie, Jr.; Jack Benny; Walter Huston; William Morris, Jr.; Abe Lastfogel; and George Burns. (Some wag referred to the AFA as the Hebrew union, since so many Jewish entertainers now dominated the comedy scene.) Sophie was so overwhelmed by this reception from fellow performers, she was unable to read her prepared speech (written by Jack Yellin). Between sobs, she confided to the audience that "this is the biggest moment of my life." No woman had ever before been recognized by an actors' group. The fact that ninety-five percent of all these groups were composed of men made Sophie's reward that much more gratifying.

The following week found Sophie in Chicago, playing the Chez Paree nightclub, for the first of many visits that would continue for more than thirty years. Newly opened, the Chez Paree charged no cover at any time and only a $2.50 minimum for the dinner. Not surprising, then, that shows featuring headliners made the Chez Paree the most popular club in town. No customer walked out feeling he or she had paid too much. Such policies quickly built up a large and faithful following.

Sophie appeared there for eight weeks. As recorded by *Variety*, every performance was like a command performance.

Sophie Tucker headlines the current show and accounts for the turnaway trade. Long an established Chicago attraction, her

A publicity photo of Sophie, appearing at the Chez Paree in Chicago. There is no indication that she knew how to ride a bicycle. Sophie was not averse to having photos taken showing her involved in activities apart from typical stage roles. (Museum of the City of New York)

arrival in Chicago for this engagement drew editorial space and front-page pictures. Always a surefire performer, a certain aura of sentiment surrounds her. But Miss Tucker doesn't need sentiment. On straight performance, she must be acknowledged as without peer on delivery and showmanship.[4]

After closing at the Chez Paree — her last night was filled with old favorites and audience sing-alongs — Sophie jumped across town to the Oriental Theater for another week of entertaining Chicago patrons.

> Nearly all La Tucker, and she's got 'em lining up again. They've grown up with the last of the red-hot mamas hereabouts, so her blue lines and songs are plenty okey. Her hottest and bluest, "I Picked a Pansy in the Garden of Love." Only a performer such as she could handle a song like this and get away with it.[5]

The accolades from all of Chicago's reviewers were warmly welcomed; but the references to her longevity — that is, her age — were not nearly as comforting. Was she now being viewed nostalgically by Chicago audiences as an old-timer? Was that bad or good for her?

Now concentrating all of her time on the nightclub scene — the only seemingly viable outlet for stage performers at the time — Sophie traveled to Florida for an eight-week engagement at the Hollywood Country Club. During the past several years, the Miami area had blossomed into a vacation capitol, with hotels adjoining the beach being erected so quickly that construction companies often ran out of building materials and were forced to wait for shipments from the north. Every hotel had a dining room and nightclub featuring its own entertainment, and performers found new venues to play. The salaries were excellent, and the engagements were long, not unlike the cabarets of earlier years.

A sizable portion of the vacationers came from the Jewish populations of major eastern cities, many of them retired people who planned to spend the entire winter in Miami's warm climate. Vaudeville might be moribund in the North, but the venues in Florida attracted many of the well-known vaudeville headliners. Sophie proved the perfect performer for this new situation.

Patrons of the Hollywood Country Club, many of whom were already familiar with Sophie, flocked to the nightclub each evening to savor her repertoire of new ballads, saucy rags, self-deprecating humor, and famous signature tunes. Every show closed with "Some of These Days" and "Yiddishe Mama." Audiences shouted to have her repeat these songs again and again. Evidently, they did not want to let go of "good-old-days" entertainment. After two weeks of two long shows an evening, Sophie's voice began to weaken, and she reduced the number of songs and encores presented. To fill the time, Sophie incorporated other acts into her program: dancers, a singing group, and a comedian, which seemed to work out well as long as she acted as emcee, introduced each act, and closed the acts with humorous patter.

The winter season over, Sophie returned to New York to appear at the Hollywood Restaurant for a ten-week stay. For April, the *Herald Tribune* chose Sophie the best-

For a change in performance format, Sophie hired a small band, led by Ted Shapiro, and a vocal chorus to back her. The experiment lasted for less than a season. The costs of carrying so many people on the payroll proved prohibitive. (Museum of the City of New York)

dressed woman in New York. Newspapers reported in detail each of the gowns she wore while performing. Her rendition of a new popular song, "The Continental," quickly set her apart from all other performers singing it. Jack Yellin had added lyrics which, sung in Sophie's style, offered an especially fresh viewpoint that audiences loved. *Variety* welcomed Sophie's return to New York, calling it a "sensational premiere."

> It was a gala occasion in superlative gobs. For one thing, she's a new Soph all over again.

Such new Jack Yellin numbers as "Right Time in the Right Clime," (a decided hit in Florida); "I Picked a Pansy in the Garden of Love," (saucy); and her own version of "The Continental" were, according to *Variety*, "socko." But "Life Begins at Forty" was the show-stopper.

> Her discourse on post-40 life and love, if perhaps too biologically detailed, was made to sound like a lyrical academic discourse on the facts of life.

They were hanging from the waiters opening night and stood up often and long to cheer, an evening which impressed the many professionals in that first-night audience on the hyper-sentimental appeal some of 'em still enjoy in the public consciousness.[6]

Sophie was quite pleased with the reception she received from New York audiences, particularly when singing those songs that challenged her longevity in the business. As she quickly grasped, the best way to deal with her age and icon status was to meet it head-on. There was no self-pity in her songs. They included self-mockery and at the same time assured her audiences she meant business. She plainly let them know that growing older was not a problem or disability to her; instead, life was good "as long as the blood flowed through the veins." Sophie was, indeed, "a new Soph all over again."

Radio appearances on WHN, New York, which featured various vaudeville acts, gave Sophie the opportunity to render a number of new songs. Of course, her radio persona had to be toned down; so she claimed she was going to give up her "red-hot mamma" image for the time being. Response to the radio show was so positive, Sophie was signed to appear on a series of programs entitled "Sophie Tucker's Music Hall," on which she emceed and sang-along with an assortment of popular guests. A few weeks later, she added doing commercials for Mulsified Coconut Oil.

The "Music Hall" series evolved into featuring not only well-known actors, but newcomers, as well. According to the Morris agency, the idea was Sophie's own. She supposedly staged daily talent auditions at the Morris offices, and those selected would appear on her radio program. To heighten interest, listeners were encouraged to vote for the best acts they heard; and those acts would later appear on other radio programs. Sophie viewed the arrangement as an opportunity for unknowns to gain exposure; WHN viewed the show as a means to increase the station's listening audience.

The "Music Hall" continued through the end of June. Like old-time theater owners' perceptions of the need for summer closings due to the heat, radio management believed that their audiences declined for the summer as well. With that factor in mind, the show was transferred to the Capitol Theater and broadcast with a live audience (likely the first in radio broadcasting). Sophie was regaled with cheers and applause, but the remainder of the bill received only mediocre response. The experiment lasted two weeks.

Variety's initial reaction to the event suggested that it "was a sock program and prestige-builder for the station," but the lack of really good talent and the inability to attract sponsors made the program short-lived. Nor did *Variety* feel that Sophie was giving her best. She appeared on stage but within the more restricted radio format; thus, she had to play down her "nightclub paprika." "Go back to the stage," they advised her, "where you can play yourself."

For her annual visit to Hartford, Sophie and a group of performers played one evening at the State Theater on behalf of the Hebrew Old Folks Home. Almost 4,000 people attended the benefit.

Sophie sang, "I Picked a Pansy in the Garden of Love," accompanied by a self-deprecating monologue on her loves and matrimonial failures, and "Life Begins at Forty," the audience loving every aside and shimmy she added to the song. She almost missed the train back to New York when she added another encore, "Baby Your Mother," which elicited sobs from the crowd.

In appreciation of Sophie's work and the collection of more than $1,400, she received a plaque of recognition that would be hung in the Old Folks Home. Among those in the audience were some of the remaining members of the founding group, who, like Jennie, had pioneered the establishment of the institution.

In accepting the honor, Sophie thanked the association and the audience and promised to return each year for a "Sophie Tucker Day."

With the conclusion of the "Music Hall" series, Sophie played at the State Theater, New York, for a two-week engagement. Everyone seemed to breath a sigh of relief when she returned to her familiar routines. *Variety* noted that audiences wanted the "real and original Sophie Tucker" and no one else. A thoughtful reviewer wrote that, while audiences continued to compliment Sophie's work, there was a concern that she might be unable to change her stage performances because audiences had, over the years, become so comfortable with her act. Being so typecast might limit her work to specific venues, like nightclubs. Sophie's response to the reviewer was "so what," yet she and Abe Lastfogel were at that moment discussing alternatives.

Nevertheless, the nightclubs continued to beckon. A week at the House of Lords, New York, and four weeks at Vivian Johnson's only reaffirmed nightclubs' interest in her; which meant high salaries. The summer crowds at these venues were treated to Sophie as both master of ceremonies and performer, as greeter and maitre d'. Dressed in a white sport suit, Sophie wandered from table to table, greeting friends and acquaintances, joking in her husky voice, slapping men warmly on the back and kissing ladies.

Once the show began, Sophie, now dressed in a long, white, sequined gown accented by a feather hat and wrist bands, came out on the stage to introduce each act and relate a brief tale of its recent triumphs. After each number, she radiantly returned to center stage, applauding and repeating, "lovely, lovely, more, more." When the spotlight swung to her, she began her set by belting out "They All Pitched a Quarter Apiece and Bet It on a Horse"; switched the tempo to a blues ballad, "Forgotten Man"; and followed with a sizzler, "I'm the Laziest Gal in Town." It was now the audience's turn to be shouting "more, more." Later, Sophie could be found at a corner table, talking with patrons, signing autographs, and having her picture taken with fans.

During her engagement at Vivian Johnson's, Sophie suffered several days of laryngitis but continued working, talking or croaking her lyrics, and indulging in repartee with resident comedians.

On to Saratoga, New York, for two weeks, entertaining at the Arrowhead Inn and Piping Rock nightclubs, in a program that also featured other stage stars, such as Ben Bernie, H.B. Slone, Bobby Crawford, and Bing Crosby. These shows were especially enjoyable because the performers ad-libbed their dialogues in between playing their numbers.

On her way back to Chicago to appear on a radio program, Sophie made brief stops at picture houses in Boston and Cleveland. NBC had signed Sophie to play the Marie Dressler role opposite Wallace Beery, doing excerpts from a recent Dressler/Beery movie. It was an interesting trial, reading lines from a script in front of a microphone without an audience, but Sophie was not sure she liked the experience. Playing at the Oriental Theater, however, returned Sophie to her favorite milieu; and audiences cheered her every gesture on stage.

Although Abe Lastfogel warned Sophie that she would not get the salary she wanted, her next stop was at the Trocadero nightclub, in Los Angeles. According to Sophie, she believed the trip to Los Angeles would be an opportunity to lobby the studios for a movie role.[7] At her opening, the nightclub was packed with movie people, performers, and studio executives. At the close of the show, Sophie was deluged with flowers and kisses. Candidly, Sophie told the crowd that she had come to town, to "find a place in the movies."[8]

Nonetheless, two highly successful weeks at the Trocadero garnered no movie offers, even though she and Abe did visit a number of studios. Sophie added another week at the Orpheum Theater, but still no calls from the studios. The Orpheum crowds, however, demonstrated their love for her.

> Reception was tremendous and the applause that greeted her every number showed real appreciation. She is the same Tucker as of old, and her material is typical of her style.[9]

Garbed in a long, black sheath dress, Sophie opened with "If It Ain't One Man, It's Another," with some soliloquizing that had everyone laughing. Then, in a more serious vein, she sang "Why Do They Call It Gay Paree" and "The Lady in Red." "Life Begins at Forty" stopped the show, as Sophie added a seemingly autobiographical tale of found and lost love and its effect on the human body.

It had been eight years since Sophie had played at the Orpheum. Yet, as *Variety* reported her engagement, "Soph has not been forgotten."

Attempts by Sophie and the William Morris office to get her into motion pictures had failed—not even a display of interest—so she decided to return to the nightclub scene in New York for the Christmas holidays. As usual, she was treated like theatrical royalty.

Was it age that prevented her from appearing in pictures? Her unique persona? Her reputation? The studios' penchant for young, pretty stars? She had time to discuss the issues with Abe on the train ride back East.

At the beginning of February, 1936, Sophie was headed for an extended engagement at the Hollywood Country Club, Hollywood, Florida, to entertain the area's vacationers. They anxiously awaited her arrival by standing in lines for days to buy tickets.

When Sophie came on stage at the Hollywood Country Club, gasps of visual delight mingled with applause filled the room. For her opening show, she was wearing a dress of silver lame, made in coat fashion, with a belt. Four glass buttons matched a velvet scarf of Dubonnet. Covering her blonde hair were folds of silver and velvet, with two diamond clips holding them in place.

Sophie played at the country club for fifteen weeks, until the end of May. Although she called the engagement "relaxing," each day was spent selecting and practicing songs in preparation for the evening's performance. As she had done for years, Sophie wished to present new material at each show, a promise well appreciated by patrons who returned to the nightclub every week. A bonus for the long engagement: Ted began dating a young woman from Miami, and the relationship appeared to be serious.

Sophie's next engagement was the Terrace Room, in the Hotel Morrison, Chicago. For this appearance, she decided to hire other performers and, along with Ted, include backing from a small band. It was part of her plan to reduce the amount of singing she did, thus save her voice. The arrangement sounded good in rehearsals. Yet, how well it would play at the Terrace Room was questionable, since the Terrace had the reputation of being a "tough spot" to attract "the smart crowd." The *Chicago Daily News* reported that Sophie was bringing a number of new songs with her and, as before, remained the "chantress of risqué ditties."

Variety' s review of Sophie's opening night dispelled any doubts of her ability to attract a crowd.

> They might as well change the name of this place to the Sophie Tucker room. The Terrace Room is no longer a bugaboo. In one night, La Tucker swept out the cobwebs and planted irresistible magnets that will continue to attract the best money and top nitery mob of the city.
>
> Sophie Tucker steps out with new ideas, new angles and greater entertainment. She comes back with her own band and her own show. Then Tucker enters: she gave 'em what they had come for; the Tucker brand of songs, some new, some old.
>
> She can fit into any spot, and, as ever, she spells surefire entertainment, and surefire box-office.[10]

Prior to the show, while patrons danced, Sophie spent time greeting her fans and giving the evening a "gala" atmosphere. Ted acted as emcee and directed the orchestra for four acts and a chorus of twelve "peaches." Ted and Sophie together had developed a routine of patter to work into numbers, with Shapiro as the foil for Sophie's comedy. Nothing stagey or theatrical, according to *Variety*: "just solid sock-on-the-nose laughs."

Six weeks into her engagement, Sophie continued to garner headlines for her performance. "Like Old Man River," said the *Daily News,* "Sophie Tucker just keeps rolling along."

> A clever playwright knows the advantage of making an audience cry one moment and laugh the next. So does Sophie. One song is serious, the next gay. She mixes spice and sugar as deftly as a pastry chef, and consequently has the audience eating out of her hand. She's a grand old gal, and capacity business in the Terrace

Room proves Chicago is as crazy as ever about her. She is the seasoning for the season.[11]

During Sophie's last performance at the Terrace Room, the management staged a gala farewell party for her. In the audience were a crowd of cafe', stage, and radio entertainers, who accompanied Sophie singing all of her favorite tunes.

After a short rest back in New York, Sophie returned to the Piping Rock nightclub in Saratoga, New York, for a brief run. Her timing was perfect. Since the close of Arlington Park, Chicago, the horse race crowd rushed to Saratoga to participate in their continuing equestrian schedule. The result of this influx of horsemen meant good business for local niteries, and particularly for Sophie. As with her show at the Terrace Room, Sophie employed an orchestra and several acts— a pair of violinists, a singer, and exotic dancers— to fill out her program. Ted emceed, led the orchestra, and helped introduce Sophie's songs.

It was during this time that Sophie and Abe Lastfogel had a disagreement regarding future bookings. Abe argued that Sophie should continue to play the nightclub circuit; Sophie sought more engagements at picture houses and the formation of a personal orchestra (like her old Five Kings of Syncopation). They could not agree; so they parted company, still friends but unable to compromise their beliefs. Sophie contacted the Music Corporation of America, a leading booking office for bands. With a band led by Ted, they played a number of dates in Midwestern cities; but Sophie quickly discovered that audiences were not interested in her band, just herself. Nor was M.C.A. able to book her into hotels or onto the radio. The experiment had flopped; suddenly, Sophie had no future engagements.

M.C.A. was successful, however, at getting Sophie booked into the Grosvenor Hotel in London for an eight-week run. Given Sophie's reputation among British audiences, the engagement seemed ideal. On September 24, Sophie opened her act to a packed house and a marvelous reception. Sophie recalled that the opening night "made me feel good all over," and that the crowd of admirers "treated me as though I had come home to my own."[12] London's *Variety* verified her sentiments,

> Sophie Tucker is still at the top of the heap of American artists who have come over to this country. When she opened at Grosvenor House cabaret last night, all the tables were occupied and hundreds turned away.[13]

The only other act on the program was a ventriloquist, Edgar Bergen. Along with his dummy (prior to his being named Charley McCarthy), Bergen was reported to have done a commendable job of entertaining, much improved over his initial performance several years earlier. After Bergen's act, Sophie returned to the stage to sing a few numbers, which required her to "warm up" the audience once again. She did not really succeed, and decided not to attempt it again.

At the request of London's Lord Mayor, Sophie, never one to turn down a benefit, agreed to organize a variety program for the King George V National Memorial, for the establishment of children's playgrounds throughout England. Sophie moved quickly with the planning for the event. An all-American show would be put on at midnight, December 10, at the Coliseum Theater, to be staged by Lew Leslie (of Cotton Club fame). Louis Sterling, a planning committee member, agreed to pay all the show's expenses and contributed a $500 television receiving set. Another committee member, Gordon Selfridge (head of Selfridge's department stores), donated a window in his store on Oxford Street to advertise the event. American actors who agreed to participate in the benefit included Marlene Dietrich; Douglas Fairbanks, Jr.; Edward G. Robinson; Ben Lyon; and Allan Hale. Sophie and a dance group planned to parody the old Floradora Sextette; and three bands entertained, as well.

The day of the show produced its own excitement for Sophie. Early in the morning, she received a telegram from Abe Lastfogel telling her that MGM wanted her for a picture. If she OK'd the deal, she would have to be in Hollywood early in January, forcing her to cancel her remaining engagements in England. Since appearing in a movie was what Sophie had been wishing for, she quickly canceled the dates. At the moment, she was elated over Hollywood's possibilities.

On the same day, King Edward VIII announced his abdication of the British throne. The news seemed to freeze all England in place, everyone awaiting further information, since, it was rumored that Mrs. Simpson, a divorcé, had been the reason for the King's abdication. Under the circumstances, there was some question whether the benefit should be staged.

Nevertheless, the event went on as planned and truly entertained a full house. The American actors did their best to make the patrons laugh and forget, at least temporarily, their country's dilemma. At the end of the show, Martin Bartlett stepped to the center stage and sang "Auld Lang Syne," with the audience joining in the chorus. He followed it with "The Star-Spangled Banner." After that, he turned to Sophie. In light of what was happening, should he sing "God Save the King?" How would the audience respond? Without hesitation, Sophie signaled him to sing the British anthem.

The audience immediately joined in, some loudly and with conviction, some so choked by emotion that they sang with muted voices. Still, it was a fitting climax to a unique event in both theater history and the history of the British monarchy. Four thousand pounds (more than $20,000) was presented to the Lord Mayor, thanks to the American performers.

A week later, Sophie received a letter from the Lord Mayor.

> I am sending a little memento with the earnest hope that you will accept it as a token of my deep appreciation of your splendid work for the King George Memorial Fund.[14]

He went on to apologize that no royalty had been in attendance at the performance, "owing to certain national matters," and closed by wishing Sophie success "in your new undertakings over the other side."

Sophie arrived in the U.S. on January 1, 1937. She and the Morris agency were working together again and Abe's first new booking on Sophie's behalf was a gala reappearance at the Oriental Theater, Chicago, on her way to Hollywood. Such a homecoming Sophie could dearly embrace.

> Sophie Tucker is at the Oriental this week. She's what they come to see, and it's a long wait between the end of the picture and Sophie's entrance. Sophie closes the bill. She switched a capacity audience from the hilarity of "I'm the Girl Who Didn't Marry Dear Old Dad" to the force of "Wanderers Must Die." Plenty socko.[15]

Sophie was in Hollywood several weeks before shooting was scheduled to begin on "Broadway Melody of 1937." She spent the time entertaining colleagues who, like herself, had come to Hollywood from the Broadway stage to continue their careers, or so they reasoned. A party Sophie put on for Fannie Brice and Charlotte Greenwood was noted in the newspapers for its extravagant menu and decorations, all prepared by the hostess. The papers also reported that Sophie, in order to prepare herself for the movie role, had engaged Laura Hope Crews to coach her for several weeks and "perfect her delivery."

Production for "Broadway Melody of 1937" (changed to 1938 to increase the longevity of the film and account for a late-in-the-year release) began in late February at MGM studios. Since studios were now under orders that all performers must possess social security cards (a recent innovation mandated by the Roosevelt administration), Sophie was required to fill out the appropriate papers for employment. These included not only social security information, but also data useful to the studio's publicity department. Her application was quite revealing for its confusion of facts and the insight it provided regarding her personal preferences.

She claimed to have been born in Boston in 1884. She described herself as being five feet, six inches tall and weighing 170 pounds. She offered no favorite childhood memories. She reported that she had been living in Hollywood for the past ten months, in Beverly Hills. Her recreation was her work, she said, although she enjoyed swimming, dogs, horses, and bicycling. Her favorite type of person: genuine, honest, truthful; her aversion: people who are insincere. Having completed the necessary application, Sophie was now ready to work for MGM.

Executive producer of "Broadway Melody" was Irving Thalberg; producer, Jack Cummings; director, Roy Del Ruth; the screenplay from an original story by Jack McGowen and Sid Silvers. Eight songs were slated for the picture, ranging from Bizet's "Toreador Song" to the 1913 hit, "You Made Me Love You." Sophie was to sing "Your Broadway and My Broadway," with lyrics that brought in the great names of past generations, and "Some of These Days."

Starring in the film were Robert Taylor (Steve Raleigh), Eleanor Powell (Sally Lee), George Murphy (Sonny Ledford), Binnie Barnes (Caroline Whipple), Buddy Ebsen (Peter Trot), Judy Garland (Betty Clayton), and Sophie Tucker (Alice Clayton).

The plot: Millionaire Herman Whipple backs a new show to be produced by Steve Raleigh. His wife, Caroline, is impressed by Raleigh. Out-of-work dancers Sonny Ledford and Peter Trot get work training Mrs. Whipple's horse, "Stargazer."

When the horse loses a race because of an injury, Mrs. Whipple decides to sell it. On the train, she has met Sally Lee, who raised "Stargazer," but Mrs. Whipple is now more upset because it seems that Steve likes Sally. When Steve sees Sally dancing, he asks her to audition for his new show; and she is soon made the star. Steve is in love with Sally and tries to help her buy "Stargazer" from Mrs. Whipple, who, in turn, is jealous of Sally. To hurt Steve, she convinces her husband not to back the show. "Stargazer" is run in a big race and wins $25,000, which Sally uses to back the show, which is a huge success.[16]

Sophie and Judy Garland played only specialty roles, but the dynamics of their performances sparked the movie. For Garland, the movie was the first in which her dramatic singing style was revealed. Her rendition of "Dear Mr. Gable" became her first success in motion pictures. For Eleanor Powell, the movie was the debut of a star dancer. As for Sophie, she had only a few innocuous lines between her two numbers.

Shooting for the movie was completed in late July. However, though her role was small, Sophie was nonetheless forced to be "on call" throughout the production because of constant changes in the plot lines. Moreover, "Your Broadway and My Broadway" was a large production number and required many takes, split off into sections, which required several weeks. Sophie was not entirely pleased with her small role, but she hoped it would survive the editing by studio executives.

In fact, the completed picture was taken to San Diego to test-market it before an audience. Decisions on what remained and what would be cut were determined by the audience's responses. To Sophie's surprise and delight, the executives reported that the test audience had loved Sophie. She was now a bona fide movie star, at least in her own perception. To celebrate her success, she purchased a new car, bought a home in Beverly Hills, and hosted many dinner parties.[17]

"Broadway Melody" was to be released in early September, its premiere at the Capitol Theater, New York. Stars of the movie were expected to attend the opening. In the meantime, Sophie was booked to play in Detroit and Chicago on her way to New York. The engagements had to be canceled when she received a call from MGM to return to Hollywood, to appear in another picture. Delighted, Sophie dutifully checked in at the MGM studio to await her new movie assignment.

On September 2, "Broadway Melody of 1938" made its public debut. The *New York Times* reviewer called the movie "a cut above the average musical chapter-play. Unfortunately, most of 'Broadway Melody' had been done before." *Variety,* on the other hand, reported that the movie was "swell entertainment and will do smash business everywhere." And what of Sophie?

The *Times* reviewer had little to say about Sophie, praising her for her vitality, "though her emoting is strictly not on the level."

Variety gave Sophie and Judy Garland a "special niche." They were praised as performers who, "with much less to do than the others, stand out like traffic lights."

> ...when she walks on the screen something happens. You can hear what the others are saying, but Miss Tucker is the only one you see. It's as if all that energy of more than a score of years in vaudeville has been recharged and sewed up in

A publicity device to promote the opening of the movie "Broadway Melody" was the appearance of the entire cast on radio. Although Sophie played only a cameo role in the movie, she was the center of attention on the radio broadcast. Front row, left to right: Igor Gorin, Judy Garland, Sophie, Eleanor Powell, Harriet Parsons, and Frances Langford. Back row, left to right: Billy Gilbert, George Murphy, Buddy Ebsen, and Robert Taylor. (Museum of the City of New York)

    one package. Most of the rest is just filler-in between the Tucker and Garland numbers.[18]

Sophie's new movie, "Thoroughbreds Don't Cry," began production in early September. This was the first picture in which Judy Garland received top billing and the first of several films in which she co-starred with Mickey Rooney. The studio had previously announced that Lewis Stone and Edna May Oliver were to co-star with Rooney. However, Stone was replaced by C. Aubrey Smith and Oliver by Sophie. Not only was Sophie not the original choice for the role, she would not be singing in the picture. From the beginning, Sophie was unhappy with the assignment.

    Harry Rapf was producer of the movie; Alfred E. Green, director; the original story was by Elmore Griffin and J. Walter Ruben. Starring in the picture were Judy Garland (Cricket West); Mickey Rooney (Timmie Donovan); Roland Sinclair (Roger

Calverton), a last minute replacement for Freddie Bartholomew; C. Aubrey Smith (Sir Peter Calverton); and Sophie Tucker (Mother Ralph).

The plot: Sir Peter Calverton, hoping to win enough money to save his estate, takes his horse, "The Pookah," to California to run in the Santa Anita Cup. His grandson, Roger, and their trainer convince Sir Peter to hire jockey Timmie Donovan. Though an excellent jockey, Timmie has a "swelled head." He lives at Mother Ralph's boardinghouse, along with her niece, Cricket West. Timmie is urged to see his estranged father, who had abandoned him as a boy. Now his father begs him to throw a race so that he can collect enough money to pay his medical bills. At first reluctant, Timmie agrees to throw the race. When "The Pookah" loses, Sir Peter has a heart attack and dies; and Timmie disappears. When he discovers that his father's illness was a lie, he takes the winnings to enter "The Pookah" in the Cup race. Timmie's father reveals his crime; Timmie admits his guilt and is banned from racing. With Mother Ralph's help, Roger qualifies and rides "The Pookah" to victory.[19]

In the movie "Thoroughbreds Don't Cry," Sophie and Judy Garland sang a duet. The movie was Judy's first starring role, and her singing created a studio sensation. Sophie, on the other hand, considered her movie role, manager of a boardinghouse for jockeys, demeaning. (Museum of the City of New York)

Sophie's role consisted of operating a boardinghouse for jockeys. She had a number of amusing lines.

"Thoroughbreds Don't Cry" was premiered November 12 at the Uptown Theater, Los Angeles. It was an inauspicious start for a movie played as farce-comedy — a few emotional moments and some thrilling racing scenes. *Variety*'s sarcasm helped sink the movie into disregard.

> They might not break down and shed tears, but the racing thoroughbreds would rise up on their hind legs and let out a neigh of protest if they knew that their instinctive urges to win were thwarted by crooked jockeys, touts and gamblers.[20]

Sophie received only brief mention, as playing Garland's aunt and a boardinghouse owner. Nothing more. She now anxiously hoped for a call from the studio for another picture. It never came.

In the meantime, Morris publicity announced that Jack Yellin was planning to write a biography of Sophie and suggested that she was very busy collecting material about her early career. Pictures in the book were to include shots of her visits to England and poses with royalty. After Sophie left Hollywood, nothing more was heard of the project.

Her distressing experiences in Hollywood made Sophie irritable and embarrassed. The studios were obviously disinterested in her. She had no immediate stage bookings. Playing benefits offered little solace. A one-time appearance on the Metro-Maxwell radio show that included a celebration of her son's birthday—he was thirty-three—only served to remind Sophie of her own aging. Being honored by the Southern California Women's Press Club for her "long years of entertaining performances" did little to improve her sense of self-worth. She believed that her role as boardinghouse matron had demeaned her, and the frustration of not being allowed to sing made her even more angry. For a brief moment, Sophie wondered about her future. Was she too old for the new media? Had her act become dated vaudeville material? Could she still find a place on the stage, where her skills and reputation were recognized? The movies might have exposed her name across the country; but, at the same time, they appeared to have smothered her stage persona. It was four frustrating months before she was able to renew her stage career.

Abe Lastfogel called Sophie to inform her that she had an engagement at the Riviera nightclub, New York, beginning May 23, 1938, with an intermediate stop at her familiar haunt, the Oriental Theater, Chicago. Sophie was packed and ready to leave in an hour. Left behind forever were an automobile, a Beverly Hills home, and servants (generously compensated).

Sophie was now back in business, her kind of business. The *Chicago Tribune* reported that Sophie was "in town" and "the Oriental is once more looking like a theater instead of a hideaway."[21] *Variety* labeled her new show "bang-up entertainment." But not everything she sang was new; some songs were taken from her recent pictures, and some were popular radio tunes. Her efforts for constant "newness" in the act had decreased, but no one seemed to notice or care.

> "Your Broadway and Mine" gets the heart tugs and she finishes with a new arrangement on "Some of These Days," telling the story of 1912 when Sheldon Brooks first brought her the song in Chicago. It's a good lead-in for the song itself. She looks like a million, as always, and her showmanship has few peers in the business.[22]

Sophie came away from the engagement refreshed, given the stage again, with enthusiastic audiences who refused to let her go.

Marden's Riviera, a roadhouse on the western banks of the Hudson River, was located in Fort Lee, New Jersey. Marden's had quickly developed a reputation for producing fine stage shows, and it attracted a large New York crowd. Sophie headed the cast, aided by old friends Willie and Eugene Howard, four other acts and two orchestras. Sophie began her act in a dialogue with Ted about a man who had attempted to seek her autograph. That led into "I'm the Girl Who Didn't Marry Dear Old Dad," a dance sequence with the chorus, and finally "You've Got to Be Loved to Be Healthy," a typical Tucker sizzler. Encores followed, with the audience shouting for all their old favorites. "She is still the last of the red-hot mamas," said *Variety*, "and puts on a fine show as m.c. and in her popular stint."[23]

In fact, Sophie was so much in demand that she played at the Riviera through early August to continually crowded houses. Two weeks in Saratoga entertained the horse racing crowd again. A visit to Philadelphia, however, was short-circuited when the AFA, Sophie's union, threatened to go on strike, forcing her to travel to New York and meet with the union council.

Members of the AFA had pulled out of an engagement at the Strand Theater, New York, featuring Ben Bernie and his orchestra. The AFA's complaint was that the members of a female choir on the bill were not being paid minimum wage. Bernie became so irate at the AFA's action that he resigned as vice president and a member of the council and threatened to speak out against the AFA and its policies. Sophie, who had recently been elected to the council, as well as serving as honorary president, attempted to resolve the argument but was outvoted. Bernie kept his promise to resign from the AFA.

Variety scolded the AFA for its prejudicial behavior and suggested that the union needed a fresh outlook about handling its business affairs. Sophie expressed agreement with *Variety'*s assessment and decided to take a more hands-on approach as president. She helped resolve the argument with Bernie, but the episode proved to be only the precursor to a welter of disagreements, both inside and outside the AFA, regarding the union's practices and internal operations.

While she was in New York, the Morris office called Sophie to attend a meeting with producer Vincent Freedley, at his offices to discuss a possible role in his new musical comedy. The meeting itself was inconclusive, however; and Sophie was unsure she wanted to deal with the usual musical comedy limitations and what they might cost her in future bookings.

In the meantime, Sophie had a week's engagement in Hartford to prepare. She was looking forward to returning home, and audiences were eager to see her again. The bill included, besides Sophie and Ted, a fresh, new comedian, Henny Youngman; five other acts; and an orchestra. Hartford's "hometown gal" was a smash hit again. The theater was sold out for the entire engagement.

Sophie sang a swing arrangement of "Annie Laurie," followed by "Your Broadway and Mine" and "Alexander's Ragtime Band." She reminisced about the old hometown and her early days, in a tear-jerker monologue, then closed the act with her old standby, "Some of These Days." Sophie also had the opportunity to visit with her brothers and sister and their families; it had been some time since they last had been together. Phil was not feeling well, but it was his wife who complained. Moses talked constantly about his family. Anna had small children to show off. Bert was not present.

A message awaited Sophie when she returned to New York: come to Freedley's office to hear the songs Cole Porter had written especially for her. The show was to be called "Leave It To Me," and plans were for it to open in November in New York.

Sophie adored the songs she would sing, as well as the script, no doubt because she would have a major speaking part. Co-starring in a musical comedy had been a longtime wish; and, after twenty-nine years, it had finally come true. Rehearsals were to begin immediately. Still, so that Sophie might protect herself, the producers granted her the option to double at a nightclub if she desired.

"Leave It to Me" was written by Bella and Samuel Spewack, based on their successful stage comedy, "Clear All Wires." The music and lyrics were by Cole Porter, coming off his award-winning musical, "Anything Goes." Sam Spewack staged the production; dances and ensembles were arranged by Robert Alton; costumes designed by Raoul Bene Du Bois. Sophie would co-star with William Gaxton (a star in Porter's "Anything Goes" and "Fifty Million Frenchmen" and Lew Fields's "Connecticut Yankee") and Victor Moore (a veteran comedian who had successfully transitioned from old vaudeville to new musical comedy). Also in the cast, playing a small part, was Mary Martin.

Theater historian Gerald Bordman had called the show "the first successful spoof of the Soviet Union on the musical stage." (When, a year later, the Soviet Union and Nazi Germany signed a non-aggression pact, the script was modified to reflect the public's changed perception of Russia.) Alonzo P. Goodhue (Victor Moore) plays a confused U.S. Ambassador to the Soviet Union, not sure how he got the job. In fact, his position is due to his ambitious wife (Sophie Tucker), who contributed $95,000 to a political party campaign fund to win him the position. Now living in Russia with his wife and five beautiful daughters, the ambassador thinks only of returning home. Buckley Joyce Thomas (William Gaxton), a newspaper reporter, is sent to Moscow to reveal Goodhue for what he really is and get him recalled. Meanwhile, Goodhue himself is purposely trying to cause trouble to get sent back home. Unfortunately, every undiplomatic episode he creates is met with congratulations from both the U.S. and Russia. When he gets serious about the job and speaks of preventing war, both countries are antagonized and Goodhue's ambassadorial career is ended. Meanwhile, Thomas falls in love with one of the daughters and wins her.

It was the demure Mary Martin, however, who stole the show. Marooned in a Siberian railroad station, swathed head to foot in ermine, she sang "My Heart Belongs to Daddy," while simulating a striptease. Although the song was filled with double-entendres, Martin's innocent, sweet, and childlike voice put the song across with gusto. Almost overnight, Martin's song turned her into one of the stars of musical comedy. It was reported that, to give the song a truly sexy impact, Sophie had taken Martin aside to teach her certain "moves" designed to enhance Porter's provocative lyrics.

Sophie sang four songs: in Act One, "I'm Taking the Steps to Russia," backed by her five daughters; "Most Gentlemen Don't Like Love" (they just like to kick it around), which was put over in Sophie's typical style; in Act Two, "Tomorrow" and

"To the U.S.A. from the U.S.S.R.," in which Moore performed the old "shuffle off to Buffalo" routine. Her comedy work with Moore was met with laughter, approval, and applause.

After a week of smoothing out the production in Atlantic City, "Leave It to Me" opened at the Imperial Theater, New York, November 9. The show was an immediate hit. It played 307 performances in New York alone, to the end of July, 1939. Sophie was excited about the success of the show, as well as her own performance. No question, the stage provided more "love" and personal gratification than any movie could hope to generate.

While Sophie was enjoying Broadway's plaudits, events concerning the AFA began to show signs of impending trouble. The aborted strike and arguments with Ben Bernie had focused attention on the AFA's operations. Now

Sophie and Victor Moore co-starred in a 1939 musical comedy, "Leave It to Me," with music and lyrics by Cole Porter. The show was a decided hit and ran in New York for an entire season, more than 300 performances. Sophie, playing the role of an domineering wife to Victor Moore's confused and malleable husband, was a natural. (Museum of the City of New York)

a series of articles in the *Hollywood Reporter* suggested that executive secretary Whitehead was mismanaging the union. Questions were being raised by the 4A's (the Associated Actors and Artists of America) regarding Whitehead's handling of funds. Some of the accusations had become quite nasty, and Sophie reacted strongly to these comments, since it appeared they were a reflection on her presidency and personal integrity.

Early in 1939, hostility between the 4A's, SAG, and the AFA broke out in the newspapers; and Sophie found herself a partner to this conflict. She had no idea what she was getting into.

13

The Labor Union Blues

During the past several years, actors' unions had made substantial progress, not only in their relations with theater owners and managers, but also with their internal affairs. It seemed that the year 1939 would likely contribute to further strengthening the performer's role in the amusement industry.

In the ranks of professional show business labor unions, all actors were governed by the American Federation of Labor (AFL), one of the country's most powerful labor organizations. The AFL had given a charter to the Associated Actors and Artistes of America (AAAA or 4As), giving them jurisdiction over the entire field of performance. The 4As member affiliates, each with its own charter, covered different fields of entertainment. These included: Actors Equity (AEA); Screen Actors Guild (SAG); American Federation of Radio Artists (AFRA); American Federation of Actors (AFA); American Guild of Musical Artists (AGMA); and a number of minor unions.

For 1939, the 4As primary objective was to strengthen its various unions so as to facilitate necessary changes in its constitution. Efforts were also being made to house, under one roof, a unified system of bookkeeping, membership, and dues-payment. While everyone agreed on the proposed changes, the actual method to bring it about remained to be worked out. Previously, strong disagreements between the AEA and SAG had stymied progress. A good deal of time, effort, and political energy were being invested to determine which of the unions had jurisdiction over certain other performing groups. AFRA had recently taken over radio rights, in which Equity, SAG, and AFMA had previously had a stake. The AFA and Burlesque Artists finally agreed to merge, bringing together all vaudeville and burlesque performers. The AFA also absorbed Chorus Equity (formerly a subsidiary of Actors Equity), thus gaining jurisdiction over chorus members in nightclubs and vaudeville houses.

While the AFA had expanded its membership by absorbing chorus and burlesque performers and winning a battle with Ringling Brothers-Barnum & Bailey circus management—forcing the show to close until it improved wages and working conditions for its employees—the AFA's forceful tactics had received a "brutal lambasting" from the press. At the same time, extensive criticism from inside the 4As itself questioned the AFA's leadership and goals.

At the beginning of 1939, the AFA officers were Sophie Tucker, president; Rudy Vallee, vice president; and Charles Mosconi, treasurer. Sophie had been selected honorary president in 1935 and had little to do except preside at events and benefits. Ralph Whitehead, the union's executive secretary, continued in his position as the chief administrator of the organization. As with most performers' unions, the AFA's officers were non-paid, their positions primarily ceremonial and prestigious. The officers were seldom aware of the operating details of their own union, since they spent most of their time "on the road." Eddie Cantor, a former AFA president, had persuaded Sophie to take on the job, believing she could improve the union's image of honesty, integrity, and assistance for destitute actors.

Early in 1939, Sophie, wishing to take a more active role in the AFA, called a general meeting to discuss a bonding system. Under this proposal, all theater operators would agree to pay performers—all of whom were AFA members—the promised wage, or the theater would be shut down. The AFA was also about to establish its own charity for destitute actors, to be called the Sophie Tucker Fund.

The bonding idea had first been suggested by Actors Equity. Henceforth, all theater operators would be obligated to post bonds to ensure payment of salaries. Some recent failures to pay actors had motivated the bonding idea. The new Tucker Fund would provide for hospitalization for sick and needy members of the AFA.

During the next several months, the AFA, under the aggressive leadership of executive secretary Whitehead, forced Billy Rose, operator of the Aquacade at the New York World's Fair, to give employees salary for rehearsals as well as performances. In addition, he sent notices to all Chicago vaudeville and nightclub operators that the AFA was demanding a closed shop. In other words, all actors performing at these theaters had to belong to the AFA. If not, the union would strike. Further, Whitehead informed the Theater Authority (TA), a committee made up of the various unions, that it had been too lax in agreeing to sponsor benefit shows, thereby depriving actors of salary. The TA had originally been formed to determine which benefit shows were for legitimate charity purposes and which were not. If a show was considered legitimate, actors were permitted to play without pay. In such cases, the TA would collect a percentage of the gross box-office receipts which was then to be divided among all the theatrical charities. Those shows not viewed as legitimate would have to pay actors' salaries. A number of the lesser unions complained that Whitehead was attempting to control the TA by threatening its operation.

When Whitehead announced that the AFA was sending letters to all West Coast operators demanding a closed shop, SAG, which was especially strong on the coast, objected to this AFA incursion into SAG "territory." In fact, SAG served notice to the 4As that it was opposed to the formation of "one big union," for fear that the umbrella group might lead to control by a small group of paid employees or by a particular faction (i.e., the executive secretaries of the various unions). SAG further pointed out that the film business was centered on the West Coast; therefore, SAG

Sophie was feted by members of the American Federation of Actors when she was elected president of the union. The position was primarily ceremonial; but when her union was investigated for financial irregularities, Sophie decided to take an active part in defending it. (Museum of the City of New York)

should be able to maintain its influence there. SAG also questioned Whitehead's official conduct and filed a complaint with the 4As, stating that SAG was "critical of Mr. Whitehead and the conduct of the AFA." Responding to SAG's accusations, Sophie wrote the 4As, explaining the AFA's position concerning its recent activities and strongly defending Whitehead's actions.[1]

Unfortunately, Sophie was totally unaware that, for the past several months, the 4As had already been examining Whitehead's activities, due to rumors regarding his handling of the AFA's finances. Information about the rumors had been passed on to Whitehead by a lawyer friend familiar with the inner workings of SAG. In his letter, the lawyer provided names of 4As and SAG members "out to take care of Whitehead." He also mentioned a reference to the effect that "they would take care of all the Jews in the 4As, and particularly the AFA."[2]

In an action ill-conceived, and without consulting Sophie, Whitehead contacted the 4As and claimed that, because he was the subject of malicious rumors, he insisted on a debate of the contested issues. When Sophie was informed of his action, she supported his position, although she was still unaware of the issues. The people out to "get" Whitehead and the AFA were delighted with the results of their surreptitious actions. Finally, Whitehead's activities would be revealed.

In light of Whitehead's challenge and the information already collected regarding his activities, the 4As published formal charges against the AFA and called for assistance from New York City District Attorney Thomas Dewey's office and the U.S. Revenue Department. The 4As claim was that the AFA had been using tax-free benefits for non-charity purposes. If the charges were upheld, the AFA could be accused of tax evasion and lose its charter. Sophie was totally taken aback by the turn of events, not really sure what to say or do, if she was in a position to do anything at all. She believed that her union was being attacked and her only recourse was to defend the AFA and Whitehead.

Sophie called a membership meeting for June 20 at the Edison Hotel, New York, hoping to give Whitehead a vote of confidence. Seven hundred people attended the meeting, which did not turn out as Sophie planned. In fact, in the early hours of the morning, the meeting devolved into a riot that had to be quelled by police.[3]

To begin the meeting, Sophie attempted to lead the discussion toward giving Whitehead a collective vote of confidence, so as to challenge the charges made against him. Nonetheless, several speakers from the floor, later identified as nonmembers and SAG "plants," attacked AFA policies and demanded Whitehead's resignation. When Sophie found herself unable to maintain order, she abruptly adjourned the meeting and was roundly booed. Sophie's refusal to recognize Peter Wells, an opposition leader, and seizure of the microphone by a showgirl precipitated a melee. Sophie, Whitehead, Vallee, Harry Richman, and Milton Berle left by a backstage exit as the riot-to-be ignited. Several fist fights broke out, and the amplifying system and lights were turned off in an attempt to halt the uproar. Police had to be called to stop the disturbance. Sophie later declared that the disorderly course of events had been plotted by non–AFA members and SAG adherents. The opposition claimed they were denied a fair hearing. SAG, in particular, was incensed by Sophie's accusations.

Eddie Cantor and Rudy Vallee, former AFA presidents, then appealed to the membership not to give Whitehead a vote of confidence. Sophie was stunned at the position they took, since both had long been loyal AFA members. Cantor also wired Sophie. As a friend for twenty years, he appealed to her to resign, so as not to become innocently involved in a situation for which she was not responsible. Still smarting from the riotous meeting, Sophie not only refused Cantor's request, but accused him of deserting his fellow-actors. Cantor shot back a telegram expressing his surprise at Sophie's charge.[4]

"Are you not being a bit hysterical, Sophie? Your bigness of heart blinds you to the fact that there is great mismanagement of the AFA." He concluded the telegram by advising Sophie: "You are an honest and sincere person and have done much to aid the actors in their many fights. You have been misled in this present controversy; and, as a friend, I plead with you to resign as quickly as possible, or you will innocently involve yourself." Other colleagues, including William Morris, wrote similar appeals to Sophie.

Instead, Sophie responded to Cantor by suggesting a thorough investigation of the situation, believing the accusations were the "result of malicious gossip spread by our enemies." She reaffirmed her support for the AFA and Whitehead and believed that the investigation would prove that Cantor had been misled. She also asked him to withdraw his intended resignation from the AFA.

Nonetheless, actions by various groups in opposition, as well as by the investigatory unit of the 4As, had already progressed far beyond Sophie's awareness. First, the 4As demanded a written answer from her regarding the charges spelled out against Whitehead and the AFA. Second, a hearing was set for July 10, at which time the AFA could present its own witnesses. Immediately, Sophie entered general denials to the 4As' charges.

Still, as the 4As explained it, their entire controversy was with Ralph Whitehead's administration as executive secretary of AFA. Sophie was not implicated in the 4As charges. Why then was she defending Whitehead and the union?

Whitehead's challenge to have the 4As examine his activities was accepted. Through its lawyers, the 4As requested the AFA's records. For the time being, the district attorney's office declined to involve itself, claiming that press reports of its involvement were untrue. A public statement by the district attorney's office clarified its position. Sophie's letter to the *New York Times* reiterated the same information, so as not to make it appear that the AFA was under governmental scrutiny.

Not so for the 4As. It soon obtained the AFA's papers and financial records "for informational purposes." The AFA's lawyer, however, refuted the 4As right to investigate by arguing that union bi-laws stated that the parent organization could not "prefer charges against one of its subordinate lodges," and that the 4As were powerless to do so. No answer would be made to the 4As' accusations until the AFA was convinced that the 4As had jurisdiction.

On June 26, Sophie wrote a letter to William Green, president of the AFL, arguing the 4As' inability to prefer charges against the AFA.[5] She suggested that the charges were rumors and stories planted by "persons unfriendly to the AFA." In responding to the charges made against the AFA, she believed they had "no merit" and had been made in "bad faith." She pointed out that, although the official charges had been made ten days previously, the AFA had not yet received copies of them. If, however, a hearing were to be convened, she wrote, the AFA would participate, unless it believed the hearing would not be "an impartial inquiry."

Once again, Sophie's friends and colleagues attempted to persuade her to disassociate herself from the growing storm of criticism against the AFA. Again she refused everyone, saying she would wait until the 4As' charges were heard. Even members of the 4As purposely withheld criticisms of the AFA for three days to permit Sophie to withdraw from the onerous situation. When she demurred, the 4As permitted the release of their unflattering report.

The 4As selected personnel to hear the charges at the July 10 meeting, among them representatives from each affiliate organization. The AFA was entitled to three delegates, but it had not yet selected them, since it had decided to boycott the hearing. The press considered this decision a grave error and blamed Sophie for preventing the AFA side from being heard. In response, the AFA lawyer threatened to go to the AFL to seek an injunction to halt the proceedings.

Nevertheless, the July 10 hearing was held, without the AFA in attendance. The findings of the 4As' investigation savaged the AFA's style of doing business. They charged gross mismanagement, misuse of charity funds, disregard of constitutional rules and membership rights, misrepresentation of the union's affairs to its members, underhanded deals with employers, failure to render service to the membership, and refusal to cooperate with affiliate unions. Since the evidence was uncontested, all charges were upheld.

Three issues were of particular consequence. First, $12,000 due to the TA for actor relief had amounted to much less because some money had been used for AFA operational purposes. Second, an annual benefit showed a profit of $7,150 after paying large amounts to salaries, expenses, and commissions; but Whitehead's books showed no expenses or commissions had been paid, nor had an accounting of all expenditures ever made by Whitehead. Third, the AFA Council had given Whitehead $1,700 to purchase an auto; but no bill of sale or payment for its purchase was found. Sophie's claim that the $12,000 had been given to the TA for artist relief was declared "untrue" by the auditor. In fact, the auditor declared that there was no evidence that any money had ever been paid to the TA. Under later questioning, Sophie had to admit she had no firm evidence of payment. In addition, it appeared that the money for Whitehead's auto had been taken from relief funds.

The report also disclosed that, although the AFA claimed a membership of 15,000, of whom 9,000 were paid-up members, there were only 5,905 membership cards in the active file and many of these people were no longer members or were in arrears. Moreover, Charles Mosconi, AFA treasurer, had been the recipient of $500 in "loans," for which no repayment was recorded. Most devastating, the auditor said that the union's books appeared to have been altered to show that the money raised from benefits had been moved from one account to another.[6]

Still, in spite of these revelations, Sophie declared she would stick by the AFA "to the finish." She and the lawyers convened a meeting to map plans for a rebuttal of the 4As' charges.

Variety reported that, due to her recalcitrance, the 4As planned to suspend Sophie from the union, the effect being that she would have to withdraw from all entertainment contracts and engagements.[7] The 4As also prepared a charter to form a new union, the American Guild of Variety Artists (AGVA), to replace the AFA, thereby forcing AFA members to convert to the AGVA if they wished to remain union members.

Sophie was staggered by the 4As' actions. Nonetheless, after recovering from the news, she announced that she refused to accept the 4As' pronouncements, that the AFA would "continue to conduct their union as before." AFA lawyers again challenged the 4As, claiming they had no jurisdiction to hold hearings or submit charges. The dispute was now headed for the courts; and Sophie found herself to be the focus of attention, even more than Whitehead's alleged misdeeds. Yet, she remained determined not to back down.

After an appeal from Whitehead, a new force now entered the dispute. George E. Brown, president of the International Alliance of Theatrical Stage Employees (IATSE), a non–4As union, sided with the AFA.[8] The IATSE threatened to strike if the AFA was not treated "with respect." Brown was the power-hungry boss of a powerful union that could affect every theater owner in the country. He looked upon the controversy as an opportunity to disrupt the 4As and grab a leadership position for himself. (An additional underlying threat was that the IATSE was being financed by the CIO, which wanted to infiltrate the artists' unions.) At the same time that AFA lawyers were attempting to secure an injunction against the 4As, Whitehead applied to Brown to be granted an IATSE charter for the AFA. When she was informed of this news, Sophie was shocked at Whitehead's actions, since she was doing everything she could to keep the AFA in the 4As' organization. Her belief in Whitehead had been dealt a blow. Now, for the first time, she believed that she might be being manipulated.

Moving quickly, the IATSE granted a charter to the AFA, stating that its council was within its constitutional rights to make such an alliance without prior approval from its membership. Of the IATSE and AFA members present to vote on the issue, Sophie was the only one to vote against the alliance. At the same time, Whitehead announced the AFA's resignation from the TA and declared that the union planned to boycott the upcoming meeting that had been scheduled to look into the AFA's use of relief funds.

In its July 26 issue, *Variety* voiced its opinions about the conflict, focusing on "the AFA's blunders."[9]

> The officials of the American Federation of Actors appear now to be making every effort to bring upon themselves another indictment—for gross stupidity."

On the AFA's resignation from the Theater Authority:

> Last week's resignation from the Theater Authority was an inexcusable blunder. If not exactly an admission of guilt, it was the closest thing to it."

Regarding the AFA riot:
Whitehead called the meeting, but when it came time to sticking a neck out it was Sophie Tucker's that lay on the block that night. Whitehead remained quiet; Soph took all the abuse and some of the saner minds began to wonder why.

Clearly articulated in the *Variety* article was a decided concern for Sophie.

> Whitehead uses the AFA; Sophie Tucker is a non-salaried president and, until the investigation started, probably as unfamiliar as any minor member of the AFA with the inner workings. Why was Sophie pushed to the forefront, while Whitehead remained in the background? Practically all of the charges against the AFA for mismanagement focused chiefly upon Whitehead, but from appearances it had been made to look as though Miss Tucker was the major target. Those who like Soph are beginning to feel that she has been "put on the spot" for selfish reasons.

Variety also pointed out that the AFA's affiliation with the IATSE was solely a Whitehead action, obtained without calling a vote of the AFA membership.

In early August, a showdown occurred when the IATSE threatened to strike against the 4As. If the strike actually took place, it would halt virtually all show business in both Hollywood and Broadway. The 4As attacked the IATSE and warned of severe punishment for anyone supporting a strike. SAG suspended Sophie.[10] Equity announced it planned to suspend Sophie at its next meeting. AFRA said it would follow suit at its meeting in a few days. It had become an avalanche of bad news for Sophie.

Still the featured star in the highly successful "Leave It To Me," Sophie planned to reopen the show August 21 at the Imperial Theater, New York. The IATSE-AFA declared that, if Sophie were barred from the show, the stagehands would strike. In addition, Sophie supposedly had a picture contract with Universal; and her suspension by SAG would short-circuit that engagement, as well. Sophie made the situation even worse by participating in the ceremonies uniting the IATSE with the AFA.

When news of these startling events hit the national newspapers, Sophie found herself deluged with hundreds of telegrams, letters, and phone calls from actors, colleagues, and theater owners across the country.[11] Those supporting Sophie were old friends and colleagues urging her to quit, although a few said she should "fight on." Those against Sophie, and they numbered three times as many as her supporters, ranged in their reactions from pleading to keep their shows running to spewing outright anti–Semitic vitriol. The members of one entire cast from a New York show each sent her a telegram begging that she consider their jobs and salaries, if she ever considered actors at all.

Indeed, Sophie was overwhelmed by these messages; and friends believed they helped her to realize her predicament and its potentially disastrous outcome. She

After a contentious meeting with the Associated Actors and Artists of America (4As), its parent union, the AFA was disbanded; and Sophie lost her union membership. Fortunately, thanks to appeals from many colleagues, she was reinstated so she could return to the stage.

would not knowingly put actors out of business, nor would she contribute to the union's vicious bickering. A meeting of the 4As, its affiliate unions, and lawyers was set for August 17 to discuss the explosive issues and, it was hoped, achieve some resolutions. SAG called a meeting for August 22 to hear the charges against Sophie.

Prior to the 4As' meeting, New York Supreme Court Judge McGoldrick ruled that the union conflict was not a labor dispute, thus clearing the way for the 4As to hold its hearing and clean up the problems internally. The decision supported the 4As' action to revoke the AFA charter and organize a new union to incorporate the AFA's former members. The ruling was a decided blow against Whitehead and the IATSE.

In addition, the 4As won a decisive victory in defense of its autonomy and jurisdiction over all affiliates. The 4As repudiated the agreement between the IATSE and AFA; then the AFA was expelled from the 4As and had its charter revoked. These actions prevented a strike but left unsettled the status of Ralph Whitehead, who was responsible for the entire controversy. Sophie's fate was yet to be determined.

Ironically, when Sophie appeared at the 500 Club (a non–4As establishment) on August 14 to begin a week's engagement, members of the 4As crowded the nightclub and "enthusiastically applauded her singing." Obviously moved by the reception she had received, Sophie went to the 4As table and thanked them for being her "best audience in the house." It was also a sign that she had been forgiven.

Meanwhile, Vincent Freedley, producer of "Leave It to Me," conferred with SAG officials, pleading to have Sophie reinstated so that he could open the show on schedule. "We could hardly play without Sophie," he told the group. He also claimed that, if the show did not go on, he could not pay the others in the cast two weeks salary — as stipulated in the contract — because he would have no funds.[12]

The day before Sophie's meeting with SAG officials, *Variety* reported that she was about to be reinstated, "without prejudice," because no one could claim that she had ever been disloyal to them. Sophie formally resigned from the AFA and sent an application to the AGVA to join the new organization. At her hearing with SAG, with little discussion, Sophie was formally reinstated. All of her friends and colleagues were greatly relieved that the internecine battle had finally been resolved. For Sophie, the entire affair had been one filled with conflicting emotions, humiliation, and embarrassment, an experience that she would never forget.

Prior to his hearing, Ralph Whitehead suffered a severe heart attack, which delayed his trial for many months. While he was ultimately convicted of "moving funds in an unauthorized manner," Whitehead was dismissed with no more than a strong reprimand.

When informed of Sophie's reinstatement, Freedley was greatly relieved and rushed her into rehearsals. "Leave It to Me" would open a week late, but the show would definitely open. In the meantime, Sophie opened at the Versailles nightclub for a four-week engagement, taking the clause in advantage of her contract that allowed her to double if she desired. She wanted the work and needed the money.

14

Fast Becoming a Legend

Only the most perceptive patrons would have recognized nervousness and anxiety in Sophie's demeanor prior to the reopening of "Leave It to Me." Yet it had been less than a week since Sophie had been reinstated by SAG in order to be permitted to perform again.

To the audience, Sophie seemed her usual flamboyant self, parading across the stage with her familiar assurance while shouting out the titillating innuendoes of Cole Porter's lyrics.

Brooks Atkinson, the *New York Times* reviewer, was genuinely pleased to see Sophie and the cast back on stage. He hoped that past hard feelings would quickly fade away once the show began.

> Out of loyalty to her beaming talents let us hope that the anger aroused by internal strife may quickly pass away. Although the venerable slogan that 'the show must go on' seems silly on certain public occasions, it seems like the commonest sort of sense just now. A good show can heal almost any kind of wound.[1]

The cast, too, seemed anxious to proceed, demonstrating an obvious "prance" in their steps and glad to be back to work.

Nonetheless, the Spewacks (writers of the show) had to deal with new creative problems, political in nature, due to the recent signing of a non-aggression pact between Germany and Russia. In effect, the Soviet Union was no longer considered an ally of the U.S., especially not as portrayed in the original script. The roles of the ambassadors had to be changed, along with U.S. loyalties. Soviet good-guys had now become bad-guys; and even Sophie was forced to modify the lyrics of her song about Russia to meet the new requirements. Another change in the show was the replacement of Mary Martin by Mildred Fenton, to sing "My Heart Belongs to Daddy." Still, first nighters believed she had done a respectable job as a replacement for Martin. Victor Moore's comedy presence seemed to be the "perfect augway" to let audiences know that good feelings had again returned to the theater.

"Leave It to Me" reopened at the Imperial Theater September 11, 1939, to a crowded house that, to show their appreciation to the cast, cheered every actor's entrance and seemed to laugh all the more heartily at the jokes. That "honeymoon" lasted throughout the entire month the show appeared in New York. Vincent Freedley, the producer, had originally planned to begin the new season on the road; but the recent union conflict and threatened strike suggested he open in New York to take advantage of the higher ticket cost and audience euphoria about the shows' reopening. His hunch was obviously correct.

For the remainder of the year, the musical comedy's tour included Philadelphia; Washington, D.C.; Pittsburgh; Detroit; Chicago; Dayton; Cincinnati; St. Louis; then two weeks of one-night stands, plus Kansas City and Baltimore, where it would finally close. The show did well in Philadelphia and Washington, D.C.; but box-office in all other cities, with the exception of Chicago, consistently declined. When the show arrived in Chicago, Sophie and the cast were met at the train and escorted to their hotel. The opening evening turned away hundreds of patrons. First week's box-office was a record-breaking $26,500.

Although the *Daily News* reviewer complained that the show had been cheapened by replacing a number of secondary leads, the stars "deployed themselves in roadshow form."

> The evening will not be for you in vain should you join the throngs which are rushing down upon the Auditorium box office.[2]

When the musical played in Philadelphia, Sophie doubled at Jack Lynch's Hotel Walton Roof. (Sophie's contract allowed her to double at nightclubs while the show was in progress.) In Detroit, she appeared at the Cadillac Hotel Casino. No Pittsburgh nightclubs booked her because they could not meet her $1,000-a-week price. Instead, the mayor of Pittsburgh honored Sophie with a key to the city. In Chicago, Sophie doubled at the Colony Club. Obviously, nightclubs still sought her, and they would continue to welcome her long after "Leave It to Me" had become history.

The weeks of one-night stands through Kansas, Oklahoma, Texas, and Tennessee were plagued by a run of extremely cold weather, which decreased audience attendance considerably. In Memphis, Victor Moore made a curtain speech about the bad weather the show had experienced; and he appealed to patrons to conduct a telephone campaign to get people to the theater. The results of his efforts were mixed.

Freedley had originally attempted to close the show in Pittsburgh; but the booking agency, UBO, refused. Poor box-office returns had persuaded Freedley to close the show prematurely. Nonetheless, UBO would not let him close until the show had been on the road for sixteen weeks, as the original contract stipulated. During the show's last several weeks, the cast had to be paid half their regular salaries just to keep the show alive until they reached Baltimore. It was a slow, sad death to what had once been a top Broadway production.

In the meantime, Sophie and the Morris office had organized her nightclub bookings for the remainder of the year. Her first stop was at Jack Dempsey's bar in Miami Beach, where Sophie played for four weeks to standing-room-only crowds cheering her every stage move. Most of her performances included songs with Yiddish lyrics because of the preponderance of Jewish patrons vacationing in Miami Beach. During one special performance each week, Sophie featured a different Hollywood star. For example, Dorothy Lamour was in town for a movie premier and was brought over to share the stage with Sophie. The pair traded acts: Dorothy sang "Some of These Days"; Sophie donned a sarong and sang a song from Dorothy's new movie. Sophie's wearing a sarong was, in itself, a show-stopper.

From Miami Beach, Sophie went to the Versailles in New York for three weeks, where she met patrons that had been following her career for, seemingly, ages. As *Variety* described her appearance, "Sophie Tucker has become a show business institution, among the best in the entertainment world." Audiences were now treating her with reverence, as well as the customary exuberance over her act. Reviewers noted that she had attained a level of elegance — "Sophie has no competition," said *Variety* — that had transformed her into an established public character in the eyes of adoring audiences. Sophie admitted that she felt uneasy with the compliment. Did it imply she was close to the end of her career, or that she had matured to serve her patrons better?

A return to Chicago's Chez Paree made her forget about veneration as audiences cheered a "new Sophie." She had slimmed down again: Her gowns were the talk of the society pages. Her songs were the type that had called out the police twenty years earlier, yet they were still met with the same degree of raucous enthusiasm.

Sophie's opening night was a smash. The *Daily News* reported that Chicago's love for Sophie had yet to cool down and that "Miss Tucker still knows best what audiences want in the nightclubs." Typically, Sophie covered all the sentiments in her song selections. In "You've Got to Be Loved to Be Healthy" (a provocative song with an added saucy monologue), she informed the audience, "I'm the healthiest gal in town." She told the tale of a bright young man whom she had loved, but who also received the contents of her purse. About the follies of husbands, Sophie noted ruefully, "I have men whose wives are beautiful creatures, but what their husbands have on their minds are double-features." Sophie's own views on life and love were expressed in "Life Begins At 40."

For the sentimental crowd, Sophie turned back to songs of other years. "After You've Gone" set hands clapping; "Sweet Georgia Brown" and "Waiting For the Robert E. Lee" were rendered in her old ragtime style. The buildup to her special encore of "Some of These Days" consisted of the story of how she had met Sheldon Brooks and how he had persuaded her to sing the song. Waving the original copy of the music, which she had owned for twenty-eight years, she launched into the song. Tucker fans went home happy and content.

One note of caution. Audiences noted that Sophie's voice was noticeably weaker.

Joseph Lauber, a longtime observer of Sophie's appearances in Chicago pointed out that "her voice was a bit worse for weather and wear." Still, he noted, to please the audience, she sang until she was hoarse.

Five weeks at the Chez Paree diminished neither audience attendance nor Sophie's enthusiastic performances. Chicago papers reported her continual success as if she was their personal star. A hastily added week at the Oriental Theater completed Sophie's Chicago engagement; and again her status was viewed as befitting a theatrical institution. *Variety* spoke in glowing terms of her recent success.

A typical publicity photo of Sophie and Ted Shapiro when they appeared at nightclubs throughout the U.S. and England.

There is no substitute for experience, and Miss Tucker's every mannerism underscores the fact that she knows her audiences and knows how to use a stage. Her appearances are no longer just "dates"; they have become "concerts."[3]

Teamed with Harry Richman's band and comedian Joe E. Lewis, Sophie played at Marden's Riviera, Fort Lee, New Jersey, to the end of October, eleven weeks. Sophie had an easier schedule here, appearing only once an evening and limiting herself to six songs, including encores. In addition to her songs, she and Lewis put on a number of comedy sketches.

While she was at Fort Lee, a story circulated in *Variety* concerning Sophie's long-term care for a fellow performer, Lora Valedon, a high-wire expert. Early in Valedon's career, Sophie had taken her on tour. In 1933, Valedon fell from the wire and, during her recovery, was found to be suffering from cancer. For seven years and several operations, Valedon fought the disease until she was cured. During this entire time, Sophie often visited her at the hospital and even took her to New York as a guest to see "Leave It to Me." The previous week, Lora Valedon had reopened her career in Boston, thanks to Sophie. "That shows what a great trooper she is," reported *Variety*, "never forgets her brother and sister performer."[4]

Sophie opened the 1941 season at the Colonial Inn, Miami, in what was now becoming an annual visit to Florida on behalf of the hoards of New York vacationers. Miami was in the process of becoming "Sophie's City" as much as Chicago claimed to be. According to *Variety*, the city had become "the Barbary Coast in Florida," a place where "everything goes," and the number one hot spot in the U.S.

Abel Green, the veteran *Variety* reporter, called Miami a cross-section of Rue Blondel, Paris's notorious sector; Greenwich Village, with its assorted sexual misfits; and Reno, with its wide-open gambling. Toss in the cream-of-the-crop from Broadway and Hollywood and "you have a case of never-a-dull moment." Due to her style of entertainment, Sophie had become a fixture in Miami. She played to full houses there through the end of March.

Unfortunately, her voice had weakened again; yet she refused to cancel her final appearances at the nightclub. Still, the problem did force her to change plans while in San Francisco, her next engagement.

Sophie had signed to appear on a CBS radio program emanating from San Francisco, prior to her engagement at the Golden Gate Theater. She was forced to cancel the job due to laryngitis and also had to delay her picture house opening for several days. Even though she was not at full voice, she drew full houses. Along with the reissue of "Devil Dogs of the Air" on screen, Sophie generated more than $18,000 in box-office receipts during the first week.

The *Chronicle's* review of Sophie's success at the Golden Gate lauded her showmanship and alluded to her now apparent icon status in popular theater. (More and more reviewers were echoing similar themes.)

> Sophie Tucker, grand ol' gal of red-hot rhythms, is doing another smash this week on the new Gate bill. A sermon of show biz could be written around this act, for here is the essence of true showmanship. The way Sophie sings a song is something they don't learn anymore. Her brilliance and magnetism may be equaled for short periods, but few indeed have the staying power, the what-it-takes of La Tucker. She's one of the reminders of what made vaudeville great.[5]

Sophie tended to use most of her nightclub material, reviewers reported, "some of which is enough to burn the ears off the family trade. But the mob here eats it up." Occupying the closing spot on the bill, Sophie sang for more than twenty minutes, bowed to a shouting-for-more audience, and then launched into her encore program. Recognizing the increased state of interest in the country's support of the Allied war effort, she urged the women to "take care of the army and navy boys."

When Sophie was playing in Saratoga Springs, she received a call from old friend and vaudeville veteran George Jessel. Would she consider appearing in a musical comedy he was putting together? The salary would not be what she normally received, and she might be called upon to help underwrite the show, but it would be a well paying job. Sophie agreed to take the part to assist an old colleague; and the show had built-in bonuses if the production did well.

Jessel had written the book for "High Kickers," a story about a young burlesque producer who is platonically protected throughout his career by a gruff but good-natured chorus girl, to whom he has been entrusted by his dying father, the owner of a burlesque company. The primary plot centered around the chorus girl's going on stage one night as a stripteaser, which caused the jailing of the entire company. The story resembled that of an old-fashioned show, full of specialty acts and parading, scantily-clad chorus girls. Jessel played the role of the young producer; Sophie played the chorus girl and his protector.

Bert Kalman and Harry Ruby wrote the songs (except for Jack Yellin for Sophie's); the dances were directed by Carl Randell; Ted Shapiro handled the musical direction; and Jessel was the producer. The entire production was designed, created, and supervised by Nat Karson. The first act contained nine songs, two of which Sophie sang, "Didn't Your Mother Tell You Nothing" and a specialty army-and-navy song. In the second act, Sophie sang one song, "I Got Something."

The show opened at the Broadhurst Theater, New York, October 31, 1941. Skeptical critics called Jessel's musical "a melange both malodorous and mediocre." Furthermore, Jessel was panned for writing about old-fashioned show business, which was more likely to convince people that the business "is infinitely keener today." They noted, however, that he succeeded in walking briskly across the stage in a series of well-fitted suits.

Nor was Sophie regarded any better. Critics accused her of "shouting some grimy lyrics" and performing an extensively costumed pseudo-striptease. Her role and her delivery were considered questionable.

> Miss Tucker is a singer in the grand manner. No matter what her material may be, she uses it with humor, deliberation and authority. The material this time is all in the key of the single entendre, written in a style that went out with mahjong, we hope. It is burlesque all right, but is it entertainment?[6]

Nevertheless, for the next five weeks, audiences shook off the poor reviews, filled the theater each night, and broke box-office records.

On December 7, while the matinee was in progress, a loudspeaker announcement was made by the management for all newsboys to report immediately to their stations. It seemed a strange request to be addressed in the middle of the show, but few patrons paid any attention to the odd appeal. Backstage, the news of Pearl Harbor had spread; but no one let on to the audience what had occurred. Only when patrons left the theater did they discover the reason for the announcement. Newsboys were dashing along the streets hawking extra editions telling of the Japanese attack.

The evening performance of "High Kickers" had a full house, but successive performances during the week were lucky to fill half the theater. People seemed in shock regarding the United States' abrupt entry into war. They spent their time reading newspapers and listening to radio bulletins in order to keep up with current events. Early reports were not good.

During the months following the attack, few new shows took the risk of opening and, of those that did open, most closed in a matter of weeks. Audiences could not be attracted or sustained. The usual word-of-mouth that shows needed to increase attendance was being directed toward other, more pressing issues. There was no question among theater managers that the war had depressed stage attractions, and there was no relief in sight.

Many companies folded, and many theaters closed. Shows in rehearsal were aborted because producers declined to gamble on entertaining a distracted audience that was already reeling from depressing war news and the country's mobilization efforts. Moreover, newly installed wartime rules inhibited travel, specified the conservation of resources (earlier evening starts to save coal and electricity), and called for theaters to solicit donations for the war effort. Theater staffs were being coached in blackout and bombing raid procedures. Worst of all for agents, many actors were drafted or voluntarily joined the military.

Nightclubs and picture houses either closed down or rushed to change their formats to meet the mood of a bewildered public. Even light comedy was met with some indifference. For almost the first six months of the war, popular theater lived a borderline existence.

"High Kickers" was as affected as any other show, in spite of its obvious popularity and well-liked entertainers. To attract audiences, various war effort activities were included at the performance. Bulletins were read to the audience between acts. The theater was decorated with American flags. Donations from the audience were solicited during intermission. At the end of the show, the headliners came on stage and urged patrons to buy war bonds, accompanied by the singing of patriotic songs.

An article by Billy Rose, an esteemed Broadway producer, called on performers to lead the calls for patriotism. "Showmen must sell aggressive Americanism to everyone to help strengthen civilian and military morale," he declared. Such calls for patriotism were being preached across all of entertainment, becoming almost a *raison d'etre* for actors. "We must provide plenty of gay evenings," said Rose, "so that people can forget the dark realities."

"High Kickers" could very well qualify for the presentation of a gay evening. Within a matter of weeks, patriotic songs and skits were incorporated into the plot and topical jokes (deriding both the Germans and Japanese) were inserted in the script. (At each insertion, the audience would cheer and applaud in recognition.) All of these features seemed to keep the show from "going down" but, at the same time, created a sizable strain on the production's finances.

Amazingly, "High Kickers" entertained audiences for an incredible twenty-two weeks on Broadway, playing to the end of March, 1942. In the process, the show had lost a good deal of money; but Jessel was determined to put the show on the road where, he believed, a profit could be made. Jessel convinced Sophie and Lewis of the show's road potential; Sophie even put some money into the show to cover its initial touring expenses. While the booking agents were pleased with Jessel's decision, Sophie was concerned about an "iffy" job environment.

On April 29, after a few weeks of trimming production expenses and cast, "High

Kickers" opened at the National Theater, Washington, D.C., to a responsive audience. The show made almost $20,000 in eight performances, thanks to its war-effort activities. Treasury bond sales were held at every performance; and, nudged by newspaper ads, local critics were "kind" to the musical. Unfortunately, a planned two-week engagement was reduced to one week when the National was forced into bankruptcy and was taken over by its insurance company.

Pittsburgh was the show's next stop, at the Nixon Theater. Reviewers gave "High Kickers" good press but the public disagreed. The show made a disappointing $14,500 for the week. Extensive efforts had been made to attract people to the theater — the selling of war stamps, the playing of veterans' hospital benefits by Sophie and Jessel — but the theater never filled up. Why did such a good show, according to reviewers, fail at the box office? Some suggested the cast seemed tired; others believed that the "blue" portions of the show likely made patrons uncomfortable. "High Kickers" left Pittsburgh in debt. Chicago was the next stop, and how well the show attracted box-office returns would determine its future.

Because of Sophie's extensive Chicago following, "High Kickers" received substantial newspaper publicity. Reports spoke of Sophie's last appearance in "Leave It to Me," when she had "raised her hearty voice and displayed her ample contours." Her upcoming show would top even that, the papers exclaimed, when she would engage in a striptease. In more subtler terms, the *Chicago Daily News* reported that "High Kickers" featured Sophie in "a take-off of a take-off."

Of course, Sophie was now even more intimately tied to the show because of its condensed plot. Moreover, her role as an aging burlesquer was amply interpolated by local reviewers.

> Thru the years — it is perfectly polite to refer to Miss Tucker's advance thru the middle years, for she is always talking about it herself — she has returned the same unabashed style of singing, though nowadays she often spares herself wear and tear by talking part of the words. For more years than she or anyone would like to count, she has been billed as "the last of the red hot mamas." This is, after all, as apt a description of her magnificently extroverted talent as anyone has ever been able to devise.
>
> Whether she has good material to work with or not, she is always worth prizing for her own sake.[7]

Of the show itself, little was described or anticipated.

"High Kickers" opened at the Erlanger Theater on May 11. All of Sophie's loyal admirers were on hand to cheer her on. Reviewers, however, saw the show differently. Cecil Smith, of the *Chicago Tribune*, declared that "it is never a satisfactory formula merely to revive the past from the point of view of the past." Nonetheless, he wrote, "Miss Tucker, still as vigorous as a pile driver, maintains a feeling of animation in spite of her mediocre opportunities."

Lloyd Lewis, of the *Chicago Daily News,* never a lover of Sophie's style, called "High Kickers" a "sooty show," and the most sooty of them all was Sophie.

> Miss Tucker is assigned the task of being bluntly sooted not only when she sings but when she speaks most of the dialogue of her role. As of old, Miss Tucker spends much of the evening close to the footlights assuring her audience with leering winks and emphatic confidences that she is a creature of vast animalistic experience. And, as of yore, many listeners, of whom, alas, your correspondent is not one, find intensely comic the spectacle of so Falstaffian a female, so rotund a matron, boasting of romances that are as limitless as they are lawless.[8]

Not a very good start for a show that was scheduled to play three weeks in Chicago. Sophie did not seem to be affected by the negative press, but patrons showed little inclination to attend the show. After two losing weeks, "High Kickers" had to close. The show was reported to be $140,000 in the red, and it was labeled "the season's most costly musical mistake." Jessel and Sophie had sliced their own salaries frequently, but the fixed charges of the show continued to build up. Salaries had been secured by a bank letter for $12,000, but the bank held up payment. Equity contributed $5,000 to bring the company back to New York and pay off those in the cast earning $100 or less weekly. How Jessel was going to handle the I.O.U.s he had passed out was open to question. Several weeks later, the notes went into arbitration. Since Jessel had no money, the backers of the show lost their entire investment. To a small degree, this included Sophie. Nor had she been paid for the Chicago engagement. Still, the show had been fun. As regarded the money, Sophie believed, that was just the sort of hazard that stage performers always faced.

A month later, appearing at a Navy Relief benefit, Sophie found her performance again heavily criticized. Playing before a crowd of 50,000 at Buffalo's Civic Stadium, Sophie and Olson and Johnson entertained townsfolk and the military. Sophie delivered her regular nightclub routine, interspersing it with some peppery dialogue. It left some of the spectators gasping. Immediate repercussions were heard throughout the stadium. The next day, thanks to front page headlines critical of Sophie, the entire city was gossiping over her act.

Variety called the episode "one of the toughest raps ever handed a stage performer in that city." The Buffalo Committee of the Navy Relief quickly issued a statement, regretting that one featured player (unnamed) had exceeded the bounds of propriety. Radio station WBNY, on its regular news broadcast, severely castigated Sophie, accusing her of bad judgment and purveying smut. Later, Mayor Kelly, referring to the incident, issued a public statement saying he would seek legislation to prevent the use of Civic Stadium loudspeakers for the dissemination of salacious, suggestive, and obscene songs and speeches.

To these accusations Sophie responded by calling the citizens of Buffalo "hypocrites." She claimed the same show had previously been given to servicemen in Toledo, at Camp Perry, and at Chicago's Great Lakes Naval Training Station. Audiences there had been highly appreciative, with no adverse criticism. "When you give your services for nothing and for charity, nobody has the right to criticize," said Sophie. "I am billed as the 'Red Hot Mamma'; and as long as I live, I'll always remain 'Sophie Tucker, the Red Hot Mamma.'"

Sophie appeared to be vindicated when, two weeks later, the *Buffalo Evening News* reported on the events of "Mayor Kelly Day." They revealed that not only was gambling present, but a cooch-dancing concession had been featured at the affair, with the emcee's comments over the public address system being "strongly on the spicy side."

Sophie returned to San Francisco in September. The *Chronicle* headlined her appearances "First, Last and Always."

> Sophie Tucker, "the last of the red hot mamas," was also the first and the best. And she still is.[9]

A month later, Sophie made her annual return to the Chez Paree, Chicago, for a ten-week engagement, running through the Christmas holidays. As usual, she "packed them in" for a record box office.

> It's a veritable triumph for the veteran star. Miss Tucker, of course, remains more than just a singer of tunes, old and new. She's still a tradition, part of the spangled history of show business, bringing to her performances the consummate artistry with which years of great performances have endowed her.[10]

In January, 1943, Sophie opened at the Copacabana, New York, her first appearance at this new, plush nightclub and her first performance in the city in two years. "Sophie hasn't changed her act," said one reviewer, "but neither has she gone 'back to the woods.'" The reviewer claimed that a new type of customer had come to the "classy eastside room" to see Sophie, a clientele that was unafraid to exhibit shrill whistling for a performer.

> They came to hear the mistress of song, and she gave them their fill — and more — by staying on at least a half-hour and running the gamut of the best and bluest in her extensive repertoire.[11]

While she was in New York, the suit against George Jessel was settled; but not to Sophie's liking. Jessel had to repay Equity for its salary loans, but the cast's high earners were disregarded by the court. Sophie lost not only two weeks salary, but also the money she had invested in the show. It was to be the last musical comedy she appeared in, although she continued to invest in future productions.

At the same time, Sophie was signed by Decca records to record an album of songs she had made famous. Quite naturally, the album would be titled "Some of These Days."

Sophie had planned to visit a number of army camps to entertain the troops; but while she was playing in Cincinnati, she fell ill. It began with a heavy cold that turned into bronchitis and laryngitis, and doctors soon confined her to quarters at the hotel. This time, the laryngitis was so pronounced, Sophie was unable to talk for a week. The illness also thwarted an appearance in Beverly Hills and a supposed cameo appearance in a Universal Studios Picture.

Miraculously, after a week, Sophie got out of bed, made her way to the train station, and headed for Los Angeles, where an extended engagement at the Florentine Gardens awaited her. A travesty of mislaid or ignored first-night reservations turned the evening into chaos, and many important Hollywood people were turned away since no seats were available. Confusion was so rampant in the room, it was reported that one famous Hollywood star left with a black eye.

Sophie performed throughout the evening as if nothing out of the ordinary was happening, but her show had lost its glitter due to the constant hubbub in the audience. After the show, she voiced her displeasure loudly to the management and threatened not to perform until they had corrected their reservation errors. The following evening, after a day full of frantic phone calls, telegrams, and apologies, Sophie presented her familiar act.

Reviewers again reminded Sophie of her tenure on the stage; this double-edged compliment was becoming commonplace now. While calling her act "a carbon copy" of previous work, they praised her for her tireless demeanor and her eagerness to work. Sophie presented a mixture of old and new songs, from "Put Your Arms Around Me, Honey" to "Mairzy Doats." Between shows, she circulated through the tables, chatting with acquaintances, answering questions, and signing autographs. As usual, she made it a point to be in touch with her audience.

Since this was Los Angeles, rumors regarding Sophie's return to the movies abounded. It was said she planned to appear in "Three Cheers for the Boys" with George Raft, but the studio denied any such agreement. In fact, no studio really cared to star Sophie in a movie, primarily because her previous pictures had netted little profit and

An ad in a Los Angeles newspaper featuring Sophie at the Florentine Gardens, a popular cabaret resort. By this time in her career, during the 1930s, she was already being called "America's beloved star."

now she was getting too old. After all, she was fifty-seven, and studios were more interested in featuring young actresses, whether talented or not, because of their appeal to the military audience.

When "Three Cheers for the Boys" was changed to "Follow the Boys" and the emphasis was on loading the picture with cameo performances, Sophie was hired to play Sophie.

"Follow the Boys" was Universal Pictures' contribution to the all-star musical revues being produced by all the major studios. Charles K. Feldman was the producer; Eddie Sutherland, the director. Several writers contributed specific scenes to the film, and various stage- and dance-managers directed the chorus numbers. Musical background included old standards like "Swing Low, Sweet Chariot," "Besame Mucho," and "Liebestraum." Songs in the picture included "Good Night"; "The Bigger the Army and the Navy" (by Jack Yellin); "Beyond the Blue Horizon"; "I'll Walk Alone"; "I'll Get By"; "Is You Is or Is You Ain't My Baby?"; "I'll See You in My Dreams"; "The House I Live In"; and "Some of These Days."

Starring in the cast were George Raft, Vera Zorina, Charley Grapewin, Regis Toomey, and Martha O'Driscoll. The guest list seemed to include everyone who happened to be on the Universal lot: Jeanette McDonald, Orson Welles, Marlene Dietrich, Dinah Shore, Donald O'Conner, W.C. Fields, the Andrews Sisters, Ted Lewis and his band, and Sophie Tucker. Three additional bands appeared; and, in the Hollywood Victory Committee sequence, such names as Maria Montez, Lon Chaney, Andy Devine, Evelyn Ankers, Nigel Bruce, Thomas Gomez, Randolph Scott, et al., made fleeting appearances.

Sophie had been hired to sing "Some of These Days" and had one line of dialogue, "Yes, too bad he was a gentleman," which the studio lawyers almost literally pounced on to make sure it was delivered without sexual innuendo. Her work amounted to one week on the set. Production for the picture began September 28 and was completed December 4, 1943. Additional sequences were added in ensuing months, mostly actual footage taken from army camp performances. The movie was released in New York, April 25, 1944. The picture was a financial success, earning more than a million and a half dollars domestically. For Sophie, though, it was like playing a one-night stand to an empty house.

During Sophie's time at the Florentine Gardens, the Morris agency set up her schedule for the entire year. From the Bal Tabarin, San Francisco, in November, she would move on to appearances in Las Vegas (her first visit), New York, Chicago, Detroit, Boston, and Philadelphia, before finally returning to Los Angeles.

All these appearances were in nightclubs or roadhouses. Sophie was said to be earning no less than $3,000 a week during the tour.

Her first appearance in Las Vegas, at the Last Frontier, broke all records for gross weekly receipts. The more "off color" her songs, the more audiences loved her.

Opening at the Copacabana in New York, Sophie experienced the aura of nostalgia that surrounded her presence. Reviewers spoke of her as "one of the great, virtually legendary, variety entertainers of the time."

Her repertoire of songs included "Never Too Young or Too Old," a laugh score in "If He's Good Enough to Fight for His Country, He Shouldn't Have to Fight for His Love," and "3-A Papa, You Can't 4-F Me." The show-stopper was "You Gotta Be Loved to Be Healthy," interspersed with comic recitations of her own life and loves. Among the oldies, Sophie sang "After You've Gone," "Blowing Bubbles," and, of course, "Some of These Days."

Over the past several years, Sophie had been blending new popular songs (not written by Jack Yellin) with her oldies. Her efforts to be constantly original had become an exhausting and demanding task. Now, Sophie gave way to using songs from "The Hit Parade" radio lineup. Audiences paid no heed to the change in her selections. It was her presentation that made them unique.

"Follow the Boys" had its premier while Sophie was in New York, and her appearance in the movie, although brief, was heavily promoted by Morris. The movie itself was panned for its "over-generosity." "Still," said the reviewer, "the galaxy of names should make it a cinch for big box-office." *Variety* reported, "A timely tribute to show business as big names are shown playing themselves as guest stars at the sundry service camp entertainments."

At the same time, *Variety* pointed out several specialty numbers that could have been dropped from the movie at no particular loss. The list included Jeanette McDonald, Dinah Shore, the Andrews Sisters, and Sophie.

Whatever feelings Sophie might have had about the movie review, her opening at the Chez Paree, Chicago, dispelled any doubts she may have had regarding her reputation. The *Chicago Daily News* called her "the empress of entertainment." The *Tribune* labeled her "Miss Show Business." As usual, audiences could not get enough of Sophie, although she tried to please everyone during an eight-week engagement.

When Sophie entered the stage, "her appearance was like turning on a light in a dark room." For a full five minutes, she had to stand to applause before she could say a word. "The show was definitely on — simply because she had come into the room."[12]

In a wistful piece of writing, Will Davidson, of the *Tribune*, bemoaned the day that Sophie would finally decide to retire, "A sad and sobering thought," he remarked. "But worry not, she is still here."

> She is the personification of the gay and gaudy world of after dark. She is a tradition, mountainously gowned in ostrich feathers and satin and mile-high orchids, shouting a lusty challenge to convention and the academic conception of a normal morality.[13]

"When will you be back?" the audience shouted. "Next year, same time," Sophie shouted back.

For the next two months, Sophie entertained at military camps west of Chicago, as she worked her way back to Los Angeles. At each of the camps where she appeared, no criticism was found for her work. Rather, the soldiers refused to let her leave the stage. In addition, she was on her way to becoming one of the top "pin-up" girls of the armed forces. She had received almost 10,000 requests from servicemen for her picture.

What awaited Sophie in Los Angeles was another musical revue, this time produced by United Artists, in which she would sing two songs. While production for the movie began in January, 1944, Sophie's scene was not shot until she arrived in Los Angeles. To compete with the other studios' military-oriented revues, production had been speeded up so that "Sensations of 1945" opened in New York on June 16, 1944, only three months after "Follow the Boys." The title was changed from 1944 to 1945 to accommodate a longer run at the theaters.

Andrew Stone was both producer and director; the screenplay was written by Dorothy Bennett; dances and choreography were directed by David Lichine. Unlike in most war-related movies, all songs for "Sensations" were written specifically for the picture, the music and lyrics prepared by Al Sherman and Harry Tobias.

The cast featured Eleanor Powell, Dennis O'Keefe, C. Aubrey Smith, and Eugene Pallette. Guest appearances included those of Sophie and W.C. Fields as themselves, Cab Calloway and his band, Woody Herman and his band, the Les Paul Trio, and twenty-one lesser stars.

In a scene at a Gay Nineties club, Sophie sang "Wake Up Man, You're Slipping" and "Divine Lady." Again, Sophie's presentation was carefully monitored to ensure her songs included no suggestiveness. Actually, the War Department delayed release of the picture because it objected to scenes showing soldiers behaving in "an undignified manner."

For one week of work, Sophie earned $15,000, minus expenses. Although there were a number of occasions when her name came up for further roles, this was her final appearance in pictures. Studios rejected Sophie because they believed her to be too old and her act passé'.

Review of "Sensations" by *Variety* suggested another film musical with popular appeal. It contained no plot, but "the specialties were all quite entertaining." Sophie was mentioned as singing "two dandy numbers with Teddy Shapiro omnipotently at the Steinway."[14]

Sophie played at the Florentine Gardens, Los Angeles, for a total of twenty-five weeks, to December, 1944. During this time, Sophie and ghostwriter Dorothy Giles collaborated on the preparation of her autobiography titled, aptly, "Some of These Days." The book spoke of Sophie's early life in Hartford, her work at the family restaurant, her mother's influence, and the frustrations of being raised in an Orthodox Jewish community. Sophie's descriptions, in her own words, were quite revealing as they explained her break with the family to pursue a theatrical career. She told about her professional development and the barriers she had to overcome to gain headliner status. After reaching her goal, Sophie spent the remainder of the book reciting her triumphs in the U.S. and England. It was interesting and informative enough to be a good read.

Nonetheless, as in most autobiographies written by stars late in life, dates were jumbled (or missing), events embellished or revised, stories left untold, important activities carefully omitted. Except for her mother, little was mentioned about the remainder of her family, including Bert. There were doubts that she even knew her true age.

The book was published by Doubleday Doran in 1945 and sold for $2.50.

A special autographed edition of 1,000 copies sold for $25 each. Several hundred signed copies were sent to Sophie's long list of colleagues and admirers, with a request to make a donation to the Sophie Tucker Foundation. Sophie had promised that all proceeds from the book would be given to charity; and, from all indications, she kept her promise. Proceeds were destined for the Actors Fund; Jewish, Catholic, and Episcopal Theatrical Guilds; the Home for the Aged in Hartford; and the Sophie Tucker Playground Camp Fund. Wherever she played, she touted the book; and it was available for sale in theater lobbies. There is no record of how many thousands of books were sold, nor how much was collected for charity; but the Morris agency claimed "considerable proportions" had been donated.

Publication of the book at this time in her career was a shrewd bit of publicity. For all those longtime admirers, it was an opportunity to lovingly recall Sophie's rise to fame. For new audiences, seeing her perform triggered an intense interest in her background and career history. Even ten years after the book had been published, Sophie was promoting and selling it wherever she could.

Sophie began 1945 by returning to the Bal Tabarin, San Francisco, for a six-week engagement. As had become her usual habit, she wrote hundreds of letters to admirers announcing her appearance at the nightclub. "Come visit me and have a good time," she suggested.

As promised, Sophie returned to the Chez Paree, Chicago, in May, almost a year to the day she had rocked audiences out of their seats. Her engagement was interrupted, however, when news came from Hartford that Phil, her older brother and financial manager, was close to death. Apologizing to the audience for her absence, Sophie rushed to Hartford.

Philip Abuza died May 9, 1945, at age 61. He left a widow (Leah), two sons (Henry and Zachary) and a daughter (Sadie). Along with being Sophie's manager, Phil had been an efficiency expert for several companies. A funeral service was held on May 11, with the entire family and synagogue friends in attendance. But because of her engagement at the Chez Paree, Sophie quickly returned to Chicago, back on stage two days later. Before leaving Hartford, she appointed her younger brother Moe, who was a lawyer, to take over her business affairs.

No mention was made in the Chicago newspapers of Phil's death, only that Sophie had taken a short trip home to handle family affairs. On stage, no one would have known she was in mourning for her brother.

The *Daily News* greeted her return with enthusiasm.

> One of the country's foremost authors, as well as entertainer, still full of flash and fire, Sophie is back at the Chez Paree, turning on the old personality and singing as only Sophie can sing. Her audiences still love her, still go wild about her. And for that they can hardly be blamed.[15]

Although admitting to being completely exhausted physically and emotionally, Sophie packed them in. When it was finally revealed that her brother had died while she continued to perform, audiences' applause showed their appreciation for her entertaining them under the circumstances.

In addition, the Chicago newspapers gave plenty of space to Sophie's book-selling activities and the charitable outcome. She netted more than $34,000 in Chicago alone. With the war seemingly coming to an end, the Morris agency believed that the New York theater scene would become one of euphoric proportions; and Sophie planned to be there to share in the festivities.

A stop in Boston on the way to New York found Sophie selling her book and selling dinner tables at the Mayfair nightclub simultaneously. She gave audiences a mixture of old and new songs, some so rowdy they pushed the limits of Boston censorship. "She still has the spirit of youth," said the *Boston Globe* reviewer. "Boston obviously loves it, particularly the old girls and escorts who think they're just as frisky as ever."

Sophie opened at the Martinique nightclub, New York, for an extended stay, well into 1946. With the war over, the city's theater business had taken on a new zest; and audiences flocked to everything that offered a chance to celebrate the victory and relieve their emotions. Sophie was greeted with lusty cheers and appreciative applause when she was honored for her efforts on behalf of the military and her publicized contributions to charity. Having become a theatrical icon, she could do no wrong.

15

The Glory Years

On February 13, 1946, Sophie celebrated her sixtieth birthday at the Latin Quarter in Miami Beach. She claimed it was her fifty-eighth, but no one would have known the difference anyway. Patrons attending the bash were just ecstatic to be among the "privileged" few in attendance during this special evening, enjoying the antics of their beloved performer.

Once the usual hubbub had diminished, several hundred patrons saw one of the most amazing theatrical phenomena of the times charging into the spotlight. Sophie Tucker was on! Her magnetism, as incredible as it had been in her youth, still literally infused the place. Into the light she came, an aigrette quivering above her spectacular hairdo, three orchids nodding on her white broadtail cape, her white evening gown blazing with rhinestones. Everyone was her confidante. She gave each of them the truth.

Sophie recited and sang a tailored rendition of "Entertaining Papa," a new tune full of topical references and pointed barbs directed at husbands who neglected their wives.

"Ladies and Gentlemen. Last night at my hotel, a couple in the suite next to mine were having quite an argument. I didn't mean to eavesdrop, but I couldn't help overhearing their conversation. And from what I overheard, I gathered...."

> (Singing) The gentleman's first name is Irving.
> His last name I'll leave you to guess.
> He's tops in New York's garment center,
> But at home he's not such a success.
> While he entertains buyers, as his business requires,
> Home alone he leaves Irma, his wife.
> So while he's out entertaining, cocktailing, champagning,
> She leads a most unhappy life.
> The other night while he was dressing

15. The Glory Years

to go out, she said, "Irving, my dear,
I know you've got a date. I don't want you to be late.
But here's a record I'd like you to hear.
It's by Sophie Tucker. Just out. Brand new.
And what she says on the record is what I've got to say to you.

(Singing) Entertaining Papa. If you want my business,
Y' got to entertain your mama tonight.
To get business from the buyers, you go out and buy them wine.
And that's what you are goin' to have to do, if you want mine.
Y' got to take your mama to a show, a nightclub,
and maybe get me just a little tight.
I want the A-one treatment; and if you don't think I rate it,
I'll give my business to somebody who'll appreciate it.
Entertaining papa, if you want that certain business,
Y' got to entertain your mama tonight."[1]

The crowd roared and begged Sophie to continue her recital. Unhesitatingly, she launched into the second chorus, talking her story before finally breaking out into the musical coda, "Y' got to entertain your mama tonight."

In this manner, at every performance, Sophie captured her audiences. It made no difference what city, or nightclub, or jaded or neophyte patron, Sophie won their hearts with a charisma no other performer was able to duplicate. At sixty, she easily accomplished the task. At seventy, her dominance continued. Even at nearly eighty, she had audiences begging for more.

"How much longer could this singing dynamo go on?," critics and patrons asked themselves. Yet even as they pondered their question, Sophie was hustling them through another barrage of her unique amusements. Yes, she was a veteran entertainer — she admitted that herself — old by any theatrical criteria. Her singing voice had steadily decreased in strength. Her litheness on stage had been reduced to occasionally using the piano for support. After more than forty years of continuous performance, critics seemed to anticipate that the zest and enthusiasm of her work would surely wane, that a time would come that represented one performance too many; and reviewers would then, in all sadness, have to report Sophie's decline. But the occasion never arose.

Yet, all of these factors made no difference to admirers, old or new. As if they had been inoculated into a timeless reverie, she was Sophie as she had been, still was, and always would be.

Back in vaudeville times, few performers like Sophie had received such enthusiastic adoration from audiences. Now, in the second half of the twentieth century, the world of entertainment was packed with visual media headliners and a never-ending succession of publicity-driven heroes and heroines. Yet, there stood the ever-present Sophie. As if performing on her own entertainment island, she had gathered about her admirers who faithfully promised to carry their legendary figure into the proverbial sunset.

The last two decades of Sophie's life were, indeed, the "glory years." Nearly everything she said and did became constant reminders of her contributions to popular theater and philanthropic organizations. Even more astonishing, all of these activities were secondary to her continuous record-breaking nightclub appearances across the country.

Sophie's engagement list read like a railroad schedule. Beginning in New York (the Latin Quarter and Copacabana), she rolled on to Boston; Saratoga Springs; Atlantic City; Baltimore; Philadelphia; Miami Beach; Chicago (Chez Paree); Las Vegas; Los Angeles (Florentine Gardens and Coconut Grove); then around the same circuit once again the following year.

Vaudeville was dead; although television attempted to revive it. Burlesque was dead, an ignominious death at the hands of self-proclaimed moral arbiters and movie studios, who unashamedly usurped its titillation. Radio had blundered into its entertainment niche as a purveyor of sports and musical programs. Movies had threatened to take over the amusement industry until that upstart, television, with its eclectic programming, moved to take over the entertainment field and dominate the public's attention.

Nevertheless, through all of these leisure-time mutations, nightclubs flourished and established themselves as a viable amusement niche. In reality, nightclubs were likely the last venue for face-to-face, indeed, in-your-face, live entertainment. The nightclub venue allowed both performers and patrons to share the stage for spontaneous and participatory enjoyment, in contrast to other, increasingly scripted, voyeuristic diversions. And it was in this unique environment—its basic form the lone survivor of the old days of popular variety—that Sophie thrived; and her admirers with her.

For forty years, Sophie had given fully of herself to audiences. In later years, what changed was that her giving included charity organizations along with theater audiences, causes along with admirers, social services along with entertainment entrepreneurs. Now, instead of always giving, Sophie found herself also a recipient, as groups of people came together to honor her as an individual.

When these events first occurred, Sophie, predictably, felt uncomfortable. "What am I doing here?" she would ask. "I'm supposed to be performing for you." But after several such events, Sophie came to enjoy the tributes and became a gracious honoree. (She admitted, however, that she was never really relaxed at such events, in fact, she felt embarrassed at the attention given her. Also, after spending so many years attempting to overcome yet embody her mother's humble value system, feelings of guilt may have lingered.)

Some tributes amounted to no more than quiet thanks; others were noisy and gaudy celebrations. Some consisted of the simple passing of a check to a needy group; others were the occasion for podium-thumping speeches in front of thousands, with the intention of selling as many Israel bonds as she was able. Some were unobtrusive visits to children's hospitals; others involved the ritual trappings of British royalty. Yet, there was no question that each of these tributes was presented to Sophie with sincerity and admiration, as only a genuine legend could be venerated.

During the late 1940s and early '50s, Sophie was consistently headlined for breaking box-office records at venues like New York's Latin Quarter and, at the same time, for dispensing thousands of dollars to charity.

In May, 1947, Sophie was given a gala testimonial dinner sponsored by the Jewish Guild of America, Inc. She was the first woman ever to be so honored by the organization. New York Mayor William O'Dwyer; Eddie Cantor; Harry Hirshfield; William Morris, Jr.; Gene Buck; and George Jessel were among the speakers, with Jessel also serving as emcee. Irving Berlin was chairman of the dinner committee.

Buck summed up the event in one short sentence: "This is the greatest one-night stand Sophie Tucker will ever play." As Sophie's inspired speech of appreciation

In 1947, Sophie was given a testimonial dinner in honor of her fortieth anniversary in show business. Sir Cedric Hardwicke presented a tribute from Britain, and Irving Berlin wrote and performed a special song for Sophie. Left to right: Irving Berlin, Jack Ruben, Sophie, Sir Cedric Hardwicke, and Eddie Cantor. (Museum of the City of New York)

reviewed her long career, the 1,500 in attendance in the Hotel Astor's grand ballroom — at $15 a head, all of it going to Sophie's various charities — unashamedly revealed their sentimental emotions. Mayor O'Dwyer paid a special tribute to Sophie; Sir Cedric Hardwicke presented her with a scroll of honor from Britain; William Morris, Jr., linked his agency's growth to its longtime relationship with Sophie.

In lieu of making a speech, Berlin wrote a song especially for Sophie. His tuneful recitation of her career ended with the phrase, "Sophie keeps rolling along." The audience both laughed and cried at this musical tribute to "dear Sophie."

Song for Sophie
by Irving Berlin

Making what you'd call a speech
Isn't up my street.
Fancy words are out of reach
When I'm on my feet.
So I've done the best I could for now,
In the only way I know how.

Chorus
I've written a song just for Sophie,
A song that I'll sing through a mike,
Just to tell her how we love her,
What we think of her
In the business there's no business like.
While others are staging their comebacks,
Miss Tucker is still going strong.
She continues to deliver,
Just like that river,
Old Sophie keeps rolling along.

Second Chorus
We know what an artist is Sophie,
'Though some say her songs aren't nice.
But her lyrics don't need cleaning;
Her double meaning
Simply means what she means, only twice.
When Jolson and Cantor and Jessel
Have finished with their final song,
They'll be rocking in their rockers,
Three alta 'yockers,'
While Sophie keeps rolling along.

15. The Glory Years

> Third Chorus
> We know of the kindness in Sophie.
> We know too that Sophie is smart.
> As a star she's made a boodle,
> Using her noodle.
> But she's best when she's using her heart.
> The Angels will watch over Sophie,
> They'll see that she keeps going strong.
> They'll say, 'tho we're wild about her,
> We'll do without her.
> Let Sophie keep rolling along.[2]

(The third chorus was Berlin's personal salute to Sophie which he preferred not to sing at the dinner.)

It was shortly after this event that Abe Lastfogel and Sophie initiated a campaign to promote a movie of her life story. It was described as an adaptation from her book, the script to be written by Jack Yellin. Query letters were sent to each studio to elicit their interest. However polite the responses, studios expressed little enthusiasm for the project. Lastfogel had estimated the cost of the movie to be over $200,000, due to several production numbers; and that figure concerned studio executives. Of even greater significance to studio execs was the daunting challenge of who could play Sophie in the movie. One studio promised that, if they were able find a performer who could "out–Sophie" Sophie, a deal could be made. For the time being, the treatment languished.

On the performance side, Sophie continued to break box-office records at the Latin Quarter (New York); Beachcomber (Miami Beach); and the Florentine Gardens (Los Angeles). Her Los Angeles stay was highlighted — scooped, one might say — by Louella Parsons, when she revealed that Sophie might wed again. Arriving from Honolulu during Christmas week was Marion Scoby, a very rich hotel owner. Scoby announced his coming for the sole purpose of trying to persuade Sophie to marry.

"He's been my boyfriend for a long time," Sophie admitted, "and has made frequent visits to see me. I haven't made up my mind about marriage. It's possible; but, of course, I wouldn't like to give up my career."[3]

When Sophie left Los Angeles for Miami Beach, she had obviously chosen to remain single. Scoby returned to Honolulu a disappointed suitor.

The Miami Beach engagement was scheduled to run through March. After a brief vacation, Sophie planned to visit London, her first trip there in twelve years. Unfortunately, her plans were abruptly interrupted in March, when it was reported that she had broken two toes in a stage fall. Actually, she had fractured her leg and remained in a hospital recuperating for several weeks. The London trip had to be delayed, although Sophie promised to arrive in Britain on crutches if she had to. Having been slated to begin her London engagement in late May, Sophie learned that advance sales for her dates were the heaviest in history for an American performer. Sophie would open on May 31, at the Casino, London. Not only was the four-week engagement sold out; but when sales opened up for an additional two weeks, tickets sold out in a matter of hours.

Still on crutches at the opening, Sophie was obliged to sing sixteen numbers, winding up with the sentimental "Yiddishe Mamma." She took bows for another fifteen minutes, while Ted was busy gathering baskets and bouquets of flowers from the audience. The Morris contingent were in attendance — they attended every one of Sophie's London openings — and were celebrating Sophie's forty-first year with the agency.

During her last week in London, Sophie was honored with a luncheon given by Foyle's, British booksellers, who made a feature of "literary lunches to distinguished writers." Three hundred people were in attendance to mark the launching of Sophie's autobiography in England. On hand was Hannan Swaffer, who had been the first to review Sophie when she arrived in London in 1922. He paid special tribute to her "sterling qualities and lovable personality," and endorsed the sincere affection with which Sophie was held in the city.

In her acceptance speech, Sophie told how the idea for her book arose and how it had developed. She concluded by singing the song that had lent the book its title.

Nor were the King and Queen ignored. Sophie sent them a copy of the book and received, in turn, a letter of thanks from the royal secretary. "Their Majesties, I know, will read this with the utmost interest; but what has given them the greatest pleasure of all is your very kind thought in sending it."[4]

Returning to the U.S., Sophie took a rare, brief rest, visiting Anna before she headed to Chicago and the Chez Paree for a September opening.

Still sporting crutches, Sophie did a forty-minute turn at her Chez Paree opening. As she entered the nightclub, she received an ovation of several minutes while negotiating the entrance staircase. She was resplendent in a white, sequined gown and a white fur cape, one side of it covered with orchids. After a nostalgic medley of old-time hits, Sophie followed up with new songs written by Jack Yellin.

> Miss Tucker has a new stock of non-nursery school songs which she sings with amazing vitality. The rest of the show, without Sophie on stage, is mainly filler.[5]

Behind the scenes, however, all was not well between Sophie and Lou Walters, the Chez Paree owner. He had forbade her from selling her book in the lobby after the show. His argument: many patrons had become irritated by Sophie's behavior when she planted herself at the door and buttonholed customers, urging them to buy the book and/or make donations for charity. Sophie became so irritated by Walter's edict, she threatened never to return to his nightclub. She claimed that no other nightclub had ever treated her in that manner. For the moment, Walters remained unapologetic.

At the beginning of 1949, in an act of great significance (at least to theater historians), Sophie presented her entire collection of theatrical memorabilia, including all of her scrapbooks since 1907, to the New York Public Library. The scrapbooks alone, one for each year of performance, filled with reviews, feature stories, cards, congratulatory letters, telegrams, and personal notes, represented a treasure trove of Sophie's career and life as a performer. Interestingly, while the accumulated material was rich in information, Sophie saved very little to record her career activities from this point to her death. In recent years, she often admitted, keeping up the scrapbook had become a sizable chore, even with two helpers. Yet it seemed indicative that Sophie stopped recording her life and career at this time, just short of her sixty-third birthday.

Her birthday, however, was not entirely forgotten. Bert, her son, now the manager of a hotel in Miami Beach, feted his mother while she was appearing at the Beachcomber. Everyone in town attended the party, from civic leaders to nightclub headliners. The guest list included Joe E. Lewis, Dean Martin and Jerry Lewis, Bill Robinson, Frances Langford, Harry Richman, and Mack Miller. After the usual round of speeches and toasts, Sophie sang a number of old-time songs, to everyone's delight.

The SRO sign was out the entire four weeks that Sophie played at the Beachcomber. "That Miss Tucker is one of the cafe' greats," declared *Variety*, "is an established fact."

> What adds to her stature is the manner in which she not only wraps up from her walk-on, but the presentation of a completely new set of materials. In spots, the material, in other hands, would be too blue; with La Tucker, however, these lines become yock comedics that spark heavy mitting.[6]

After a summer of sold-out nightclub dates and on her return to Los Angeles, Sophie was feted with a "roast" sponsored by the Hollywood Friars' Club. She was the first woman to be so honored in their hallowed halls. The event was filled with toasting, comedic skits, jovially barbed speeches, and, at times, general mayhem. Yet, tribute in loving words from those who had known her for years was the order of the evening.

Ronald Reagan described Sophie as the Whistler's Mother of Show Business. Phil Silvers called her the equal of any man. Joe Schenck said that she was one of the greatest women he had ever known—"even though she turned me down for marriage"—and also the most generous woman, because she donated both money and talent for charity. Joe Howard serenaded Sophie with an old favorite, "Hello, My Baby; Hello, My Ragtime Girl."

When George Jessel announced that Sophie's first husband would be present, a hush came over the audience. A venerable figure in an old Prince Albert coat, sporting gray hair, mustache, and stooped shoulders, marched down the aisle. It turned out to be Eddie Cantor, depicting Louis Tuck. Al Jolson debated with Sophie which was the elder. George Burns and Jessel made final tributes to this "great woman whom everybody loves."

When Sophie was allowed to respond, she talked about the importance of people loving one another. "We should all live gracefully, which I will do," she added, "until the next time the Friars give me a similar salute." She concluded by singing "Some of These Days," and was joined in song by the enthusiastic audience.

After almost two years of nonstop nightclub engagements, Sophie took time off in early 1950 to rest and furnish her new New York apartment on upper Park Avenue. It was an environment filled with career memorabilia and simple but elegant furnishings.

Plush, padded chairs and sofa highlighted the living room, with enough lamps to keep the entire room bright. A Japanese designed rug adorned the floor. In the dining room, there was seating for twelve around a large, oblong table, adorned with place settings of a kind resembling her mother's. There were three bedrooms and three baths set aside for guests or relatives, which happened rarely since Sophie was almost continually on the road.

Of the theatrical memorabilia, one large wall contained a montage of pictures of herself, from childhood to her most recent nightclub appearance. A large framed piece housed the medals she had received. Another piece framed all of the monetary notes she had collected from the countries she visited. Above a small, polished desk was a section of shelves for Jewish awards. A bookcase contained an assortment of knickknacks Sophie had received from other performers. Another bookcase housed all of her record albums. A large picture of her mother hung on one wall and several oils, done for Sophie early in her career, adorned another. Photographs of favorite friends and fellow artists hung on her bedroom walls. When Sophie entertained at home, it was done in grand style. Family get-togethers found the dining room crowded with conversation and rounds of food. Sophie seemed to enjoy these family gatherings but often apologized for their infrequency.

Her "rest" at home gave *Variety* reporters the opportunity to interview Sophie on a number of subjects. One humorous piece, concerning what she did not like about show business, nevertheless gave readers insight into the trials and tribulations performers faced when on the stage. The comments obviously mirrored many of Sophie's personal complaints.

- The act who comes in year after year with the same material.
- The infrequent times when I am overweight.
- The squawks from billing.
- The blasé customer.
- A waiter dropping a tray of dishes.
- Total strangers maneuvering themselves into my dressing room to O.K. their personal checks.
- The grandmother who greets me, "I remember seeing you at the Palace when I was a little girl."
- The sport who is always giving me a horse that can't lose unless it breaks a leg.
- The trunks and suitcases that never close when I'm rushing to make a train.

- The Hollywood producers who insisted on making me a Marie Dressler, when, for forty-five years, I've slaved to make the name of Sophie Tucker.
- The inconsiderate ringside patrons who blow cigar smoke while the star is singing a ballad.
- Acts who "dog it" when the house isn't packed.
- The inevitable drunk who calls for "Melancholy Baby."
- Last year's costumes.[7]

Sophie received numerous letters from performers about the article, most of them supporting her remarks and a few adding to the list. The article seemed to have struck a poignant note among actors, who rarely get the chance to voice their own opinions about working on stage.

In July, 1950, Mercury Records announced that they had signed Sophie to record a 12-inch, long-play disk. She would be one of the first entertainers to use this new delivery system. The platter was designed to feature a complete show presentation on one side, simulating her nightclub routine. The alternative side would feature seven tracks of old, familiar standards, The record would be priced at $4.85. Of course, Sophie's nightclub routine had to be "purified" for record customers.

Sophie planned to sell the record in the clubs where she appeared. Like her book, she announced that the record's proceeds would go to charity. In support of the new album, Mercury Records published full-page ads in Variety and New York newspapers promoting the new recording, calling it "her latest and greatest spicy saucy songs" and "a masterpiece of Sophie Tucker's half century in show business." The hype helped produce good sales at retail outlets. Yet Sophie's own record selling did even better at her shows.

Although Sophie had planned to visit London in early 1951, her doctors dissuaded her from making the trip. She had still not fully recovered from the leg fracture — she was now walking with a cane — and was currently taking physical therapy for it. Nevertheless, the infirmity did not prevent her from a record-breaking engagement in Boston and a holiday bash in Houston, where she shared honors with Julie Wilson. The Hotel Shamrock had two ballrooms, so each performer entertained in one room at the 10 P.M. show, then switched rooms for the midnight show. Texas law forbade the sale of hard liquor but placed no restrictions on champagne. Not surprisingly, the later show was much more raucous, the songs saucier, the jokes bluer, and the audience more demonstrative.

> Sophie Tucker scored the greatest sock ever recorded in the Shamrock's lively life. From the moment she comes on, glittering with jewels and a sequined gown, wearing a black mink stole and orchids and a fantastic new hair-do, Texans take to her and raise the roof with encores.[8]

Unfortunately, Sophie was unable to finish the Houston run because of a severe cold. Still, on the evening of her show, she had herself wheeled onto the stage, where she apologized to the audience for her inability to perform. Sophie then had to return to New York due to the seriousness of the illness, reported to be a heavy case of the flu. It was actually pneumonia, and she had to recuperate for several weeks. Nor was she in full health when she opened at the Copa City, Miami Beach. During her first show, after a couple of numbers, she stopped and leaned on the piano. She told the audience she would return shortly; and she did, to complete the show. The following night, she made it through the entire show but was so fatigued, she had to return to New York for further rest. Newspapers reported these events and wondered what was really wrong with Sophie.

Yet no sooner had she returned home than Jimmy Durante wanted her to appear on his radio show. Against doctor's orders—after all, this would be her first radio show in several years, and on NBC—Sophie did not refuse the offer. The April 18 show featured Sophie and Jimmy performing a skit on old times in vaudeville and Sophie singing several songs, the finale of which was, of course, "Some of These Days." Playing with Durante, an old vaudeville veteran himself, was hilarious, as both improvised from the script and ad-libbed most of the routine.

In the fall of 1951, a special tribute that gained national newspaper headlines was made to Sophie. The American Jewish War Veterans named her "Woman of the Year," and a special dinner in her honor was held at the Statler Hotel, Buffalo, New York (where she happened to be appearing). The previous year, the vets had similarly honored Eleanor Roosevelt. Sophie received hundreds of telegrams and letters congratulating her, but the most important letter of best wishes came from Mrs. Roosevelt herself. Sophie later added the plaque to her honors wall at home.

Sophie's return to the Latin Quarter, New York, was met with some concern. The nightclub was owned by Lou Walters—who also owned the Chez Paree in Chicago and had refused to allow Sophie to sell her books—and there was question whether Sophie would fulfill her engagement. As far as the newspapers were concerned, opening night answered all their concerns. The seemingly repentant Walters not only gave Sophie as much time as she wanted on stage, but also allowed her to sell both her books and records. Moreover, in honoring her record-breaking performances at the Latin Quarter, he presented her with a new Cadillac. On stage, Sophie's audience was kept rapt the entire show and "they rode with Sophie all the way."

A special feature of her run at the Latin Quarter was the introduction of a new Yellin song, "My Mother's Sabbath Candles." Segueing into the new song, Sophie recalled, "It was a block from the Palace Theater where I introduced 'Yiddishe Mamma' a quarter century ago." Tears and cheers combined to make the song a hit overnight. To take advantage of the song's appeal, Mercury Records had the record in the stores a few days later. Sophie herself had them available for sale at the club, the proceeds destined for charity.

London called again in early 1952, and Sophie was now healthy enough to meet the challenges of a British tour. Her plan was to leave for London in April and return to the U.S. in August. Bookings would give her few breaks during the tour, and Lastfogel wondered whether Sophie could do it. She claimed she could.

Sophie was to open at the Palladium April 21 and would double at the Bagatelle, a nightclub, at the same time. Then, she would launch a tour of the "provinces," including Glasgow, Leeds, Liverpool, and Birmingham, before returning to London.

The schedule was no sooner announced than the tour was extended to include an appearance in Paris and a trip to Israel, her first, to give concerts in Tel-Aviv, Haifa, and Jerusalem. The Israeli portion of the tour would benefit various charities, including two that Sophie had herself sponsored. Abe Lastfogel shook his head in consternation and immediately assigned a doctor to accompany Sophie, if only for his own peace of mind.

As everyone expected, Sophie's opening at the London Palladium proved the largest the theater had ever experienced. She received "a roof-raising reception" and concluded her act forty minutes later "to a tremendous ovation."

> She filled her turn with sock numbers in which she created humorous as well as nostalgic moods and wound up on a powerful note with "Mother's Sabbath Lights," a tear-jerker.[9]

The appearance was Sophie's first at the Palladium since 1935. After receiving a tremendous welcome, she had to give a speech of thanks even before she performed. Her gowns sparkled; her humor and sentiments captured the hearts of patrons; and when she was finished, the audience would not let her go until she had given another speech. At the Bagatelle, down the street, Sophie drew the largest crowd there of the post-war era. In spite of advanced prices, her four-week stay was a complete sellout. Some patrons rushed from the Palladium to the Bagatelle to see Sophie perform again.

For Sophie, her first trip to Israel was a revelation. Daily luncheons preceded tours of requested sites, including the children's home she had funded and the forest planted in her honor. The concerts featured Sophie and Ted alone on stage, where she ran the gamut of nostalgic songs and modern tunes, with many of which the audience sang along. She recited her life story and gave helpful hints to women about how to treat their men. She promoted Israel bonds. "Some of These Days" ended her act, but the audience demanded encores until her voice was hoarse. Sophie came away amazed at the dedicated commitment the Israeli people were making to their country, and she promised to return soon to contribute what she could to their cause.

While Sophie was cementing relationships in Israel, Abe Lastfogel was attempting to cement a contract with a studio for "The Sophie Tucker Story." Months of negotiation had netted little progress. Warner's believed they had found a suitable actress to play Sophie — the effervescent, energetic Betty Hutton — but screen tests did not seem to impress the studio. Universal, MGM, and Fox had already turned down the idea. Warner's was about to send Lastfogel a letter with similar news. "The Sophie Tucker Story" was about to die a neglected death. Of course, Sophie was disheartened to hear the news and quite disappointed that her life story might never reach the screen. As Jack Warner had written, "Who wants to see an impersonator on the screen when they can see the real thing in person."

Her return to the U.S. brought Sophie back to the Chez Paree (Chicago), an engagement at the Latin Quarter (New York), and a holiday booking at the El Rancho (Las Vegas). There, Sophie joked about running for president, sold records in the lobby, and announced that her golden anniversary in show business would be celebrated next year.

During this period, with the advent of television shows featuring variety performers—Toast of the Town, All-Star Revue, and the Ed Sullivan Show—Sophie had her first opportunities to perform in the new medium. In many ways, television variety shows in 1953 resembled vaudeville olios, with numerous acts introduced by an emcee (who extolled the virtues of each performer like a circus barker), and an afterpiece in which the guest performers together sang or put on a brief skit.

Unlike vaudeville, however, these shows were highly scripted, and performers, particularly those who had been nightclub entertainers, found it difficult, if not inhibiting, to play on television. Some appeared rarely because they were unable to duplicate their usual nightclub routines, subject matter and lyrics now scanned by network censors. Others more easily adapted to the medium and used these appearances to enhance their other theatrical interests. Still others, like Eddie Cantor, Jack Benny, and Milton Berle, took to television so readily, they were soon featured on their own shows and found new audiences to entertain.

Sophie was part of the group that found television restricting, her repertoire limited and subject to scrutiny. She was allowed to sing a few popular songs and, occasionally, signature tunes. She rarely appeared in skits. Program censors often "crossed their fingers" in the hopes that Sophie would not stray from the script and interpolate her own lyrics or offhandedly mention her views on relationships between men and women. Television shows at the time were transmitted in "real" time and performed before live audiences, so it was indeed possible that the emcee could lose control of the proceedings.

This accounts for Sophie's rather infrequent appearances on television, only twenty-five times during a fourteen-year period, 1951 to 1965. Of these occasions, two were interviews (one of them a ridiculously staged "home" interview with Edward R. Murrow), four were done in England, and two were part of all-star telethons.

Sophie's first appearance on television was April 25, 1951, on the "Four Star Revue." She sang several songs, engaged in a brief dialogue about her long career, and ended with "Some of These Days." She was getting so tired of this same routine, she began to believe that she was becoming a parody of herself. Worse, she believed that her audience was coming to perceive her in the same fashion.

She appeared briefly on "Toast of the Town" three times in 1951 and 1952, the last show a tribute to Sophie. After two appearances on the "All-Star Revue" in 1952 and 1953, Sophie returned to "Toast of the Town" (by popular demand, whatever that meant) in 1953 and 1954, these last two appearances promoting her forthcoming Golden Jubilee celebration.

In early 1953, the Jewish Theatrical Guild announced they were planning a testimonial dinner for Sophie to celebrate her 50th year in show business. The dinner would be held on October 4, at the Waldorf-Astoria Hotel, New York. It would be the first of several jubilee celebrations to take place during 1953 and 1954. (Actually, these events were two years premature, but public relations won out over accuracy.)

Over the last several years, Sophie's charitable contributions had been as numerous as her nightclub engagements. Much of the money collected came from the sale of her autobiography and records, but personal investments also contributed a certain amount. In 1946, Sophie gave $1,000 each to the Community Hospital, Philadelphia (on behalf of the Waiter and Waitress Union), and the Betty Bachrach Home. The following year, $1,000 donations went to the John Tracy Clinic for deaf children; the Lou Costello, Jr., Youth Foundation; and the Duarte Foundation. In addition, Sophie had collected more than $14,000 in 1947 from book sales. Most of these funds were given to various Jewish organizations, which included the synagogue in Hartford and the Ladies Home for the Aged, in honor of her mother.

After being honored by the Variety Clubs of Texas, Sophie pledged $100 a month for the remainder of her life to the Boys' Ranch. An equal amount was pledged to a children's hospital in Denver. Additional funds went to the Sophie Tucker Foundation and the Sophie Tucker Playground Fund; and $1,000 donations were given to the Catholic and Negro Actors' Homes. Still another $1,000 went for an electric drinking fountain for the Tumor Clinic at the Rhode island Hospital (in honor of Lora Valadon). Further, a considerable amount of money was given to the Youth Center at Beth Shemesh, a kibbutz in Israel, one of Sophie's favorite places. It was estimated that, between 1945 and 1953, Sophie had donated more than a million dollars to charitable groups. As long as she was alive, she promised, she would continue to make charitable donations.

From October 1953 to late 1954, Sophie's Golden Jubilee was to be celebrated by many events in numerous cities across the country. Thanks to the efforts of the Morris agency, everyone, it seemed, was demanding an opportunity to recognize Sophie.

Likely a precautionary measure, Sophie's first decision was to budget her appearances at nightclubs and reduce the number of shows she would perform at each. She had decided to "take her time" and not spread herself so thin as to jeopardize her health and her voice. Even though some nightclubs offered Sophie $7,500 a week, she refused so that she could rest for two or three weeks between engagements. She wanted to fulfill all her contracts, so her stamina had to be carefully monitored. Sophie readily acknowledged that age was playing an influential role in her planning.

Second, Sophie turned down appearances at theaters and movie houses, stating that she did not have an act for such houses. She declared that she was staying strictly with nightclubs "where they know me and know what to expect of me. If I did my act in a picture house, I'd be criticized severely; and I just couldn't take it." Further, Sophie emphasized that she had found a niche for herself and that she had come to be regarded as an institution in that particular niche. No one could really argue with her reasoning. Other performers should have been more perceptive and self-aware.

As the October 4 Golden Jubilee dinner approached, work had already begun to sell tickets and tend to all the special requests coming in to the hotel management. As early as July, more than $10,000 worth of reservations had been received. Regarding the box-office receipts, Sophie made it very clear that all proceeds were going to actors' guilds of various denominations.

By September, the figures for tickets and advertising had exceeded the $97,000 mark. Capacity for the upcoming dinner was 1,500, but $50-a-head donors were being told that their tables would not provide good vantage points. A souvenir journal would contain byline pieces by Walter Winchell, Ed Sullivan, Quentin Reynolds, Louella Parsons, Hedda Hopper, Earl Wilson, Herb Caen, Irv Kupcinet, Louis Lobol, and others.

A week before the dinner, Mercury Records announced that they had just cut a special, long-play album that would include tributes from show biz personalities, as well as a Tucker songalog. Guests would receive copies of this album and donations for it would be welcome.

Under the Jewish Theatrical Guild's sponsorship, a high-class bash was staged on October 4 to honor Sophie's fifty years in show business. A record $150,000 was collected, all of the proceeds to go to the Negro, Catholic, Episcopal, and Jewish Theatrical Guilds, the Will Rogers Memorial Hospital, Motion Picture Relief Fund, and the American Guild of Variety Artists' welfare fund. A well-planned version of "the Sophie Tucker Story" was presented, a wealth of talent to reprise, in vignette fashion, the fifty-year span of the guest of honor. As was often the case for these

In 1953, Sophie was given a Golden Jubilee dinner. More than 1,500 people — performers and admirers — crowded the Waldorf-Astoria Hotel to honor her. Sophie's entire family was on hand to celebrate the occasion. Left to right: Moe; Blanche, his wife; Lillian, Bert's wife; Charles, Sophie's nephew; Bert; Sophie; Julius Aronson; Anna Aronson, Sophie's sister.

events, George Jessel served as the emcee and narrator. The list of participants represented the elite of American popular theater.

Gertrude Berg began the recitation, describing Sophie as a kid. "Sonya Abuza, the confused, bewildered girl who, just a half-a-century ago, left her home, her husband, her child, to follow, blindly, stubbornly, the irresistible beckoning of a dream." Jack Pearl recalled her as a vaude novitiate. Adolf Zukor told of his first booking of Sophie in vaudeville. Gene Buck reminisced about Sophie's Ziegfeld experiences. Sheldon Brooks, whose "Some of These Days" was now Sophie's trademark song, played and sung his tune.

Deborah Kerr and Tallulah Bankhead, representing British theatrical interests, brought best wishes for Sophie. Milton Berle recalled the multiplicity of Sophie's "new act" reviews. Joe E. Howard, Blanche Ring, Smith & Dale, and Harry Hirshfield followed with nostalgic salutes. A singing tribute from Jane Froman preceded kind words for Sophie's humanitarian endeavors from Dr. Ralph Bunche, the Nobel Laureate for Peace. Joe E. Lewis told a number of humorous stories about himself and

Featured at the Golden Jubilee celebration were Betty Hutton, supposedly selected to play Sophie in a proposed film of her life, and Sheldon Brooks, the composer of "Some of These Days." (Museum of the City of New York)

Sophie—"I admire her war work, but for a time I was afraid the Confederates captured her"—and he saluted Sophie as the "Betty Hutton of the Stone Age."

William Gaxton sang "You're the Tops." Edward G. Robinson told of the many charities Sophie had endowed. General James A. Van Fleet saluted Sophie for her wartime entertainment of the troops. Betty Hutton (still hoping for a movie role as Sophie Tucker) belted out "Some of These Days."

Finally given the chance to respond to the myriad tributes, Sophie spoke of her career in a manner reported as "frank in self-analysis and revelation of character." She singled out William Morris, Sr.; Abe Lastfogel; Ted Shapiro; and Jack Yellin as the men who had helped make her a headliner. "I've been real lucky in life," she admitted. Then she went on for a half an hour, baring her inner feelings, noting that the love of her friends and her public had had to compensate for the more personal love she had never quite found.

Prior to the dinner, Sophie made her entrance to the Waldorf-Astoria in a 1903 Ford, rolling down from her Park Avenue home to the hotel. This event was the climax to a series of intra-show-biz fetes—Friars' Club, Variety Club, radio, TV, and press salutes—that were afforded her. Finally, a group of religious leaders presented scrolls and plaques to Sophie, who, by this time, was crying openly in response to the many emotional and tangible gifts she had already received.

The following week, Sophie opened at the Latin Quarter (New York) and received renewed recognition for her fifty years in show business. At the Latin Casino, Philadelphia, audience reactions were similar, as they were at the Beachcomber, Miami Beach. In between engagements, as she had promised, Sophie made a quick trip to Hartford to participate in a fund-raising drive for the new Hebrew Home for the Aged.

For the next several months, it seemed that Sophie was going to be honored at every engagement. Special tributes were made to her in each city; menus were printed in gold; early photos of her were distributed to the audience. In Philadelphia, Sophie was feted by local charities, at which events local and state politicians were in attendance. Noble Sissle, Negro Actors' Guild president, presented Sophie with a plaque thanking her for her efforts on behalf of the Guild.

For Sophie, the years leading to 1953 had been enchanted. Now, 1954 seemed primed to offer more of the same. "Take a deep breath, Soph," advised George Jessel. "If you thought 1953 was a frolic, next year will blow the sequins off your gown."

16

A Fabulous Character

The ever-perceptive George Jessel had been correct in his assessment. Sophie spent the next six months celebrating her Golden Jubilee wherever she appeared. Of course, she enjoyed every minute; and the attention she received brought renewed interest in her performance and career.

During the first part of 1954, Sophie spent fourteen weeks at the Beachcomber, Miami Beach, with one evening set aside each week to reprise her fiftieth anniversary celebration. Old, favorite songs and a recitation of Sophie's long career were interspersed with tunes sung by other performers on the bill, among them Nat "King" Cole and Dick Shawn, singing Sophie's hits. For two shows a night at the Beachcomber, Sophie earned $7,200 a week.

Sophie instituted two new variations during these engagements. First, she took off several days every few weeks as new acts were being set up, thus treating her strained voice to a brief rest. Second, she and Jack Yellin revived a number of old songs with new lyrics, retaining the familiar melodies but adding modern, topical stories to make them fresh. Occasionally, afterpieces were added to include the entire cast for a "swinging" conclusion to the act.

The pattern was much the same at the Chez Paree, Chicago, where her engagement was advertised as "Sophie's Golden Jubilee Revue." An appearance on Ed Sullivan's "Talk of the Town" featured Sophie's fifty years in show business, although she was allowed to sing only two songs. Visits to Las Vegas, Reno, Los Angeles, Seattle, and Portland were all billed as part of Sophie's Golden Jubilee tour.

In early May, the entire, yearlong commemoration was musically highlighted when Mercury Records, with great hoopla, released a special Golden Jubilee album, entitled "50 Golden Years." The printed tributes ran sixteen pages, with a galaxy of pictures, two beautifully rendered watercolors of Sophie in regal attire, and many photos of Sophie with colleagues Jimmy Durante, Irving Berlin, George M. Cohan, and Judy Garland, as well as pictures of her mother and family. Included was an essay, written by Jack Yellin, called "The Sophie Tucker Story," apparently a shortened version of the treatment sent to movie studios. On one side of the record were George Jessel's introduction, "Hi-Ya Soph!"; Pattie Page's interpretation of "Yiddishe Mama"; Eddie Cantor's "If You Knew Sophie Like I Know Sophie"; Georgia Gibb's takeoff on "Some of These Days"; Jack Benny's telephone greetings; Vic Damone's "Who Cares?"; and Rusty Draper's "Hard Hearted Hannah."

On the other side were five of Sophie's specialty hits: "Inhibition Papa"; "Vitamins, Hormones and Pills"; "It's Never Too Late to Have a Little Fun"; "Sophie Tucker School for Red-Hot Mamas"; and "There's No Business Like That Certain Business." For disk jockeys, some of Sophie's songs demanded editing if they wished to play them over the radio. Still, they said, "It is to her distinction that she can blend the romantic and nostalgia with the saloon stuff and make both jell."

The Tucker album was heralded as a "special edition," to be sold for fifteen dollars. The beautifully adorned album quickly became a collectors' item.[1]

After a brief trip to Hartford to attend High Holy Days services and visit her parents' graves, Sophie returned to the nightclub circuit. Since her trip to Israel, she had expressed renewed interest in the Jewish religion and its age-old rituals, which, when she was able, she observed. During the Christmas holidays, Sophie visited Dallas and Las Vegas, where she was fast becoming an annual visitor. Another appearance on Ed Sullivan's show, where Sophie was again feted for her long career in show business, culminated a year of tributes and triumphs.

Sophie's usual round of nightclubs was highlighted during her visit to the Latin Quarter, New York, where she entertained enthusiastic SRO crowds for four weeks. *Variety*'s review offered special insights into Sophie's stage presence, as they perceived it, and described her audience appeal "even at this late date in her career."

> Sophie Tucker is now launching her second half-century in show business and, if anything, the "last of the red-hot mamas" is hotter than ever. Miss Tucker's grip upon the customers, even when they are jam-packed so closely is underlined by the almost hypnotic silence which she commands when she does her stuff. It was a demonstration of respect from the youngsters and veneration from the oldsters which few other performers could have duplicated.[2]

At this time, another movie version of Sophie's life made its appearance, this time due to her personal efforts. She had hired Norman Lessing, an already well-known, successful screenwriter, to prepare an entirely new script for her to submit to the studios. Sophie also revealed that she would dub all the tunes in the picture, hopefully making it easier for the studios to select an actor/impersonator, as had been done for "The Jolson Story."

Unfortunately, even this new version was rejected by studios. It seemed a strange decision for, at the same time, they were churning out biographies of musical stars and songwriters at unprecedented speed, depicting such talents as Gus Kahn, Eva Tanguay, John Philip Sousa, Stephen Foster, Lillian Roth, Sigmund Romberg, and Joe E. Lewis. Among current releases were The Eddie Cantor Story, The Gene Krupa Story, The Benny Goodman Story, the Glenn Miller Story, and others. "Why not The

Sophie Tucker Story?," she wanted to know. No one seemed willing to provide a reasonable answer.

Some observers suggested that the studios, in their rush to produce dozens of movie musicals, had already saturated the market. It was possible, said some movie critics, that the studios guessed that the era of film musicals was nearing its end. Or maybe, it was speculated, the studios believed that Sophie was past the point of general audience recall and familiarity. For some time now, she had appeared only in nightclubs and a few television, vaudeville-style shows. Other performers who made it to the screen had obtained considerable exposure to the general public via their own radio and television programs. Whatever the reasons, despite all her efforts, Sophie's story failed to reach the movies; and this failure remained a major disappointment. Yet, undeterred, she turned her efforts to seeing her story presented on the stage, a friendlier, more willing venue, she believed. This, too, however, would prove to be a long and, in the end, unfulfilling and expensive labor.

In late 1955, Sophie suffered another bout of laryngitis, which caused her to cancel several engagements. She had to be moved from Winnipeg to Los Angeles to obtain the care she needed. Newspapers again questioned the state of Sophie's health. Nevertheless, she was back in Las Vegas by December, in spite of doctors' warnings that she needed further rest.

At this time, Sophie and Abe Lastfogel announced that she had been booked for a farewell tour of England in 1957. (It was an ominous sign to old-time critics; successive farewell tours had not yet become publicity events to draw crowds.) Four weeks at the Café de Paris nightclub and a tour of the "provinces" suggested a more limited schedule than in the past. There was also talk that she might appear in a number of television programs while in England.

To her surprise, Sophie was again called to Hollywood, this time by Paramount Pictures. Would she appear in a scene showing her introduce Joe E. Lewis (played by Frank Sinatra) at the old Frolics Theater, Chicago? Although the event to be depicted was fictitious, Sophie agreed to the cameo appearance. A day off from a Las Vegas engagement allowed her to fulfill the studio's request.

A hard day's work again went for naught. When the film was edited, the scene was omitted, lying dead on the proverbial cutting-room floor. The effect on Sophie was again disappointment, an emotion she had often experienced when working with movie studios.

The year 1956 ended with another appearance on the Ed Sullivan show, at which time she was required to sing "Some of These Days," which she had sung on every previous Sullivan program. She also gave several benefits for underprivileged children and donated $100 a month to the Variety Club for its Heart Fund.

In March 1957, Sophie sailed on the H.M.S. Queen Elizabeth for England. She had dearly wished to visit Israel again, but the Suez Crisis prevented that part of the trip. Billed as her farewell appearance in London, the engagement at the Café de Paris was sold-out in days. Her four-week run there was to open April 1.

A capacity crowd, the room filled with movie and stage stars, turned out for

Sophie's opening. "More than unique," reported *Variety*'s London correspondent, "it was memorable."

> As she descended the stairs from the balcony to the main restaurant, she was cheered for minutes on end in a spontaneous demonstration of affection and admiration.[3]

Beginning with the song, "Starting All Over Again," Sophie proceeded to entertain and delight the crowd for a solid forty-five minutes.

"You Can't Deep Freeze a Red-Hot Momma" began a cycle of sexy songs that also included "No Business Like That Certain Business," "How to Hold a Man," and "A One-Man Girl." Then came a group of sentimental ballads, followed by a number of nostalgic songs Sophie had sung to English audiences in past appearances. By way of diversion, Sophie presented a two-language version of "Mama Goes Where Papa Goes," first in English, then a reprise in Yiddish.

> In style, appearance and staying power, Miss Tucker doesn't seem to have changed much since she last played London some five years back. And she's certainly lost none of her popularity.[4]

Another week was added to her stay in London, and Sophie also appeared on the BBC-TV show "A–Z." A *London Times* personal interview revealed that Sophie claimed to have lost thirty-nine pounds before coming to England; and she now weighed 184. She had brought over nine trunks of new dresses and admitted to be earning 2,000 British pounds a week. She told of spending 20,000 pounds a year on clothing and $25,000 a year each for Ted Shapiro, her accompanist for thirty-five years, and Jack Yellin, her exclusive songwriter.

Sophie declared herself a "pal to all the world" and devoted to charity. In the last ten years, she stated, she had raised over $3 million for various charities. Her songs were mainly "moral carrying" ones, not to be taken too seriously; yet within their lyrics "a wealth of good sense abounds."

"They carry the results of my own early hardships," she revealed, "and the lack of real marital happiness which I've sought for myself." Asked about her future, Sophie answered jokingly, "Red hot mamas never fade away. They just go up in smoke."

"My song repertoire can be divided into three categories," she explained: "spangled sentimentality; noisy vulgarity; and brassy nostalgia. You may think I'm an old one, but I'm not a cold one."

As Sophie was leaving London to return to the U.S., the *Evening Standard* reviewer summed up her latest triumph.

> Sophie sailed on the floor liked a gayly bedecked battleship. She opened her plump arms, smiled that infectious smile, and let forth with that rollicking voice of hers and, taking you to her ample bosom, practically defied you not to love her. She kicked sex around with an inoffensive bawdiness that breaks down all barriers.

People know when they are in the presence of an artist of such assurance and authority they are going to be disarmed. And they like it.[5]

One decision Sophie had to change, or likely it had been changed for her. Instead of this trip being her farewell tour, Sophie promised everyone she would return again soon.

In October, Sophie visited the Chez Paree, Chicago, to help them celebrate their twenty-fifth year in business. Elaborate silvery ornamentation inside and outside the nightclub was augmented with silver cakes and silver spangles covering the walls and tables. Silver columns and floodlights added to the showiness of the setting. Even Sophie promised to wear only silver gowns on stage. In response, management allowed Sophie to sell her wares in the lobby and request audience support for her charity work.

Sophie had first appeared at the Chez Paree shortly after they had opened; so her act carried a nostalgic theme throughout. Indeed, her entire routine was made pertinent to the nightclub's anniversary.

While playing in Denver, Sophie made several speeches at the Denver children's hospital she had endowed, raising more money for new projects. At local synagogues, she also took the opportunity to raise funds for Israel bonds. Sophie's speaking engagements were increasing, as more and more organizations, especially those to which she had already made donations, vied for her time to assist at benefits. In fact, Sophie was an excellent speaker, with her personable manner and bits of humor mixed with the seriousness of the topic; and she projected a sales pitch that matched her dynamic stage presence. Yiddish phrases were often used, and her mother's philanthropic values invoked. She may not have had all her audiences crying, but she certainly had them buying.

Months of nightclub dates caused only one bout of laryngitis in 1958 and only a few weeks lost to bed rest. The rests between engagements and the reduction in show length definitely helped her voice. Moreover, upon the advice of her doctors, Sophie reduced her smoking habit, at least temporarily.

At Abe Lastfogel's sixtieth birthday bash, Sophie announced that she was going to Israel next year to dedicate the Sophie Tucker Youth Center and, maybe, put on a few benefit performances. Sophie talked of the strong emotional bond she had formed with the people of Israel and hoped she could continue to donate to Israeli causes. In fact, when she appeared on the Jerry Lewis Show and again with Ed Sullivan, she made impromptu pitches for Israel bonds.

The year 1959 opened with Sophie's usual appearance in Las Vegas, this time at the new Sahara Hotel, where she played through February. She was sharing the stage with the Ames Brothers; together they represented the most expensive opening act in Las Vegas history. She was also allowed to set up her charity booth to sell her books and record albums.

As a new feature, expressly for the Las Vegas crowd, Sophie's last number sported a Western theme to a new Yellin song, "I'm a Wild Wicked Woman From the Badlands." Sophie dressed in a colorful cowgirl outfit, replete with sequins, broad-brimmed hat and six-guns at her ample hips. The number brought a standing ovation and was considered "one of the best acts to hit Las Vegas in a long time."

A short visit to the Coconut Grove, Los Angeles, preceded preparations for the Israeli trip, scheduled for the beginning of April.

Welcomed by large crowds at the Israeli airport, a motorcade to her hotel, and a dinner honoring her arrival, Sophie was quickly caught up in a nonstop schedule filled with speeches, kibbutz encounters, hospital visits, benefits, and appearances at various theaters. When she spoke at a ceremonial Passover supper, she acknowledged that, "for the first time in my life, I have known and felt the true meaning of the Passover seder." At the Youth Center in Beth Shemesh, Sophie presented a check and invited the children of the kibbutz to visit her in New York. As she kissed the youngsters surrounding her, she remarked jokingly but with affection, "Don't worry about the lipstick. All my boyfriends tell me it comes off very easily."

Speeches at Hadassah installations and the Hebrew University drew crowds of cheering people. Sophie presented both institutions with checks, at the same time marveling at the accomplishments she observed. A luncheon at the university commemorated the establishment of the Sophie Tucker Chair of Dramatics at Brandeis University. In her speech, she hoped she would be able to "do something similar for the Hebrew University."

At a reception camp for newcomers, Sophie welcomed them to Israel "where a happy life awaits you among your wonderful brothers and sisters, who have taken you into their arms and their hearts." No question that Sophie was fast becoming an unabashed spokesperson for Israel as she toured the country and met the people. The experience also appeared to confirm her own religious commitment, not so much to a particular deity as much as to a "home," a place she could identify with.

As she prepared for her departure from Lydda Airport, Sophie's last words to the crowd emphasized her affinity with them. "I'm so grateful, so thankful, dear God, for giving me the life and the strength to come here — home — to Israel — to the land of my people."[6] The crowd cheered her in unison.

Returning to the U.S. with the accolades of an entire country sustaining her, Sophie prepared to open her annual nightclub visitations with a stop at the Chez Paree, Chicago. At the last moment, however, Abe Lastfogel informed her that the new owners of the nightclub had canceled her appearance there. It was the first time in decades that Sophie had been dropped from a bill. Abe reported that the new bosses felt that Sophie simply did not pull enough audience to validate her price. Of course, Sophie was incensed at the implications, citing a long list of past sellouts at the Chez Paree. When the nightclub hired a number of not yet well-known young singers instead, Sophie could easily surmise that the combination of her price and her age had played an important role in the termination of a longtime relationship with the nightclub.

Instead, Sophie was booked for four weeks into the Palmer House Empire Room, Chicago, where she scored well. At the same time, Lastfogel was working on an arrangement to unite Sophie and Ted Lewis at venues that could accommodate their joint financial demands. Together they had played at the fortieth anniversary celebration for Victor Moore and had been so well received that their services were quickly in demand. The highlight of their improvisational act was when they performed "Me and My Shadow," with Sophie playing the shadow.

Their appearance at the Moulin Rouge, Hollywood, California, brought out the duo's feelings of nostalgia when they reminisced about the "good old days."

> A combined hundred years of entertainment are wrapped up in an effervescent red hot mamma named Sophie Tucker and an unhurried, tophatted clarinet player named Ted Lewis who, for the first time, have joined forces to chronicle that century.[7]

After each performed a solo act—Sophie sang "Some of These Days" and Lewis "When My Baby Smiles at Me"—they came together to sing "There's Only a Few of Us Left," as they counted the few show biz greats who were still entertaining at that time.

Sophie's second appearance at the Palmer House attracted many of her longtime partisans, who vowed from the start that, despite the new venue, Sophie remained their beloved entertainer.

> The toniest setting has not altered her stuff one whit, nor is there reason it should from the hefty reaction of the crowd. Other considerations aside, there's the plain wonder of vintage Tucker. Her vigor, going on 72, is somewhat astonishing.[8]

After songs about sex, which represented a sizable musical part of her life, Sophie switched to a synopsis of the Tucker saga, to tunes associated with her career. A misty thank-you speech by Sophie sent the audience off into the night satisfied that they had been a part of a special evening.

Sophie ended the year as she had done previously, with an appearance on the Ed Sullivan Show. A reviewer wondered whether it was Sophie he had seen on television or a ghost. In any case, she continued to "attack the audience like a bulldozer gone berserk."

For a CBS radio show, Sophie and Irving Berlin collaborated on a number of old, familiar songs she had sung in the "good old days."

Nineteen sixty appeared to be Sophie's year for donations, awards, and benefits. At the same time, she continued her usual round of nightclubs, from Las Vegas to Miami Beach to New York. During all these scheduled events, in September, sister Anna died, causing a brief but significant respite in Sophie's hurried timetable.

Sophie was made a lifetime Hadassah member and honored by the Beverly Hills chapter for "her outstanding philanthropies." She donated heavily to the Happiness Club for crippled children. To the Variety Club International, Sophie pledged $100 a month; likewise to the Greater New York Fund. Further donations went to the Nathan Goldblatt Society for Cancer Research, Chicago, and the Home of the Sons and Daughters of Israel, New York.

Boy's Town received a sizable gift. Speeches at the Hadassah chapters in New York obtained funds for a new Sophie Tucker Playground. Sophie joined the Actors' Temple (just off Broadway) and immediately solicited them to purchase Israel bonds. The American Guild of Variety Artists gave a dinner dance for Sophie, and she used the opportunity to sell her book and record albums. She also received an award from the Catholic Actors' Guild. Traveling to Hartford from Las Vegas, Sophie headed a benefit for the hometown synagogue that collected more than $20,000.

At most of her nightclub engagements, she teamed with Ted Lewis; and the combination broke box-office records wherever they appeared—Las Vegas, Pittsburgh, New York, New Orleans, Miami Beach. The show at the Riviera, Las Vegas, typified the duo's success.

Variety became part of the script for the show, as the paper's articles tied together the Tucker-Lewis careers for five decades. To begin with, Sophie impersonated Lillian Russell, then went on to develop her specialty to the present red-hot mama. Lewis, likewise, reprised his career from Reisenweber's pre–Prohibition era "lobster palace" to date.

> Nostalgia and showmanship in massive doses are the result of the combined efforts of Sophie Tucker and Ted Lewis. Together they represent nearly a century of show business; they are holdovers of a golden era in entertainment having savvy and polish that in these days are difficult to develop.
> Both are names of unmatched longevity in their sphere. Their merger results in the entertainment apex for the old-timers and a lesson in techniques for younger viewers.
> Sophie is a durable breed of performer, and a star whose lustre has not dimmed. Both of these stars add to the stature of the other. It's a happy combination.[9]

The duo played to eight weeks of SRO crowds. Sophie could not have been more pleased with her recent success, thanks again to the introduction of a new act and new material.

Anna's death (September 29, at age 68) delayed Sophie's opening at the International Casino, New York, for several weeks. Family lore suggested that Sophie had provided funds over the years for Anna and her family and that Anna had lived a quiet and unassuming life, seemingly content with her position. Of course, Anna had raised Bert; and Sophie was ever-grateful for her efforts. Moe called Sophie to tell her of Anna's death, and she immediately left for Hartford to attend the funeral. The customary Jewish rituals followed and Sophie helped attend to them. Before returning to New York, Sophie promised the rabbi she would help the synagogue at its next benefit. Yet, Anna's death seemed but a brief interlude in Sophie's busy life, as did visits with brother Moe and his family.

Sophie opened at the International Casino on October 26 to SRO crowds.

> This is Soph's 58th year in show biz and she admits to being in the septuagenarian age bracket. She has the vibrancy of the 40s and the socko appeal of any contemporaneous giant in the box-office sweepstakes.[10]

The reviewer's dates were wrong, but the information made Sophie's efforts seem all the more amazing. She was reported to be earning $8,000 a week at the Casino, similar to what she was earning at the Las Vegas resorts. Not having appeared in New York for several years, her act included material recently developed, so everything was new to New York audiences, from her high-style gowns to her talk-songs to her cowgirl routine. As expected, after the show, Sophie was found in the lobby, selling her book and LPs for charity.

Sophie also revealed she was working on a sequel to her autobiography to serve as a new commodity for her charity work. Shortly after the book was published, Sophie had bought from Doubleday the rights to "Some of These Days." Since then, she had used the plates to continue the book's production to ensure its continued availability at all of her nightclub appearances. Sophie stated that, to date, she had collected more than $3,500,000 from book sales, all of the proceeds going to charities in the U.S. and Israel.

Speaking of Israel, Sophie seized the opportunity to promote her 1961 touring schedule, which would include another visit to London and Israel, where she planned to dedicate a second youth center in her name. Both prior to and following the trip, Sophie would be making the rounds of the usual nightclubs. "And how about a round-the-world tour in "62", she proffered. No one questioned her claims; history had already demonstrated that whenever Sophie promised to fulfill a commitment, she always carried through.

The year began with engagements in Detroit, Chicago, Miami Beach, and New Orleans. A brief rest at home in New York prepared her for the London and Israel visits. In May, she began a six-week engagement at London's "Talk of the Town," to the familiar audience excitement and full houses. Called by a London reviewer, "that living legend of show biz," Sophie was said to hold the audience "in the hollow of her expressive hands." It was reported that many younger performers, some of them pop stars, attended Sophie's opening, obviously not based on nostalgia "but on sheer admiration for the technique of this veteran performer."

Dressed majestically in a white, sequined gown with matching hat and gloves, Sophie commanded the floor with an act that was not so much singing as rhymed monologues to a musical background, with Ted Shapiro at the keys. Incidentally, Ted had only the previous week celebrated his fortieth year with Sophie—"without a contract," he noted.

Actually, Sophie's presentation was no different than what she had given at U.S. nightclubs, ending the routine with her cowgirl skit, sung while wearing a flamboyant Wild West outfit. For an encore, she sang English and Yiddish versions of "Yiddishe Mamma," as a final audience appetite appeaser. It had not been too many years before when Sophie first introduced this song, that she had been berated for using Yiddish in front of English audiences.

Given an opportunity by the press, Sophie lauded English audiences and suggested that more American performers should visit the British Isles to take advantage of their hospitality, even though the salaries were not as large as back home. "Treat it as a working vacation," she advised. "You'll learn something. You'll meet new audiences and friends. For those who haven't played to British audiences, there's a great new experience awaiting you." But as some American actors pointed out, who could entertain British audiences as well as Sophie?

While in London, Sophie emceed "The Sophie Tucker Show" on BBC-TV. The show was nothing more than a revue, a string of musical acts, with Sophie winding up the event in a brief performance. Critics called the show "somewhat unenterprising" and filled with "so-so entertainment," lacking in surprise and quite empty of humor. Of Sophie, they reported:

> The Tucker personality was as forceful as ever, but the matter seemed embarrassing and thin, okay for nostalgies but holding little for those with short memories.[11]

As Sophie perceived the show, it seemed a mirror of her U.S. television experiences, heavy on scripted material and short on spontaneity, limiting her skills. Television again proved problematic for Sophie.

In early July, Sophie arrived in Israel and made stops at all the places to which she had donated. Included was a stop at the new youth center that she dedicated in her name. Her speech, similar to those she had made during a previous trip, reflected her optimism for and excitement about Israeli pioneers and the vitality of the young country. The welfare of Israeli children was her favorite activity; and, while she apologized for not paying more attention to adults, Sophie believed children to be the future of the nation. In explaining why she favored children, Sophie discussed her immigrant upbringing and growing up on the streets among hostile neighbors. She talked about her early married life, her son, and her decision to make a career in show business, thereby leaving everything youthful "back home." Sophie called the children at Beth Shemesh her "first-born"; and she stated, "in Jewish tradition the first-born has always had special privileges." In a concluding admission, Sophie alluded to her newfound discovery of God "and the strength to serve Him and this glorious, beloved Land of Israel."[12]

Sophie arrived back in the U.S. in late August, after what she considered to have been a rewarding and heart-lifting experience. Indeed, her adventures in Israel had strongly reminded her of her own Jewish heritage. Now, she seemed to be rushing to recapture her heritage after having neglected it for years. In ensuing years, Sophie

16. A Fabulous Character

tended to focus most of her philanthropic activities on Jewish enterprises, both in the U.S. and Israel.

The remainder of the year featured engagements in Chicago, Minneapolis, New York, and Miami Beach, as well as Omaha and Hot Springs, Arkansas, both new locations. In New York, Sophie appeared at the Waldorf-Astoria Hotel for three weeks, to crowded houses made up of the city's elite. In Miami Beach, at the swanky Diplomat Hotel, Sophie entertained old-timers with a history of her hits, to their distinct delight. At the end of her shows, in both New York and Miami Beach, Sophie made emotional appeals on behalf of Israel bonds.

At the beginning of 1962, Abe Lastfogel confirmed that Sophie was going to tour "around the world" for the summer and fall of the year. He took the occasion of Sophie's seventy-fifth birthday (actually seventy-sixth) to make the announcement, reaffirming her previous statement of intentions but also praising her for such an ambitious schedule at her age. Lastfogel alluded to the fact that there were few performers today who could, or would, undertake such an assignment.

Sophie's tour was to begin in Australia — Sydney and Melbourne — go on to various cities in South Africa, take a short respite in Israel, and conclude with a month of performances in England before returning home.

Visits to Miami Beach; New Orleans; Washington, D.C.; and San Francisco preceded the international tour. In Washington, D.C., besides leading an Israel bond celebration, Sophie introduced new personal stationery that heralded "a musical play based on the life of Sophie Tucker, slated for Broadway next fall." The information was not entirely a surprise to theater insiders, since Sophie and Abe had been negotiating with directors, choreographers, writers, and composers for some time to prepare the musical. While most of them were willing to offer their services to the project, there was a lack of adequate funds to finance the production. Sophie promised Abe that, when she returned from her tour, she would obtain the necessary funds to produce the show.

Although Sophie was not to open at the Tivoli Theater, Melbourne, until June 27 and in Sydney July 19, she was already the recipient of heavy press coverage, which, in turn, drove heavy ticket sales. When she did arrive, she was met by a sizable crowd of newspaper and radio-TV reporters. Having flown into Melbourne, Sophie declared she would have been there twenty years before only she disliked boat trips. Incidentally, there was a clause in Sophie's contract that she had to travel to Australia by jet. Australian agents now complained that other performers demanded similar clauses. In fact, Sophie's press coverage was reported to have topped that of any other headliner to come to Australia.

Sophie was also revealed to be the highest-paid female entertainer to visit Australia, with a salary of $2,240 weekly for ten performances a week. The Tivoli, Melbourne, audiences were said to be "enthralled" by Sophie, which, among Aussie critics, meant she was "a wow." In Sydney, she had the audiences "yelling for more."

> Sophie Tucker, a show biz legend here via her records and imitators, had the Tivoli outfronters yelling for more after working solidly for 45 minutes despite a

heavy cold. She drew a four-minute ovation on her initial bow. Nothing to equal Miss Tucker's performance has ever been seen in this area, especially her handling of sexy numbers before a mature audience.[13]

Sophie's act consisted of "The Saga of Sophie Tucker" (her life history in song); "How Ya Gonna Keep 'Em on the Farm"; "Some of These Days"; "Life Begins at Forty"; and "After You've Gone." She concluded her songfest with "Yiddishe Mamma," but not in Yiddish, since the promoters believed an unfamiliar language would confuse the audience.

While playing in Sydney, Sophie participated in two television programs, both variety shows in which she reprised songs she was using at the theater. Although she was interviewed during each show, Sophie's comments were generally restricted to how much she was enjoying Australia.

A week off and a long jump to South Africa. On August 24, Sophie opened in Capetown to a house full of admirers, although the majority of them were seeing Sophie for the first time. Visits to Durban, Port Elizabeth, and Pretoria preceded a series of gala performances in Johannesburg. On the day she opened in the city, patrons began lining up in front of the theater well before dawn. Surprising to promoters, not only were old-timers besieging the box office, but the responses from younger patrons was equally enthusiastic. Critics marveled both at her performance and her durability.

> Taking a heavy schedule of twice-nightly performances, an attack of laryngitis, and an itinerary covering half-a-dozen cities in as many weeks in her stride, Sophie Tucker has been showing South African audiences that the last of the Red Hot Mamas is still sizzling. And her admirers here are proving warmly responsive to the Tucker treatment.[14]

Two personal notes of interest. Sophie brought Moe along to serve as her companion at social gatherings. And, although she argued strongly to have her black maid accompany her to South Africa, the apartheid government refused to let the woman enter the country. From Australia, Sophie's maid was sent directly on to Israel.

After a three-week vacation in Israel, Sophie and her entourage headed for London. The Israeli vacation was typical for Sophie, her time filled with luncheons, tours, visits to the youth centers and kibbutzim, and dinner tributes. In the meantime, London's Palladium was selling out Sophie's two-week engagement.

Yet, the ultimate highlight of Sophie's stay in London far surpassed any previous engagement and, in terms of personal recognition, surpassed any accolades she had received in decades. When she arrived in the city, Sophie was notified that she had been invited to play before Queen Elizabeth and Prince Philip at a Royal Variety Performance. Included in the show would be Bob Hope and several other American and British stars. Sophie and Bob, however, were to be specially honored by the Queen for their longtime contributions to the amusement industry in England. Sophie was alternately surprised, honored, gasping with delight, nervous, and scared she would not perform well before royalty. The event, as perceived by Sophie, would be the crowning achievement of her career entertaining British audiences since her first appearance in 1922.

Sophie grew even more nervous when she learned that her place on the bill would be near the end of a long evening. Coming on first was a contingent of American headliners that included Edie Adams, Eartha Kitt, and Rosemary Clooney. Then followed a host of British acts: singers; dancers; a comedian (Harry Secombe); an acrobatic group; and a facsimile of a minstrel show. According to reviewers, by this time in the evening, the show was showing signs of "drooping," that is, until Sophie was announced to appear. The announcement literally changed the demeanor of the audience, who suddenly sat up attentively in anticipation of her entrance.

> Disk stars may be idols of the teenagers, but it took a pro like Sophie Tucker to surmount the resistance of the toughest audience in the world to win acclaim at the Royal Command Variety Gala.
>
> Her performance, toward the end of a long and star-studded bill, was an object lesson to any entertainer. Miss Tucker was the only artist to have this sedate audience begging for more. The timetable of the Royal show precludes any encores, but the determined patrons would not be silent until Miss Tucker returned for an extra bow. It was a unique tribute to a triumphant performance.[15]

Sophie began with what she described to the audience as the Sophie Tucker saga, a nostalgic songalog that illustrated her rise to fame, from her mother's restaurant to international stardom, with such numbers as "Down on the Farm," "After You've Gone," and "Life Begins at Forty." She ended with her signature tune, "Some of These Days."

Bob Hope followed Sophie, having the advantage of coming on to an audience already roused to enthusiasm. Reviewers, however, reported his comedy act to have run too long.

The reception after the show was primarily taken up by the Queen's talking to Sophie and Bob. What was said is unknown, but the broad smiles on their faces and the number of bows they made suggested a plethora of compliments. A few days later, Sophie was hand-delivered an elaborately printed and signed commission from the Queen, thanking her for entertaining the audience and participating in the benefit to aid variety artists. The show had netted more than $100,000 and was taped by BBC-TV to appear on television the following Sunday.

Under the headlines "Soph 'Steals' Command Show," "Sophie's Big Click," and "Sophie Tucker 'Saga' Wows," ran an acclaim from reviewers that "Sophie Tucker is the wonder of the music hall and cabaret stage."

> Never, in my time, has a star nearer 80 than 70 been one of the smash hits of the Royal Variety Show. But American Sophie Tucker had the audience yelling for more at the Palladium last night — the only performer on the bill to do so.
>
> What a marvelous and well-deserved tribute it was to this fabulous character who, as she told us in her musical saga, was 'born with a song in my soul.'[16]

In 1962, at the Royal Variety Performance, Sophie and Bob Hope were honored by Queen Elizabeth and Prince Philip for their contributions to British entertainment. (Museum of the City of New York)

As Sophie enjoyed the ego-satisfying reviews and the relaxation of her voyage home, news of a musical comedy to open on Broadway the following year spread through New York theatrical circles. The musical was to be called "Sophie," with music written by Steve Allen. According to reliable sources, the show would deal with the early part of Sophie's life, from 1906 until she became a star. Now all Sophie had to do was raise sufficient funds to make the show a reality.

Sophie wasted no time seeking funds. On the Ed Sullivan show in January, 1963, Sophie talked about the musical and mentioned its need for financing. While in New Orleans for two weeks, Sophie visited scores of potential "angels" with some success. Back at the "Town and Country" in Brooklyn, she had time to meet several New York investors who, she reported, had expressed interest in the show. Funds were collected, but not as much as she would have liked. The show would have to begin with limited funding, not an auspicious way to launch a new production.

After two months of rehearsals, "Sophie" opened March 3 in Detroit, to a full house and mediocre reviews.

> Sophie, a musical about that red hot mamma, is pretty much cold potatoes on the basis of its Detroit opening. The musical looks too flat for Broadway, and this version wouldn't make an acceptable scenario. The heroine is depicted as a coldly calculating career-happy dame. As a result, the song "Red Hot Mama," a Sophie Tucker signature, seemed forged and out of place.
>
> Libi Staiger, in the title role, has a loud voice and makes no effort to ape Miss Tucker's mannerisms. She sounds more like Ethel Merman and acts like the Meadows Sisters. "Sophie" is an uneven show, a collection of No. 2 spot vaude acts, only some of which were meant to actually be vaude sketches.[17]

The reviews prompted Sophie to drop her current nightclub revue and rush to Detroit. Changes in the script and cast were made, for which Sophie had to spend an additional $25,000 to keep the show going out-of-town. Unfortunately, at its next stop, the Erlanger Theater, Philadelphia, reviews were only slightly improved.

Because of changes in scheduling for other shows at the Winter Garden in New York, "Sophie" was being forced to open there several weeks before it was ready. The three-week engagement in Philadelphia had been cut to two weeks, and a proposed booking at the Shubert Theater in Boston had to be canceled to meet the Winter Garden's new schedule. Sophie knew the show was not ready — would it ever be ready? — and a premature New York opening could prove disastrous.

A revised and heavily reworked "Sophie" opened April 15, 1963, at the Winter Garden Theater, New York, its mediocre reviews preceding it. While curious audiences filled the house to see what was being done with Sophie's life, reviewers with sharp pencils were preparing to write the show's obituary, although Sophie begged them to be "fair."

The show's quick entrance to New York had short-circuited a planned advertising campaign and a host of pre-opening parties to promote the show, its music, and its stars. Nor did the music from the show receive sufficient exposure on local radio stations (a common practice for musicals about to open).

"Sophie" was purported to be a musical biography of Sophie Tucker, with music and lyrics by Steve Allen and book by Phillip Pruneau. The show was directed by Jack Sydow, who had replaced Gene Frankel in Detroit, and choreographed by Donald Siddler. It was produced by Len Bedsow and Hal Grossman, in association with Michael Pollack and Max Fialkov, supposedly the money men behind the show. Still, it was Sophie who had contributed as much if not more at this point.

Libi Staiger played the role of Sophie and proved again that no one could impersonate her, on the screen or on stage. The characters of William Morris, Sr.; Marcus Loew; Julian Mitchell; and Nora Bayes appeared in the script, along with that of Frank Westphal, who was played by actor Art Lund. "Sophie" closed its doors in one week, after a number of devastating reviews.

Robert Coleman, of the *Daily Mirror* wrote: "Soph, we're sorry. We had hoped

Sheet music for the song "Red Hot Mama," written by Steve Allen, featured in "Sophie," a Broadway musical based on Sophie's early life and career. The show closed after one week. It reminded everyone that no one but Sophie could play Sophie.

to ring bells and dance in the streets this morning, but it just wasn't to be. 'Sophie' is no Sophie."[18]

Walter Kerr, the esteemed critic of the *Herald Tribune,* lamented: "There were ghosts at the Winter Garden Monday night, but not one of them was Sophie Tucker's." Kerr observed that Sophie had been in the audience and got up to take a bow. "Before the show started," Kerr noted, "was the time to do it."[19]

New York Times critic, Howard Taubman, felt sorry for Sophie. "Not only did Miss Tucker have her story turned into a musical of shattering dullness, but she also had to sit through it." For the most part, reviewers felt sorry for Sophie, since the "real her" had been so distorted and defiled.[20]

Seemingly as a last resort, full page ads for "Sophie" were run in *Variety* and New York papers with the headline, "What the Critics Say About the Score of 'Sophie.'" Ten (partial) reviews were quoted, some from the very critics who had panned the show. In addition, several reviews came from Dallas and Columbus, leaving readers to wonder how they had anything to do with the show. In any case, the ads did no good.

For Sophie, the experience was a devastating, if not totally unexpected, failure, as well as a substantial financial loss. For years, she had attempted to get her story in movies or on stage; now, finally, she had to admit defeat. Her insurmountable barrier: no one else could really play Sophie, not as audiences expected her to perform and entertain them.

A trip to London served as an escape from the barbs of Broadway. A six-week engagement at "The Talk of the Town" restored Sophie's self-pride, although not to the extent she would have liked. London reviewers now spoke more of Sophie's age and long career than her actual performance, and she could sense that perceptions of her were shifting.

> New words or phrases to praise Sophie Tucker are difficult to find, for they have all been used before. They will probably all be used again before she makes her retiring bow.
>
> Okay, Miss Tucker has slowed down a little. She possibly declaims rather than sings more now than in the early days. But, immaculately gowned and in complete control of what is one of her favorite floors, she is supremely show biz.[21]

Sophie's triumphal appearance, however, was marred by a severe cold and laryngitis she acquired near the end of her engagement. She continued to perform, but under personal duress.

Back in the States in August, Sophie spent the remainder of the year visiting Cleveland, Pittsburgh, and New York, then playing a new Christmas holiday date in San Juan, Puerto Rico. While in New York, a brief illness, described as "stomach trouble," put her in a hospital for a four-day checkup. Nothing more was revealed of her ailment. In Pittsburgh, her illness was noticeable to the extent that "there was evidence of many tears being shed in the audience, many of whom were ready to give Soph credit for just being able to walk out to the mike." Still, Sophie persevered.

In a booking breakthrough, the Morris agency announced that Sophie was being united with Ted Lewis and George Jessel to play the Latin Casino, in Cherry Hill, New Jersey. Salaries for all the three combined were said to amount to $20,000. If the show was well received, other locations would be considered. It seemed inevitable to show biz observers that these people would ultimately get together. Veteran performers from a previous era, they were some of the last of the best who remained on stage.

Before the trio could get together, however, Sophie made another six-week trip to London to play "The Talk of the Town." As before, she was received with great acclaim from audiences, although reviewers noticed she was "less torrid," did a shorter act, and seemed "more strained" than usual. Still, when Sophie took the stage, she "enveloped the room with her zest, know-how, and socko star quality."

Another engagement at the Latin Quarter, New York, postponed the proposed Tucker-Lewis-Jessel act to late 1964. Sophie had not performed at the Latin Quarter in several years, and show biz people wondered if she would ever return. Not to disappoint them and her host of admirers, she played there for almost two months. "A grand lady is Sophie, and its a privilege to welcome her back to New York," declared the *New York Journal-American* reviewer.[22]

In spite of her age and longevity in the business, the reviewer pointed out, "Miss Tucker is one of the more amazing entertainers and a prime example of showmanship." The reviewer observed that people were now going to see Sophie as if it might be the last time they would be able to see her in person.

The Tucker-Lewis-Jessel revue appeared for only one week, but two shows a night generated capacity crowds. "Instead of young fathers bringing their kids, as they did with the Three Stooges, we now see young fathers bringing their parents," noted one reviewer of the new bill. Bus parties came from as far south as Wilmington. Regular bus tours, full of old-timers, came from Philadelphia and Trenton. Together, the trio represented close to two centuries of stage experience.

Jessel told his stories like the toastmaster he had become in recent years. Lewis still extracted mileage with his battered hat and clarinet. High point of his revival of "Me and My Shadow" was Sophie's trailing him, as she had once before. Another Lewis standby, "When My Baby Smiles at Me," won audience approval.

One could see and feel the excitement in the audience rise when Sophie took the stage. She quickly reminded audiences that she knew her business.

> Miss Tucker, always a commanding figure, enunciates nonsense as though it were Shakespeare. She gets an impressive silence from the huge house with the unabashedly sentimental rhymes, draws roars with rowdy lyric advice to those males who let moneymaking interfere with their boudoir obligations. And, of course, she still belts out with major response one of the greatest get-off numbers of the century — "Some of These Days."[23]

Shortly after, Morris announced that the trio would again appear at the Latin Casino later in the year. In the meantime, Sophie had her own nightclub schedule to keep.

In April, 1965, Sophie was given a testimonial luncheon by the United Jewish Appeal Women's Division, marking her sixty-second anniversary as an entertainer.

During the last years of her life, Sophie often played at the Latin Quarter, New York. On October 25, 1965, on this stage, she last appeared before an audience. (Museum of the City of New York)

(Actually, it was fifty-nine years; but with such longevity, a few years difference surely did not deny the tribute.) At the luncheon, Sophie announced that she had begun to fund a new high school in Israel, at a frontier town in the Negev desert, to go along with her playground and children's hospitals.

With booking agent demand so great for the trio, the Morris agency reported they were setting up an engagement in Detroit in July, with others to follow. Still, Sophie worked in another four-week visit to London in June. Unfortunately, the planned engagement in Detroit was canceled. Sophie complained she was not feeling well and felt fatigued. She spent several weeks at home resting, but unspecified "stomach problems" continued to annoy her.

In late October, Sophie opened at the Latin Quarter, New York, for a three-week engagement. She received a heartwarming and admirable reception.

> Sophie Tucker is the grand beldame of the niteries. At an age when most headliners of her era are in pasture and beefing about the current state of the entertainment world, Miss Tucker remains one of the top stars of the café belt. She personifies authority and stature and, more important, has an innate ability to communicate and project in the great traditions of the profession. She's out for fun, and so is the audience coming to see her.[24]

Although quite ill on opening night, Sophie performed her entire act. Yet, startlingly, she missed a few bars of her signature song and was unable to return to the stage to acknowledge the prolonged applause.

In her dressing room, Sophie collapsed to the floor in great distress and was quickly rushed to the hospital. She would never again appear on the stage.

Epilogue

Sophie Tucker died on February 9, 1966, at age eighty. The causes of death were lung cancer and kidney failure.

The final four months of Sophie's life were filled with the wasting away of a once robust body and the increasing pain of encroaching death. Sophie refused to reveal her condition publicly, telling only immediate family members of her condition when she returned home from the hospital. She had been aware of her condition for several months, yet was determined to perform until she could no longer physically bear the strain. That fateful day arrived during her opening show at New York's Latin Quarter.

In early November, newspapers reported that Sophie had canceled the remainder of her Latin Quarter engagement, slated to have included Jessel and Lewis during its second week. Several days later, spokespersons from Mt. Sinai Hospital reported that Sophie was undergoing tests "to make sure she recovers from the flu brought on by physical exhaustion." Of course, the announcement was a cover-up, carefully orchestrated for public consumption. Sophie herself told reporters (by phone) that she was planning to rest until January 1 and then resume work, scheduled to appear at the Fontainbleau Hotel, Miami Beach, February 15.

Sophie returned home in early December under a nurse's care. She had lost considerable weight and remained exhausted. Shortly after returning to her Park Avenue apartment, she announced that she was canceling all of her nightclub bookings, since she needed more rest. To theater insiders, her notice of cancellations was an ominous sign. She made it more difficult by refusing to have any newspaper reporters visit her. Sophie began chemotherapy treatments and, later, radiation treatments at the hospital, although she demanded that she return home after each treatment. When she lost her hair, she donned a wig.

As she visibly wasted away and the pain increased each day, only Sophie's immediate family were allowed to visit her. During the last few weeks, she was confined to a wheelchair and had twenty-four-hour nursing care. Moe, his son

Charles, Sophie's favorite nephew, and her son Bert were present when she quietly died.

Obituaries appeared in almost all the U.S., British, and continental newspapers. Articles in the New York, Chicago, and Hartford papers covered her life and career. These were compiled from all the available sources, including her autobiography. No one seemed to be able to agree on her age, the newspapers offering a range from seventy-eight to eighty-two. They unanimously agreed, however, that she had been one of popular theater's greatest stars for more than fifty years.

Two funerals were held to honor Sophie. The first, on February 11, was held at Riverside Chapel, Amsterdam Avenue and Seventy-sixth Street, New York. The marquee lights of the Palace Theater were darkened while this service was being held.

Nearly 1,000 friends and admirers crowded the chapel. On the side streets, behind barricades, more than 3,000 others strained for a glimpse of the service. Rabbi Isidore A. Aaron of Mt. Sinai Congregation, Brooklyn, a longtime family friend, presided. Standing before an enormous array of floral tributes, Rabbi Aaron declaimed: "I had a feeling that Wednesday afternoon there must have been a great deal of excitement in heaven — the trumpets must have been blaring."

Rabbi Aaron went on to pay tribute to Sophie as a "warmhearted individual who gave of herself freely to all. Everywhere she went, she lit a bright candle in a dark corner."

A second eulogy was given by Sophie's old friend and colleague, George Jessel. "The Lord gave Sophie many blessings that few women have enjoyed," Jessel declared. "A full life, a life of being loved and respected, from the tipsters to the tycoons, from the chambermaid in a small hotel to a Queen of England in Buckingham Palace." Throughout his eulogy, Jessel often stopped, choked up, and wiped tears from his eyes.

Honorary pallbearers included Abe Lastfogel, president of the William Morris Agency; Abel Green, editor of *Variety*; Barney Balaban, chairman of Paramount Pictures; Ted Shapiro; Ed Sullivan; William Morris, Jr.; Charles "Honi" Coles, president of the Negro Actors Guild; and Horace McMahon, president of the Catholic Actors Guild.

Also attending the services were Jack Haley, Harry Hirshfield, Ted Lewis, Jack Yellin, Van Johnson, Jack Pearl, Blossom Seeley, Joey Adams, Spyros Skouras, Jules Stein, Dinty Moore, and representatives from various theatrical and actors' unions.

Following the services, Sophie's casket was taken to Hartford for another funeral and for burial. A special railroad car had been hired by the Morris Agency to take the casket and a party of thirty-six people — family and show business colleagues — back to Sophie's home town.

In London, hundreds of theater people turned out for a memorial service for Sophie at the Crawford Street Synagogue, in the Edgeware Road district, not far from where Sophie had frequently entertained.

On February 13, sixty years after she had left Hartford as a poor girl, to seek fame as an entertainer, Sophie was buried in Emanuel Cemetery.

The mortuary was filled to standing-room-only with 600 mourners. Several hundred more waited quietly outside in a cold wind and sleeting rain. Even inside, a decided winter chill etched faces already reddened from crying. At 1:30 P.M., Cantor Arthur Koret began the services with the familiar Jewish psalm, "Lord, what is man?"

In the eulogy, Rabbi Noveck spoke of Sophie's strongly-held inner determination. "She was a unique and unusual personality; a woman blessed with great success and a long span of career." Solemnly he observed: "Sophie Tucker made entertainment a real profession; she became an institution in her lifetime."

Rabbi Aaron, who had officiated at the Riverside Chapel, noted that thousands of people from all walks of life had gathered to pay their last respects to Sophie. "They represented many denominations, many creeds. They came to that chapel because they, too, had been touched by the woman's goodness, by her capacities as a gifted personality."

"The person blessed with three score and ten years leaves something lasting in life," Rabbi Aaron continued. "And in Sophie Tucker's life, it was a friendship, a kinship, for actually millions of people — heads of state, presidents, and people in the street. She set out to accomplish many things and she did these many things."

The mourners rose as the Cantor chanted the "Kaddish," the prayer for the dead, and the casket was borne out of the chapel. Television cameras and newspaper photographers caught the long procession of family, admirers, and theatrical people who walked silently in the rain to waiting limousines. The cortege wound slowly through the traffic and heavy rain to Emanuel cemetery. Close to 1,000 people had gathered along the roads and paths of the cemetery grounds to say goodbye to Sophie in their own way. A brief prayer was chanted by the two rabbis and the cantor next to the family plot, and the casket was lowered into the ground. In accordance with Sophie's orders, in neither funeral service had the casket been opened.

A week later, Sophie's will was filed in Surrogate Court.[1] It was a twenty-two-page document, dated March 25, 1964. Her estate was estimated to be somewhere between a half-million and $1 million. Those funds not allocated to specific people or organizations were to be divided three ways: among her son, Bert; brother, Moe; and nephew, Charles. The money to Bert was left in trust. Fifty percent of the total amount would derive to him on the fifth anniversary of Sophie's death; the remainder on the tenth anniversary of her death, if he was still alive. Bert died on October 25, 1982, after a long illness. He was survived by his wife, who inherited what remained of the estate.

Bert's wife, Lillian, received a $5,000 bequest outright, plus $5,200 annually. Moe's wife, Blanche, received "my Rogers 1847 set of flatware silver and my Worcester dinner set." Regrettably, Blanche had died two weeks before Sophie. Furs and jewelry and "other personal adornments" went to Bert and Charles.

Anna's husband, Julius Aronson, was given $10,000; Ted Shapiro was willed $25,000; and four members of Sophie's staff each received $1,000. Thirty thousand dollars went to the Sophie Tucker Foundation, and $10,000 to the Hebrew Home for the Aged. The Screen Actors Guild was willed Sophie's stage clothing, except furs and stage jewelry, "for distribution to members."

Sophie had not forgotten her immediate family, nor the organizations closely associated with her mother's philanthropies.

The time that Sophie had so often sung about had finally arrived. "Some of these days, you're gonna miss me, Honey," she had prophesied. "Some of these days, you'll feel so blue."

Sophie was missed by multitudes. In show business, the world had literally become her stage; and the audiences her friends. For almost sixty years, from beer halls to nightclubs, she belted out those gutsy songs and revealed openly what was in her heart. Her gay ribaldry, her infectious good humor, and her high spirits, combined with the earthy liveliness and zest with which she delivered every song, kept her at the top of her profession.

More than any other city, Hartford loved her; and she, in turn, remembered her old home town. Many Hartford organizations were recipients of her largesse. They served as symbols of dedication to her Jewish heritage. Her memorial to her mother was always to remember other people in need.

Sophie was also viewed as a champion of women's new-found freedom in the early twentieth century. Her stories of love gained and lost, of romance and fulfillment no matter one's age, portrayed woman as strong and independent. Her songs, filled with humorous innuendo, broke down taboos between the sexes. Although the songs were in fun, even self-deprecating, their fundamental seriousness shone through. Sophie was able to subvert the sexual mores of the day, and her audiences loved it.

During the era in which she lived, Sophie was unique as an artist and distinctive as a person. When she died, her era died with her. Although we often dream of embracing such pleasures again, sadly, we are faced with the realization that these joys will likely never be revived.

Notes

Chapter 1

1. Gilbert, M., *Atlas of Russian History*, London, Dorset Press, 1972, pp. 69–71.
2. A description and history of Tulchin can be found in *International Jewish Cemetery Report-Ukraine*, on the Internet at www.jewishgen.org/cemetery/e/europe/ukra-t.html
3. Naturalization papers, *National Archives and Records Administration*, Waltham, MA, 02452. Reaffirmed by 1900 Census Index, Department of Commerce, Bureau of the Census.
4. Philip and Sophie's birth dates were listed differently in various census and city directories. Philip's naturalization papers give his birthdate as January 5, 1884, Court of Common Pleas, State of Connecticut. Sophie's birthdate is derived from the landing manifesto recorded at Castle Garden, U.S. Immigration Processing Center, upon the family's arrival in the United States in May, 1886. Sophie's age was given as four months old.
5. Howe, Irving, *World of Our Fathers*, New York, Harcourt Brace Jovanovich, 1976, particularly Chapter 8, pp. 256–286.
6. For a description of Front Street at the turn-of-the-century, see: Dalin, D.G. and Rosenbaum, J., *Making a Life, Building a Community*, New York, Holmes and Meier Publishers, Inc., 1997, Chapter 4: Hartford's Jewish East Side.
7. Howe, 261–263, 265–271.
8. Springfield, Massachusetts Vital Records, Marriage Certificates, 1903, Vol. 537, p. 157, #187.
9. Hartford Vital Records, Births, 1905.

Chapter 2

1. Tucker, Sophie, *Some of These Days*, New York, Doubleday Doran, 1945, pp. 21–22.
2. Tucker, p. 30.
3. Tucker, p. 31.
4. Tucker, p. 37.
5. *New York Clipper*, December 14, 1907.
6. *Clipper*, April 11, 1908.
7. *Variety*, April 6, 1908.
8. *Clipper*, May 30, 1908.
9. *Clipper*, September 13, 1908.
10. *Clipper*, November 22, 1908.
11. Tucker, p. 45.

Chapter 3

1. *New York Clipper*, June 26, 1909.
2. *Clipper*, August 28, 1909.
3. *Clipper*, September 4, 1909.
4. *Chicago Daily News*, September 24, 1909.
5. *Clipper*, October 2, 1909.
6. *Clipper*, October 30, 1909.
7. *New York Sunday Reviewer*, October 31, 1909.
8. *Clipper*, November 13, 1909.
9. Tucker, p. 101.
10. *San Francisco Chronicle*, August 8, 1910.

Chapter 4

1. *New York Post*, January 11, 1911.
2. *New York Clipper*, April 29, 1911.

3. *Chicago Tribune,* April 20, 1911.
4. *Chicago Daily News,* April 21, 1911.
5. *Chicago Examiner,* June 2, 1911.
6. *Clipper,* September 16, 1911.
7. *Chicago Daily News,* September 4, 1911.
8. *Daily News,* May 7, 1912.
9. *Clipper,* November 2, 1912.
10. *Clipper,* July 5, 1913.

Chapter 5

1. *Hartford Courant,* October 19, 1913.
2. *Courant,* October 19, 1913.
3. Tucker, p. 119.
4. *Courant,* October 21, 1913.
5. Tucker, p. 125.
6. Tucker, p. 123.
7. Spitzer, Marion, *The Palace,* New York, Atheneum, 1969, p. 34.
8. *New York Clipper,* August 1, 1914.
9. *Clipper,* November 2, 1914.
10. *Clipper,* April 10, 1915.
11. *Clipper,* November 13, 1915.
12. *Clipper,* December 18, 1915.
13. *Clipper,* January 15, 1916.
14. *New York News Tribune,* June 22, 1916.
15. *Clipper,* July 8, 1916.
16. *Clipper,* December 27, 1916.
17. Letter: Sam Gerson to J.J. Shubert, February 6, 1917.
18. Letter: Sam Gerson to J.J. Shubert, February 6, 1917.
19. Letter: Sam Gerson to J.J. Shubert, February 12, 1917.

Chapter 6

1. Segal, H.B., *Turn-of-the-Century Cabaret,* New York, Columbia University Press, 1987.
2. Erenberg, L.A., *Steppin' Out: New York Night-Life and the Transformation of American Culture, 1890–1930,* Westport, CT., Greenwood Press, 1981, pp. 180–185, 248–249.
3. *San Francisco Chronicle,* November 19, 1917.
4. *New York Clipper,* March 18, 1918.
5. Letter: Frank Westphal to *New York Clipper,* March 27, 1918.
6. *Clipper,* March 30, 1918.
7. *The Chicago Show World,* June 6, 1918.
8. *Clipper,* June 26, 1918.
9. *Clipper,* March 12, 1919.

Chapter 7

1. *New York Clipper,* September 26, 1919.
2. Letter: Sophie to J.J. Shubert, November 9, 1919.
3. *Clipper,* November 26, 1919.
4. *Clipper,* December 17, 1919.
5. A full description of the divorce proceedings can be found in the Supreme Court of Cook County files, October 20–27, 1920.
6. *Variety,* September 20, 1920.
7. *Variety,* November 19, 1920.
8. *Chicago Examiner,* February 23, 1921.
9. *Variety,* October 10, 1921.
10. *Variety,* January 4, 1922.
11. *Clipper,* January 18, 1922.
12. *Dramatic Mirror,* January 21, 1922.
13. *Clipper,* March 15, 1922.

Chapter 8

1. *London Times,* April 9, 1922.
2. *London Times,* April 16, 1922.
3. *London Daily Mail,* June 14, 1922.
4. *London Evening Standard,* June 10, 1922.
5. *Evening Standard,* June 21, 1922.
6. *New York Clipper (London),* July 26, 1922.
7. *Clipper,* August 23, 1922.
8. *Clipper,* September 20, 1922.
9. *Variety,* September 21, 1922.
10. Tucker, p. 216.
11. *Clipper,* October 4, 1922.
12. *Clipper,* October 18, 1922.
13. *Chicago Daily News,* December 2, 1922.
14. *Chicago Herald Examiner,* December 6, 1922.
15. *Herald Examiner,* December 13, 1922.
16. *Daily News,* December 18, 1922.
17. *Clipper,* April 25, 1923.
18. *San Francisco Call,* April 21, 1923.
19. *San Francisco Chronicle,* May 3, 1923.
20. *Los Angeles Times,* May 22, 1923.
21. *Daily News,* December 18, 1923.
22. White, M., *You Must Remember This: Popular Songwriters, 1900–1980,* London, Frederick Warne Ltd., 1983, p. 16.
23. *Daily News,* June 23, 1924.
24. *Variety,* August 6, 1924.
25. *Variety,* September 17, 1924.
26. *Variety,* September 24, 1924.
27. *Variety,* October 8, 1924.
28. *Variety,* October 8, 1924.

Notes

29. *Daily News,* January 31, 1925.
30. *Encore,* September 24, 1925.

Chapter 9

1. Tucker, p. 224.
2. Tucker, p. 225.
3. *Variety,* April 7, 1926.
4. *Variety,* August 4, 1926.
5. Letter: Sam Gerson to J.J. Shubert, August 14, 1926.
6. Letter: Sam Gerson to J.J. Shubert, August 17, 1926.
7. Letter: Sam Gerson to J.J. Shubert, August 19, 1926.
8. *Chicago Examiner,* August 11, 1926.
9. *Chicago Daily News,* August 21, 1926.
10. *Variety,* November 28, 1926.
11. *Chicago Herald Examiner,* May 23, 1927.
12. *Daily News,* May 23, 1927.
13. *Examiner,* May 23, 1927.
14. *Los Angeles Times,* October 18, 1927.
15. *Variety,* December 7, 1927.
16. *Variety,* December 7, 1927.

Chapter 10

1. *Variety,* February 8, 1928.
2. Tucker, p. 241.
3. *Variety,* April 4, 1928.
4. *Variety-London,* May 6, 1928.
5. *Variety-London,* May 23, 1928.
6. *Chicago Herald Examiner,* November 6, 1928.
7. *Chicago Daily News,* November 6, 1928.
8. Tucker, p. 247.
9. *Variety,* January 9, 1929.
10. *San Francisco Chronicle,* March 26, 1929.
11. *Los Angeles Times,* April 12, 1929.
12. *Variety,* May 22, 1929.
13. *Variety,* May 29, 1929.
14. *Daily News,* May 25, 1929.
15. *Variety,* June 12, 1929.
16. *New York Times,* June 5, 1929.
17. *Variety,* June 12, 1929.

Chapter 11

1. *Variety,* October 29, 1930.
2. *Variety,* May 10, 1930.
3. *London Times,* September 25, 1930.
4. *Sunday Times,* September 18, 1930.
5. *Variety,* October 8, 1930.
6. Tucker, p. 261; *Variety,* June 16, 1931.
7. *Variety,* October 13, 1931.
8. *Variety,* November 3, 1931.
9. *Variety,* December 22, 1931.
10. *Variety,* March 7, 1932.
11. Tucker, pp. 266–67.
12. *Variety,* September 3, 1932.
13. Tucker, p. 265.
14. *Variety,* September 5, 1933.
15. *San Francisco Chronicle,* December 12, 1933.
16. Tucker, p. 269.

Chapter 12

1. *London Times,* May 9, 1934.
2. *Times,* August 22, 1934.
3. *Times,* September 12, 1934.
4. *Variety,* December 18, 1934.
5. *Chicago Daily News,* January 10, 1935.
6. *Variety,* April 16, 1935.
7. Tucker, p. 282.
8. Tucker, p. 282.
9. *Variety,* November 20, 1935.
10. *Variety,* May 20, 1936.
11. *Daily News,* July 1, 1936.
12. Tucker, p. 284.
13. *Variety-London,* October 7, 1936.
14. Letter: Lord Mayor of London to Sophie, December 17, 1936.
15. *Variety,* January 7, 1937.
16. Excerpted from the *American Film Institute Feature Films, 1931–1940,* p. 241.
17. Tucker, p. 297.
18. *Variety,* September 4, 1937.
19. Excerpted from the *American Film Institute Feature Films, 1931–1940,* p. 2189.
20. *Variety,* November 17, 1937.
21. *Chicago Tribune,* May 8, 1938.
22. *Variety,* May 11, 1938.
23. *Variety,* July 6, 1938.

Chapter 13

1. Letter: Sophie to William Green, president, AFL, June 15, 1939.
2. Letter: I.B. Padway to Ralph Whitehead, executive secretary, AFA, July 3, 1939.
3. *Variety,* June 21, 1939.
4. Telegram: Eddie Cantor to Sophie, June 21, 1939.

5. Letter: Sophie to William Green, June 26, 1939.
6. *Variety,* August 9, 1939.
7. *Variety,* August 9, 1939.
8. *Variety,* August 16, 1939.
9. *Variety,* July 26, 1939.
10. *Variety,* August 16, 1939.
11. Copies of these letters and telegrams were obtained from The Jacob Rader Marcus center of the American Jewish Archives, Cincinnati, Ohio.
12. *Variety,* September 6, 1939.

Chapter 14

1. *New York Times,* September 10, 1939.
2. *Chicago Daily News,* November 13, 1939.
3. *Variety,* June 12, 1940.
4. *Variety,* December 4, 1940.
5. *San Francisco Chronicle,* June 18, 1941.
6. *New York Times,* November 1, 1941.
7. *Chicago Sunday Tribune,* May 10, 1942.
8. *Daily News,* May 13, 1942.
9. *Chronicle,* September 11, 1942.
10. *Variety,* November 11, 1942.
11. *Variety,* January 20, 1943.
12. *Daily News,* May 13, 1944.
13. *Tribune,* May 14, 1944.
14. *Variety,* June 21, 1944.
15. *Daily News,* May 5, 1945.

Chapter 15

1. One of Sophie's routines featured at the Latin Quarter celebrating her 60th birthday, February 13, 1946.
2. *Variety,* May 7, 1947.
3. *Los Angeles Examiner,* September 22, 1947.
4. Letter: Queen Elizabeth to Sophie, June 12, 1948.
5. *Variety,* September 8, 1948.
6. *Variety,* January 26, 1949.
7. *Variety,* ? , 1950.
8. *Variety,* January 10, 1951.
9. *Variety-London,* April 22, 1952.

Chapter 16

1. A copy of this beautiful album can be found in the Cinema Library, University of Southern California. Universal Music, currently the owner of Mercury Records, possessed no copy of the album nor had records of its publication.
2. *Variety,* April 20, 1955.
3. *Variety-London,* April 10, 1957.
4. *Variety-London,* April 10, 1957.
5. *London Evening Standard,* May 2, 1957.
6. Speeches that Sophie made to various Jewish organizations in the U.S. and during her trips to Israel can be found in the collection of letters at The Jacob Rader Marcus Center of the American Jewish Archives, Cincinnati, Ohio.
7. *Variety,* August 12, 1959.
8. *Variety,* October 21, 1959.
9. *Variety,* June 15, 1960.
10. *Variety,* October 26, 1960.
11. *London Times,* June 12, 1961.
12. Speech at Sophie Tucker Youth Center, July 6, 1961, from American Jewish Archives.
13. *Variety-Sydney,* August 3, 1962.
14. *Variety-Johannesburg,* September 25, 1962.
15. *Variety-London,* November 7, 1962.
16. *London Times,* October 30, 1962.
17. *Variety,* March 6, 1963.
18. *New York Daily Mirror,* April 16, 1963.
19. *New York Herald Tribune,* April 16, 1963.
20. *New York Times,* April 16, 1963.
21. *Variety-London,* June 30, 1963.
22. *New York Journal American,* August 21, 1963.
23. *Variety,* December 2, 1964.
24. *Variety,* October 20, 1965.

Epilogue

1. *Variety,* March 9, 1966.

Selected Bibliography and Source Material

Archives, Collections, Libraries

Museum of the City of New York
Harry Ransom Humanities Research Center, University of Texas
Universal Music
The Museum of Television and Radio
Connecticut Society of Geneologists
Hartford Vital Records Office
Superior Court of Cook County, Illinois
Connecticut State Library
State of Massachusetts Marriage Records
Declarations of Intent, United States Immigration Papers
Russians to America (CD), 1850–1896, Passenger and Immigration Lists
Passenger Lists for the Port of New York, 1886
Jewish Historical Society, Hartford, CT.
Chicago Blue Book
Hebrew Home for the Aged, Hartford, CT.
The Jacob Rader Marcus Center of the American Jewish Archives, Cincinnati, Ohio
University of Southern California, Special Collections Library
University of Southern California, Cinema Library
New York Public Library, Performing Arts Division, The Sophie Tucker Collection
National Archives, Boston, MA.
Brandeis University Libraries
Shubert Archive
The New York Historical Society
Connecticut Woman's Hall of Fame
Academy of Motion Picture Arts and Sciences
Connecticut Historical Society
Hartford City Directory, 1895–1900

Periodicals, Newspapers

New York Clipper, January 1906 to July 1923.
Variety, December 1905 to March 1966.
Selected newspaper articles from 1907 to 1966 — *Chicago Daily News, Chicago Tribune, Chicago Herald Examiner, New York Times, Hartford Courant, San Francisco Chronicle, Los Angeles Times, London Times, London Evening Standard*

Books

Allen, R.C. *Horrible Prettiness: Burlesque and American Culture.* Chapel Hill, University of North Carolina, 1991.
Antler, J. *The Journey Home: Jewish Women and the American Century.* New York: Free Press, 1997.
Atkinson, B. *Broadway.* New York: Macmillan, 1970.
Cashman, S.D. *America in the Twenties and Thirties.* New York: New York University Press, 1989.
Coffin, C. *Vaudeville.* New York: Mitchell Kennerlly, 1914.
Cohen, S.B. (ed.). *From Hester Street to Hollywood.* Bloomington: Indiana University Press, 1983.
Dolin, D.G., and Rosenbaum, J. *Making a Life, Building a Community.* New York: Holmes and Meier, 1997.
Dunn, L.C., and Jones, N.A. (eds.) *Embodied Voices: Representing Female Vocality in Western Culture.* Cambridge: Cambridge University Press, 1994.
Erenberg, L.A. *Steppin' Out: New York Night-Life and the Transformation of American Culture, 1890–1930.* Westport CT: Greenwood, 1981.
Fields, A., and Fields, L.M. *From the Bowery to Broadway.* New York: Oxford University Press, 1993.
Gilbert, D. *American Vaudeville: Its Life and Times.* New York: Whittlesey House, 1940.
Glenn, S.A. *Female Spectacle: The Theatrical Roots of Modern Feminism.* Cambridge MA: Harvard University Press, 2000.
Goldman, H.G. *Fanny Brice: The Original Funny Girl.* New York: Oxford University Press, 1992.
Green, A., and Laurie, J., Jr. *Show Biz from Vaude to Video.* New York: Henry Holt, 1951.
Howe, I. *World of Our Fathers.* New York: Simon & Schuster, 1976.
Jasen, D.A. *Tin Pan Alley.* New York: Donald I. Fine, 1988.
Kenney, W.H. *Chicago Jazz: A Cultural History, 1904–1930.* New York: Oxford University Press, 1993.
Kibler, A. *Rank Ladies: Gender and Cultural Hierarchy in American Vaudeville.* Chapel Hill: University of North Carolina Press, 1999.
Laurie, J., Jr. *Vaudeville: From the Honky Tonks to the Palace.* New York: Henry Holt, 1953.
Raymond, J. *Show Business on Record from the 1890s to the 1980s.* New York: Frederick Ungar, 1982.
Silverman, M. *Hartford Jews, 1659–1970.* Hartford: Connecticut Historical Society, 1970.
Snyder, R.W. *Voice of the City: Vaudeville and Popular Culture in New York.* New York: Oxford University Press, 1989.
Tucker, S. *Some of These Days.* New York: Doubleday Doran, 1945.
Whitburn, J. *Pop Memories, 1890–1954.* Menomonee Falls WI: Record Research, 1986
Young-Tulin, L. *Sophie and Me.* New York: iUniverse.com, 2001.

Playbills, Magazines

Playbill: "Follies of 1909," Ziegfeld revue, Jardin de Paris, New York Theater, 1909.
Playbill: American Music Hall, vaudeville, Chicago, January, 1910.
Playbill: "Merry Mary," Whitney Opera House, Chicago, April, 1911.
Playbill: "Louisiana Lou," La Salle Opera House, Chicago, September, 1911.
Playbill: "Louisiana Lou," La Salle Opera House, Chicago, September, 1912.
Playbill: "Le Maire's Affairs," Wood's Theater, Chicago, July, 1926.

Playbill: "Leave It To Me," Auditorium Theater, Chicago, November, 1939.
Playbill: "High Kickers," Erlanger Theater, Chicago, May, 1942.
Playbill: Florentine Gardens, Los Angeles, 1943
Antler, J., "So Big and Ugly," *Lilith,* Spring, 1997, pp. 30–35.
Chung, M., "Our Golden Girl," *Fabulous Las Vegas,* October 17, 1953.
Dunray, W.R., "Sophie Tucker in Another Smoke Bit," *The Chicago Show World,* Vol. 1, No. 2, June 6, 1918.
Edison Phonograph Monthly, March, 1910.
Engle, W., "The Magnificent Sophie Tucker," *The American Weekly,* April 16, 1950, p. 12.
"Golden Jubilee Fete For 'Last of Red Hot Mamas,'" *American Jewish Ledger,* September, 1953.
"Herman Swaffer Demands the Truth From Sophie Tucker," *London Sunday Times,* May 24, 1928.
Hays, M.B., book review of "Some of These Days," *Connecticut Circle,* 1945, pp. 60–61.
Millstein, G., "First of the Red Hot Mamas," *New York Times Magazine,* September 27, 1953.
Pennybacker, S.D. and Albert, N., "East Side Story," *Northeast,* July 2, 1995.
Proclamation for "Sophie Tucker Day" in San Francisco, February 5, 1957.
Program: *Promises Kept,* celebration for the new Hebrew Home and Hospital, October 29, 1989, pp. 34–36.
Stevens, A., "When Sophie Tucker Kissed a Critic," *Actorviews: Intimate Portraits by Ashton Stevens,* Chicago, Covici-McGee, 1923.
"Sophie Tucker Spanked For Flirting With Stage Hands," *PIC,* October 3, 1939, pp. 24–27.

Index

Abuza, Anna 9, 17, 24, 31, 39, 48, 55, 62–63, 98, 101, 109, 120–121, 124, 138, 143, 181, 224, 234–235
Abuza, Charles Poltiel (Kalish) 8, 11–12, 16, 18, 55–57, 62–63, 95
Abuza, Jenny Linetsky (Kalish) 8, 11–12, 16–18, 48, 55–57, 62–63, 69, 98, 109, 113–114, 121–124, 171, 208, 227
Abuza, Leah 48, 55, 98, 181, 208
Abuza, Moses (Moe) 9, 15, 40, 48, 55, 57, 62–63, 98, 114, 123, 181, 208, 224, 234–235, 238, 246, 248
Abuza, Philip 7–9, 11, 15, 48, 55, 57, 62–63, 67, 98, 107, 112, 114–115, 121–124, 135, 137, 181, 208
Abuza family restaurant 3, 11, 18, 106
Actors' Equity Association (A.E.A.) 84–86, 150, 184–185, 191, 203
Adams, Maude 2
After You've Gone 196, 206, 238, 239
Ager and Yellin 110, 116, 143, 145–147, 151
Albee, E.A. 53, 59–60, 77–78, 82, 84, 115–116, 127, 150, 157
Alexander's Ragtime Band 181
Alhambra Theater (London) 121, 140, 166
Alhambra Theater (New York) 99, 116
All Night Long 52
"All-Star Revue" 222
Allen, Lester 127–129, 131, 133, 162
Allen, Steve 240–242

American Federation of Actors (A.F.A.) 167, 181, 183–193
American Guild of Variety Artists (AGVA) 190, 193
American Music Hall (Boston) 37
American Music Hall (Chicago) 37, 39, 42
American Music Hall (Rockaway Beach, Long Island) 36
The Angleworm Wiggle 44
Annie Laurie 181
Another Male Hitched in Your Stable 98
Araby 65
Aronson, Julius 138, 248
Arrowhead Inn (Saratoga) 171
Ash, Paul 129–130
Associated Actors and Artists of America 4As) 183–185, 187–192
Atkinson, Brooks 194
Atlas Advertising Company 29

Babes in Toyland 32
Baby Your Mother 171
Back Home 66
Bacon, Lloyd 144, 146
Bad Little Boys Aren't Goody-Good to the Goody-Good Little Girls 108
Bagatelle (London) 220–221
Baker, Belle 41, 162–163
Bal Tabarin (San Francisco) 205, 208
Balaban & Katz 119, 135, 149, 156
Ballin' the Jack 66
Barrymore, Ethel 5, 59
Bayes, Nora 4, 5, 33–35, 125, 127, 241
BBC-TV: The Sophie Tucker Show 236

Beachcomer (Miami Beach) 215, 226–227
Beck, Martin 76–78, 112, 159
Benny, Jack 167, 222, 228
Berg, Gertrude 225
Bergen, Edgar 174
Berle, Milton 187, 222, 225
Berlin, Irving 19, 53–54, 127, 159, 213–214, 227, 233
Bernie, Ben 133, 156, 171, 181, 183
Blackface acts 22, 25–28, 33, 48
Blowing Bubbles 206
Bluebird Blues 108
Brice, Fanny 5, 42, 49
Broadway 1–3
Broadway Melody of 1938 176–177
Bronx Theater (New York) 58
Brookhurst Theater (New York) 199
Brooks, Sheldon 41–42, 68, 76, 97, 180, 196, 225
Brown Elementary School 9, 12–13
Buffalo Evening News 203
Bunche, Dr. Ralph 225
Burns, George 167, 217

Cabarets 53, 71–75, 88, 159
Cadillac Hotel Casino (Detroit) 195
Calloway, Cab 207
Can't Get Enough of It 52
Cantor, Eddie 159, 167, 185, 188, 217, 222, 228
Capitol Theater (New York) 158, 170, 177
Carnival Time 53
Carr, Alexander 48–51
Carroll, John 100–101, 107, 112, 117, 119–120

259

Casino (London) 216
Casino de Paris (London) 229
Century Theater (San Francisco) 110
Chez Paree (Chicago) 167–168, 196–197, 203, 206, 208, 212, 216, 220–221, 227, 231–232
Chez Paree (New York) 159–160
Chicago Daily News 37, 45, 50, 109, 113, 130, 173, 195–196, 201, 206, 208
Chicago Examiner 45, 95, 109, 142, 156
Chicago Tribune 39, 44, 180, 201, 206
Chutes Theater (San Francisco) 41
Civic Stadium (Buffalo) 202
Coconut Grove (Los Angeles) 212, 232
Cohan, George M. 50, 227
Coliseum (London) 138, 175
College Inn (Chicago) 156
Colonial Inn (Miami) 198
Colonial Theater (New York) 88
Colony Club (Chicago) 195
Columbia Records 119, 142
Columbia Theater (Far Rockaway, Long Island) 90
Columbia Theater (San Francisco) 51
The Continental 169
Coon shouter 27, 29, 37, 41, 46, 54
Coon songs 14–15, 21–22, 27–28, 37–38, 41
Copa City (Miami Beach) 220
Copacabana (New York) 203, 205, 212
Corbett, J.J. 58, 97
Crews, Laura Hope 176
Cross-Eyed Papa Look Straight at Me 112
Curran Theater (San Francisco) 111

The Daily Mail 105
Dance Hall Doll 156
Dancing Shoes 65
Darktown Strutter's Ball 42, 76
Delmonico's restaurant 79
Desmond, Florence 165
Didn't Your Mother Tell You Nothing 199
Diplomat Hotel (Miami Beach) 237
Divine Lady 207
Do I? 108
Double-entendre songs 39, 44–45, 47, 59–60, 73, 76–78, 84, 111, 116, 129–130, 133, 173, 199–201–202, 205

Down Home Rag 52
Durante, Jimmy 220, 227

Earl Carroll 116–117, 162
Earl Carroll's Vanities 116
"Ed Sullivan Show" 222, 227–229, 231, 233, 240
Eddie Foy and the Seven Little Foys 58, 97
Edelweiss Gardens (Chicago) 90–91, 93
Edison Phonograph Company 38, 47–48
Edison Phonograph Monthly 39, 46
El Rancho (Las Vegas) 222
Eli-Eli 98
Elkins, Mollie 35, 99
Emerson, Harry 28, 30
Empire Theater (Paris) 154
Empress Theater (San Francisco) 61
The Encore 120–121
Entertaining Papa 210
Erlanger, Abe 5, 49, 131, 150
Erlanger Theater (Chicago) 201
Erlanger Theater (Philadelphia) 241
Euson's Theater (Chicago) 30
Evening Standard (London) 230
Experience Will Teach You How 46
Extraordinary Girl 157

Family Theater (New York) 23
Fields, Lew 2, 110, 131, 151
Fields, W.C. 2, 27, 207
Finsbury Park Empire Theater (London) 104, 165
"First Lady of Show Business" 6
Floating Down the River 53
Florentine Gardens (Los Angeles) 204–205, 207, 212, 215
Follow a Star 151–153
Follow the Boys 205–206
Forgetting Vows 142
Forgotten Man 171
Four Marx Brothers 5, 76, 97
"Four Star Revue" 222
Freedley, Vincent 181–182, 192–193, 195
Friganza, Trixi 58, 97
Froman, Jane 225
Fulton Theater (Brooklyn) 37

Gaieties of 1919 87
Garland, Judy 176–179, 227
Garrick Theater (Chicago) 133–134
Gaxton, William 182, 226
Gay Love 165
Gay Masqueraders 23, 28, 30, 32

Gay Paree 132–134
General Phonograph Company (Okeh Records) 101, 114, 119
The German Village 19–21
Gerson, Sam 128
Gibson, Charles Dana 1
Giles, Dorothy 207
Glad Rag Doll 145
Golden Gate Theater (San Francisco) 112, 198
Golden Jubilee (Jewish Theatrical Guild) 222–224, 227
Grand Central Station 3, 6
Granville, Bernard 48, 50
Green Mill (Chicago) 147–149
Greenwood, Charlotte 132, 176
Gresham, Herbert 32, 35
Grosvenor Hotel (London) 174
Guinan, Texas 74, 125

Hammerstein, Arthur 150, 155, 159
Hardwicke, Sir Cedric 164, 213–214
Hart, Max 52–54, 59, 63–65
Hartford Daily Courant 55–56, 162
Hathaway, Phil 27
Haviland, F.B. Publishing Company 38–39
Hebrew Home for the Aged 226, 249
Hebrew Ladies Old People's Home 12, 124, 162, 170–171
Heidt, Horace 156
Held, Anna 15, 35
Hello, Alexander 84, 86–87
Hello My Baby! 12, 21
Herbert, Victor 32
Herman, Woody 207
He's a Good Man to Have Around 146
High Kickers 198–202
Hill, Gus 27–28, 110
Hippodrome (London) 104–105, 107
Hippodrome (New York) 2, 80
Hirshfield, Harry 213, 225, 247
Hollywood Club (Hollywood, Florida) 161, 168, 172
Hollywood Reporter 183
Hollywood restaurant (Los Angeles) 161
Homesick—I'm Glad to Be Back Home 107
Honky Tonk 141, 144–147, 151
Hope, Bob 238–240
Hotel Morrison (Chicago) 173–174
Hotel Shamrock (Houston) 219
House of Lords (New York) 171
How to Hold a Man 230

Index

How Ya Gonna Keep 'Em on the Farm 238–239
The Howard Brothers 5, 18, 51, 96, 99, 145, 181,
Hutton, Betty 221, 226

I Am Married 46
I Can Never Think of Words 151
I Don't Want to Get Thin 146, 151
I Got Something 199
I Picked a Pansy in the Garden of Love 168–169, 171
I Want Someone to Call Me Dearie 30
I Wonder Where My Easy Rider's Gone 58
If He's Good Enough to Fight for His Country, He Shouldn't Have to Fight for His Love 206
If I Had You 146
If It Ain't One Man, It's Another 172
If Your Kisses Can't Hold the Man You Love 151
I'm a Real Kind Mama Lookin' for a Lovin' Man 75, 77
I'm a Wild, Wicked Woman from the Badlands 232
I'm Doing What I'm Doing for Love 146
I'm Feathering a Nest for a Little Bluebird 146
I'm Funny That Way 146
I'm Taking the Steps to Russia 182
I'm the Girl Who Didn't Marry Dear Old Dad 176, 181
I'm the Last of the Red Hot Mammas 113–115, 119, 121, 139–144, 146, 242
I'm the Laziest Gal in Town 171
Imperial Theater (New York) 183, 191, 195
Influenza epidemic 80–81
Inhibition Papa 228
International Alliance of Theatrical Stage Employees (IATSE) 190–192
International Casino (New York) 234–235
The International Rag 58
Islesworth Hotel (Atlantic City) 74
Israel, visits 221, 231–232, 236, 238
It Takes a Good Girl to Do That 112
It's All Your Fault 65
It's Never Too Late to Have a Little Fun 228

Jack Dempsey's Bar (Miami Beach) 196
Jack Lynch's Hotel Walton Roof (Philadelphia) 195
Jardin de Paris (New York Theater roof) 33–34, 71
Jazz 64–65, 67, 69, 74, 87–88
Jessel, George 97, 156, 158, 198–200, 202–203, 213, 217, 225–228, 243–244, 246–247
Jewish benefits, donations 81, 96, 121, 153, 162, 170, 223–224, 231–232, 234–235, 237, 249
The Jewish community 8–17, 31, 63, 98
Jewish Theatrical Guild of America 213, 224
Jolson, Al 5, 49, 217

Keith, B.F. 53, 59
Keith circuit 53–54, 57–59, 64, 107–108, 115, 132, 147
King and Queen of England 164, 216, 238–240
King Edward VIII (Mrs. Simpson) 175
Kiss 'Em and Run Girls 113
Kit Kat Club (London) 120–121, 138–140, 152–153, 155

Lacky (Lackeyman), Al 108–109, 120, 123–124, 130, 140, 142–143, 148, 151, 153, 155, 160
The Lady in Red 172
Lait, Jack 40, 81
Lamour, Dorothy 196
The Land of Bom-Ba-Loo 47
La Salle Theater (Chicago) 48
Last Frontier (Las Vegas) 205
Lastfogel, Abe 159–162, 167, 171–172, 174–175, 180, 215, 221, 226, 229, 231–232, 237, 247
Latin Casino (Cherry Hill, New Jersey) 243
Latin Casino (Philadelphia) 226
Latin Quarter (Miami Beach) 210, 212–213, 215, 220, 222, 226, 228
Latin Quarter (New York) 243–246
Learning 96
Leave It to Me 182–183, 191, 193–195, 197, 201
Le Maire, George 110–111
Le Maire, Rufus 127–129, 131–132
Le Maire's Affairs 127–128, 130–133
Le Marne (Atlantic City) 97
Les Paul Trio 207
Leslie, Amy 37, 45, 47, 49–50, 110–112, 115, 119, 130, 133, 142, 145, 149

Leslie, Lew 155, 175
Levant, Oscar 133
Levi, Maurice 32–33
Lewis, Joe E. 197, 200, 217, 225, 229
Lewis, Ted 127, 129, 131, 133, 136, 158, 205, 233–234, 243–244, 246–247
Liberty Theater (New York) 2
Life Begins at Forty 169, 171, 196, 238–239
Lillian Russell 4, 15, 234
Lindsey, Walter O. 45, 47
The Little Minister 2
Loew circuit 59–61, 148–151, 158
London Citizen 166
London Times 103, 152, 230
Lopez, Vincent 89, 96
Lord, You Made the Night Too Long 157, 165
Lorraine, Lillian 33–35
Los Angeles Times 112
Lost, a Wonderful Man 107
Louisiana Lou 48–52
Louisville Lady 165–166
Lovin' Sam, Sheik of Alabam 107
Lyric Theater (Newark) 37

"Madame Sophie Tucker" 115–117
Mairzy Doats 204
Majestic Theater (Chicago) 50, 65, 76, 93, 95
Mama Goes Where Papa Goes 230
Marbro Theater (Chicago) 149
Marden's Riviera (Fort Lee) 180–181, 197
Marigold Gardens (Chicago) 90
Martin & Lewis 217
Martin, Mary 182, 194
Martinique (New York) 209
"The Mary Garden of Ragtime" 40–41, 51, 54, 56, 68
Maryland Theater (Baltimore) 97
Mayfair Theater (Boston) 209
McIntyre & Heath 84, 111
McVicker's Theater (Chicago) 61
Me and My Shadow 244
Mercury Records 219–220, 224, 227
Merry Mary 46–47
Metro-Goldwyn-Mayer Studios 176–177, 221
Metropole (London) 105
Metropole Cafe (New York) 19
Missouri Joe 48
Mitchell, Julian 32–33, 35, 241
Mollie, Dear 65
Mollie, Dear, It's You I'm After 66

Moonlight on the Mississippi 53
Moore, Victor 182–183, 194–195, 233
Morning, Noon, and Night 66
Morris, William, Jr. 102, 134, 141, 144, 159, 162, 167, 188, 206, 213–214, 244, 247
Morris, William, Sr. 35–36, 38–40, 45–47, 50–54, 57, 62–67, 70–71, 74, 78–79, 81, 84, 87–90, 93, 96–98, 102, 107, 110, 112, 115–116, 120–121, 124–125, 132, 135–138, 141, 148–149, 151, 153, 155, 157–159, 226, 241
Mosconi, Charles 185, 189
Moss theater group 98, 102
Most Gentlemen Don't Like Love 182
Mother 65
Moulin Rouge (Hollywood, California) 233
Moulin Rouge Cafe (Atlantic City) 90
Mounds Country Club (East St. Louis) 149
Moving Day in Jungle Town 32–35
Murder at the Vanities 161–162
Murray, Mae 33, 66
Murrow, Edward R. 222
My Extraordinary Man 165
My Heart Belongs to Daddy 182, 194
My Husband's in the City 39
My Mother's Sabbath Candles 220–221

Nat'an, for What Are You Waitin', Nat'an? 66
National Theater (Washington, D.C.) 201
National Vaudeville Association (N.V.A.) 80, 82
Naughty Eyes 30
Never Too Young or Too Old 206
New York Clipper 26, 36, 38, 46, 48, 54, 58–59, 64–65, 68, 77–80, 82, 87, 89, 95, 106, 108, 110
New York Daily Mirror 241
New York Herald Tribune 242
New York Journal-American 243
New York Post 46
New York Public Library 217
New York Sunday Reviewer 38
New York Times 2, 116, 146, 177, 188, 194, 242
Nixon Theater (Pittsburgh) 201
Nobody Much 75
Norworth, Jack 33–34
Now Am de Time 48

Ochs, Adolph S. 2
O'Dwyer, Mayor William 213–214
Oh, You Georgia Rose 52
Old Home Town of Mine 65
116th Street Theater (New York) 25–26
125th Street Theater (New York) 22
A One-Man Girl 230
Oriental Theater (Chicago) 129–130, 149, 156, 168, 172, 180, 197
Orpheum circuit 67–69, 75, 97, 99, 112, 114, 132
Orpheum Theater (Brooklyn) 117
Orpheum Theater (Chicago) 145
Orpheum Theater (Los Angeles) 112, 145, 172
Orpheum Theater (Memphis) 75
Orpheum Theater (San Francisco) 145

Palace Theater (Chicago) 64, 93, 109, 113, 115, 117, 119, 142, 147–148, 160
Palace Theater (Hartford) 99
Palace Theater (New York) 59–60, 65, 79–80, 99, 108, 110, 117, 119, 125, 141, 147, 150, 157–158, 247
Palladium (London) 153, 155, 164, 220–221, 238
Palmer House Empire Room (Chicago) 232–233
Pantages, Alexander 132, 134
Pantages circuit 39, 41, 132, 134, 137
Paramount Pictures 229
Paramount Theater (Brooklyn) 156
Paramount Theater (New York) 136, 156, 158
Park circuit 22, 25
Pastor, Tony 26–27, 53
Pepper Box Revue 110–111
Phoebe Jane 46
Picadilly Hotel (London) 121
Piping Rock (Saratoga) 171, 174
Plaza Theater (New York) 38, 46
Pleasure Man 142
Poli's Theater (Hartford) 14, 54–56
Porter, Cole 182–183, 194
Powell, Eleanor 176–178, 207
Primrose, George 50
Prince Edward Theater (London) 165
Prince of Wales 106, 121
Publix circuit 160

The Puritan Prance 48, 51
Put Your Arms Around Me Honey 204
Put Your Paws Around Me and Be My Bear 46

Raft, George 133, 204–205
Ragtime songs 21, 37, 39–40, 46, 48–50, 53
Rector's restaurant 71, 79
Reisenweber's restaurant 71, 79–81, 83–84, 86–88, 92, 96–97, 99–100, 105, 108, 234
Rendevous (Chicago) 131–132
Reuben Rag 46
Richman, Harry 187, 197, 217
Right Time in the Right Clime 169
Riverside Theater (New York) 108
Rivoli Theater (London) 106
Robey, George 104, 106, 164
Robinson, Bill "Bojangles" 162–163, 217
Rogers, Will 58, 80
Rooney, Mickey 178
Rosie, My Dusky Georgia Rose 22, 29
Rossiter, Will Company 41–42, 58–59, 65–66, 82
Round in Fifty 104–105
Royal Command Variety Gala 238–240
Royal Theater (New York) 66–67

The Saga of Sophie Tucker 238
Sahara Hotel (Las Vegas) 231
San Francisco Call 111
San Francisco Chronicle 76, 111, 114, 134, 198, 203
San Souci Park (Chicago) 47
Screen Actors Guild (SAG) 183–185, 187–188, 191–194, 249
Sensations of 1945 207
Shanley's restaurant 71, 79
Shapiro, Ted 100–101, 107, 112, 117, 119–121, 123, 127, 134, 139, 142, 145, 151, 154–156, 158, 165, 169, 173–174, 181, 197, 199, 207, 216, 221, 226, 235, 247–248
Sherbourne Hotel (Brighton Beach) 97
Sherman Hotel (Chicago) 52, 91–93, 149
Sherry's Dance Hall (New York) 165
Shine on Harvest Moon 30
Shubert, J.J. 69–70, 87, 129
Shubert, Lee 133
The Shuberts 5, 66, 69, 71, 84, 86–87, 128, 131–134, 150

Siegal, Al 98–100
Silverman, Sime 146, 159
Smith, C. Aubry 178–179, 207
Smith, Harry B. 32–33, 35
Smith, Kate 156
Some of These Days (book) 207, 216, 220, 235
Some of These Days (song) 41–42, 48, 118, 130, 142, 146, 152, 154, 156, 161–162, 166, 168, 176, 180–181, 196, 203, 205–206, 218, 220–222, 225, 229, 233, 238–239, 244
Somebody's Coming to My House 53
Somebody's Wrong 113
Something to Be Thankful For 157
Sophie (musical comedy) 237, 240–242
Sophie Tucker and Her Five Kings of Syncopation 67, 69, 74, 79–80, 98, 100
Sophie Tucker Foundation 208, 223, 248
Sophie Tucker garage 67–68, 75, 92, 112
Sophie Tucker Music Hall (radio) 170–171
Sophie Tucker School for Red Hot Mammas 228
"The Sophie Tucker Story" 221, 224, 227, 229
Sophie Tucker Youth Center 231–232
Sophie Tucker's Playground (New York) 125, 127
Sophie Tucker's Tobacco Fund 76, 78
Sophisticated Lady 165
The Spewack's 182, 194
Staiger, Libi 241
Star and Garter Theater (Chicago) 30
Starting All Over Again 230
State Theater (New York) 150, 171
Stay at Home Papa 159, 165
Stevens, Ashton 45, 47, 95, 129–131, 133
Suffering Suffragette 65
Swaffer, Hannan 152, 216
Sweet Georgia Brown 196
Swing, Swing, Swing 53

Talk of the Town (London) 235, 242–243
Tanguay, Eva 4, 15, 34–35, 42
Tears Won't Bring Him Back 157
Temple Theater (Detroit) 64
That Lovin' Rag 39
That Lovin' Soul Kiss 48
That Lovin' Two-Step Man 39

That Old Gang of Mine 113
That's Something to Be Thankful For 158, 165
That's What Keeps Me Broke 107, 109
That's Where the South Begins 151
Theater Authority (TA) 185, 189–191
There's More Music in a Grand Baby Than There Is in a Baby Grand 108
There's No Business Like That Certain Business 228, 230
They All Pitched a Quarter Apiece and Bet It on a Horse 171
They Sent for Me 47
Thoroughbreds Don't Cry 178–179
3-A Papa, You Can't 4-F Me 206
The Three Keatons 2, 57–58
Tick, Tack, Toe 89–90, 112
Timberg, Herman 89
Tin Pan Alley 2, 3, 5, 12, 14, 17–18, 20–21, 25, 44, 60, 64, 66, 89, 144
Tivoli Theater (Melbourne) 237
To the U.S.A. from the U.S.S.R. 183
"Toast of the Town" 222
Tomorrow 182
Tony Pastor's Theater (New York) 26
Town & Country (Brooklyn) 240
Trocadero (Los Angeles) 172
Trocadero (New York) 124
Trocadero Theater (London) 154
Tuck, Albert (Bert) 16–17, 24, 31, 48, 55, 62–63, 96, 114, 117, 129–130, 135–137, 143, 149, 153, 155–156, 180–181, 208, 217, 234, 247–248
Tuck, Louis 15–17, 52, 108, 217
Tucker Terrace (Cleveland) 114, 137
225 Club (Chicago) 160

United Artists 207
Universal Pictures 205, 221
Uptown Theater (Los Angeles) 179

Valeton, Lora 197
Vallee, Rudy 185, 187–188
Variety 26–27, 65, 97, 99, 108–109, 125, 127–129, 135, 137–138, 140–141, 147, 150–151, 153–154, 156–157, 161, 167, 169–174, 177, 179, 181, 190–191, 193, 196–198, 206–207, 217–219, 228, 230, 234, 242, 247
Vaudeville Manager's Association (V.M.A.) 82, 84–85
Vernon Country Club (Los Angeles) 136–137
Versailles (New York) 193, 196
Victoria, Vesta 46
Victoria Palace (London) 140
Victoria Theater (New York) 53, 58–59
Vitamins, Hormones, and Pills 228
Vivian Johnson's (New York) 171

Waiting for the Robert E. Lee 196
Wake Me Up, You're Slipping 207
Waldorf-Astoria Hotel (New York) 223–226, 237
Walking the Dog 42, 68
Walters, Lou 216, 220
Wanderers Must Die 176
Warfield Theater (San Francisco) 161
Warner Brothers 141, 143–144, 221
Weber & Fields 5, 159
Westphal, Frank 52–53, 57–59, 64–65, 67–68, 75–79, 81, 87, 91–93, 95, 108, 241
What Do You Say 48
When My Baby Smiles at Me 233, 244
When the Leaves Comes Tumbling Down 110
When They Get Too Wild for Everyone Else — Perfect for Me 98
Where Does My Daddy Go? 108
White, George 93, 95
White City (Chicago) 53
Whitehead, Ralph 183–185, 187–193
Whiteman, Paul 89, 121
Whitney Theater (Chicago) 46–47
Who Cares 109
Who Paid the Rent for Mrs. Rip Van Winkle When Rip Van Winkle Was Away 59
Who'll Take My Place 109
Why Do They Call It Gay Paree 172
The Wild Cherry Rag 37
Wild, Wild Women 87
Willard Theater (Chicago) 52
Wilson's Music Hall (New York) 22
Winter Garden (London) 140, 152–153, 165

Winter Garden (New York) 81, 241–242
The Wizard of Oz 32
Women's impact on theater 4–5
Wood's Theater (Chicago) 127–129, 131
"World Renowned Coon Shouter" 6, 22
Wright, Frank Lloyd 90–91

Yazoo Rag 87
Yellen, Jack 113–114, 119, 127, 146, 152, 158, 167, 169, 180, 199, 205, 215–216, 220, 226–227, 231, 247
Yiddishe Mamma 119, 121, 142, 154, 161, 166, 168, 216, 220, 228, 236, 238
You Can't Deep Freeze a Red Hot Mamma 230
You Can't Expect Kisses from Me 50
You Made Me Love You 176
Youngman, Henny 181

Your Broadway and My Broadway 176–178, 180–181
You're the Kind of Girl Men Forget 113
You've Got to Be Loved to Be Healthy 181, 196, 206
You've Got to See Mamma Every Night 110

Ziegfeld, Flo 5, 30–35, 71, 150
Ziegfeld Follies 32–36
Zukor, Adolf 159, 225

www.ingramcontent.com/pod-product-compliance
Lightning Source LLC
Chambersburg PA
CBHW081546300426
44116CB00015B/2778